Praise for *At the Cutting Edge*

"The first comprehensive look at Canad[...]
[...]hed and lucidly presented, it makes a compelling case for an urgent
[...]tional debate...aimed at saving our forests before it is too late."
—OTTAWA CITIZEN

"We may be a forest nation, but *At the Cutting Edge* shows we are
damn casual and careless at it.... [May] is astute enough to
[re]cognize that the nation's political morass, combined with Ottawa's
[ge]nuine disdain for anything green, is actively feeding an immense
[e]cological crisis and another big bad news story for taxpayers. Just
how many cod-like fiascoes can ordinary Canadians finance?"
—CANADIAN FORUM

"[Eli]zabeth May makes her case with a lawyer's attention to the evidence,
[citin]g study after study showing overcutting of cheap wood, wildly inaccu-
[rate] forest inventories, looming wood shortages and, ultimately, the sort of
[sc]ientific and technological hubris that is all too familiar to the people
[wh]o used to stake their livelihoods on the Atlantic cod fishery.... Anyone
who thinks that all is well in the woods should read this book."
—THE GLOBE AND MAIL

"[At] the Cutting Edge is a meticulously researched plea to save what forests
[rem]ain.... 'We're battling human nature,' May says. 'But if we're not capable of learning as a species from our mistakes, we won't survive.'"
—TIMES COLONIST (VICTORIA)

"May is to be applauded for bringing to the attention of the public the
[gr]oss mismanagement of our forests.... Forestry is the biggest industry in
Canada and the debate is often couched in terms of the environment
[v]ersus jobs. In reply, May points to the East Coast fishery: 'It has proved
that without a healthy environment, there can be no jobs.'"
—WINNIPEG FREE PRESS

"A wake-up call to alert people to the devastation of Canada's forests....
May hopes to heal polarities between the two extreme positions on this
issue: business and the environmentalists."
—QUILL & QUIRE

"...she challenges those who are entrusted with the management of our forests to do better."
—SUMMERLAND REVIEW

"Elizabeth May decodes the technical language and explains in a st forward manner why Canadians should be concerned about what is happening to the forests. In doing so, she shatters the m that our forest resources are inexhaustible or that the Canadia government has the logging situation well in hand."
—ATLANTIC BOOKS TODAY

"This extensively researched book provides, for the first time, an across-Canada survey of forests and forestry that deals with ecological, economic and political issues."
—THE GAZETTE (MONTREAL)

"This thorough and clearly written text will certainly be part of the public debate about our forests' future."
—THE DAILY GLEANER (FREDERICTON)

"...an exhaustively researched look at how the logging industry is going to put itself out of business if it's not careful."
—THE COAST (HALIFAX)

"*At the Cutting Edge* is a meticulously documented lament for a forest legacy lost. If this book doesn't make you weep, your heart has turned to stone."
—MAUDE BARLOW, THE COUNCIL OF CANADIANS

"What we decide about the future of Canada's remaining forests will indicate whether we will try to find a balance with the ecological treasures that sustain us."
—DAVID SUZUKI

At the Cutting Edge

The Crisis in Canada's Forests

REVISED EDITION

Elizabeth May

KEY PORTER BOOKS

Library and Archives Canada Cataloguing in Publication

May, Elizabeth

   At the cutting edge : the crisis in Canada's forests / Elizabeth May.—Rev. ed.
ISBN 1-55263-645-3

1. Forests and forestry—Canada.   2. Forest policy—Canada.   3. Logging—Canada.
4. Deforestation—Canada.   5. Forest conservation—Canada.   6. Crown lands—
Canada.   I. Title.

SD567.M39 2005   333.75'0971   C2005-900651-X

The publisher gratefully acknowledges the support of the Canada Council for the Arts and the Ontario Arts Council for its publishing program. We acknowledge the support of the Government of Ontario through the Ontario Media Development Corporation's Ontario Book Initiative.

We acknowledge the financial support of the Government of Canada through the Book Publishing Industry Development Program (BPIDP) for our publishing activities.

Key Porter Books Limited
Six Adelaide Street East, Tenth Floor
Toronto, Ontario
Canada M5C 1H6
www.keyporter.com

Text design: Peter Maher
Electronic formatting: Jean Lightfoot Peters

Printed and bound in Canada

05 06 07 08 09 6 5 4 3 2 1

CONTENTS

For those leaders in the movement to protect
Canada's forests who helped me with the book in
1998, and who have since been taken from us, far
too soon: John McInnis, Alice Chambers, Stan Rowe,
Colin Stewart, Ron Burchell and Don McAllister

FOREWORD BY FARLEY MOWAT

Our species has demonstrated a singular and ever-expanding ability to eradicate its fellow species, and to erode the support system upon which life depends. We are clever creatures. Yet for all our vaunted brilliance we seem incapable of realizing that our prime endeavour, making money, will not enable us to go on eating, and breathing, and in fact, existing.

Nowhere is our tendency to trash this planet for short-term gain more obvious than in what we have done, and are doing, to the forests. Their ongoing destruction at our hands is not only an ecological abomination in itself, it may well be a huge wooden nail in our coffin. And yet the forest industry responsible for this degradation seems to be immune to reason. Furthermore, it has been able to distance itself from the damage it does, at least partly through the connivance of government at all levels. The butcher has become sacrosanct.

What Elizabeth May has done in this book is to shine a new and powerful light on what modern industrial forestry is really all about. By dissecting the Byzantine computer models, double-speak, and selected scientific data used by the industry to conceal its crime, she reveals not only a naked emperor, but an evil one. Her hope, and mine, is that revelation of the smoke-and-mirror charade employed to justify the destruction of the forests may help shock the nation into acting now to save what remains of the forests...and ourselves. She shows us that the long-term costs of allowing the rape to continue are so horrendous as to be almost inconceivable, not just for us, but for all life on earth.

The forest industry will hate this book. But it cannot pretend it is based on false premises, or that its argument is just another ideological expression of environmentalism. The book is thoroughly grounded on a mountain of government-generated, as well as independent, data that inexorably demonstrate that, beyond all rhetoric, the forest industry is culpable of committing an atrocity against the living earth. This book sounds much the same warning for the forests that was sounded by committed environmentalists about the East Coast cod fisheries. If we have learned anything from that ecological, human, and economic tragedy, we will not fail to heed what May tells us, and take preventive action.

Now. Before it is indeed too late.

PREFACE TO THE REVISED EDITION

It has been eight years since I studied the research of twelve dedicated experts in forest policy from across Canada to write the first edition of this book. Once again, Sierra Club of Canada has found experts from every forested jurisdiction and asked them the same questions. The basic concerns still hold true: the forest is not protected against overcutting. Forested ecosystems across Canada such as old-growth forests in British Columbia, Acadian forests in the Maritimes and intact boreal forests are still at risk. Forest-dependent species such as the woodland caribou, spotted owl and pine marten are in trouble due to loss of habitat.

Some goals have been realized. The debate has become more open, and the level of vitriol has been reduced. A few provinces have made remarkable changes, such as developing policies that require the forest industry to preserve intact "core" areas for species that depend on unfragmented habitat. Others are considering the reduction of clear-cutting. But for each provincial government that has improved, another has become dangerously reckless with the environment within its borders.

Nevertheless, the new research is encouraging. The threat to Canada's forests clearly remains, but environmental groups have found new tools. There is greater sophistication in market-based campaigns. Individual companies, and a large number of them, are seeking environmental certification in order to ensure a green seal of approval. Retail companies and publishers are increasingly looking for forest products that pass the tests of environmental groups.

Key to any sense of progress and optimism on my part is the continuing and growing engagement of Canadians in decisions about our forests. The base for that engagement must be information and education. It is for concerned members of the public that I hope this expanded and revised edition will be helpful. After all, Canada's forests belong to the people of Canada.

Consider this your owner's manual.

INTRODUCTION

For twenty years or more we've worried about running out of oil. Now we're faced with the fact that we may end up running out of wild forests and fish first.

It's not surprising that we've concentrated on the preservation of non-renewable fossil fuels such as oil and natural gas. After all, the very origins of the conservation movement lay in the sustainable use of forests. It was over one hundred years ago that Sierra Club's founder, John Muir, joined with the founder of the Yale School of Forestry, Gifford Pinchot, to expound the theory of forest conservation. Muir wrote, "The forests must be, and will be, not only preserved, but used; and...like perennial fountains...be made to yield a sure harvest of timber, while at the same time all their far-reaching (aesthetic and spiritual uses) may be maintained unimpaired."[1]

Gifford Pinchot led the movement for forest conservation in the 1890s in the United States. The term "sustainable-yield forest management" dates back to those times. The goal was simple—the efficient use of natural resources—in other words, never cutting more in one year than could be replaced naturally.

Ultimately, John Muir and Gifford Pinchot parted company. Pinchot's utilitarian view was incompatible with Muir's fierce devotion to wildness. Pinchot wrote, "The object of our forest policy is not to preserve the forests because they are beautiful...or because they are refuges for the wild creatures of the wilderness...but for the making of prosperous homes.... Every other consideration comes as secondary."[2] As leading ecologist Aldo Leopold, an early graduate of Yale School of Forestry who also rejected the utilitarian view, wrote of his work with Pinchot "a stump was our symbol of progress."[3]

For one hundred years the debate has continued, hinging on the question of whether forests should be managed for timber production or set aside as wilderness. Now, at the beginning of the twenty-first century, a more fundamental question needs to be asked: Are we capable of sustaining our renewable resources?

Around the world, it is the renewables that are in scarce supply. According to the United Nations, of the world's major seventeen fisheries, thirteen have collapsed or are collapsing. Deforestation around the world has global implications, not only in lack of firewood for the burgeoning population of the developing world, but in reducing our planet's ability to cope with the ever-increasing release of carbon into our atmosphere. Forests have acted as carbon sinks, holding these greenhouse gases out of the atmosphere. Could we be felling and burning at rates significant enough to affect the global climate?

We have learned little in Canada from the disastrous mismanagement of the immense marine resources of our East Coast fishery. One of the richest fisheries in the world—with legendary abundance that hundreds of years ago made it difficult for ships to ply the waters or come to harbour for the sheer pressing mass of cod—has all but disappeared.

The evidence of overfishing is clear enough. Beyond the shallow public pronouncements of "too many fishermen chasing too few fish," a number of lessons are worth noting. Technology was probably the driving force behind the collapse of the fishery. New, highly efficient draggers, with nets capable of scooping up twenty 747s, wasting as much as they caught, plied the ocean floor year-round. With radar, sonar and a ship's bridge that would have done the starship *Enterprise* proud, these draggers could fish until they hunted down the very last fish in the area. The technology exceeded the ecosystem's ability to recover.

This massive harvesting power was matched by overcapacity in the fish plants. A bonanza of new fish processors throughout Newfoundland created constant pressure to keep up the volume of the catch, no matter the ecological consequences. All this was buttressed by government subsidies and short-term corporate profit motive.

Of course, the Canadian fishery was also regulated. It has been said that the roughly $9 billion spent on fisheries management between the extension of Canada's territorial limit to 200 miles (320 kilometres) in the late 1970s and the collapse of cod stocks was the best management system in the world. We had extensive scientific expertise. Catches were set by theories of conservation and sustainable harvest.

But there were problems. The commitment of the government scientists to their own models was so strong that early indicators of problems were discounted. When the small in-shore fishers complained that the cod were gone, it was assumed that these people, who had fished for generations, were not good fishermen. Bigger boats were built. Better sonar and radar. Technological solutions and science outweighed the voice of experience.

As the fishery began to collapse around them, the scientists and the government ministers who set quotas and catch rates went into a state of denial.

In the late 1990s, Greenpeace ran a newspaper ad. It pictured a clear-cut running as far as the eye could see. Below was the caption: "They said we could never run out of cod, either." This book will examine whether Canada's forest ecosystems and the full range of species they support are at risk of going the way of the cod.

Ultimately, it is a question of vital concern to the thousands of Canadians who make their living in the forests or in forest products. It is not a debate about the environment versus jobs. As in the case of the East Coast fishery, it is about the fact that without a healthy environment, there are simply no jobs at all.

Part I
At the Cutting Edge

1 | A FOREST NATION

Canada's forests have always seemed inexhaustibly vast. The endless forest is part of the national mythology, and the wealth it represents is one of the cornerstones of the country's economy. Canada is the world's largest exporter of wood and wood products, and produces a third of all the newsprint used in the world. In 2003, exports of forest products netted nearly $40 billion.[1] Three hundred communities depend on the forest industry—often a single mill in a small town—with 376,300 Canadians directly employed, and an additional 738,000 indirectly, in cutting down the forests and converting them to pulp, paper, chips and lumber.[2]

"Canada is a forest nation" is a truism voiced by Canadian politicians. And indeed, this vast geographical area was once almost completely forested below the treeline. Even now, after centuries of clearing for settlement and logging for economic growth, Canada still has fully 10 per cent of the world's forests and a full third of the planet's boreal forests within its borders. British Columbia alone contains more temperate forest wilderness than anywhere else in North America and 20 per cent of the global total.[3] For most of our history it has been easy to believe that it doesn't matter how many trees we cut down: there will always be more.

Canada is a forest nation in another sense as well: forests balance the climate, protect fresh water, purify the air and provide food and shelter to a myriad of species. As the global effort to reduce carbon intensifies, credits for carbon storage will provide a tangible economic value to what was previously an economic "free good." In fact, the storage of carbon by Canadian forests may soon provide economic value greater than their value as pulp.

Forests generate wealth for Canadians far beyond the forest industry. Tourism, fishing, hunting and trapping—all of which are heavily dependent on healthy forests—bring billions of dollars into the Canadian economy. All have real economic value, although the economics of *forests* in Canada is always presented as the economics of *forestry*.

A 1997 report from the World Resources Institute (WRI), a non-profit environmental think tank based in Washington, D.C., puts Canada's role as a forest nation in a global perspective. WRI set out to map the last remaining primary forests, identifying "frontier forests" found in large, intact ecosystems. Of all the world's remaining frontier forests, 25 per cent are in Canada's boreal region.[4] Nearly half of Canada's huge land mass is forested, a total of 401.9 million hectares.[5]

But these numbers can be misleading. Of that 417.6 million hectares, only 294.7 million hectares are considered "productive" or commercial forest land, although the meaning of such terms varies from province to province.[6] Yet many Canadians still believe in the myth of inexhaustibility. The expanse of forest from coast to coast has created the illusion of an endless, self-renewing resource. The same false belief led to the collapse of the cod fishery: overfishing of the Grand Banks off Newfoundland continued until the fish were gone.

When technology was limited to cross-saws and axes, the ability to annihilate forest ecosystems was limited as well. Even with saws and axes, Canadian logging did alter ecosystems. The practice of "high-grading"—taking the best trees and leaving weaker trees and less valuable species behind—gradually eroded the wealth of large regions. It was not until the last decades of the twentieth century, however, when the industry began to use large-scale mechanized equipment, that logging operations became capable of fundamentally altering whole landscapes.

The myth of inexhaustibility—the curse of the cod fishery—persists in government and in the public perception of Canada's forests. Primary jurisdiction over forests is vested in the provinces; provincial governments continue to offer incentives for new development. Year after year, Natural Resource departments across the country produce reassuring statistics to prove that, even if it takes "creative accounting," Canada has enough forest to maintain its industry—at least on paper.

Giving away the forest

Like the fishery, Canada's forests are largely a public resource—publicly owned. And, as in the East Coast fishery, the allocation of harvest rights over a common property resource is essentially a form of privatization. But when you hear industry spokesmen talking about the threat a park represents to the pulp supply or read about the compensation that industry demands if forest is set aside for a park, it is easy to forget that industry, for the most part, does not own the forest it logs.

Leases are cheap. Industry never pays an amount that even approximates the commercial value of the forest it converts to cash, let alone its greater value in terms of ecological services, habitat and biological diversity. Short-term gain—logging the forest and building the mills— is subsidized, while long-term interests—the sustainability of the resource itself and all other future values—are heavily discounted.

Compared to other forest-industry dependent nations, Canada has very little forested land in private hands. Only 7 per cent of Canada's forest is privately held, compared to roughly 70 per cent in the United States and Sweden.[7] While some provinces have significantly more privately owned forest, the reality is that the vast majority of Canadian forest is owned by the Crown. For the non-Canadian reader, this may sound perfectly delightful: visions of Her Majesty taking tea in the midst of the boreal come to mind.

The term Crown land simply means that the land is owned by the people of Canada, with jurisdiction over forests vested in the provinces. Thus, Canadians can exert a special interest, indeed a proprietary interest, over the management of their forests. The irony is that for many years there has been virtually no public oversight of forest policy.

Leases come in a profusion of categories: TFLs, TSAs, CAAFs, and FMAs. But they all add up to the same thing—they hand over rights to public timber to private companies. There are two basic types of leases: those based on a specific *area* and those based on a designated *volume*. Area-based tenure arrangements tend to go to large companies over an extended time period. Volume-based leases (except in B.C.) tend to go to smaller operators for shorter periods.

Historically, provincial governments in Canada have made cozy deals with large forest industries in hopes of luring foreign investment to the area. While modern examples, such as the Alberta government's decision to grant long-term leases over nearly 9 million hectares to two Japanese companies—5.8 million hectares to a consortium of Mitsubishi and Oji Paper (known as Al-Pac) and 2.9 million hectares to Daishowa Marubeni—created alarm and media interest,[8] this was entirely consistent with Canadian forest policy since the turn of the century. In 1913, for instance, New Brunswick leased timber rights to forest companies for periods of up to fifty years on the basis of annual payments of three cents per hectare for the first year, and 1.5 cents per hectare for every year thereafter.[9] Newfoundland offered ninety-nine-year leases, renewable at the request of industry, with no stumpage fees for pulpwood and with water and mineral rights thrown in for good measure. Some of these leases still apply.

What does the public get out of this? Unless you subscribe to the belief that "what's good for Abitibi-Consolidated is good for Canada," the answer is surprisingly little. Two types of payments occur: the actual price paid at the time the lease is negotiated, sometimes paid as annual "rent;" and second, payment for the volume of wood cut from the leased land, known as "stumpage." The initial cost of a lease is usually minimal. The Tree Farm Licence (TFL) held over critical ecosystems of the Queen Charlotte Islands in British Columbia by Western Forest Products was purchased in the 1930s for $35,000. To protect those ancient forests from industrial exploitation and place them within what is now a national park, tens of millions of dollars had to be paid in "compensation."[10]

Low stumpage rates are part of the ongoing dispute between U.S. forest industries and Canadian exporters. The U.S. firms claim, and not without reason, that Canadian forest products are heavily subsidized: low stumpage rates—that is, cheap trees—are either part of our "competitive advantage" or our ongoing "undervaluing of our forests." It all depends on how you look at it.

Historically, stumpage rates paid by forest companies in most provinces have not approached the costs of running the provincial forest departments. For example, in 1994 British Columbia charged as little as $22 per cubic metre, which after adding the costs of reforestation is still less than the $111 price south of the border.[11] The same pattern held true across Canada through to the late 1990s, with Quebec stumpage at $5 per cubic metre, while Eastern U.S. prices were $16.[12] Recent reforms have increased stumpage, and some provinces have moved to a more market-based system, which also increases costs. Quebec, for example, has more than doubled its stumpage fees, now charging $12, and British Columbia, relying on a market pricing system, has increased fees by $5 to $7 per cubic metre throughout its rich coastal forest.

Despite advantageous arrangements, forest industry spokesmen traditionally complain about "insecurity of tenure." They argue that longer-term leases are required on more favourable terms if the industry is going to be able to reinvest. There is a certain persuasiveness to the argument. After logging, forests require anywhere from forty to eighty years to grow and mature, depending on the ecosystem. Private companies argue that if they have a long-term stake, such as they would have in their own land, they would be more likely to take responsibility for the future productivity of the forest. The reality is that large holdings of private land are most often poorly managed. Approximately one-third of Vancouver Island is privately owned due to old railway grants. These forests are overcut, creating eroded hillsides and damaged fish streams. And the timber from private forests is routinely shipped out as whole logs.

At least one Canadian environmental group has argued for privatizing Crown lands to obtain better forest management.[13] But in the twenty-first century, in a world of stateless capital and transnational companies bestriding the globe like so many Colossuses, it no longer follows that ownership conveys values of responsibility and good stewardship. If shifting operations to Indonesia or Brazil is less costly than regrowing a Canadian forest, nationalism will not be the factor that drives the business decision.

In 1997, as MacMillan Bloedel's CEO, Tom Stephens, cut the ribbon on a new $13-billion pulp mill in Indonesia, he noted that B.C.'s wages and forestry rules "can't be tolerated in a world where free-market forces will decide the winners and the losers."[14]

What? Me worry?

Some voices in industry can already be heard shaking the house of cards on which Canada's logging rates are based. John Roblee, head of the Forest Group Ventures Association of Nova Scotia, told a legislative committee in March 1997: "It's time to wake up.... We're in a crisis." Roblee explained that without accurate inventory information and with no regulations to ensure that cut levels are not exceeded, the province's industry was unsustainable. "Add her up, folks," he said. "We don't have the data of what is leaving the province by rail, by truck and by boat. It's going on twenty-four hours a day... It's just clear-cutting."[15]

While clear-cutting is an appropriate harvesting method for some forest types, since the 1950s it has been used across the board in 80 to 90 per cent of Canada's forests for one simple reason: it is the cheapest way to get the most fibre per hectare. Under the old model, forests have been managed primarily for fibre values, with little to no attention paid to other values such as wildlife or the maintenance of natural forest composition, structure and function.

Demands from mills across Canada have entrenched overcutting, since a reduction in the volume of trees, without a change in the system, results in job losses. As a result, forestry companies in rural areas across Canada (including British Columbia, Ontario and Prince Edward Island) have overcut forests for decades, and are now running out of easily accessible forests and closing mills, citing timber supply shortages. (Other factors, such as the rebounding Canadian dollar, softwood tariffs and increasing energy costs have also contributed to mill closures.) Industry is responding in many provinces by pushing for short-term solutions, such as a greater access to wood, increased tenure rights and more subsidies.

Despite such warnings and the demise of many forest-dwelling wildlife species, governments continue in a state of denial, avoiding the uncomfortable conclusion that a series of "local" wood shortages and a growing list of species at risk may actually constitute a national crisis. The only level of government capable of seeing the big picture, the federal government, is loath to do or say anything critical of either the provinces or the forest industry.

The federal government and the provinces have established the Canadian Council of Forest Ministers (CCFM), comprised of the ministers with responsibility for the forests. Collectively, they have produced statements of principles, several National Forest Accords and a report entitled "Criteria and Indicators for Sustainable Forest Management." Reading such documents, a reasonable person might well be convinced of a deep and abiding commitment to ecological values across Canada. But the reality in the forest is far different. Even if the federal government were concerned about provincial levels of overcutting, Canada's federal-provincial politics means that the federal government has no real power to change provincial policies.

While the federal government has done much useful work in international forums and in forest science research, budget cutbacks have reduced the impact of these efforts. Through the 1980s, the federal government role in forests expanded somewhat through funding programs for intensive silviculture in partnership with the provinces. But those came to an end in the mid-1990s. In fact, the federal government, having increasingly circumscribed its previously limited role in forest issues, now acts primarily as a propaganda arm of Canada's forest industry, helping to protect Canada's trade in forest products from nasty rumours of environmental malfeasance. Canada's 1997 report to the United Nations Commission on Sustainable Development went so far as to offer the website address of the B.C. forest lobby, the Forest Alliance of B.C., as a reliable source of information about sustainable development in Canada.[16]

International negotiations toward a binding convention to arrest global deforestation are presented as a trade-protection measure. The former federal Minister of Natural Resources, Anne McLellan, defended her government's commitment to such a convention as a way to silence environmental critics: "It's to ensure we're not held hostage to environmental terrorism," she said in early 1997.[17]

While the federal government pumps out propaganda claiming that forestry in Canada is sustainable, the reality on the ground is far different. As a national average, approximately 80 per cent of everything that is logged in Canada is clear-cut, while 90 per cent of the cut comes from primary and old-growth forests.[18] The area cut annually has steadily increased. From under 500,000 hectares in 1950 to 600,000 hectares in 1970 to the 2000 total of just over one million hectares, Canada is constantly reaching into previously unlogged areas to meet the demand for wood.[19] The voracious appetite for forest products pushes new roads into wilderness, felling areas that were once pristine and ancient forests.

Canada is conducting a vast and reckless experiment. The basic fact that nearly all the cutting is in the natural forest confirms that Canada is converting forest ecosystems to fibre farms. It supports the concern that Canada has not mastered any tried and true forestry formula. For the most part, logging is not taking place in areas previously logged. There is no track record of ecologically healthy second- and third-growth forests following heavily mechanized clear-cutting.

In the 1980s and early 1990s, the increasing proportion of land "not satisfactorily restocked" (NSR)—areas that have failed to re-establish healthy forests after logging—was one of the driving forces behind the massive federal government subsidies for tree planting, stand tending and other silviculture efforts to bring back areas ravaged by clear-cuts. The goal was, of course, to regenerate degraded land with commercially useful species, rather than the successional stages that would normally follow a disturbance. The area considered

NSR reached a peak in 1991, at 2.8 million hectares, but it remains high, with a 2001 total of 2.5 million hectares.[20]

The experiment is on shaky ground. Local wood-supply shortages are already occurring due to mill overcapacity, yet cutting and over-cutting are justified on the basis of future forest investments in silviculture. Increasingly, however, foresters are questioning the reality of the alleged benefits of future silviculture, the so-called "allowable cut effect." British Columbia's Chief Forester, Larry Pederson, has said that "most current research indicates that while such [intensive forest management] practices improve the *quality* of timber within a forest stand, they have little effect on the actual *volume* of timber produced, in most cases."[21]

But it is precisely the volume that is consistently increased in the mathematical models for calculating annual allowable cut (AAC) rates across Canada. Underpinning the current rates of cut is the belief that silviculture investment in the future justifies overcutting in the short term. Meanwhile, federal silviculture subsidies have ended and the rates of cut have not declined. There is no proof for the hypothesis that increased silviculture would produce a larger volume in second-growth forests. For the most part, Canada is still working its way through original forest.

Foresters commonly understand that the primary, virgin forest contains more wood than the younger forest that will replace it. The reduction of volume in a second-growth forest and the impact on future cut-rates is called "the fall-down effect." The impact is particularly significant in British Columbia, where commercial logging is moving through some of the tallest and largest trees on earth. The fall-down effect of a future supply restricted to second-growth forest, when it hits, will hit hard.

Too much Canadian forest is being cut and cut too fast. The flora and fauna of the forests have fewer and fewer places to call home. And fewer and fewer people are being employed per tree that is cut. Canada is eroding the ecological diversity of its forests, while reducing their economic value.

These trends are disturbingly reminiscent of the cod fishery. Technological innovation in the large draggers finds its terrestrial equivalent in clear-cutting. As in the fishery, a reduced labour force exploits more of the resource. As in the fishery, as supply of wood fibre has gone up through overcutting, so too have the number of mills. The political dynamic that stayed the hand of Fisheries ministers, who should have reduced fishing quotas, now maintains excessive logging levels. Wood must flow to mills or jobs will be lost. Built-in overcapacity and blinkered, short-sighted politics risk destroying the ecological integrity of the forests.

Canada's old-growth forests in many regions are already going the way of the cod. As the ancient trees are cut down, so too does natural species composition of forests become simplified, shifting to different species, eliminating habitat for forest-dwelling creatures. The woodland caribou is now at risk throughout its range in Canada. Forest-dwelling species, such as the wolverine and pine marten, are in trouble. Our endangered species laws are weak and ineffective, with the federal minister unable or unwilling to step in even for the most endangered of all birds in Canada—the spotted owl.

Change is happening across the landscape. More and more forested lands are being managed by their traditional stewards—the First Nations peoples of Canada. Reform is taking place, whether driven by the ongoing softwood wars with the United States or by market-driven campaigns demanding ecologically certified forest products. Never before has the Canadian public been as engaged in protecting our forests, with hearings and public consultations overwhelmed by the response of citizens, whether in Newfoundland, New Brunswick, Ontario or British Columbia.

But the forests are increasingly besieged not just by the forest industry, which in many places is moving toward better practices, but by other resource-based industries. Oil and gas exploration and development is destroying boreal forest with no thought of replanting or restoration of any kind. The mining industry is taking forests in its quest for minerals, while massive hydroelectric projects continue to threaten large forests from Newfoundland to Manitoba.

Speculation by industry on future forest conditions leads to optimistic projections of enhanced productivity. The potentially negative impacts of climate change, such as increased fires and shifts in species composition, could be mitigated by ensuring that there are forested areas set aside that are large enough to buffer change. But climate change is rarely recognized as a variable in forest management planning.

Our forests are not inexhaustible. Recently the Forest Products Association of Canada began an ad campaign designed to reassure

Canadians that we have more trees than ever. And it is true that old farm fields are reverting to forest cover. More of the landmass in Canada has trees than forty years ago. But the trees on the landscape are not of the same quality, ecologically or economically, as the original, primary forest. It is not true that current forest practices will sustain a healthy forest ecosystem. We are losing whole ecosystems— the Carolinian forests, old-growth Acadian and Garry oak. We are losing the boreal forests and wetlands that migratory birds depend upon, home to hundreds of millions of warblers.

We have long used the metaphor of "not seeing the forest for the trees." Seeing a forest is more than seeing trees. Seeing a forest is seeing the rich myriad of species and their interrelationships. It is understanding the role of forests in moderating climate, making soil and protecting water. Seeing the forest for the trees is seeing that life depends on the ecological services of the forest in holding carbon from the atmosphere and purifying water. We can have a landscape of trees, but lose the complexity of original forests. Industry ads deceive us with this sleight of hand.

Old-growth, intact and diverse forests are at risk. We are still at the cutting edge.

2 | MYTHS AND PROPAGANDA

In the 1990s, public-opinion surveys demonstrated that people don't like or trust the forest industry. Whereas forty years ago the term "threats to forests" brought to mind fires and insect plagues, more recently the term has become associated with the forest industry itself. Moreover, public disapproval of the industry was growing. In 1989, 33 per cent of Canadians identified acid rain and pollution as the number-one threat to forests, with forest industry mismanagement and overcutting a close second, at 31 per cent. By 1991, concern about overcutting had increased: 79 per cent of Canadians believed that clear-cutting was a poor forest management practice. Not surprisingly, the forest industry itself was identified as the greatest threat to forests, among 49 per cent of those sampled, while acid rain and pollution were in second place, at 18 per cent.[1] And while only 25 per cent of professional foresters agreed with the statement that "most old-growth forests should be protected," 86 per cent of the public supported that view.

When the chemical industry faced similar polls in the 1980s, the Canadian Chemical Producers' Association was horrified to realize that most Canadians would be happy to see the whole lot go out of business. So they organized an industry-wide policy, "Responsible Care," and started moving the industry to higher standards of performance. While its record is far from perfect, the chemical industry does have a functioning public advisory committee and has markedly improved its performance over the last ten years.

The forest industry, on the other hand, has always viewed its low public-approval rating as a communications problem. It has never thought that if 86 per cent of the public think clear-cutting is unacceptable, use of the method should be reduced. The response to every complaint from environmental, conservation and Aboriginal groups is a new assault of slick propaganda. If the Canadian public thinks the forests are in trouble, then the appropriate response is to make people believe that clear-cuts are "temporary meadows," that they mimic natural disturbance patterns and reflect the best ecology that money can buy.

Treating the forest crisis as a problem of perception, in the 1990s the forest industry turned to the world's best and largest public-relations firms. Burson-Marsteller, the PR giant called in to help Tylenol through the poison caplets crisis, and Union Carbide through Bhopal, gave the B.C. forestry industry its marching orders. To persuade the public of the industry's environmental bona fides, a neutral-sounding front was needed. The industry created the B.C. Forest Alliance and placed pro-clear-cutting spokesmen, such as Jack Munro and Patrick Moore, both of whom were previously affiliated with labour and environmental organizations, at the forefront. Its $2-million annual budget was nearly entirely funded by the forest industry.[2]

The B.C. and federal governments have worked closely with industry to promote Canadian forest practices abroad. During the 1990s, it is estimated that the government-industry propaganda effort totalled in excess of $68 million.[3]

In another effort to blunt environmental criticism, the industry has helped spawn groups that project the appearance of grass-roots community organizations. Throughout the United States, such groups go by the name Wise Use. In Canada, they are more likely to be called "Share" groups, as in "Share the Stein [Valley]."

Working with media experts, the industry developed a series of messages. The key, from an industry point of view, is to neutralize the response to horrific visuals of clear-cuts. Convincing people to deny the evidence of their own eyes takes a lot of work. But the industry has one element of human nature working in its favour: most people would rather believe everything is all right. It is deeply disturbing to hear that the ozone layer is thinning, that the climate is dangerously disturbed and that forests and the wildlife that depend upon them are dwindling. Any counter-argument that sounds convincing will be welcomed. Outrage takes energy, and most people have enough to worry about just paying their bills in the absence of job security.

Environmentalists tend to call such industry propaganda "myths." But myths generally speak to some larger cosmic truth, which is conveyed to mere mortals through allegory. While they are not scientifically true, myths have more veracity than the fictions that industry concocts. Such messages lock the debate about forest practices into polarized and entrenched positions.

In the last decade, a pronounced shift has occurred: dialogue and discussion have begun to take place. Some companies are working collaboratively with local environmentalists, establishing research projects and environmental benchmarks to better protect the non-timber values of a forest. The tone of public debate has been reduced in volume and intensity. Many within the forest industry know perfectly well that overcutting must stop. Such individuals are working to stop the propaganda war and find a common ground for the sake of the forests. All parties with a stake in the economic and ecological future of Canada's forests need to exchange views—reasoned as well as impassioned ones. Getting to that sensible discussion was not possible so long as industry and government created public-relations smokescreens.

The dynamics of denial and propaganda were in operation on the East Coast during the final years of the cod fishery. No one wanted to face up to what was clear to see from the poor catch rates of inshore fishers. No one wanted to admit that there were flaws in the mathematical models and biomass calculations. No one wanted to admit that dragging the ocean floor with 1.5-ton steel doors might have an impact on marine habitat. No one wanted to think about the fact that draggers were scooping up half of the total catch with only 10 per cent of the workforce. Draggers were modern and efficient; small fishers were outmoded and inefficient—and, once they couldn't find any cod, they were deemed inept to boot. Myth-making and an advanced state of denial allowed the industry to wipe out the fishery.

Many authors have done a brilliant job of unmaking the forest industry's myths.[4] But, as so many of these myths continue to be repeated in forest debates and statements to the media, it is important to put the major ones to rest once and for all.

Myth 1: "Environmentalists are urban dwellers who don't understand forests. They don't like clear-cuts just because the aftermath is ugly."

Most of the forest activists in Canada happen to be people living and working near forests. In fact, in contracting with the best forest researchers in Canada to assist with this book, Sierra Club of Canada drew on expertise from a logging contractor, a logger, a forester and people concerned about logging because they live with the consequences of bad logging practices, whether through loss of water supply as a result of poor road construction, eradication of valuable salmon runs, or contamination of crops from forest-spray drift.

While it is easier to motivate people about visible forest damage from clear-cutting than about damage to the ocean floor, that does not mean that aesthetics are the problem; rather, it's damage to bio-diversity, loss of soil, and reduced ecological productivity. As ugly as clear-cuts may be, if a forest could re-establish itself and be left for the requisite time to develop all the varied characteristics of a natural forest, the issue would be quite different. Clear-cuts, on a planned rotation of seventy to one hundred years, do not allow a forest to replace itself. The evidence from across Canada is that clear-cutting leads to conversion to lower-value species—more balsam fir in the east, more aspen in the prairies.

In Newfoundland, for example, the relative proportion of black spruce has declined through clear-cut logging. Tracking the reduction of black spruce is difficult, as the province's forest service lumps species together and indicates densities by individual species only if the volume is above 25 per cent. But regeneration surveys show a worrying decrease in black spruce after logging, reflecting the greater ability of balsam fir to regrow after a logging disturbance. "Regeneration failure is a problem on black spruce cut-over sites," reported a government survey. Less than 32 per cent of logged-over black spruce areas were adequately recovering in black spruce.[5]

In Ontario, the original boreal forest was dominated by white and black spruce, jack pine, balsam fir, trembling aspen and white birch. In recent years, the effects of widespread clear-cutting are being felt. And, unlike the natural fire suppression regime, removing all the trees over vast areas through clear-cutting is leading to a massive species conver-sion across the landscape. A 1992 government-commissioned study that examined more than 1,000 clear-cuts across Ontario's boreal found that softwoods were being replaced by lower-value small hard-woods. In fact, regenerating spruce had dropped by 77 per cent, while the proportion of poplar and birch had increased by 216 per cent![6]

Clear-cutting is simply the single most damaging way to log. As mentioned in Chapter 1, the term used by Canadian foresters for forests destroyed to the extent that new growth has a hard time tak-ing hold is "not satisfactorily restocked." NSR lands are generally priority areas for replanting. Nationally, in 2004, 2.4 million hectares were "officially" in this category.[7]

The reason that the number of NSR areas continues to rise is that clear-cutting on a massive scale makes it increasingly less likely that natural seed stock will reach usable soil. In comments that would foreshadow the criticisms made in the 1990s of clear-cut logging practices, Nova Scotia's 1958 inventory bemoaned that

> Clear-cutting...of medium-aged, high-density stands for pulpwood or small logs has effected a sudden and excessive exposure of the forest floor. The resultant drying from this exposure, and the scarcity of seed, has delayed natural reforestation of some lands for many years. Where seedlings have become established, the regeneration is frequently very light, and uneven under these circumstances.[8]

In a descriptive caption under a photo of a red spruce stand being clear-cut, the inventory report noted critically: "A thinning would have produced pulpwood and increased the diameter growth of those trees [remaining]...Also with maturity the remaining stand seed production would have ensured better chances of red spruce reproduction in the future."[9] Such candid appraisals of the risks of clear-cutting have been purged from more recent government reports. Currently, clear-cutting is defended by both government and industry as an acceptable "silvicultural tool."

In 1975, 585,000 hectares of Canadian forest were considered NSR. By 2004, the area classified NSR was officially 2.4 million hectares.[10] This was the case after more than ten years of federal-provincial subsidies for tree planting. Clearly, it's not working.

Myth 2: "Clear-cuts mimic nature."

This was the industry's first and most clever defence of clear-cuts. Large-scale disturbances do happen naturally in forests. They don't occur on seventy-year rotations, however, and they don't do the same amount of damage as clear-cutting. Fire disturbance patterns vary a great deal across Canadian ecosystems. They were never as prevalent in the Atlantic provinces as in the Prairies, and not at all a disturbance factor in the Pacific coastal rainforest. If any natural event actually resembles a clear-cut, one provincial biologist suggested that the only thing that came close was a landslide.

The key differences between fire damage and clear-cuts are:

- Fires do not leave behind a network of logging roads, landings and skid trails, opening the area to hunting and other exploitation and creating the risk of landslides. Logging roads themselves have been a significant cause of ecological degradation. As the Newfoundland Poole Royal Commission noted in 1980: "Bulldozing for access roads and wood landings causes deep mineral exposure on an estimated 10 per cent of the area harvested, and compaction by stockpiling of wood and by heavy vehicular traffic affects an additional 26 per cent or about 4,000 hectares per year."[11] It is a simple equation: roads destroy wilderness. If it's not roadless, it's not wilderness.

- Fires usually do not consume every tree on a site. The more fire-resistant survive, creating stronger genetic characteristics.

- Fires "may kill trees, but they leave the bodies on the site," says Herb Hammond, one of Canada's leading ecological foresters.[12] The diversity of structures left behind—fallen trees, snags (standing dead trees)—provide habitat for a range of species. The decomposing organic matter left behind rebuilds the soil.

- Fires generally do not occur every fifty to eighty years over the same area.

- Fires and other natural disturbances rarely do substantial damage to the soil. Clear-cuts do. Heavy mechanization often removes the top layer of organic material and exposes mineral soils, compacting the soil beneath the equipment. Ruts from the logging equipment increase erosion. And other than extremely hot fires, fire disturbance generally does not destroy the subterranean mycorrhizal fungi. These fungi and other soil bacteria perform essential functions, deriving nutrients from the tree roots, while giving the tree a vast network of threads, drawing water from a huge soil area. Thus, fungi and tree enjoy a perfect symbiotic relationship. Without the fungi, the soil is nutritionally and functionally impoverished. Clear-cuts destroy this fungal network. Erosion follows.

- Fires do not revisit recently burned-out areas to extend the damage through new fires, as progressive clear-cuts do.

- Fire is a chemical process; clear-cuts are a mechanical one.

- We cannot eliminate fires and choose to have clear-cuts instead.

Damage to forests is increased through the action of clear-cuts, adding to the damage from forest fires we are increasingly unable to control. Is it in anyone's interest to practise resource management that can be defended only by comparison with a natural disaster?[13]

The Clayoquot Sound Scientific Panel summarized the ecological impacts of clear-cutting as follows:

1. Clear-cutting affects streamflow by significantly changing patterns of evapotranspiration, snow accumulation, and snowmelt;
2. Clear-cutting leads to increased instability and soil erosion on steep slopes. This often results in increased sediment in streams, which degrades aquatic habitats and creates long delays in re-establishing forest cover, with attendant losses in productivity;
3. Clear-cutting exposes organic soils (folisols) and other thin soils to sunlight and wind, resulting in desiccation [extreme dryness] and subsequent soil loss from steep rocky areas, fissured limestone and bouldery ground;
4. Clear-cutting removes all trees older than the length of the cutting cycle. Therefore, all plant and animal species that require old trees can no longer be sustained on that site;
5. Clear-cutting replaces naturally uneven-aged forests with even-aged forests that greatly reduce structural age-class diversity and, often, changes tree species composition;
6. Clear-cutting removes all living trees and standing dead trees, thereby removing both present and future sources of large, decaying trees. This removal affects many wildlife and fish species that require specific structural components of forests (for example, snags, downed wood, woody debris in streams), as well as other organisms such as epiphytes and fungi;
7. The large tracts of young, even-aged forest that grow following clear-cutting have fewer gaps than natural, uneven-aged forests. These gaps are important to a variety of species;
8. Clear-cutting has damaged areas of cultural significance to Native peoples and has removed "culturally modified trees," that is, trees with evidence of prior use, primarily of the bark.[14]

Myth 3: *"Modern industrial forestry does not reduce biological diversity."*

High-grading in the past mined the most valuable species from the forests. The forest industry now vilifies high-grading in the defence of egalitarian clear-cutting: everything must go.

But clear-cutting inevitably leads to the loss of biological diversity, especially when one considers that under current industrial forest plans, every clear-cut will be logged again as early in its rotation as possible. As Canada cuts the last of its old-growth forests, ancient forest characteristics will be lost forever. Any logging regime that dictates that there will never again be vast areas of old-growth forest is guaranteed to have a negative impact on biodiversity.

Certain species need old growth. Without it, they do not have a home. As Dr. Bill Freedman of Dalhousie University has put it: "Old-growth stands are never managed by foresters as renewable, natural ecosystems. Rather, old-growth forest is always 'mined' by harvesting, which along with silvicultural management converts the ecosystem to one of younger, second-growth character."[15]

Clear-cuts also remove the biodiversity you do not see—that is, the life underground. Northern temperate forests hold a healthy web of life in the earth surrounding root systems. Plantations established after clear-cuts suffer from significantly reduced soil biodiversity. For example, a healthy Douglas fir has between thirty and forty species of ectomycorrhizal fungi, compared to only three to five species on Norway spruce found in Germany's intensively managed plantations.[16]

There are a number of variants of this myth:

- "Herbicides do not cause a loss of biodiversity."
  Herbicides kill trees and bushes. That is their purpose. Industry argues that just as many species end up on the site, and that using herbicide to kill weed species on recently clear-cut land does not lead to species conversion. In fact, it is part and parcel of the industrial forest intensive-management regime. "Weeds" are a symptom of clear-cutting. Herbicides are used only because clear-cutting has been so damaging that natural regeneration either needs "help," or has failed, and plantations need protection. But the so-called "weeds" are actually part of the healing process after disturbance. Some hardwood trees and bushes,

such as alders, are nitrogen fixing, improving the fertility of the soil. They hold the soil against erosion and provide micro-climatic shelter to new growth. These benefits are removed by chemical defoliants.

- "Clear-cuts *increase* biodiversity."
This is a clever argument. What it alleges is that biodiversity is protected, because when you add up the species growing on a clear-cut site, you get big numbers. A post-clear-cut area may change from an apparent war zone to a riotous proliferation of wildflowers, weeds and bushes. The area may actually have a higher number of species. But that does not mean that biodiversity has been enhanced, much less preserved. It is essential to understand the difference between counting species and protecting biological diversity. The *number* of species present may be high. But, if the *kinds* of species are fundamentally different, biodiversity has been affected negatively.

Research in New Brunswick found as many songbirds in a second- as in a first-growth forest, but the species differed. Those in the second-growth forest were the more common species that did not require mature- and old-forest attributes.[17] As Dr. Chris Pielou, a member of the Clayoquot Sound Scientific Panel, wrote: "Protecting common species is like saving old newspapers from a burning house, while leaving irreplaceable documents and the family photo albums behind.... Common species will come back—their ability to make a quick comeback is what makes them common. But a much larger number of comparatively uncommon true forest species will take much longer to return, and a good many will probably never make it."[18]

- "Clear-cutting and planting do not reduce genetic diversity."
There is evidence that plantation and second-growth forests lack the genetic variations of the natural forest. The most extreme cases would be those of large clear-cuts with subsequent planting of nursery-reared and genetically engineered seedlings. But research also suggests that even shelterwood and selection-cutting may have a negative impact on the genetic diversity of the trees themselves.[19]

Forest geneticist Roy Silen has noted that large-scale clear-cuts represent a risk to genetic diversity: "Our native tree populations, which we seem to thoughtlessly waste, may be our prime resource when the world of the twenty-first century must once again return toward truly sustainable yields."[20]

- "Clear-cuts are a temporary meadow."
Industry sources don't claim authorship of this myth; however, it is clearly trademarked by Patrick Moore, the Greenpeace founder who has changed sides and found his niche as the industry's most effective flack.[21] The tactical skill of an anti-seal hunt campaigner has been let loose on a pro-clear-cutting campaign.

Dr. Chris Pielou focused many of her arguments on Patrick Moore's proclamations. In response to this one, she wrote: "A meadow is a level expanse of water-logged soil that floods in wet periods and supports a rich growth of moisture-loving plants, chiefly sedges and grasses. The conditions are so ideal for these plants that trees are crowded out. It's hard to believe that anybody who has ever strayed off a sidewalk could mistake a clear-cut for a meadow."[22]

Myth 4: "Clear-cutting is a regeneration tool."

Clear-cutting is often defined as though it were a tree-growing system. For example, consider this common definition from the Canadian Council of Forest Ministers: "Clear-cut: A method of regenerating an even-aged forest stand, in which new seedlings become established in fully exposed microenvironments after removal of most or all existing trees."[23] The definition could be from a rewrite of Orwell's *Animal Farm* or *Nineteen Eighty-four*. In an Orwellian world, names often convey the opposite of what they seem to mean: the government censorship department is called the Bureau of Information. And clear-cutting is a "tree-growing system."

No one would have invented clear-cutting if the goal was to grow a forest. The definition of clear-cutting is efficiently logging vast areas quickly for short-term profit. Clear-cutting stresses the ecosystem beyond its natural capacity to maintain a forest. While trees can and will grow back, a forest, in all its complexity, often cannot replace itself.

Industry apologists will argue that a forest is imperiled if left alone in the shade, without the liberating effect of a clear-cut. While it is true that some trees regenerate better in bright sunlight, others do not. Those that do, such as Douglas fir, are perfectly capable of re-growing in the patches of sunlight that strike a forest floor after a single tree has fallen.

Clear-cuts are necessary if the goal is even-aged stands. But even-aged stands are not ecologically desirable. They are more vulnerable to insects and disease, and lack the habitat opportunities that the mixed structures of a natural forest offer to a range of species.

Even-aged stands are desirable only from a forest-fibre point of view. Clear-cutting one stand of same-aged trees maintains fibre flow to the mill. Selection logging of a mixed-age stand for those trees old enough for harvest is more costly in terms of labour, but leaves relatively intact forest with ongoing value.

Myth 5: *"If it greens up, it's fine."*

This is a variant of the "temporary meadow" myth. The fact that something will grow back in Canadian forests after clear-cutting is a tribute to the resiliency of the natural world. Trees may re-establish themselves naturally. Plantation trees may take root, and what was a scarred bit of ruin will likely be green again.

But the forest that existed before the clear-cut will not come back unless the area is given adequate time to re-establish itself before the next clear-cut logging. Second-growth forests have neither the ecological variety nor the economic value of first-growth forests. Canada is fortunate: its climate, water, soil, and species of flora and fauna are such that logged sites in most areas do not become moonscapes. But that is not an argument against the valid concerns that the forest is impoverished, and biodiversity lost, by clear-cutting on a short rotation.

The resilience of the natural world is not a legitimate justification for continued damage. Imagine if violence against another were justified because the victim was strong and could recover. Given therapy and counselling, many victims can regain their health and lead full, if somewhat compromised, lives after abuse. In other words, there is no need to stop the violence as long as we establish a program of intensive counselling. The silviculture equivalent of this perverse argument is manifested as tree-planting programs.

Myth 6: *"More than 12 per cent (50 million hectares) of Canada's forests have been protected from harvesting by policy or legislation."*

This myth also has authorship. The statement is from *The State of Canada's Forests, 1995–1996*, published by the federal Department of Natural Resources, Canadian Forest Service. It is intended to suggest conformity to the goal, adopted by all provinces and the federal government, of meeting the World Wildlife Fund (WWF) target for protected areas. The WWF Endangered Spaces Campaign calls for the protection of *at least* 12 per cent of Canada's land base in a network of representative protected areas.[24] The 12 per cent figure was drawn from the 1987 Report of the World Commission on Environment and Development (the Brundtland Commission). When the 12 per cent target was a floor instead of a ceiling, WWF emphasized that the goal was of an ecologically viable system of representative protected areas by the year 2000. But the 12 per cent target achieved such salience that the federal government claims it has accomplished the goal.

In fact, far less than 12 per cent of Canada's forests are protected within parks. Much progress has been made in protecting forests over the last decade, and by 2000, 7.6 per cent of Canada's forests were adequately protected.[25] Nevertheless, Manitoba still allows logging in some of its provincial parks. In Ontario, where only 1 per cent of the original old-growth white pine remains, only 37 per cent of that is currently protected within parks.[26] British Columbia has made the most progress in protected areas, but protection has been skewed toward rock and ice. Of the province's widely varying forest types, only 10 per cent have been protected and not in all key forest types. Particularly poorly represented in British Columbria's parks are the boreal white and black spruce, coastal Douglas fir, interior Douglas fir, ponderosa pine, sub-boreal pine spruce and sub-boreal spruce zones.

The claim in numerous federal government publications that 12 per cent of Canada's forests are protected is designed to mislead. When the CCFM originally made the claim, only 4 per cent of Canada's forests were in protected areas. The 12 per cent figure is generated by including all the buffer zones along waterways, beauty strips along highways, deer yards, steep hillsides and otherwise unlogged and inaccessible areas. Many of these buffer zones are suggested or mandated by provincial guidelines and regulations. It is not known whether these guidelines, regulations and policies are actually observed. But if areas of true protected forestlands are added to the hodgepodge of buffer zones and deer yards, the total allegedly equalled 12 per cent of Canada's forests in 1995.

Collections of 30-metre buffer zones do not constitute viable ecosystems. They are not part of a protected-areas strategy of representative ecoregions. They are not connected by wildlife corridors.

Indeed, most of these areas would be too small to support large species. The government's 12 per cent claim is analogous to saying that city green space constitutes 12 per cent of the downtown, based on adding up the areas of median strips between highway lanes. Children cannot play on the median strip, even if it is grassy. As well, biodiversity is not protected through minimal restrictions, such as those placed on logging next to large streams or on very steep slopes.

Myth 7: *"Clear-cutting is a carefully designed system used only in the appropriate ecological conditions."*

This argument attempts to create the impression that the decision to clear-cut is always site-specific: based on a thorough assessment of the particular ecosystem in question, the stand age and species mix, and other considerations. The big hole in this claim is that 85 per cent of the forest logged in Canada every year is clear-cut. This shows some improvement, as just ten years ago the proportion clear-cut was over 90 per cent.

Given the diversity of Canada's forests, the claim that the choice to clear-cut is tailored to local conditions is absurd. Patrick Moore, a proponent of clear-cutting, has perfected this argument. When pressed, he said he considered 90 per cent clear-cutting "about right" for all of Canada.[27]

Myth 8: *"Clear-cutting is the only economical way to log."*

The blanket response that there is no alternative to clear-cutting is implicit in much industry propaganda. Government efforts to achieve more ecologically sustainable logging often focus on reducing the size of clear-cuts, responding to the public outrage at clear-cuts visible from satellites out in space. But simply reducing the size of clear-cuts can actually worsen ecological damage, by increasing fragmentation of wildlife habitat. More roads are required for smaller clear-cuts, or "cutblocks." Of course, the use of the term "smaller" to describe clearcuts of up to 100 hectares is quite relative.

Proponents of clear-cuts have argued that any opening is a clear-cut, reducing anti-clear-cut arguments to an absurd position. Such semantic hair-splitting also obscures the alternatives. No environmental group has ever argued that no clearings, of any size, should be allowed in a forest. Their position is that the opposite extreme—indiscriminant reliance on clear-cutting—is unacceptable.

The alternatives to clear-cutting are many. In some ecosystems, shelterwood cutting, or even-aged forest management, could be an appropriate method. In the shelterwood system, two cuts are made: first, a "regeneration cut," leaving trees at intervals; and second, a "harvest cut," made when the trees left after the regeneration cut are old enough for logging. Like clear-cutting, this method has the disadvantage of leaving trees at more or less the same age after the two cuts have been made. Irregular shelterwood, or partial-cut, techniques can be used to maintain higher quality habitat for wildlife.

In contrast, the selection logging method, or uneven-aged forest management system, more closely approximates a natural forest. As defined by ecological forester Herb Hammond: "Single stems in a single tree selection system or small groups of trees in a group selection system are cut at each entry, with careful regulation of crown closure, species composition, health and vigor of the remaining stand."[28] The selection system ensures that new trees will continually grow to replace those removed. As openings fill with young trees, new ones are logged. Thus, there will always be at least three different age classes in a forest that remains available for logging on a sustainable basis.

While short-term logging costs may be higher, the forest maintains healthy growth and generates higher economic benefits in the long term.

The Clayoquot Sound Scientific Panel recommended a "variable retention silvicultural system." The primary objective of this selection method is to establish what elements of a forest should be left behind after logging. In Ontario, the government developed a new policy of retaining 10 to 36 per cent[29] of a forest within a logged section, or cutblock, to better emulate natural patterns after a forest fire.[30] Although many companies have adopted variable retention, some have used it to assert that clear-cutting no longer takes place, while retaining only unwanted trees.

Practicing ecosystem-based logging and retaining essential elements of the forest reduces the volume that is cut. But increasingly, "green" certification, such as certification from the Forest Stewardship Council, gives forest managers a competitive edge in the marketplace.

For woodlot owners, there are even more options. In Oregon, Individual Tree Selection Management, Inc. (ITS), works with small landowners to ensure a steady cash flow from their woodlots. Years of using selection management have generated reams of data establishing the system's profitability. On one Oregon woodlot of 172 hectares, thirty years of logging has yielded an average annual profit, after costs, of $4,000 (U.S.), and the standing volume of timber has more than tripled. The land was originally purchased for $17,250 (U.S.).[31] Similar success has been achieved by B.C. forest operator Merv Wilkinson, by the Menominee Nation of Wisconsin, by Leonard Otis of Quebec and by Donald George of Algonquin Provincial Park, to name a few. There is no particular magic to the notion that a standing forest will produce more wood than bare ground.

With many of the above alternatives, there is no need for costly and environmentally destructive replanting efforts, herbicide treatments, or the rehabilitation of fish habitat and other corrective measures after devastation by poor logging.

"I cut for the forest, not for the trees," observed the head of ITS forestry consulting, Scott Ferguson, in an article published in 1988. "Then I maximize the value of the product through marketing. Trees grow in groups, not in a grid pattern. I try to maximize what the group can do."[32] But whether called "variable retention" or "selection system," to quote Herb Hammond, "it is not the words that matter, but the ecological impact on the forest."[33]

Myth 9: *"Variable retention is not clear-cutting."*

In response to opposition to clear-cutting, a number of companies have made the announcement: "We are no longer clear-cutting. We are now using variable retention." Retention has been recognized as an important component of ecosystem-based logging. The islands of trees left within a cutblock retain some of the diversity and habitat value of the harvested land. However, some companies leave single trees or small groups of trees standing within a cutblock. With little buffer from the wind and weather, these trees most often blow down and offer little genetic, structural or habitat value. Variable retention can mean good forestry, but it can also amount to very little depending on the percentage of trees retained.

Myth 10: *"Canada keeps its international commitments."*

Canada has signed and ratified the United Nations Convention for the Protection of Biodiversity. This, in itself, is a significant achievement. The United States signed, but has not ratified, due to the anti-environmental forces on the rise in the U.S. Congress since the Earth Summit in 1992.

A key element to commitments under the Biodiversity Convention is protecting endangered species. Canada finally enacted legislation to protect species at risk in 2003. First introduced in 1995, after two failed attempts, it finally became law eight years later. When the act finally passed, it was so weak that it applied to only approximately 40 per cent of the endangered species in Canada. The fundamental flaw was a refusal on the part of the federal government to accept its responsibility to protect any species in Canada threatened with extinction, no matter where it lives. By protecting only those species found on federal lands or waters, it left the bulk of Canada's lands and species without any legal tools to halt extinctions.

While the so-called "safety net" is relied on by government to protect the majority of terrestrial species, it is politically and constitutionally problematic. The safety net is theoretically available any time a species at risk is not receiving adequate protection from a provincial government. When the federal Minister of Environment determines that the species is sliding toward extinction on a provincial watch, the minister must go to Cabinet and seek a regulation to protect that species. In 2004, a number of environmental groups petitioned the Minister of Environment, demanding protection for the northern spotted owl by way of an Emergency Order. Only fourteen adult owls were recorded in the old-growth forests of British Columbia in 2003, making it the most endangered bird in Canada. The minister declined. Many Canadian provinces have brought in provincial legislation since the ratification of the Biodiversity Convention, but not Alberta, and not British Columbia. The B.C. government continues to approve cutting plans even in the few areas known to harbour these few animals.

The Biodiversity Convention also requires buffer zones with reduced logging adjacent to parks and protected area. But across Canada, clear-cut logging takes place right up to the borders of our national parks, from Wood Buffalo to Gros Morne, Fundy to Pacific Rim.

Canada has created a Biodiversity Strategy, but it is only a non-binding statement of intent, and does not have the force of law. Similarly, Canada has a National Forest Strategy. The 2003 Strategy has clear and measurable targets to improve the ecological management of forests. Thus far, some industry and environmental groups have embraced the Strategy. Every provincial government, except Alberta and Quebec, has signed on. First Nations are active participants in the implementation, although not signatories owing to a weakening of language around First Nations issues. But for all its good intentions, living up to the commitments of the Strategy is purely voluntary. Jurisdiction over forests in Canada remains provincial; a national policy has no teeth.

Myth 11: "We need to keep clear-cutting to maintain employment."

This is The Big Lie. It's the old "jobs-versus-environment" argument, which falsely divides the workforce from the environmental movement. In fact, both groups should focus on a common enemy: an economic system that rewards reducing labour while increasing the liquidation of natural capital.

The modern corporation works with ruthless determination to become more efficient, and hence more competitive. Corporate logic has deduced that efficiency is a matter of reducing employment. To be competitive, companies have become increasingly resource-, capital- and energy-intensive. Labour has been drastically reduced per unit of production. Industrial agribusiness, fisheries, manufacturing of all kinds, and, increasingly, even the service industries, are running their companies as if there were a significant shortage of people and an abundant supply of energy, water, soil, fish and trees.

As Paul Hawken put it in *The Ecology of Commerce*, CEOs of large corporations do not awaken each bright new day and ponder gleefully how they can rape and pillage the planet.[34] Nor are they particularly venal or amoral. In fact, on an individual basis, many forest-industry executives share the concerns expressed in this book. Why, then, does the environment suffer while jobs disappear? As Paul Hawken's brilliant insight has it, what we have here is a "design problem."

The reason that corporate logic leads to such tragically flawed conclusions is that the market and fiscal indicators by which businesses steer their course dictate the wrong direction. The taxation system makes corporations pay a hefty price for every employee, but not for the machine that replaces that person, nor for the gas to run the machine. We tax the things that in themselves are harmless or even beneficial, such as corporate profit and individual income, and accord tax holidays to activities we ought to discourage. If we had deliberately designed our economic signals to ensure high unemployment and maximum ecological damage, we couldn't have done it better.

Of course, what we design, we can redesign. A whole new field is opening up called "ecological tax reform." Advocates of redesigned tax policy even suggest we could remove all taxes on personal income and corporate profit to sweeten the pot as the tax burden gets shifted to resources and energy. According to Ernst Van Weizsacher of the Wuppertal Institute—tax expert and now Green Party member of the German Parliament: "If we could increase the productivity of resources and energy in anything like the same way as we have increased the productivity of labour since the turn of the century—in other words, twenty times—there would be a veritable revolution."[35]

It sounds like such a wonderful idea: the root causes of forest devastation and high unemployment could be removed through something as apparently easy as tax reform. However, anyone who has ever tried to convince a Finance Department bureaucrat of the value of changing anything knows that even minuscule changes to tax policy are hard won, and major change of the kind suggested here might take decades.

Over the last forty years, Canada's forest industry has undergone substantial technological change, with significant implications for the workforce. It cannot be overstated that the role of mechanization is the overriding cause of ecological devastation by the industry. It is the driving force behind the degradation of the natural biodiversity of our forests. It is also the major reason that Canada exports jobs along with its pulp.

The technological revolution in Canada's forests transformed logging. What was once a picturesque but dangerous trade performed by individual loggers—hacking at the forests with cross-cut saws and axes and then hauling the wood with horses and oxen—has become a model of space-age technological efficiency. Today, a logger is likely to be in an air-conditioned cab, listening to the CD player, monitoring the species in front of him through his on-board computer and accessing satellite data.[36]

The first major shift occurred when the handsaw was replaced by the chainsaw. With the chainsaw came the skidder, essentially a modified tractor with a cable winch, or grapple, that was used to pile the logs. Bulldozers were brought in to create trails for skidders and grapple-yarders, with overzealous operators doing serious damage. Then came the forwarder, the trailer that could replace the horse and ox. By 1970, another wave of innovations hit the forest industry, with machinery that became increasingly complex and capable of performing several functions. The feller-buncher was introduced in this period, capable of actually chopping down a tree, cutting it up into even lengths, delimbing it, and piling the logs neatly in an attached trailer. The feller-buncher became immediately popular, allowing a single operator to replace between twelve and fifteen workers. Of course, feller-bunchers could cut down only trees of a smaller diameter. The feller-buncher grasps the tree and, like some bionic lobster claw, snaps it off like a twig. The forest giants of British Columbia could not be felled with claws suited to the boreal. Loggers there still used chainsaws, but increasingly it was not men who mowed down Canada's forests, but machines.

When trees were delimbed at the stump, much of the organic material was left on site. This method was known as "tree-length logging." But, in this period, loggers also began a different approach, called "full-tree logging," in which the entire tree was taken to the roadside or the mill yard and delimbed there. This method avoided having to take de-limbing equipment into the woods at all. The machines have a simpler time cutting the whole tree and delivering it somewhere else for delimbing and cutting into even lengths. As Jamie Swift observed in his classic book *Cut and Run*, "Under a full tree system, wood can be delivered to the mill untouched by human hands. Silviculture treatments could now include use of fertilizer to compensate for lost nutrients from logging. All of these developments were facilitated by the new machines. Limbs and other woody debris could be put through a chipper for use as biomass fuel."[37]

By the 1980s, forest companies and contractors had newer and more devastating types of equipment. The trend was still toward bigger and better machinery. The feller-forwarder joined the feller-buncher and grapple-skidder.[38] Less and less organic material was left on the site. Due to the weight of the logging equipment, soil compaction became a problem. More permanent roads were built for the heavy equipment. More soil was lost to erosion—the result of both poor road construction and the giant ruts left by heavy equipment, some with wheels as large as 3 metres in diameter.

Lack of regeneration following logging increased. Where the poor forest practices of the past, such as high-grading, had involved lots of labour and few machines to accomplish one type of ecological damage, modern logging was devastating huge areas. No one could accuse mechanical harvesters of choosing only the best. They took everything.

Large mechanized harvesting was economical only if it was used for clear-cutting. Bringing in the largest heavy equipment for selection logging just doesn't work. For the really big logging machines, the ideal type of cut is a huge land area through which the feller-forwarders, feller-bunchers and grapple-skidders can move with ruthless efficiency. Clear-cutting went from a small portion of total logging prior to 1940 to about 70 per cent in 1970 to over 90 per cent in the 1980s.[39] Largely due to public demand for more ecological forestry, coupled with the loss of markets for Canadian forest products in Europe and the United States, the proportion of forest clear-cut has begun to decline—to 85 per cent in 2003. Yet, in 2003, Ontario announced it was removing any restriction on the size of individual clear-cuts.

As logging became increasingly capital-intensive, pressure increased to log more trees faster. With the use of headlights, logging crews could now work around the clock. With huge tires and greater mobility, logging became less susceptible to seasonal changes and weather.

Read advertisements for this new wave of forest equipment and realize how far Canada has come from the days of long-saws and axes, or even from chainsaws. The Timbco T415-B is hailed as "the best and most versatile feller-buncher available today! Built by loggers for loggers." Standard equipment includes the Caterpillar tractor undercarriage, track shoes like a tank, the Timbco 28" barsaw "with directional felling capabilities," as well as an air conditioner and heater. Optional equipment includes the full halogen-light package for night logging and the AM/FM cassette radio with headphones. The Thunderbird TMY-70 has 4 outriggers, 430 horsepower, 5-speed transmission and yarding capabilities of 2,700 feet. The DDC 5000 ads proclaim: "Delimb, debark and chip with one machine and one operator. Whether in the woods or in the yard . . ."

Individual contractors with hundreds of thousands of dollars' worth of bank loans hanging over their heads were forced to continually find ways to make the maximum dollar each month, just to break even. At the same time, the number of jobs per unit of production tumbled. In New Brunswick, the number of people employed in the forest industry dropped from 4,756 in 1966 to 2,057 by 1993.[40] Over the same period, logging increased. The same is true in Newfoundland. In 1925, for every 725,000 cubic metres cut, 8,000 Newfoundland loggers had jobs. By 1995, fewer than 1,500 loggers felled more than 3 million cubic metres.[41] The trend is the same across Canada.

As a measurement of employment per unit of production, jobs have been lost across Canada. It took 5 workers to produce 1,000 tons of wood pulp in 1971. By 1990, only 3.1 workers produced that same volume. In 1971, 2.3 workers were required to produce 1,000 cubic metres of dimensional lumber (lumber mechanically shaped to standard dimensions); the number dropped to 1.2 workers by 1990. And the number of people required to produce 1,000 tons of paper and paperboard fell from 10.9 workers to 7.4 over the same period.[42]

Many of these job losses have been offset by increases in production. Canada is producing a much larger volume of wood products with fewer people. But, even accounting for the larger volumes of wood logged, the number of jobs in the forest industry has been reduced in absolute terms by mechanization. Between 1971 and 1990, total employment in the manufacture of wood pulp decreased by over 17 per cent, while production volume went up by 32 per cent. Employment in the dimensional-lumber sector fell by 25 per cent, while production volume increased by an astronomical 153 per cent! And jobs in the manufacture of paper fell by 9 per cent while production volume rose by 34 per cent.[43]

In the words of the union of Pulp and Paper Workers of Canada, "If we keep cutting trees at current rates, our forests will disappear forever. Forest company methods, like clear-cut slashing and burning, are wiping out our forests.... *Forest companies use technological change to make less people cut more trees faster.* Production goes up, while jobs are disappearing throughout the pulp and wood industries" [emphasis added].[44]

Jobs in the forest industry are typically subject to extreme fluctuations based on worldwide pulp supply as well as recessions. The industry is used to wild cycles of highs and lows, in production, sales and jobs. In 1970, more than 260,000 people were directly employed in the forest industry in Canada. Between 1970 and 1991, employment figures rose to a high of nearly 310,000 jobs in 1979, and fell to a low of 250,000 jobs by 1991.[45] In 2002, 361,400 people were directly employed in forestry in Canada. The total numbers are unquestionably large, but the employment-generating capacity of Canada's industry does not compare well to other countries. Overall, despite a 60 per cent increase in production, the ratio of worker to volume has been steady at only two workers for every 1,000 cubic metres for the last thirty years. Sweden's industry creates three jobs for every 1,000 cubic metres. Even the United States, that bastion of economic efficiency, produces 2.62 jobs for the same volume.[46]

The forest industry has been one of the major beneficiaries of Canada's unemployment insurance (officially known as Employment Insurance, or EI), laying off workers to save money in the short term and rehiring as it suits them. This is yet another type of "subsidy" that irritates competitors.

The average percentage reductions hide big impacts in particular communities. For example, the Special Job Creation Commissioner for Port Alberni, British Columbia, relying on logging within Clayoquot Sound and adjacent areas, found that, between 1980 and 1990, 2,200 forestry direct jobs were lost in the district. Most of the job losses were from MacMillan Bloedel. By 1993, a further 590 jobs were lost in the Port Alberni area.[47] These losses were caused by mill closures as well as mechanization. Overall, in British Columbia, employment per 1,000 cubic metres dropped from 1.5 people in 1977 to 1.0 people in 1987. It has been estimated that since 1970, 22,000 forest industry jobs have been lost in British Columbia, primarily because of mechanization. Recently, the employment picture has improved, as it now takes 1.4 workers to produce 1,000 cubic metres of forest product on the coast, but still only 0.9 workers as a provincial average.[48]

The new boom in oriented strand board (OSB, a type of chipboard), will not generate much new employment, either in logging, which will be mechanized clear-cuts, or in production. OSB plants have become increasingly mechanized. What took 7.2 workers to produce in 1978, will take only 1.8 workers in the proposed new OSB mills.[49]

New types of machinery have been developed, primarily in Scandinavia, that allow fully mechanized selection cuts. It is possible to log a forest with a piece of equipment that leaves it looking as though it had been horse-logged. Flotation tires and lighter-weight equipment makes it possible to advocate selection logging methods without advocating hazardous working conditions.

Competitiveness is an interesting phenomenon. It has driven Canadian industry to significant increases in the productivity of each employee by eliminating his or her co-workers and providing the most efficient machines ever invented for removing trees. It has encouraged downward pressure on regulations and on stumpage prices, and mitigated against protected areas or regulations to protect ecosystem values. The competition has been a race for the bottom. Canada has been prepared to move heaven and earth to ship out more wood faster, with fewer people. The forest industry in Canada has become largely volume-driven and is quantity-based. But what would happen if Canada's competitive drive was harnessed in a race for the top? What if a quality-based industry could develop, focusing less on the volume logged and more on the value-added forest product—the violin case instead of the roll of toilet paper.

The reality is that competition to produce the world's cheapest raw forest products is destroying jobs, impoverishing forest environments and fuelling drastic overcutting of our national forests.

Myth 12: *"Clear-cutting is the best way to log if you have an entirely mechanized operation and government subsidies, and want a short-term profit."*
Actually, this is not a myth. It is true.

3 | VOODOO FORESTRY

Canada is overcutting. The rates of cut are set to meet industry demands for fibre, not to ensure sustainability. Yet government and industry publications present a facade of rigorous scientific data to promote the illusion that they are working toward sustainability. To understand the true state of Canada's forests, it is essential to penetrate the smoke and mirrors of modern "forest management."

Just as the management of the fisheries employed a dizzying array of acronyms and complicated formulas, from Total Allowable Catch (TAC) to estimates of spawning biomass, so too do the forest industry and its regulators. Once these concepts are explained and examined, the intimidating technical facade crumbles. And it becomes clear that the little boy is right—the emperor has no clothes.

Over the last decade, the definition of ecological sustainability has broadened from ensuring that the level of wood that is cut does not exceed what the forest can grow to ensuring that harvesting maintains intact forested areas, for the protection of both wildlife and the natural forest. Most provinces have not yet moved to this new model. In addition, it is clear that the information needed to ensure ecological sustainability is not readily available.

Working with the old model to determine whether Canada's forests are sustainably managed, managers have traditionally looked at two key figures: the supply of wood and the rate at which it is cut. This should be a rather straightforward analysis, but in fact, Canada's estimates of how much wood is in the forest (the forest inventory) and how much is considered a sustainable rate of cut in any given year (the annual allowable cut) are subjective and open to interpretation and manipulation.

Counting the trees
The public can be forgiven for assuming that basic facts about Canada's forests are known. Government documents report confidently on wood supply and categorize it as "available," "commercial"

or "protected." While anyone can imagine the difficulties of counting masses of fish in the open ocean, trees are, after all, visible and do not move. Hence, logic suggests they should be easy to count accurately.

They are not. The problem is that Canada's forests cover such a vast area that the business of counting them is crude and the results unreliable. Overall, Canada's forest regulators have only a general idea of the nature and extent of the forest. The most recent forest inventory, released in the autumn of 2004, differed significantly from the previous tree-counting exercises. With satellite interpretation, suddenly, a lot changes. The federal government issued the inventory with the disclaimer that it "cannot be compared meaningfully" with the other inventories. The reality is that if one did compare the data, Canada's territories would appear to have mysteriously lost more than 30 million hectares of forest. But somehow Canada's newly classified "forest and other wooded area" now contains 60 million hectares more commercially available forest than a decade ago. As one knowledgeable writer and forest industry commentator, Ken Drushka, commented, the inventories are "more often than not...outdated, speculative, or just plain wrong."[1]

Canada's forest inventories are made using aerial photographs. The photographs are examined to differentiate tree species, but it's often guesswork as to what is really on the ground. Species that look alike—for instance, aspen and balsam poplar—are lumped together. Species occurring at low densities are often simply omitted.

The bird's-eye view doesn't even begin to give a picture of volumes on the ground. Trees grow at widely varying rates, depending on soil, climate, water and the extent of damage done to the forest by disturbances, whether insect, fire or logging. To determine how much can be cut, it is critical to know how fast the forest is growing, how much wood is in any given stand, and how the forest breaks down along age categories.

In order to come up with even general estimates of rates of growth, as well as to verify whether the species identified based on aerial photos actually exist on the ground, provinces establish Permanent Sample Plots (PSPs). These are revisited over the years to provide some benchmarks of how the forest grows in local conditions. But maintaining PSPs is expensive. Some provinces have relatively good coverage, while others have only scanty access to the data from too few plots.

Richmond Hill Public Library
      Check OUT Receipt

User name: ZHUANG,
KATHERINE (MS)

Item ID: 32971013566991
Title: Forests and grasslands

Date due: May 30, 2014 11:
59 PM

Item ID: 32971006999977
Title: At the cutting edge :
the crisis in Canada's fore
Date due: May 30, 2014 11:
59 PM

Item ID: 32971009599162
Title: Forestry
Date due: May 30, 2014 11:
59 PM

Total checkouts for session:
3
Total checkouts: 3

www.rhpl.richmondhill.on.ca

But even data from those few areas that have received the personal attention of a forester can be wholly unreliable. Recently a number of studies have been conducted to assess the accuracy of foresters' assessments. Uniformly, these studies found significant rates of error.[2]

Field crew mistakes are increasingly recognized in the forestry literature as a significant cause for concern. Major problems exist in estimating the height of trees, but data can even be unreliable when remeasurements are taken of the tree trunk diameter at the height of a man's chest. This measurement, called DBH or "diameter at breast height," is clearly the simplest and least open to interpretation. You just need to use a tape measure around the trunk of a tree. But errors of 5 to 15 per cent have been reported for remeasurements of DBH.[3] The impact of a series of faulty estimates of tree age, size and height only compound the lack of precision in estimating how much forest can be sustainably logged.[4]

Stand measurement errors are particularly dangerous because they tend to *overestimate* rates of growth and stand volume coming from younger forests and plantations.[5] Cutting more now based on a false sense of security of how much forest remains is highly risky. Yet inventory data, especially once codified and issued in impressive reams of statistics, are not treated with caution. As Ken Drushka remarked in his book *Stumped*, "...so frequently have these [inventory and measurement] inadequacies been revealed that one can only marvel at the assurance with which politicians and bureaucrats quote the latest inventory data."[6]

While some provinces are marginally better than others at some aspects of compiling data, the overarching reality is that the data represent best guesses—not absolutes. Overall, Canada doesn't have much better science to figure out how much wood is available than to figure out how many fish were in the waters off Newfoundland.

Log now, pay later

Once government foresters decide how much wood they think there is, they then estimate the "timber supply." The inventory is "netted down" to exclude areas that are unloggable. The "unloggable" include barrens, lakes and areas that are too rocky or are unavailable for economic reasons (trees too small or too far from any mill), as well as those areas protected in parks. There is an exception to every rule, of course, as some provinces allow logging in parks. In fact, clear-cutting was allowed in every provincial park in Manitoba until 1997, when it was banned in most of the parks.[7]

Once the amount of wood considered commercially available is determined, the province sets the level of logging, or annual allowable cut (AAC). This should be an estimate of what can be safely and sustainably cut now so that nature can replace the loss from year to year.

The AAC is usually defined as it was in *The State of Canada's Forests*: "The amount of timber that is permitted to be cut annually from a specified area. The AAC is used to regulate the harvest level to ensure a long-term supply of timber."[8]

But it is hardly ecologically based. The AAC is influenced by a whole range of maneuvers. For example, any tree species in a Canadian forest not already slated for logging is considered "under-utilized." As soon as new technologies to use these trees are developed, overnight what had been a forest running out of commercially valuable species becomes an industry boom. Hardwood, of course, is considered "underutilized" and now forms the basis of the bonanza for clear-cutting across Canada to feed OSB and chipboard mills.

Many provinces factor in totally inaccessible wood when they set the AAC, which is supposedly based on the available wood-supply base. Quebec and Ontario's AAC benefit enormously from remote northern forests, while Newfoundland's provincial inventory includes the overcut forest of the island of Newfoundland as well as the far less disturbed forests of Labrador. The lumping together of the wood supply from these different forests, and the corresponding calculation of an annual cut based on the composite forest, is quite misleading.

Voodoo forestry

There are other tricks played with the AAC. One easy way to allow more logging without increasing the number of trees is to change the age at which trees are logged. If the AAC has been calculated assuming that it will take ninety years before a new forest will be old enough to clear-cut, the simple expedient of reducing the harvest age to seventy will allow more logging now.

Dr. Chris Pielou, a B.C. ecologist, has warned of the impacts of the rotation ages chosen by government and industry. She ridiculed the concept of logging at maturity in what she calls "the maturity scam." Through this device, overcutting is accelerated: a Douglas fir, for example, which can live 750 years, is declared ready for logging at sixty to eighty years old.[9]

The most outrageous way to justify overcutting is the "log now, pay later" plan, the so-called "allowable cut effect." Here's how it works. If a forest company commits to a range of measures known as intensive forest management—tree planting, spraying herbicides and insecticides, and thinning the growing trees over time—then it can cut more now based on the speculative increase in growth later.

This approach was developed by large forest companies in the late 1970s and early 1980s. As C. Calvert Knudson, President and CEO of MacMillan Bloedel recalled, "The way the annual allowable cut is calculated, as you harvest large old growth and second growth comes in, your annual allowable cut drops substantially in proportion to the reduction of the annual volume of fibre growth in the area, *unless you do something about it*" [emphasis added].[10]

What he did was actually *increase* the AAC at a time that it would otherwise have declined. "I knew," Knudson continued, "that unless we adopted a more intensive management program to offset the forecast decline in harvest we would wind up without enough timber for our mills. If you conduct an aggressive forest management program you can *accelerate your old growth harvest* in the knowledge that the growth of the next crop will be accelerated. In fact, you can even expand your annual allowable cut.... You offset the lack of standing inventory with rapid growth" [emphasis added].[11]

Overcutting now, based on the belief that you can grow more trees faster later, is rolling the dice on the future outcome. The forest companies get credit for silviculture not yet even begun. Moreover, even if the companies did the range of energy and chemical inputs called "intensive silviculture," *there is absolutely no proof the forest would grow faster and better trees*. This is simply voodoo forestry.

Tree planting has already been shown to be unreliable in boosting the "future forest." According to a federal Forest Service eleven-year review of silvicultural statistics:

An awareness that regeneration success rates based on
stocking or density are inadequate to assess regeneration performance is developing in Canada: *mounting evidence casts doubt on the premise that yields of second growth stands will at*

least equal the yields of the natural stands they replace [emphasis added].[12]

The companies are given credit as though intensive silviculture had been proven capable of pushing production to even higher levels in the second-growth forest than in the old growth; yet plenty of evidence suggests it cannot equal the primary forest. As 90 per cent of everything logged in Canada today is in previously unlogged areas, any projected reduction in second growth will be cause for concern.[13]

Moreover, there is no proof that the use of herbicides will speed growth. The theory that herbicide spraying should allow forest companies to cut more trees faster is based on an argument that humans can improve on natural succession. Industry foresters argue that since pioneer hardwood species are the first to recover on a site after logging, and since they shade the new softwood seedlings, they should be removed by herbicides as quickly as possible to boost the growth of the commercial species. The practice is called "conifer release," as though young pin cherry and birch were holding the softwood seedlings hostage. In fact, herbicides can damage the new seedlings they are designed to liberate. The shade from alders and other early successional species protects the conifer seedlings from UV rays, while providing shelter from winds and storms. And, of course, the future forest is deprived of the positive ecological role of hardwoods and bushes, which give nutrients to the soil and help prevent erosion.

Most provinces calculate estimates of increased forest yields in "allowable cut effect" (ACE) accounts. Such accounts include projected accelerated growth, supposedly to be gained through future intensive forest management, as if the putative forest growth were already part of the standing inventory. As long ago as 1976, the British Columbia Royal Commission on Forestry report, by resource economist Peter Pearse, described the allowable cut effect as "...so obviously perverse that the degree of acceptance of the system is surprising."[14] So confident is New Brunswick, for example, of future increased productivity—or so desperate is the industry for increased AAC now—that 35 per cent of the province's cut is based on the hypothetical future forest. If the forest does not somehow grow 35 per cent more on the same land in the future, then New Brunswick's current AAC is 35 per cent too high.[15]

Voodoo forestry is everywhere. All the provinces manipulate figures on the rate of growth to accommodate overcutting now, in order to guarantee wood supply to mills. Meanwhile, it is not only the environmental community that worries that AACs are too high across Canada. A 1990 opinion survey of 4,500 Canadian professional foresters, conducted by the federal Forest Service, found that over 60 per cent of them believed that the AAC in their province was definitely or likely too high. And more than three-quarters agreed with the statement "There is a growing scarcity of timber in Canada today."[16]

Sustainable, until it's gone

Government regulators reassure the public. They urge the concerned citizen not to worry about sustainability if the AAC is too high or if it is exceeded. The key, they claim, is in the "long-run sustained yield" (LRSY), sometimes called the "long-term sustained yield" (LTSY) or "long-run harvest level" (LRHL). The bafflegab can be quite entertaining in expressing the differences between unsustainable cutting within an AAC and the long-range view. For example, one Forestry Canada publication claims that: "The AAC is not necessarily equal to the long-run sustained yield (LRSY) level, nor is it necessarily sustainable in the long run, although sustainability is usually a long-run objective."[17]

Or this priceless example from the Newfoundland timber supply analysis:

> Although the AAC is used synonymously with sustained yield, it does not imply a wood supply that can be harvested in perpetuity. Rather, the AAC concept refers to a level of harvest over the specified analysis period only. It makes no statement about the availability of wood beyond that period.[18]

In other words, forestry in Canada is sustainable until it's gone. The LRSY can differ from the AAC and be explained away by government and industry as follows: As Canada moves through its old growth and converts the whole forest to what they like to describe as a "thrifty, productive young forest,"[19] there will be a reduction in the AAC.

This drive to force the natural forest into convenient rotational ages for the forest industry has its origins in the earliest days of forestry, as advocated by the University of Toronto's first Dean of Forestry, Bernard Fernow. He believed that the "proper" distribution of ages in the forest—with no over-preponderance of young trees and equally no oversupply of the very old—is essential if the forest industry is to have a steady, even flow of timber. Since the early twentieth century, it has been the goal of "sustained yield forest management" to produce a forest with age distribution to meet the model. With widespread clear-cutting, the ideal is not mixed ages within the same stand. Rather, over a patchwork of vast landscape, the goal is to have roughly equal amounts of young, nearly mature and mature forests.

Some analysts have pointed out that creating this ideal of single-aged stands at different age levels gives the government a strong incentive to have the full AAC cut in every year. "From the government's point of view, unused allocated cut...delays the conversion of old-growth forests to faster-growing plantations."[20]

Old-growth forest has large trees with high volumes of wood. A second-growth forest is not going to build up those volumes. So the AAC for an area of old growth will have to drop when that same area comes back as second growth. This is called the "fall down effect," and plays a large part in the recent reductions to some of British Columbia's AACs in certain Tree Farm Licences. Government regulators claim that it is fine to have high AACs until the last of the old growth is mowed down. Theoretically, all of this will be sustainable as soon as the second growth comes in with lower AACs. Just what is supposed to happen to an industry operating at full tilt and dependent on levels of wood fibre no longer available does not enter into the equation.

Rates of logging are set based on optimistic assumptions; the possibility that future conditions may threaten or damage forest health is not factored into the equation. But we have no way of knowing if the present rate of regrowth and survival will continue. Through widespread clear-cutting, Canada has reduced the biological capacity of the forest to respond to new stresses. As Canada's former Minister of Environment, the Honourable John Fraser, found when reviewing West Coast fisheries policy, the resource is being "managed" to the upper limits of what we think is there. Calculations for the annual allowable cut rest on faulty data and questionable assumptions. But there is no margin for error in this situation.

We have known for many years that environmental stresses, such as airborne toxic chemicals and acid rain, reduce forest health and make it less resilient. Global climate change will have an even greater impact on the forests.

The regulating system for the engine of life

Plants are air purifiers. Urban tree planting improves air quality in cities, while massive tree planting is suggested as a solution to the greenhouse effect. Forests are part of the global carbon cycle, intimately connected to the planet's climate. They are, in the language of the international negotiations to forestall the most disastrous impacts of climate change, "carbon sinks." As a sink, forests sequester carbon from the atmosphere. The planet's boreal region is estimated to hold 65 million tons of carbon in its trunks, branches and leaves, and a further 270 billion tons in its soils and decaying matter. Every single year, the boreal region absorbs roughly 0.4 to 0.6 billion tons of carbon from the atmosphere.[1] But humans are releasing far more carbon into the atmosphere than can be recovered by forest and ocean sinks. We are liberating millennia's worth of stored carbon. Locked away in plants when dinosaurs roamed the earth, the fossil fuels we are burning now are creating previously unknown changes to the chemistry of the atmosphere.

In 2000, more than 7 billion tons of carbon was released into the atmosphere from burning oil, coal and gas, as well as from deforestation.[2] Since massive releases of carbon dioxide to the atmosphere are the number-one cause of the "greenhouse effect" or climate change, the role of forests in reabsorbing tons of carbon is critical.

Just as forests are part of the regulating system for the giant engine of life called Planet Earth, so, too, are they vulnerable to air pollution. Ever since the maple diebacks of the mid-1980s, the health of Canada's forests has been linked to air pollution, in that instance, to acid rain. The long-range transport of sulfur dioxide leads to acidification, not just of rain, but of fog and snow, and even to the dry deposition of acid. The relationship between acid rain and tree health is complex. One explanation for damage to forests from acidification suggested an indirect connection. Acidification increases the leaching of heavy metals from the soil. Research at the University of Toronto found that dying trees had high levels of soluble aluminum in their soil. The soil was also deficient in nutrients, with low levels of phosphorus and calcium. Tom Hutchinson, an ecologist at Trent University, concluded that maple seedlings "do not like growing on the declining soil."[3] Other research in the Appalachian Mountains found damage to forests at high and low altitudes when trees were exposed to acid fog and high levels of ground-level ozone. Again, as in the Canadian research, toxic heavy metals such as aluminum were more available to plants, while nutrients such as calcium and magnesium had leached out of the soil.[4]

But the air carries more than precursors of acid rain. Toxic chemicals are also carried by air, and cause stress to trees, impeding growth and imperiling forest health.[5] So, too, does ground-level ozone, drifting from urban and industrial areas, reduce the health of forests. Some trees are more sensitive than others, but, in general, the impact of ground-level ozone on forests is negative.

Ironically, while ground-level ozone is a threat to both plants and animals, including humans, the stratospheric ozone is critical to protecting forests, and, indeed, all life on earth, from the sun's most harmful rays. Stratospheric ozone screens out most of the ultraviolet radiation that otherwise would make Earth inhospitable for life. Increased ultraviolet radiation does affect tree growth and health. In Canada's boreal, research on jack pine demonstrated a 25 per cent loss of biomass from UV-B exposure, while white spruce and black spruce biomass dropped by about 50 per cent.[6] Similar experiments found that loblolly pine seedlings grew 20 per cent less when exposed to ultraviolet radiation.[7] In 2000, an Environment Canada study concluded that "Reduced tree vigour, reduced photosynthetic activity, sun scalding, and premature aging of needles are among the multiple impacts of rising UV-B radiation on coniferous trees."[8] While the ozone layer still requires more complete protection, substantial efforts have been made to eliminate ozone-depleting substances.

Much research points to the impacts of multiple stressors from different sources. A forest can be and is hit with several environmental problems all at once. It is affected by ground-level ozone and the toxic chemicals deposited on its leaves, for example, while it tries to cope with increased ultraviolet radiation and acid rain.

Dr. David Schindler of the University of Alberta has studied the synergistic impacts of these multiple stressors on aquatic ecosystems. His work has demonstrated that where increased UV reaches water that is warmer due to climate change and more acidic due to acid rain, the damage from the increased UV can be ten times worse than if that one factor was at play in isolation. Looking at all of Canada's boreal, Dr. Schindler concludes:

> When the combined effects of climate warming, acid deposition, stratospheric ozone depletion and other human activities are considered, the boreal landscape may be one of the global ecoregions that changes the most in the next few decades. Certainly, our descendants will know a much different boreal landscape than we have today.[9]

But, for all the stressing of Canada's forests by air pollution, the next wave of pollution-induced impacts on the forest environment is predicted to result in actual climate change. This disruption in the global climate brings with it a host of interconnected threats to the forests.

Climate change and Canada's forests

"Climate change" is a term for "global warming" or the "greenhouse effect." It refers to the scientific reality that releasing vast amounts of greenhouse gases into the atmosphere causes a significant disruption in the global climate. The primary greenhouse gas is carbon dioxide; most CO_2 is released when fossil fuels, such as oil, coal and gas, are burned. Currently, greenhouse gases have increased the atmospheric concentration of carbon dioxide from a pre–Industrial Revolution level of 275 parts per million (ppm) to over 379 ppm—more than a 30 per cent increase in the cosmic blink of an eye.

It is important to keep in mind the distinction between emission rates and concentrations. *Emissions* of climate-warming gases have increased four-fold in just the last forty years. The measurements of *concentration* reflect the total impact of those increased emission rates on the chemistry of the atmosphere. Oceans, forests and all green life on Earth are constantly pulling carbon out of the atmosphere, and are referred to as carbon sinks. The concentration figure is what remains after all absorption of carbon by natural sinks. It is extraordinary to realize that the difference between Planet Earth being warm enough to sustain life and being too cold is that small concentration of about 275 ppm carbon dioxide, leading to the beneficial natural greenhouse effect. In the previous 20 million years, the levels of CO_2 had never been above 280 ppm.[10]

Thanks to some fascinating science, we know how much carbon dioxide was in the planet's atmosphere millennia ago. Scientists draw information going back several hundred thousand years from Antarctic ice core data, where carbon dating determines the age of air bubbles, which are then analyzed for carbon dioxide concentrations. The data going back millions of years is drawn from "proxy" sources—trees rings, fossilized records, sea shells. This means that we have a clear baseline record, proving that humanity has already changed the chemistry of our atmosphere. By burning fossil fuels and clearing forests, we have increased the concentrations of carbon dioxide by over 30 per cent. That change is irreversible within the human time scale. So no matter what we do to reduce wasteful use of fossil fuels, we are committed to a destabilized climate regime. But the situation is worse than that. Given that the carbon we emit now remains with us in the atmosphere for a century, and given the increasing levels of greenhouse gas that we are pumping into the atmosphere, scientists are projecting that carbon dioxide concentrations will double to 550 ppm, or even to higher levels.

Globally, the impact of climate change on forests is alarming. The Hadley Centre for Climate Prediction and Research, part of the Meteorological Service of the U.K. government, has projected, based on a doubling of carbon dioxide, the conversion of the northern

Amazon from forest into desert. The process would be driven by changes in the ocean currents, affecting rainfall on the Amazon side of the Andes, combined with the effect of rapid growth of forests due to more available carbon, followed by an equally rapid die-back.[11] Changes are already being observed in the Amazon: for example, woody vines are growing at an unprecedented rate. Research published in the journal *Nature* documented the dominance of liana vines over slower-growing trees. The scientists speculated that the lianas were increasing due to more available carbon in the atmosphere, but that the impact was to weigh down the trees, damaging and sometimes killing them.[12] Forest fires have already started to occur in areas of the world known for their wet rainforests. While many Canadian ecosystems are fire-driven, the rainforests of Malaysia and Indonesia certainly are not. And yet, due to recent droughts, there have been out-of-control fires in the planet's rainforests.

Climate modelling by the federal government's Forest Service and Environment Canada has attempted to predict the impact on Canadian forests of the anticipated atmospheric doubling of carbon dioxide. The results are sobering. The climatic zone appropriate for boreal forests would be reduced to areas of northern Quebec and Labrador, with a small section in the Yukon and Northwest Territories. Nearly all of Saskatchewan and three-quarters of Manitoba would have a climate more suited to grassland than to forest. Semi-arid sections of Canada would spread, and the tundra would shrink. The climate disruption would render most of the country where boreal now thrives an inhospitable range. Meanwhile, climate would warm the north, creating the potential for expanded boreal toward the tundra. But, although the weather may shift, it may take centuries for soil quality to improve. The thin soils of the far north will not be able to support forests, even if the thermometer readings suggest they should. The stress created by changing temperatures, shifting rainfall patterns, drought where rain used to be abundant, increased rainfall in areas adapted to a dry climate, all point to a lengthy period of readjustment for Canada's forests. It is possible that, with time, forests will adapt to the new regime. After all, much of the forest stands on areas once covered in ice. But such transitions usually move at geological speed. Human-induced climate change occurs far more rapidly—arguably too fast for societies and ecosystems to adjust.

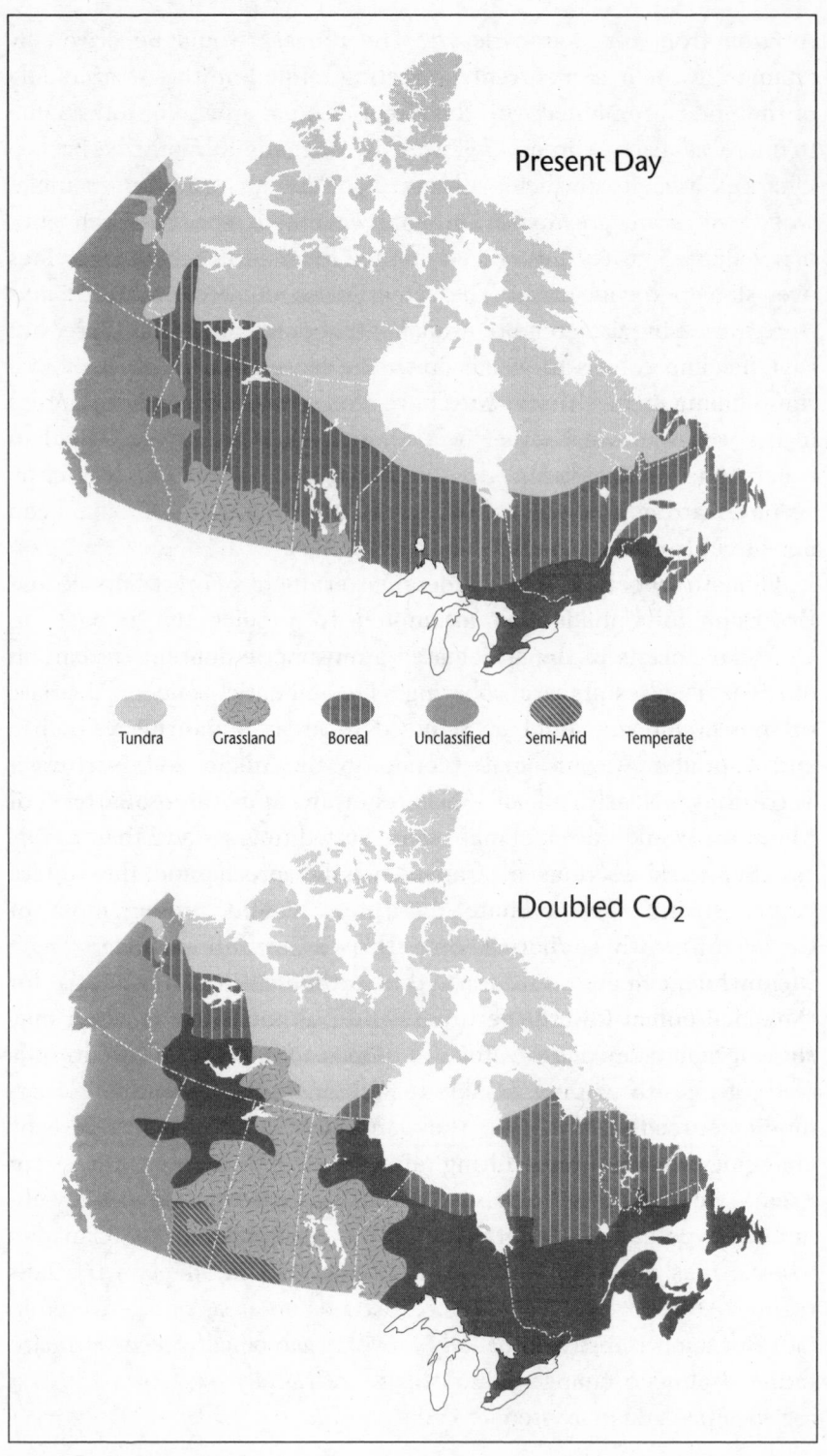

Present Day

Tundra Grassland Boreal Unclassified Semi-Arid Temperate

Doubled CO$_2$

Source: Environment Canada

Given that we are condemned to some level of climate change, the prudent course is to pursue adaptation strategies at the same time as we dramatically reduce emissions. A logical adaptation strategy for forests is to keep the forests healthy and resilient, but we do the opposite. Industrial forestry practices stress natural systems to such a degree that many areas of forest will be unable to recover from intensive logging. In the collapse of the East Coast fishery, climatic stresses helped push an overexploited ecosystem over the edge. As the climate models predicted, the waters off Newfoundland and Labrador have become colder due to changes in the ocean currents. So, too, does climate change threaten to push Canada's forests over the edge. As one early research effort by Canadian Forest Service scientists concluded: "The rapid rate of climate change that is predicted to occur could also have a significant impact on the flowering, pollination, seed formation, germination, and competitive success of tree seedlings. This may result in the increased failure of regeneration and restocking done in harvested areas."[13]

Climate change is upon us. Although no single severe storm can be conclusively blamed on climate change, there is no question that the world is experiencing more intense and more extreme weather events that are consistent with climate change trends. In the 1990s, the costs of weather-related disasters in Canada grew five-fold, totalling $2.5 billion in 1998.[14] While the insurable claims do not include loss of forests, a number of these storms were devastating to forests. The 1998 ice storm killed or damaged millions of trees in eastern Ontario, southern Quebec and New Brunswick; it damaged Christmas tree operations and dealt a severe blow to the maple syrup industry.[15]

In September 2003, Hurricane Juan slammed into Nova Scotia, doing far more damage than previous storms. Normally, cool water off the Nova Scotia coasts slows and moderates the impact of tropical storms. But with warmer ocean water offshore, Nova Scotia received the full impact of a tropical hurricane. Scientists described Juan's impact as "wind bombs" that did serious damage to the area's forests. "We noticed how some stands were completely flattened, but others a few yards away were left standing," said Dave Sutherland of Nova Forest Alliance.[16]

The stress visited upon Canada's forests is not simply the result of extreme weather. Increased risk of fire and insect assault are having significant impacts as well. Recent years have already demonstrated the threat to Canada's forests posed by fires resulting from climate change. Less winter snowfall, due to warmer winters, combined with hotter summers, more evaporation and drought conditions all conspire to increase the risk of forest fire. Decades of forest fire suppression efforts also play a large role. One study found that, since 1970, "natural" disturbances, such as insects and fire, in Canadian forests have doubled.[17] Since 1980, Canada has experienced five of the seven worst forest-fire seasons in recorded history. Nine of the ten hottest years on record have occurred since 1990.[18] 2003 was the third hottest year in 150 years.[19] Canada's second-worst year for forest fires was 1995, when, all told, 8,467 fires burned over 7 million hectares of forest. The fires stretched from the Yukon, which lost over 3 million hectares of forest, through the Northwest Territories, Quebec, Manitoba, Saskatchewan and Alberta.[20] In 1999, 7,591 fires burned a total of 1,705,645 hectares across Canada.[21]

In 2003, fires raged across Canada, but were particularly devastating in the Okanagan interior of British Columbia. Within British Columbia alone, there were 2,500 fires that summer, consuming 265,000 hectares of forest, destroying 334 homes and killing three people.[22] The movement of more and more suburban homes to within range of large tracts of forest, a function of poor land-use planning and urban sprawl, was clearly a factor in the number of homes that were lost. But the hot dry summer and the tinder-dry conditions of the forest are consistent with climate trends brought on by increasing greenhouse gases.

Of course, the connection between any particular forest fire and climate change is still only conjectural. One major confounding factor is the work of decades of fire suppression. Government efforts have been increasingly successful in reducing losses to fire, leaving large areas that would naturally be part of a fire cycle. As one of Canada's senior forest scientists explained, "In some cases, when stands are mature and overmature and not harvested, then forest fires will play a role in rejuvenation."[23]

Still, the climate change models suggest conditions that will increase the severity, the area burned and the frequency of major fires. Forest fires in recent years have already caused losses far in excess of that lost through logging. Nevertheless, annual allowable cut calculations and wood-supply analyses continue to be modeled as though forest fires will be held at low levels, and as though no provision need be made for increased losses to fire.

The same is true for the risk of new insect migration into Canada's forests. Climate scientists and public-health experts are concerned that the shifting climate will allow vector-borne diseases to migrate north. Malaria and West Nile Virus, for instance, have expanded their range in recent years, with climate change believed to be the main culprit. The same trends can be seen with insects that damage trees, since these insects are able to rapidly colonize areas with a newly hospitable climate. What's worse, the trees in these regions haven't had the chance to develop genetic resistance to the new arrivals, so they are especially vulnerable.

The wood-chewing Asian longhorned beetle (*Anoplophora glabripennis*), for example, attacks deciduous trees, mostly maple, but also poplar, birch, willow, elm, ash and horsechestnut, among others. It attacks healthy trees and has no natural controls in North America. The emerald ash borer, also from Asia, killed between 100,000 and 200,000 ash trees in the Windsor area in 2002.[24] Both of these pose an enormous economic and environmental threat.

Even endemic insects, ones native to Canada, can become more devastating with climate change. The mountain pine beetle is well known to B.C. foresters. It burrows into lodgepole pine and transmits a fungus that leaves a blue stain on the wood, reducing its market value. The fungus can also destroy the connective tissues within a tree, ultimately killing it.[25] Ordinarily, the cold B.C. winters would knock back pine beetle populations. The beetle is not found on sites where the winter temperature goes below $-40°C$.[26] Cooler fall and summer temperatures also slow the beetle's growth and limit its range. Six warm winters in a row, plus hotter summers, catapulted the pine beetle infestation to new levels. By 2000, the head of the pine beetle task force declared the infestation an "emergency" that could cost the industry $3.6 billion in lost timber.[27] Over 1.46 million hectares of B.C. forest were infested in 2003 and 2004. In 2003, Premier Campbell announced that he was ready to log in parks to combat the pine beetle. In the same speech, he also discussed the devastating impacts of the summer's fires. He did not mention climate change.[28]

Finally, there are significant ways in which the impacts of changes wrought on Canada's forest by climate change will themselves worsen climate change disruption, leading to yet more negative impacts on the forest. The most obvious of these is the massive release of carbon when Canada's forests go up in smoke. Due to increased fires, logging and insect attack, Canadian forests have already shifted from being a sink, holding carbon and keeping it out of the atmosphere, to being a net *source* of greenhouse gases. Making matters worse still, scientists in Germany have discovered that burning forests release a chemical that is a deadly ozone depleter, methyl bromide. Thus, the increase in forest fires may well throw off projections for the repair of the ozone layer due to international action in prohibiting ozone-depleting commercial chemicals.[29]

In the face of mounting evidence of the threat to the forests from climate change and of the crucial role played by forests in holding carbon out of the atmosphere, Canada's forest industry has attempted to jump on the bandwagon. It has argued that replacing old-growth forests with plantations will accelerate the absorption of carbon by our forests. The reality is to the contrary. While the rate at which young trees absorb carbon exceeds that of old forest giants, the young forest simply does not have anywhere near the biomass to replace the carbon-sink abilities of an old forest. Research published in *Science* concluded that logging and replanting an area "does not approach old-growth storage capacity for at least 200 years. Even when sequestration of carbon in wooden buildings is included in the models, timber harvest results in a net flux of CO_2 to the atmosphere."[30]

Furthermore, clear-cutting itself increases the release of carbon dioxide to the atmosphere. Exposed soil on clear-cut land, intensified through scarifying before replanting, may decompose more rapidly, thus releasing increased levels of carbon to the atmosphere.[31] Nevertheless, the forest industry and every province except Alberta and Quebec have signed on to a significant pledge found within the 2003–2008 National Forest Strategy: "On a national basis, maintaining carbon reservoirs and managing the forest to be a net carbon sink, over the long term."[32]

Operating with an awareness of carbon cycles, sinks and sources of carbon from within the forested land base of Canada is a huge step forward. But delivering on a commitment of no net loss of carbon is a bigger challenge than any the forest industry has yet faced.

Carbon for sale

The whole idea of trading in a greenhouse gas may strike the average person as bizarre. Pollution trading sounds unsavoury, with images of false reporting and buying the "right" to pollute. Nevertheless, assigning dollar values to carbon is essential in the effort to reduce greenhouse gases. We can give it value through carbon taxes, or allow the market to set carbon prices. The international negotiations process has chosen the latter route. Already, the market is trading in carbon futures. The Chicago Stock Exchange trades in carbon. Individual companies are formulating their own carbon deals.

The Kyoto Protocol takes all this one step further. Kyoto includes the first binding commitments to reduce emissions, stemming from the overarching UN Framework Convention on Climate Change, signed and ratified by Canada in 1992. The Framework Convention commits the nations of the world to reducing greenhouse gas emissions, while Kyoto sets targets for industrialized nations.

In December 1997, when Canada signed the Kyoto Protocol, Canadian diplomats were patting themselves on the back for forcing the Europeans to accept carbon credits for forests. The creation of what environmentalists called "loopholes" and Canadian diplomats called "flexibility mechanisms" was highly controversial. Kyoto allows for the trading in carbon in a number of ways, and only some of them involve forests. As noted, the net atmospheric impact of Canada's vast forests is a source of carbon. Still, it was Canada that pushed hardest to allow credits for forests in Article 3 of Kyoto. It took years of subsequent negotiations to iron out the rules for how forests might be worth money as carbon sinks. For countries in the developing world, it is possible to benefit from Kyoto's Clean Development Mechanism (CDM) by selling credits for planted forests to industrialized countries, offsetting their ongoing carbon dioxide emissions.[34]

Credits for trees in a poor country being used to offset ongoing pollution in a rich country is a fairly unpalatable trade-off. Fossil fuel use needs to be dramatically reduced. The UN Intergovernmental Panel on Climate Change has concluded that to avoid an atmospheric doubling of carbon, global emissions of carbon dioxide must be reduced by 60 per cent against 1990 levels. Canada's Kyoto target is 6 per cent. Reducing greenhouse gas emissions is the top priority. Enhancing sinks has a lesser role. Forests should be protected, but their long-term reliability to offset increasing greenhouse gases is dubious. Stored forest carbon poses serious accountability issues. Forests burn down. What happens then? Already, international watchdog groups have sprung up to monitor the types of projects advanced by the World Bank and others. SinksWatch and Greenpeace International participate in the negotiations. A Greenpeace communiqué following the 2003 negotiations urged those engaging in CDM projects not to "give Kyoto a bad reputation by using monocultures or genetically modified organisms in the name of climate protection."[35]

In Canada, our forests can be worth money as carbon sinks. Sad to say, Canada has been pursuing the cheapest options rather than the ones that offer the most benefit in addressing the climate change crisis. Canada actually tried to have post-logging regrowth counted for credit, while not counting the carbon lost when the forest was logged. Fortunately, this subterfuge never made it past early negotiations. By 2001, at the meeting of the parties in Marrakech, the rules for how forests could be counted in the Kyoto Protocol had been set.

If, after 1990, an area of land is reforested (such as land converted from forests to agriculture in the past) or afforested (where forests were not present in the past, but are now introduced) a carbon credit is possible under Kyoto. Any "deforestation," meaning conversion away from forests, would have to be subtracted. In addition, Canada has the option of including in its Kyoto accounting framework an area that it defines as the "managed" forest, potentially a huge expanse of about 1.3 million square kilometres, but still much smaller than the entire forest. Once any credit is ascribed for changes in land use by increasing carbon sequestration through expanded forest cover, those forests remain on a country's account. Should those forests burn down, be logged or be destroyed by insects or storms, the carbon lost in the fire would count as an emission.

There is clearly some potential for forest plantations as carbon sinks. From the viewpoint of enhancing biodiversity, however, such plantation schemes are not terribly attractive. But where plantations occur over a degraded land base, such as poor agricultural land, there is a plausible conservation basis for supporting the scheme. Many caveats apply. Even degraded land may have some vegetation which, once removed, results in a net loss of carbon. Some argue that plantations are a good option if coupled with protected areas in the primary forest. New Zealand has gone that route, not for carbon reasons, but to enhance biodiversity. In a great trade-off, the commercial areas of forest are tree farms, intensively managed without concern for enhancing biodiversity within them. In exchange, most of the nation's forests are set aside in protected areas. Canada's forest service has suggested a Canadian version of such an approach in its

Forests 2020 proposal.[36] Unlike the New Zealand example, Canada's approach fails to include any new measures to protect old forests.

Nevertheless, no plantation lasts forever. Claiming carbon credits for plantations is not acceptable when the real effort must be focused on reducing emissions. Some members of the Forest Sector Table, an extensive consultation engaging the forest industry, environmentalists and other stakeholders, concluded "there is little point in highlighting fast-growing plantations as a distinct option, because while there is a short-term advantage to using fast-growing species, there is no demonstrated long-term advantage to generating afforestation credits with fast-growing species as opposed to traditional native species."[37]

Although Kyoto itself will have little impact on the monetary value of Canada's forests as carbon, it is quite possible that the domestic implementation of Kyoto will generate interesting possibilities. There have been many consultations and negotiations on the possibility of a domestic carbon trading system. Under Kyoto, which became legally binding on February 16, 2005, Canada is required to monitor our carbon balance. Increasing sequestration through changes in land use, agricultural practices and forestry could become part of a domestic trading scheme. Should Canada go down that road, it is quite possible that standing forests would be more valuable as carbon offsets than as board feet to a mill. The global price of carbon has been speculated at various amounts. The World Bank has set an initial price of $15 per ton.

Sierra Club of Canada conducted an analysis of the ways in which valuing carbon could create positive opportunities for ecological forest management.[37] For the purposes of the study, Conservation Director Martin von Mirbach chose a conservative value of $10 per ton for carbon. That valuation would give a cubic metre of wood an economic value of $6.85 as standing forest. Using this reasonable estimate of a forest's carbon worth, von Mirbach ran a number of projections for how changes in forest practices could yield profits as carbon credits. A number of ecological forest practices have the double benefit of increasing stored carbon while also increasing biodiversity. For example, increasing the rotation age of a forested area from eighty years to a hundred years results in significant additional storage of carbon. Selection logging techniques, more environmentally sensitive, also have the advantage of increasing the carbon stored on the landscape. Finally, simply reducing the amount of wood logged can pay dividends in carbon sequestration. A study by the Canadian Forest Service applied their carbon budget model to a 1.2 million hectare forest in the Alberta foothills. By reducing the cut to 75 per cent of the annual allowable cut over a 150-year period, significant additional carbon would be stored: 1.6 megatons. Should such methods become available for credits under a domestic trading scheme, the forests could well benefit.

Many issues would need to be addressed, particularly the potential for scams of all sorts. Logging less in one area to gain carbon *credits* while logging more in another without carbon *debits* is just one of the concerns that would require careful accounting and monitoring. Windfall credits would have to be discounted, where a company claimed credit for a change that occurred naturally. Any domestic trading system would need rules at least as rigorous and convoluted as the international rules that took years to negotiate under Kyoto. It is all too easy to imagine forest carbon "get rich quick" schemes that offer money for forest carbon without the accountability to make it real. But despite the obvious difficulties, applying carbon trading for forest conservation benefits has significant potential.

As Mike Apps, one of the leading government scientists on forests and climate change impacts, has observed, "the Kyoto Protocol may be even better for forests and forestry than it is for the atmosphere."[38] Given the enormity of the threat posed by climate change, preserving old-growth forests as carbon sinks arguably gives them their highest value to the economy—and to the future.

5 | POLLUTION, PESTICIDES AND POLITICS

Pollution from the industrialized world threatens Canada's forests, but, so, too, is the forest industry itself a significant source of pollution. First, it is a source of toxic contamination, both in its logging practices and from its mills. In the woods, the use of chemical insecticides and herbicides is part and parcel of the intensive forest management used to justify overcutting in the short term. In the mills, a witches' brew has fouled the waters around Canada's older mills. Mills have traditionally been built along rivers, providing ease of access to logs brought down in booms along watercourses, as a source of water for production process, and as a place to dump the waste. Battles over the destruction of downstream water quality between the pulp-and-paper industry and their neighbours led to some of the earliest cases in Canadian environmental law. The case of Reed Paper's pollution of the White Dog and Grassy Narrows Reserves was recorded in one of Canada's first environmental exposés, *No Safe Place* by journalist Warner Troyer, published in 1977.[1]

Pulp-and-paper pollution

Depending on the type of processing used, pulp mills produce a toxic cocktail in their effluent, which can have devastating impacts on the aquatic ecosystem, as well as on other resource industries. Overall, the pulp mill industry uses vast amounts of water and consumes prodigious amounts of energy. It is the largest consumer of energy of any Canadian industry.[2] In 1990, it was estimated that the pulp-and-paper industry was responsible for fully half of all the waste dumped in Canada's waters.[3] In fact, "One kraft mill discharges oxygen-demanding substances equal to a city with a population greater than 120,000 people."[4]

There are two primary types of pulp-and-paper manufacturing—chemical and mechanical. Making pulp and paper is basically a process of breaking down wood fibres. This can be done either by grinding the wood into pulp through a mechanical process, or by "cooking" the wood with a mix of chemicals to break down the lignin fibres. More chemicals are used if the fibres need to be brightened for that extra-white sheet of paper. Many pulp-and-paper operations use a mix of chemicals and mechanical processing.

Chemical pulps are stronger and brighter than mechanical pulps, as the chemical cooking removes the lignin fibres from the wood. On the other hand, mechanical pulping produces a larger volume of pulp for the wood used, so trees are more fully utilized.

Within the chemically produced pulp, there are two primary types of process: sulfate or kraft mills, and sulfite pulp. You can tell a kraft mill from miles away by the sulphurous odour. The major chemicals used in the kraft process are sodium hydroxide, the main cooking chemical, and sodium sulfide. The resulting paper is then often bleached with chlorine. The sulfite pulp is generally produced without bleaching chemicals. The main cooking chemical for sulfite pulp is a bisulfite-sulfurous acid solution.

New types of processing use both chemical and mechanical pulping. The method developed by Repap is a bleached chemi-thermal mechanical pulp (BCTMP) mill. The BCTMP process was developed to manufacture bleached pulp without the environmental hazards of chlorine bleaching.

For many years, Canadian mills built before 1971 were exempt from effluent controls on a range of polluting discharges. Unenforced guidelines applied to the waste from pre-1971 mills for everything from dioxins and furans to suspended solids and oxygen-depleting substances. Public concern began to focus on the widespread distribution of dioxins and furans in the environment in the mid-1980s.

Dioxins are a large family of chemicals related to the furans, both within a chemical group called "organochlorines." They are produced in the bleaching process whenever chlorine is used. Some members of the dioxin and furan family are highly toxic. In fact, the most toxic human-made chemical is a dioxin isomer—2,3,7,8-tetra-chlorodibenzo-para-dioxin (2,3,7,8-TCDD). Studies around the Great Lakes demonstrated unacceptable levels of dioxin in gulls' eggs. Reproductive failure and unusual birth defects were also on the rise.[5]

In 1987, Greenpeace decided to run tests of sediments and shell-fish in the vicinity of mills in Howe Sound, British Columbia. The Greenpeace reports were sent to the federal government for comment prior to release to the media. It happened that, at the same time, Environment Canada had been running tests. While Greenpeace's sampling had detected some startling dioxin and furan contamination, some of the government testing showed even higher levels. The Greenpeace tests had the positive impact of moving the federal results up to the minister's desk. It is an unhappy reality of large bureaucracies that, when faced with bad news, no one wants to be the messenger. Greenpeace got the minister's attention. Former Environment Minister Tom McMillan made the decision to release the government's test results and begin work to control dioxins and furans from pulp mills.[6]

It took years to promulgate regulations under the Fisheries Act for improved controls on oxygen-depleting substances that imperilled fish, and, through the Canadian Environmental Protection Act, for controls on dioxins and furans. Before the federal government could bring forward new laws, the Howe Sound shellfish industry was closed because of the unacceptable levels of toxic contamination. Other shellfish closures near B.C. mills followed. British Columbia responded by bringing out its own effluent regulations in the spring of 1989. B.C. mills faced the toughest laws in Canada, with a requirement of no more than 1.5 kilograms of total organochlorines per ton of pulp produced. At the time, mills were releasing an average of four to eight kilograms of organochlorines per ton of pulp.[7] Industry howls of protest could be heard all the way to Sweden, where chlorine bleaching had already been banned.

In 1988, the federal government assessed the effectiveness of guidelines to control mill pollution. The assessment found significant pollution at levels far beyond the guidelines. Stora's effluent in Nova Scotia, for example, had so consistently failed toxicity testing that Environment Canada officials told the local press that they no longer bothered to run such tests, knowing that Stora would fail. With only guidelines, instead of regulations, they could do nothing about it.[8] Stora's then president, Tom Hall, did not strike an apologetic chord when it was revealed that his mill was one of the two worst polluters in Atlantic Canada. "There are no government regulations enforcing the company to [limit effluent]," he said. "We are not in non-compliance."[9] The internal review of 1988 confirmed that, of the 122 pulp mills in Canada at the time, 83 were violating the pollution-control guidelines.[10]

Finally, in 1992, the federal government announced its new regulations. After years of consultation, the regulations were no surprise, but they did not demand immediate compliance. The government set a deadline of the end of 1993 for the reduction of dioxins and furans to non-measurable levels from kraft mills.[11] These pollution laws would impose regulations for the first time on mills built prior to 1971, the very mills most likely to be polluting because of the older technologies in use. They would reduce dioxin and furans, but not require total elimination. Government regulators claimed the target levels would prevent toxicity in fish.

But new science continues to emerge about the risks of organochlorines and a larger group of chemicals known as "endocrine disrupters." Endocrine-disrupting chemicals actually mimic the human hormones released through our endocrine system, such as estrogen and testosterone.[12] Studies on fish downstream from pulp mills have revealed that, even at very low levels, and even with mills that do not use chlorine, endocrine-disrupting chemicals are having a widespread impact on wildlife. A review in 1996 of the fish in Alberta's northern rivers, for instance, found increases in abnormalities such as tumours, lesions, deformities and parasites downstream from the pulp mills. The study also found significantly lower sex hormones in the burbot within 100 kilometres downstream, while both burbot and long-nose suckers had significantly higher levels of sexual immaturity compared with fish upstream from the mill.[13] The impacts on all forms of wildlife and humans from endocrine-disrupting chemicals remains controversial, but clearly points to health effects ranging from sterility to reproductive difficulties, birth defects and cancers.[14]

The reaction from the pulp-and-paper industry to the announcement that mill effluent would be regulated was to immediately issue calls for an extension. Ultimately, the federal government agreed to give pulp mills until the end of 1995 to put in place the required pollution-control technology. Mills across the country claimed that the pollution controls would drive them out of business. Some mills managed to get financial assistance as well as time extensions before complying. Nevertheless, between 1988 and 1993, the amount of dioxins and furans in kraft-pulp-mill effluent decreased by 98.4 per cent.[15] As of 1993, of the 145 pulp mills in Canada, 46 were still using bleach to whiten their pulp in the kraft process. Mills are continuing to look for substitutes for bleach, and some are moving toward "closed-loop" systems, involving the recovery of useful by-products traditionally discharged into the environment as waste.

Discharges of other effluent, from all types of mills, also fell due to the regulations under the Fisheries Act. Total suspended solids (TSS) and oxygen-depleting substances, measured as levels of bio-chemical oxygen demand (BOD), also fell, down 7.9 per cent and 6.8 per cent, respectively, between 1983 and 1993.

Meanwhile, the oriented strand board (OSB) industry is introduc-ing a whole new group of toxic chemicals into the forest industry. When Louisiana-Pacific decided to open a mill in Manitoba in 1995, there were no regulations dealing with its emissions. The company volunteered to comply with standards that prevail in the United States after public concern about its poor pollution record began to make headlines.[16] Canadian jurisdictions have yet to catch up with the volume of waste that can be expected from the burgeoning OSB industry. Manufacture of OSB involves phenol, formaldehyde and, sometimes, methyl isocynate. Not only does the manufacture raise new pollution issues, but use of OSB as a building material creates concerns for indoor air quality as well.

While much remains to be done to reduce forest-industry pollution, the lessons of the early 1990s are instructive. The use of voluntary guidelines for two decades resulted in millions of tons of pollution to Canada's waterways. When caught with triple the acceptable levels of pollution, most corporate CEOs would have responded as did Stora's then president Tom Hall: "We're not in non-compliance."

In the last ten years, the pollution from pulp mills has significantly decreased. To meet the new emission regulations, the forest industry invested $5 billion. Through more advanced effluent treatment, the dis-charge of chlorinated dioxins and furans has been nearly eliminated.[17]

Voluntary measures just don't work. Regulations and enforcement do. All the political trends and budgetary pressures run counter to strong regulation. In fact, to date Canada's only response to the threat of global climate change is a voluntary program. Devolution of powers threatens to remove the Fisheries Act as an effective tool for environmental protection. Recent slashing of budgets for silviculture at both the federal and the provincial level, and the substantial reduc-tion of Forest Department staff in Alberta and Ontario, suggest another set of worrying national trends.

Greenhouse gas emissions

As the largest industrial consumer of energy, the forest sector plays a multi-faceted role in the climate change issue. It is a massive producer of greenhouse gases, and at the same time, its primary resource, the forests themselves, are at risk from climate change impacts.

Initially, the government's approach to emissions reductions in industry was through an exercise called Voluntary Challenge Registry (VCR). Not surprisingly, the voluntary approach has not reduced Canada's carbon dioxide emissions to the announced targets. In fact, Canada's emissions of carbon dioxide have increased by about 14 per cent since 1990, the base year for Kyoto measurements. The pulp-and-paper industry claimed credits for switching from fossil fuel to biomass (wood-based) fuel. But it did not include the carbon released from burning the wood-based fuel, claiming that the forests are managed sustainably and that therefore carbon input and output balance each other out. However, they provided no evidence that this is the case.[18]

By 2000, the forest industry realized that it would have no difficulty meeting Canada's Kyoto Protocol targets of 6 per cent below 1990 levels by 2010. Overall, between 1990 and 1997, the industry's greenhouse gas emissions declined by about 10 per cent, although production levels went up. This was primarily accomplished through increases in energy efficiency and by switching to more biomass fuels.[19] The Forest Products Association of Canada put out its own Kyoto plan, and the industry geared up for implementation. In fact, the forest sector stands to gain if Kyoto results in breaking down the barriers to full utilization of the industry's waste heat into energy potential.

For many years, pulp and paper mills tried to interest provincial utilities in buying power from them. The monopolistic power companies refused. Ontario Hydro, for example, had no interest in diversifying supply and buying from small power producers, whether small-scale hydro, windmills or pulp and paper plants. Post-Kyoto, however, new pressures are growing to force utilities to change. Power from co-generation, or using the waste heat from one process to generate energy elsewhere, holds tremendous potential for meeting energy needs while reducing greenhouse gas emissions.

In the fall of 2002, most industries in Canada joined a powerful group lobbying against Canadian ratification of Kyoto. The Canadian Chamber of Commerce and the Canadian Council of Chief Executives exerted enormous pressure on companies and industry associations to join their effort to block Kyoto. To its credit, the Forest Products Association of Canada refused. Frank Dottori, CEO of Tembec, went further and spoke out in favour of Kyoto ratification.

The Canadian Parliament overwhelmingly ratified the Kyoto Protocol on December 17, 2002.

Pesticides

Pesticides are the only chemicals in use in industrial society that can be treated as hazardous waste in one context and deliberately dispersed over the ecosystem in another. Their introduction to modern forestry is a fairly recent phenomenon. The province that led the way, adopting pesticide spraying as an annual rite of spring, was New Brunswick.

The only province to have experienced anything like the controversy that spraying created in New Brunswick was Nova Scotia, the recipient of budworm from New Brunswick's permanent epidemic. Battles over the use of herbicides and insecticides have flared up in Newfoundland, Quebec and British Columbia, but they lacked the epic-like quality of Nova Scotia's Spray Wars (related in greater detail in the Nova Scotia chapter of this book), in which local environmentalists clashed with Stora Kopparberg, a major Swedish pulp-and-paper multinational, over a period of nearly a decade. Initially, the environmental and community groups were successful in blocking the planned aerial spraying of all forested parts of Cape Breton Island with insecticides. Once the insect outbreak had collapsed, Stora, joined by the province's other large pulp mills, embarked on a planned herbicide spray program to kill "competing" vegetation and deciduous trees. That conflict led to a protracted court battle in which small communities and environmentalists suffered a punishing loss.

Animosity between local environmentalists and the Nova Scotia and New Brunswick pulp companies was fierce. Environmentalists were often personally attacked by company representatives, ridiculed and threatened in the press with lawsuits that were never filed. In the end, it is in Cape Breton that change is readily apparent. Stora now has a community liaison committee. Local volunteers who used to deride Stora, like filmmaker Neal Livingston, are now proud to work on the Stora community committee. It no longer sprays herbicides on its regenerating softwood.

Quebec has banned the use of pesticides in forests. Pesticides continue to be heavily used in other areas, especially in advance of tree planting. Students pursuing quick money by tree planting need to consider herbicide exposure before signing on to a non-unionized, poorly regulated summer job.

Across Canada, too little attention is paid to forest industry pollution. In assessing the real cost of society's addiction to wasteful paper consumption, the whole process must be included—from clear-cutting to herbicide spraying of plantations, to pulp mill effluent and OSB emissions in homes. There is no such thing as cheap paper.

6 | THE SOFTWOOD
LUMBER DISPUTE

Canada is the world's largest exporter of pulp and newsprint and one of the leading exporters of forest products of all kinds.[1] It was not long ago that Canada could boast it was the world's largest exporter of forest products.[2] By a large margin, Canada's forest product exports have headed primarily for U.S. markets.

Canada's overall share of all the imported softwood lumber in the United States is enormous and thus influences the ability of U.S. lumber companies to make a profit. Since 1989, this overall share has varied between 63 per cent and 74 per cent. Canada's share of newsprint imported by the United States has declined from a high some thirty years ago of nearly 70 per cent to a current level of 56 per cent. Part of this decline is attributable to legislation in a number of U.S. states requiring newsprint to have recycled-paper content.

After the United States, the next-largest importer of Canadian forest products is Europe. Canada also exports significant amounts of forest products to Latin America and Japan.

But it is the trading relationship with the United States that registers on the political Richter scale. For one thing, the United States is Canada's largest market, but it is also Canada's toughest competitor. Moreover, our trading relationship is a two-way street, and an increasing number of Canadian forest companies have been purchased by American companies.

While Canada ships raw lumber and pulp to the United States, it imports higher-priced U.S. structural lumber, such as large-dimension Douglas fir, hemlock and other high-value products such as doors and windows. Canada exports far more pulp and newsprint than higher-value paper products. Canada's ratio of pulp-and-paper exports is two to one, low to high value. This is the opposite of the ratio of Sweden and other Nordic countries.[3]

The United States had been reducing Canada's share of the global marketplace in several forest-product areas, increasing the U.S. proportion of imports from Europe and the Pacific Rim. But Canada

maintained and increased its market share within the United States—
all of which led to the biggest ongoing trade battle between the two
nations: the softwood lumber dispute.

During the 1990s, a number of things combined to help Canadian
exports: low stumpage rates, increased post-recession demand and a
lower Canadian dollar. In 1991, after several bad years, the total
value of Canada's forest exports was $20.6 billion. By 1994, this fig-
ure had climbed to a new all-time high of $32.4 billion—an increase
of 57 per cent in three years. And it kept climbing. In 1997, the value
of exports was $39 billion;[4] in 1998, $39.8; in 1999, $44.2 billion;[5]
and by 2000, exports hit a record $47.4 billion. The low Canadian
dollar had boosted pulp sales, even as the value of softwood lumber
exports declined.[6]

But as they say, what goes up must come down. The early years of
the new century were tough for the Canadian forest industry. A number of factors combined to knock back Canada's overall share of the
global forest products market. In 2001, it was low commodity prices,
combined with a new softwood tariff that was levelled when the previous agreement expired. A stronger Canadian dollar made our
products less of a bargain globally. In 2002, things did not improve,
with global overproduction leading to lower prices for pulp, newsprint
and softwood lumber. For three consecutive years, 2001–2003, the
value of Canadian exports declined. In 2002, it was down to $42.9
billion. Faces were gloomy at shareholders' meetings, even though the
total value of exports was identical to that which had champagne
corks popping in the late 1990s.[7]

In 2003, the industry claims it lost $635 million due to the U.S.
softwood lumber duties. Those losses were not as large as the impact
of a stronger Canadian dollar, which cost the industry another
$800 million.[8] The losses continued into the first quarter of 2004,
with giants such as Domtar, Tembec and Abitibi-Consolidated closing
mills, laying off thousands of workers and announcing plans for further cost-cutting.[9]

The consolidation of corporate control intensified in the late
1990s and into the 2000s. Big companies were swallowed up by
even bigger ones. Weyerhaeuser bought up MacMillan Bloedel.
Canfor bought Slocan Forest Products. Riverside bought Lignum,
and Tolko bought Riverside. Recently, Weyerhaeuser has been seeking buyers for its enormous B.C. operations. Bowater bought mills in

Quebec and Ontario. Laurie Cater, the publisher of a Vancouver newsletter that tracks wood prices, commented, "Bigger is always better in the lumber industry right now."[10]

The ups and downs of the forest industry are well known, with pulp gluts in a global market and a seesawing Canadian dollar making the difference between profit and loss. Investors looking for high returns did better with dot coms. But as hard as it may be to make a lot of money in the forest industry, historically it has been a major source of wealth.

The additional vulnerability of the industry to trade rules and retaliatory measures from the U.S. government drives Canadian industry to distraction. Canadian politicians are forever promising an end to the softwood lumber wars. It is our longest running conflict—170 years and counting.[11] Is a solution possible?

A short history of the dispute

One of the most significant trade irritants between Canada and the United States over the last two decades has been the growing share of Canadian lumber in the U.S. market. For Canadians unfamiliar with the forest industry, the crisis over "shakes and shingles" in the mid-1980s seemed too arcane to generate much interest. Besides, it sounded like some sort of nasty disease.

For people in the forest industry in both Canada and the United States, the softwood lumber dispute was about economic survival. But, for all the time occupied by trade negotiators, the one aspect of the forestry trade disputes that has been utterly ignored is the environmental impact of Canadian subsidies.

In a nutshell, the trade dispute erupted once again as Canadian lumber exports began to make significant inroads into the U.S. market. In the United States, these gains were seen to be at the expense of American forest companies, particularly in the western states. From 1975 to 1985, Canadian exports expanded their share of the market from 18.7 per cent of U.S. softwood consumption to nearly double that at 33.2 per cent.[12]

U.S. industry representatives lobbied hard in Washington. They claimed that Canadian imports violated fair-trade rules through the low stumpage rates for Canadian wood. Low charges for government-owned wood seemed to them to be an unfair subsidy. In terms of trade rules, if one country is unfairly subsidizing its exports, then countervailing duties are the appropriate response to level the playing field. As well, U.S. trade reviews noted the high level of government subsidies for the construction of mills and roads.

Canadians reacted with rage to news of a preliminary duty placed on Canadian exports by the United States in October 1986. This was U.S. protectionism at its worst. The former CEO of Noranda Forest, Adam Zimmerman, recalled that "a portion of the American lumber industry and a fair number of American politicians indulged in acts of outrageous protectionism, bolstered by highly spurious arguments and the selective use of dubious 'facts' and figures."[13]

Canadians could be forgiven for assuming that Uncle Sam was in the wrong. For the most part, media commentators in Canada never actually compared the stumpage rates. In 1986, stumpage equivalents in the U.S. Northwest came to $130 (Can) per thousand board feet of timber. In the same year, stumpage in British Columbia's forests came to $18 (Can) per thousand board feet.[14] The conflict was particularly focused on B.C. lumber, which was so much a part of Canadian export success. But stumpage rates right across Canada were at bargain-basement levels. Canadian costs for access to publicly owned trees were roughly one-half to one-third of what they were in comparable U.S. states.

Industry countered that labour costs in Canada were higher, that trees were farther from mills, and that, overall, they had a hard time even making a buck. Canadian industry pointed out that the U.S. lumber industry was the author of its own misfortune by valuing timber through an auctioning system that locked them into excessive lumber prices.[15]

The imposition of the preliminary duty set the stage for desperate bargaining leading up to the deadline for a negotiated settlement at the end of December 1986. What the Canadian negotiators managed to do was better for Canadian forests and the environment than previously had been the case. It was also better for Canada. But you would never have known it from the abuse hurled at Pat Carney, the Trade Minister who signed the deal. The negotiated Memorandum of Understanding (MOU) converted a duty imposed by the United States, with funds paid into the United States, into a 15 per cent duty collected in Canada, to be used for forest management in Canada. In exchange, the United States agreed not to pursue its case against Canada. Within the year, the 15 per cent Canadian duty was converted into an equivalent increase in the value of provincial stumpage collected. Thus, the increased stumpage more closely approximated market value and potentially reduced the overexploitation of Canada's forests. By 1987, the percentage of the U.S. softwood market occupied by Canada began to slip toward the pre-1975 norms.

The federal government collected a 15 per cent lumber-export tax, with revenues targeted in British Columbia for forest worker retraining and replanting. In 1987, the B.C. Minister of Forests redirected the approximately $375 million in the silviculture fund to reduce the provincial deficit. British Columbia's senior ranking federal Cabinet member at the time, Pat Carney, denounced the state of the province's forests in the House of Commons: "Every British Columbia Member of Parliament knows that our forests are a silvicultural slum."[16] A further $500 million was spent on silviculture as part of the federal/provincial Forest Resource Development Agreements (FRDAs).

Subsidies to the industry come in many forms. Across the country, cheap power is a common indirect subsidy to the energy-intensive pulp-and-paper business. In Newfoundland, for example, where hydroelectric rights are thrown in for free along with the lease, power rates are subsidized. B.C. Hydro, a Crown hydroelectric corporation, provides power to the forest industry at giveaway rates, often less than the cost of production.[17]

Traditionally, trees have also been given away. For many years, British Columbia's stumpage rate was so low that, even when British Columbia produced a volume of timber equal to that of the rest of the provinces combined, the stumpage collected did not offset the cost of running the Forest Service. As recently as the early 1980s, the average stumpage rate for a large B.C. forest company was less than $2 per cubic metre. By 1995, the average provincial stumpage rate on Crown timber was $26.46 per cubic metre, but most of the huge increase in forestry revenues actually went back to forest companies through the Forest Renewal B.C. program. As of 1992–1993, Ministry of Forest revenues, at long last, actually exceeded costs.

Still, Canadian industry was deeply unhappy about the "voluntary" Canadian imposition of a 15 per cent increase in the costs of production for export. By 1991, the Canadian share of the U.S. softwood market had fallen to under 27 per cent. Under industry pressure, the Canadian government decided to terminate its 1986 memorandum. The U.S. Trade Representative responded swiftly with a temporary duty on Canadian softwood, pending completion of an investigation by the U.S. Commerce Department. But Canadian share of the U.S. market began to climb. By 1995, the Canadian market share had surpassed its mid-1980s high of 33 per cent and had reached just over 36 per cent of the U.S. market.[18] Meanwhile, the U.S. lumber industry claimed that Canadian subsidies were responsible not only for their loss of market share, but for downward pressures on U.S. lumber prices.

To resolve the 1995 trading impasse, Canada once again negotiated an export duty, but with far more wrinkles. In exchange, the U.S. government promised not to launch any more trade complaints against Canadian softwood exports for five years.[19] In the words of former Trade Minister Art Eggleton, the agreement bought "five years of peace."[20] The Canadian government agreed to police the amount of lumber and the timing of shipments. Exports were allowed on a duty-free basis within a certain quota. No more than 14.7 billion board feet of duty-free exports could be shipped to the United States from British Columbia, Alberta, Ontario and Quebec in any year. Furthermore, to prevent Canadian lumber from flooding the U.S. market, the government ensured that no more than 28.5 per cent of that annual allotment would be exported in any quarter.[21] The new agreements actually increased the "flooding" of U.S. markets. Under this regime, as soon as a new quarter arrived, Canadian forest industries rushed to ship into the United States to avoid risking an export duty imposed if total shipments exceeded the limits.

The "five years of peace" ended in 2000. During this time, no one ever asked how the trade war affected the forest environment in Canada and the United States. While admittedly trade relationships and the environmental content of trade are an immensely complex subject, it is clear that undervaluing environmental resources—such as energy, water or forests—leads to waste and environmental damage. Free trade agreements, from the original Free Trade Agreement to NAFTA to the global market policed by the World Trade Organization, put downward pressures on the environment. They do so because current economic indicators fail to value anything not currently traded in the marketplace. Pure air, fresh water, wildlife habitat or the very existence of great-great-grandchildren are outside the market and, hence, without value. Globalization of trade could lead to improved standards, if and only if the full value of resources was included in the equation.

Adding in the environmental costs of logging and the environmental and economic benefits of a standing forest will lead to higher prices for forest products. Thus, past Canadian subsidies did harm to the environment in both countries. Canada's low stumpage rates led to lower prices, not only in Canada, but in the United States as well, with downward, competition-driven pressure on the forest environment.

The environmental impacts of the 1985–2000 quota system were mixed. From a biodiversity viewpoint, the forests of British Columbia benefited, as logging pressures were reduced. But in those provinces not covered by the quota system, unsustainable rates of logging accelerated. The pressures for clear-cut logging of privately owned forests in Nova Scotia and New Brunswick increased drastically. In the absence of adequate regulation, truckloads of logs travelled over the border into Maine without any tracking of how much wood was exported.

On March 31, 2001, the five-year Canada-U.S. Softwood Lumber Agreement came to an end. Not missing a beat, the U.S. Coalition for Fair Lumber Imports filed suits demanding countervailing and anti-dumping penalties. The United States slapped on preliminary duties totalling 32 per cent. Negotiations began to reduce or remove the penalties.

As always, the negotiators saw no need to include environmental considerations in the discussion. In August 2000, thirty-five environmental groups and First Nations wrote to the Minister of International Trade, Pierre Pettigrew, to request a meeting to present the conservation issues embedded in cross-border trade. They were rebuffed. While public interest groups were frozen out of any negotiations, the forest industry received frequent briefings. In the United States, in contrast, environmental and community groups were invited to briefings by the U.S. trade representatives.

A coalition of environmental groups on both sides of the border petitioned the environmental watchdog created with NAFTA, the North American Commission for Environmental Co-operation, to investigate forest management practices. The coalition, including Sierra Club of Canada and the U.S. group Natural Resources Defence Fund, argued that "current high-level talks to resolve the softwood lumber dispute are not properly informed by the environmental effects of trade."[22]

In numerous dispatches through the media, the environmental groups attempted to point out how creative responses to the U.S. complaints could lead to better forest policies. There was simply no way, in their view, to defend the stumpage rates. Not only were the absolute prices set very low, but the whole process lacked either transparency or a market logic. The groups argued that moving toward a pricing system, such as that in the United States, would be better for forest health. A regional log market could ensure that companies wanting high-quality logs for secondary processing would be able to get them. Monopolistic practices requiring all wood within a lease to go to the mill owned by the leaseholder made it difficult for smaller operators to buy logs. Moreover, it ensured that even high-value wood was shipped to pulp when it could have become furniture.[23] The groups also argued that lax environmental laws constitute an indirect subsidy to production, in both Canada and the United States.

In mid-March 2002, Prime Minister Chrétien met with President Bush and promised to resolve the dispute by "next week." "We are making good progress," said Bush.[24] Less than two weeks later, the talks failed. In late March 2002, the United States imposed duties of 27 per cent on Canadian exports.[25] Both nations sought support from the trade arbitration bodies within NAFTA and the WTO. In cases that defied easy interpretation, both countries claimed victory when NAFTA panels ruled. Meanwhile, efforts to restart the talks led to more optimistic announcements from politicians. The *Globe and Mail*'s Washington correspondent, Barrie McKenna, wrote this priceless description of one politician's optimism in October 2003:

> Despite the pelting rain and wind that nearly blew him out
> the White House gates, B.C. Premier Gordon Campbell was
> giddy with optimism after his 15-minute chat with U.S. Vice-
> President Dick Cheney.... Forget the decades of acrimony
> over softwood lumber and the repeated failures to settle the
> thorny dispute, Mr. Campbell sees the light at the end of the
> tunnel. Alas, it was only the glare of the television lights.[26]

Campbell was ready to promise a swift resolution of the impasse, only to backtrack within hours. But it was true that quiet diplomacy had once again begun. Canadian and U.S. officials were back at the negotiating table. On December 6, 2003, just before the transfer of the prime minister's office from Jean Chrétien to Paul Martin, a new trade deal was proposed. This time it had forestry companies and provinces at odds with each over the acceptability of the proposed pact. Ontario industry was first to announce its opposition. Tembec took the lead in opposing it, with Domtar also against it because it does not support reform of subsidies. Meanwhile, Slocan, Abitibi-Consolidated and Canfor supported the terms. Some B.C. companies expressed desperation. Any deal to stop the duties was needed immediately to keep them from going out of business.[27] While seeing it as a large compromise, the U.S. industry indicated it could live with the new terms for trade.

Proposed was another five-year deal, with quotas limiting exports to 31.5 per cent of the U.S. market. Unlike the last agreement, this one would apply to all provinces in Canada. The 27 per cent duty would be ended and the $1.6 billion collected would be split between U.S. and Canadian firms. Canadian firms would be repaid only 52 per cent of what they had paid out. All NAFTA and WTO suits and countersuits would be dropped. Of course, there was no reference to the environmental impacts of the trade in forest products. And it could be argued that the tariff money, or at least a portion of it, should go to provincial coffers instead of to the companies. If stumpage prices had been higher years ago, the price of lumber in the United States would have been high enough to avoid a tariff.

Susan Casey-Lefkowitz, a trade expert and lawyer with the Natural Resources Defence Council, summed up the lost opportunities: "Millions of dollars, years of legal wrangling and public relations by both countries have led right back to square one: a proposal for another ineffective softwood lumber agreement."[28]

Canadian companies claimed victory in the spring of 2004, when two rulings, one each from the NAFTA and WTO trade panels, ruled in Canada's favour. But of course, none of these rulings is easily interpreted. In fact, the WTO upheld the right of the United States to place duties on Canadian imports. It simply ruled that the United States had miscalculated the proper rate. A U.S. official hinted that the proper recalculation might be even higher.[29] As for the NAFTA ruling, it confirmed an earlier decision that the U.S. lumber interests had not proven that Canadian imports had substantially damaged them. But that is a long way from a ruling that Canada's stumpage rates were not trade-offensive.

Canadian officials began a new round of talks with the provinces to prepare a counter-offer to the December 6 package. By mid-2004, trade officials were promising a deal by year-end. But industry and knowledge-able commentators no longer really believed them. Maybe by the end of 2005? No one knows. Increasingly, the five-year peace from 1995–2000 looks like a good deal from a purely economic point of view.[30]

Newly elected Prime Minister Paul Martin urged that the United States stop filing new complaints under NAFTA until the softwood duties could be resolved. He complained that NAFTA had not resulted in the free trade zone anticipated by Canada: "Open markets should mean open markets. There has to be some court of final appeal," said Martin in a speech in July 2004. With six legal chal-lenges filed by Canada under both NAFTA and the WTO, Canada asked the United States to postpone moving on a related WTO appeal until the NAFTA cases could be resolved.[31]

A clearer victory for Canada came from the NAFTA panel on August 31, 2004. It was the third time the NAFTA panel had ruled on the impo-sition of countervailing duties by the United States. At the heart of the ruling was not the question of whether Canada subsidized its exports, but whether the U.S. Commerce Department had provided evidence that the Canadian softwood coming in to the United States created an injury sufficient to justify the 27 per cent duty. In the two previous hear-ings, the five-person NAFTA panel had sent the issue back to the Commerce Department with a request for evidence. The Commerce Department provided no fresh evidence, and the panel essentially low-ered the boom. Echoing Prime Minister Martin's frustration, the panel chided Commerce for being "simply unwilling to accept this panel's review authority." The panel complained that the United States had "consistently ignored the authority of this panel in an effort to preserve its finding of threat of material injury." Asserting that any further review of the issues would be an "idle and useless formality," the panel said that this ruling was final. Except, of course, the United States does have a right of appeal. And no finding was made on other matters of Canadian subsidies, leaving the door open to further complaint. It was, however, good news for Canadian companies staggering under the weight of the $1.5 billion in duties already paid out, raising hopes that duties at that level cannot be justified. Carl Grenier, executive vice-president of the

Montreal-based Free Trade Lumber Council, was euphoric, "It cannot get any better than this. It's total victory."[32]

As the history of NAFTA and WTO rulings has shown, however, there is a slim potential for a clear, unequivocal win for Canada. Despite some efforts at reform, the fundamentals of the stumpage system are hard to defend in a NAFTA context.

A sensible start to resolving the trade dilemma would be to calculate subsidies in both countries. The United States subsidizes logging in its national forest, particularly the biologically significant Tongass National Forests of Alaska. Quantifying the value of all subsidies to the Canadian forest industry is extremely difficult. From stumpage rates that go uncollected if the forest regenerates naturally to road building, silviculture programs and insecticide spray programs, the industry has benefited from a wide range of federal and provincial handouts. The indirect assistance is even harder to quantify, such as the industry's reliance on unemployment insurance programs that allow them to lay off workers seasonally without losing them from the available pool of labour. World Resources Institute (WRI) attempted to quantify the indirect assistance in 2000, as part of a review of all forest subsidies within the G-8 nations. By its own estimation, the method of quantification was somewhat crude, extrapolating from B.C. data. WRI's best estimate was a total of $6 to $8 billion, of which they classified $3 to $4 billion as "perverse." A perverse forest subsidy is one that causes forest loss or degradation without any lasting positive impact on economic development.[33]

Meanwhile, some provinces, largely due to pressure from the U.S. trade dispute, have been reforming the stumpage rate system. The B.C. government transferred some of its stumpage to an open auction system, claiming it had the effect of raising stumpage, a claim disputed by some critics. Quebec has significantly increased its stumpage prices. But these changes are unlikely to stem the U.S. complaints until there is a full and defensible system that places reasonable prices on public resources consumed by private companies.

Basic protectionism is more than enough to explain U.S. complaints. Canada's ability to deal with these complaints depends upon a transparent, ecologically sound approach. On the other hand, perhaps the best take on the ongoing softwood battles was that of former Prime Minister Jean Chrétien, "It's never won. As the great U.S. philosopher Yogi Berra said, 'It's never over until it's over.'"[34]

Reports of poor logging practices and widespread clear-cutting have led to boycotts of Canadian forest products in Europe and the United States, which have succeeded in drying up markets for some Canadian forest companies. German newspapers and California telephone books are just two of the end products for which non–Clayoquot Sound pulp was demanded. Recent boreal forest campaigns, targeting markets in the United States and Europe, have extended the potential green-market impact of Canadian forest practices. Clear-cutting Canada's forests increasingly creates an economic threat to the industry's markets.

The response from industry has been to fund a major process under the direction of the Canadian Standards Association (CSA). For over seventy-five years, the CSA has been responsible for developing technical standards for everything from toasters to televisions. The CSA is, in turn, a member of the International Standards Organization (ISO). With over $1 million in funding from the forest industry, the CSA began what was advertised as a multi-stakeholder consensus-based process to develop standards for certifying sustainable forest management.

The difference between setting safety standards for toasters and sustainability standards for forestry should have given CSA pause. They more or less stumbled into an area for which they had no professional competence and little political sensitivity. But, based on what had seemed a successful formula for standards of consistent quality, the ISO 9000 series, the CSA approached the quagmire of forest certification with misplaced confidence. In 1994, CSA set up its Technical Committee on Sustainable Forest Management.

Early in the process, the CSA managed to alienate most of the environmental and Aboriginal communities.[1] But it persevered in developing a systems-based approach similar to the approach used in ISO standards. The ISO 9000 (quality control) and 14000 (environmental management systems) series allowed certification for adopting a management system rather than for any particular outcome. While it was readily accepted by industry, critics pointed out that, under ISO 9000, if you make a lousy widget, you could be quality-certified as long as your widget is consistently lousy.

Like the ISO 14000 approach, the CSA sustainable forest certification would accredit companies committed to a management system.[2] The corporation doing the logging would receive certification for the adoption of a systems-based process. In each instance, the forest company would develop its system with reference to a set of criteria endorsed by the Canadian forest ministers, through the federal and provincial Canadian Council of Forest Ministers (CCFM), as well as recommendations received from the public through a company-led consultation effort.[3]

It would remain the exclusive decision of the company forest manager to develop the approach to sustainable forest management. If he or she decided that goals of preserving biodiversity were best met through clear-cutting and using herbicide, then those practices would be part of the Sustainable Forest Management System, certified by the CSA. CSA boosters like to point out that the system is a mixture of systems- and performance-based approaches. Once the forest management system is in place and CSA-certified, there would be independent audits every few years to ensure that the certification terms were being met. The certification applies to a "defined forest area."

This is a growth industry for independent audit firms, as well as for QMI, the revenue-generating auditing branch of CSA. But the auditors would be assessing only whether the company did what it said it would do in its plans. Hypothetically, if a CSA-certified plan was based on intensive logging, and the company subsequently shifted to an ecosystem-based approach, they could lose the Sustainable Forest Management Certification. Recently, a review of CSA certifications found that the performance requirements were not being consistently implemented, undermining its value as a label assuring ecologically harvested forest products.[4]

Nevertheless, a significant number of Canadian forest companies have sought and received the CSA stamp of approval for forest management. Over 47 million hectares of forest are now certified under CSA's Sustainable Forest Management system, covering forests from coast to coast.[5] Abitibi-Consolidated, Canfor, Stora, Weldwood, Western Forest Products and Weyerhaeuser have all obtained CSA-SFM approvals.

In the United States, the American Forest and Paper Association has developed its own certification system, also denounced as bogus by most environmental organizations. Nevertheless, its system, dubbed the Sustainable Forestry Initiative (SFI), is being applied on a widespread basis in Canada, with more than 35 million hectares in Canada certified by the end of 2004.[6] Although initiated by the U.S. forest industry and controlled by American interests, the SFI system is recognized by the Forest Products Association of Canada, as well as by the provincial governments of Ontario and New Brunswick.

As the CSA process started to generate public debate about forest eco-labelling, another approach to forest certification was receiving increased attention in Canada. The Forest Stewardship Council (FSC) had been started internationally by the World Wildlife Fund and other environmental groups in 1993. Despite the key role played by environmental groups, the council was always structured to include an equal balance of corporate and economic interests, as well as Aboriginal and other social concerns. The FSC used many of the same words as the CSA, but had a different approach. The FSC certifies products from a specific forest area based on the ecological acceptability of practices on the ground. The FSC actually certifies the certifier, who is then allowed to use the FSC name to attest that practices in a particular area meet FSC international and, where they exist, regional standards. It is a performance-based, rather than systems-based, approach.

The FSC met with early success through the strong participation of a group of retailers in Britain. Many of Britain's largest stores, including the do-it-yourself home-supply stores, committed to using only FSC-certified wood. The market for FSC products was immediately guaranteed at £4 billion a year. But finding enough certified wood to meet this market demand would prove difficult.

The FSC process has taken off in Canada. On the ground, ecosystem-specific indicators to match the vague international principles of the FSC have been developed by working groups that brought together industry representatives with academics, scientists, activists, community members and First Nations representatives. Specific Canadian ecosystem-based standards have now been approved for the forests of the Maritimes, British Columbia and all of the boreal zone. The development of the boreal standard engaged over two thousand people and 175 committee members on fifteen committees in over seventy meetings.[7] The landmark guidelines for logging standards in the boreal forest were accepted by FSC International in August 2004. The Great Lakes–St. Lawrence forests of southern Ontario and Quebec have a draft standard that is not yet approved. At every stage, the FSC process involves the environmental, Aboriginal, economic and social sectors. Large industrial forest companies, such as Al-Pac and Tembec, are also at the table. Thus far, only 4.2 million hectares, or 1.4 per cent of Canadian commercial forest has been FSC-certified.

FSC standards are different from other certification standards because they are much more specific about what is required. For example, the FSC Canadian boreal standard requires an applicant to maintain and/or restore the forest's key natural characteristics, especially its old forests. Logging operations must leave 10 to 50 per cent of the forest in conditions similar to those following a natural disturbance. Plans must be in place to maintain or restore large areas of wildlife habitat. Special management provisions apply within 65 metres of all permanent bodies of water, and applicants must take steps to reduce their use of chemical pesticides. If an Aboriginal community is affected, companies must reach agreement with the community; that agreement must include the acceptance of the management plan, opportunities for the community to participate in long-term economic benefits, assessment of Native rights and traditional land use, measures to protect Native values, and a dispute resolution mechanism. No other certification standard comes close to matching these rigorous requirements.

In January 2001, Tembec and the World Wildlife Fund jointly announced that Tembec was committed to the FSC certification of all the lands it leases across Canada.[8] Within two years, the first of Tembec's forest operations was successful in meeting FSC requirements, the Gordon Cosens Forest of Ontario. Nipissing Forest Resource Management followed in 2003. In 2000, the first certification awarded to a First Nations community was for the forests of the Pictou Landing Mi'kmaq in Nova Scotia. J.D. Irving achieved certification in one of its units in New Brunswick based on the general international standard, only to abandon it when the more regionally specific Acadian forest standards came into effect.

The acceptance of the Canadian boreal standard by FSC International clears the way for certification of 20 to 30 million hectares of forest. Currently, Tembec, Al-Pac and Domtar are actively seeking FSC certification over their boreal holdings.[9]

In international campaigns urging companies to adopt greener practices, it is FSC certification that is demanded. In 2003, Home Depot accepted the challenge from environmental organizations to buy only wood and paper products that have been FSC certified. The increasing focus on boreal conservation has led to demands on major catalogue and tissue product manufacturers to purchase only FSC-certified sources of pulp. Many of North America's largest catalogues and tissue products come from pulp logged from virgin boreal forests.[10] If the FSC becomes the only route to large markets, smart forest companies don't want to be left out.

Certification is a mixed blessing. It is purely voluntary. Its assurance to consumers of an ecologically sound product is only as reliable as its verification and certification system.

The potential to rush to a green-wash has been too tempting for some in Canada. In March 2001, the Ontario Minister of Natural Resources, John Snobelen, in the former Conservative government, issued a new release headlined: "Ontario first in world to receive environmental certification." In a joint release with the FSC, Snobelen claimed that all of Ontario's forests were *already* sustainably managed by FSC criteria. This was far from the truth. The FSC had agreed to work with the Ontario government and industry to achieve certification on as much Ontario forest as possible. No certification had actually been conferred. No site-specific audit of Ontario's forests had been conducted by independent certifiers. "Hopefully, this will lead to a more formal agreement," said Dr. Maharj Muthoo, FSC's Executive Director, based in Mexico, "whereby Ontario's forests could become eligible for FSC certification, but we are not there yet."[11]

Forest certification continues to develop rapidly, and there is a risk of consumer confusion with multiple certification labels. However, a few things have been true from the outset and will likely remain valid. Most forestry companies have come to recognize that independent certification is here to stay. Many will seek the easiest way to obtain certification—the industry-driven schemes of the CSA and SFI. Meanwhile, the FSC system continues to be the only system that has the confidence of most environmental organizations, and therefore is the only one that has a reasonable chance of achieving "peace in the woods." It continues to be the preferred system for most of the large buyers with green purchasing policies. Other certification systems continue to try to "close the gap" with the FSC, but the FSC system will likely maintain its progressive lead for the foreseeable future.

The World Trade Organization

A further complicating factor is the possibility that the adoption by governments of voluntary eco-labelling will be restricted through decisions at the World Trade Organization (WTO). With the ongoing erosion of the United Nations, the WTO is becoming the most powerful organization in the world. The WTO was created to provide an organizational home for the General Agreement on Tariffs and Trade (GATT). GATT rules are the most extensive codification of the laws of trade liberalization and globalization. They have been called a Bill of Rights for Transnational Corporations. Based in Geneva, the WTO has been examining whether certain environmental measures actually constitute unlawful barriers to the free flow of goods.

The issue of whether voluntary eco-labelling violates the GATT has been the subject of much discussion within the WTO Trade and Environment Committee. The idea that labelling produce as "certified organic," or forest products as "sustainably harvested," could violate international trade agreements would certainly surprise most citizens. But governments have been frustrated in international forums with the inability to control consumer boycotts. Pressures from non-legislated political actions threaten the essence of GATT rules.

The most recent round of GATT negotiations, the 1986–1994 Uruguay Round, included an Agreement on Technical Barriers to Trade. This agreement actually dealt with voluntary certification schemes. The member governments have committed to use "their best endeavors" to ensure that such labelling is "WTO-compatible" and adheres to principles developed by the ISO.[12] Thus, the ISO has the inside track to WTO acceptability. It remains possible that the ISO, which has received recognition from the GATT, may ultimately be recognized as the only legitimate source of voluntary eco-labelling standards. Should this occur, then even voluntary consumer efforts to obtain environmentally sustainable forest products will be undermined.

For as much as certification schemes may be attractive in lieu of regulation, their primary benefit to the forest industry is in securing export markets. Trade in Canadian forest products is under increasing pressure from environmental campaigns, as wood shortages force the logging of increasingly remote and valuable wilderness.

Legitimate, well-monitored certification holds the potential for moving forest management in Canada out of the often dangerous hands of provincial governments and toward an ever-rising bar of global consumer demand. Illegitimate, sloppy efforts, on the other hand, could legitimize intensive forestry and loss of habitat with a green stamp of approval. In a clear case of the rise of responsibility and the clout of civil society, environmental groups, having harnessed market forces, must now keep tight hold of the reins.

Certification and deregulation

In recent years, industry self-regulation has accelerated at an alarming rate. What was once a trend only in Ontario and Alberta has now spread to British Columbia. The change in government in Ontario, from Conservative Harris and Eves governments to Liberal Premier Dalton McGuinty, may herald an effort to reverse such trends in Ontario, but the damage is far advanced.

Budgetary pressure has resulted in two very different approaches. Some provinces, such as Alberta, Ontario and now the Campbell government in British Columbia, have taken the view that drastic reductions in forest service staff is an acceptable way to decrease governmental deficits. Government statements suggest confidence in the forest industry's ability to police its own operations, gather its own data and report on the sustainability of its forest operations to a much smaller group of provincial forest bureaucrats. Other provinces are taking a more practical, long-term view: they are recognizing the need to increase revenues from forest companies that benefit from low-cost tenure over Canada's forests.

Budget cuts, particularly where they result in less silviculture, should automatically translate into decreases in the annual allowable cut. But although silviculture expenditures have been reduced across the country, nowhere has this led to fundamental rethinking of the rates of cut. By the government's own modelling exercises, AAC levels are totally dependent on growing more trees, faster. But in Nova Scotia, even when 70 per cent of the silviculture targets were not met, the AAC based on that crucial silviculture investment remained unchanged.[13]

As budget cuts lead increasingly to voluntary measures and industry self-regulation, the climate is ripe for a new method of assuring that forest practices are sustainable—voluntary eco-labelling, or certification. In fact, interest is growing in voluntary approaches, not just in forestry, but across Canada's environmental scene. Pollution regulation, for example, is threatened as companies make the pitch that "regulations don't work." Industries like to argue that they respond better to carrots than to sticks. But historical evidence does not bear this out. Certainly the record on pulp-and-paper effluents in Canada makes an excellent case for "command and control." Without regulations, tons of toxic effluent would still be entering Canada's waterways, while voluntary guidelines would be thwarted by industry CEOs who could honestly say, "We're not in non-compliance."

Coupled with the overriding pressure to devolve federal responsibilities to the provinces, reduced regulatory "burdens" have become an extremely popular political rallying cry. As Ontario's former Minister of Environment Brenda Elliott put it when explaining why she did not believe in further efforts to reduce health threats from smog, "We were elected to get government out of your face."[14]

8 | OTHER PRESSURES ON CANADA'S FORESTS

Canada's forests face significant threats from other types of industrial activity, such as large-scale hydroelectric development, mining, oil and gas exploration and development, as well as agriculture and urban sprawl. These activities make no effort to address issues of sustainable forest management; in fact, they bring about virtually permanent conversion of forests to non-forest uses. The rate of removal of forest is not regulated or included in the calculation of annual allowable cuts. In many cases, the same area of forest under logging pressure is also experiencing pressures from oil and gas development, from mining or from hydroelectric dams. Cumulative impacts are rarely included in environmental reviews. Without integrated land-use planning, the forest is squeezed between competing industries.

The earliest deforestation in Canada occurred with human settlement and clearing the land for agriculture. Many of the forested areas of southern Canada disappeared in this way, although in some areas, abandoned farm fields are returning to early successional species. The Carolinian forests of southern Ontario, the Great Lakes–St. Lawrence forest, the montane and the Acadian forests have all been significantly impacted by clearing for agriculture. The southern boreal, particularly in the grass and tree belt through the prairie provinces, continues to experience alarming rates of deforestation. In some parts of the prairies the rate of loss of forest to agriculture, 1 per cent per year, rivals that in the Amazon.

Population pressures and poor land-use planning allow important forest biodiversity to be lost to shopping malls, parking lots, suburban subdivisions and highways. In Ottawa, the Leitrim Wetland, a provincially significant wetland with open fens, bogs and areas of old-growth Great Lakes–St. Lawrence forest, is threatened by a housing development. Urban sprawl has cleared remnant old-growth Acadian forest near Halifax, and Carolinian old growth near London, Ontario. Those small forests near urban areas need to be vigorously protected. Urban forests (such as Stanley Park forest in Vancouver), whether recently planted or protected over centuries, can make an important contribution to improved air quality, carbon sequestration, micro-climactic cooling effects, habitat opportunities, retention of rainfall and improved urban life.

Far north of agricultural and urban Canada are huge flooded reservoirs where once there were forests. Thousands of square kilometres of boreal forest have been drowned as a result of hydroelectric development in northern Quebec, Labrador, Manitoba, British Columbia and Ontario. Canada generates more power from damming its rivers than any other country in the world, with more water diverted by more dams. The first phase of the Hydro Quebec dam at James Bay alone flooded 11,345 square kilometres of forest. The total area of impounded reservoirs in Canada is equal to the size of Lake Ontario, with future dams poised to flood additional areas half that large.[1] Plans are on the drawing board for more dams in northern Manitoba, along the Churchill River in Saskatchewan, the Rupert River in Quebec, the Churchill in Labrador. While most of the current plans of Manitoba Hydro involve relatively small reservoirs totalling up to 42 square kilometres of inundated lands, the potential for the revival of the massive Conawapa project is always a concern. The Rupert River diversion would flood over 400 square kilometres of boreal forest in northern Quebec.

While hydroelectric developers attempt to promote electricity from the damming of wild rivers as environmentally acceptable, the reality is far different. Hydroelectricity cannot truly be described as "renewable." Neither is it carbon-neutral. The drowning of forests and other organic material has a significant impact on carbon, releasing vast amounts as methane. The environmental impacts, besides loss of habitat, include the creation of methyl mercury and its uptake in the aquatic life of the reservoir. The Cree of northern Quebec experienced mercury contamination as fish, a traditional part of their diet and culture, were poisoned by this "clean" source of energy. The manipulation of water flow impacts entire water systems, changing hydrology with impacts on wetlands and habitats along the stream and river edges. These areas are among the most productive for a wide range of species. Already, hydroelectric developments have dramatically changed the Peace–Athabasca Delta near Alberta's border with the Northwest Territory and the Saskatchewan River Delta near the Manitoba-Saskatchewan border.[2]

Mining activities also overlap with forested areas. Although mining impacts directly on a very small portion of the forested land base, indirect impacts can extend over a much larger area. Surface water may become contaminated, as can ground water. Cyanide is used to remove gold from the ore and can enter the environment from mine sites. Air pollution from mines is also a problem, while the disturbance of aquatic ecosystems through sedimentation is quite common.

Most of the mining activity in Canada occurs in the boreal region, with active mines for uranium, asbestos, copper, zinc, iron, gold, silver, nickel and coal in forested areas. Canada is the world's largest exporter of gold. The new pressure for diamond mining in the Northwest Territories generally occurs in areas of tundra. The production of uranium in northern Saskatchewan makes Canada the number-one global exporter of this radioactive material, with huge areas contaminated with the radioactive tailings from the mines. Asbestos mining in Quebec continues despite the fact that the only remaining asbestos company is under bankruptcy protection and its product is inherently dangerous. Canada is a major global exporter of asbestos to developing countries, where this hazardous material is still used.

Coal is mined in Alberta from open pits. Currently, the Cheviot Mine, operated by Cardinal River Coal, is beginning construction, despite the lack of all required governmental approvals. The Cheviot Mine is within 3 kilometres of Jasper National Park in the prime grizzly bear habitat of the Cardinal River Valley. Whole watercourses will be eliminated to make room for the mining of metallurgical coal from one of the most important areas for biodiversity in the province. The forests removed in that area for the coal mine, haul roads and related developments are in addition to those within the approved logging plans for the Weldwood paper mill in Hinton, Alberta.

There are over seven thousand abandoned mines in the boreal region, with sixty-nine operating mines and fifty-three that have recently closed.[3] The legacy of poor past practice remains an environmental threat throughout the boreal region. Mines open rock to the elements, creating a serious problem known as acid mine drainage. As well as those releasing toxic materials that had been locked away in mineral deposits, mining makes use of toxic materials such as cyanide to extract metals. A huge volume of earth and rock is transformed into waste in Canadian mining, giving the industry the dubious distinction of generating more solid waste than any other industry—95 per cent of the national total. Every year, 650 million tons of solid waste are generated by mining, of which at least one-fifth is estimated to be toxic. The abandoned mines pose a range of serious environmental risks, from pooled arsenic to acid mine drainage, cyanide and despoiled landscapes.

Increased environmental damage occurred in Ontario as the former Conservative government rolled back regulations to protect public lands and control mining. Ontario has the largest mining sector of any province and produces one-third of all the minerals and metals mined in Canada.[4]

The mining industry has tried to clean up its act in recent years, participating in extensive consultations with environmental and community groups, First Nations and other stakeholders to develop conservation planning. The Whitehorse Mining Initiative was a first step in the mining industry's stated willingness to respect important ecosystems as protected areas. In some cases, support from the mining industry has been the key difference between protected status and industrial exploitation. Nevertheless, some mining companies in British Columbia have walked away from land-use planning processes and have opposed new protected areas.

The legacy of abandoned mines and the damage done by small "junior" mining companies is a problem throughout the boreal. As most of the more readily accessible minerals have been mined, the ongoing exploration and development of mines through the boreal region represents frontier activity, taking roads and development into previously inaccessible areas and representing a significant threat of fragmentation to the intact boreal forest regions.

The largest of the non-logging threats to Canada's forests is clearly that posed by petroleum development. The development and expansion of the petroleum deposits of the Western Canadian Sedimentary Basin, coupled with the proposed Mackenzie Valley gas pipeline, present the largest current threat to the intact boreal forest from northern Alberta to the Northwest Territories. Other than the gas production facilities at the Mackenzie Delta, virtually all of this development is in the boreal region. From the devastated moonscapes of the Athabasca Tar Sands to the proposed Mackenzie Valley pipeline, the largest ecological footprint hovering over Canada's boreal is the giant boot of the fossil fuel industry.

The business of drilling for oil and gas is primarily concentrated in Alberta, but petroleum prospecting and development is actually occurring in nearly every jurisdiction in Canada. Coal-bed methane is being pushed in British Columbia, threatening high levels of ecological damage, while drilling is occurring across the country for oil and gas. According to the Canadian Association of Petroleum Producers, 16,000 wells are drilled in Canada every year.[5]

Nevertheless, it is Alberta that clearly is most exploited for oil and gas. With over 150,000 wells already, its forested areas have been criss-crossed with seismic lines and roads for testing, while its northern deposits of bitumen are the site of the largest strip mines in Canada.[6]

The Athabasca Tar Sands are the target of $51-billion worth of current and planned investment between 1996 and 2010.[7] The tar, or oil, sands are the second-largest source of oil anywhere on the planet. With more oil than Saudi Arabia, Alberta's tar sands have 300 billion barrels of proven reserves. Previously, the costs of transforming tarry mud to barrels of petroleum crude made the deposits of little commercial interest. But as oil hits $50 a barrel and oil supplies from the Middle East are threatened, Alberta's tar sands are booming.

The production of oil for export from the bitumen is devastating ecologically. Unlike the problems associated with drilling for oil and gas, the tar sands are essentially open-pit mines. The whole surface of the landscape—forests, wetlands, streams, peat lands—must be peeled back so that the heavy equipment can shovel out the bitumen muck. Each tar sands operation clears thousands of hectares. The largest and most environmentally responsible companies promise that there will be reclamation after the mines shut down, with the replanting of forests and even the recreation of streams.[8] To date, no mine site has undergone reclamation. Most are just getting started. The production of oil from bitumen is hugely energy-intensive and uses vast quantities of water. It has been estimated that for each barrel of oil produced, six barrels of water are consumed.

The energy needs of the Athabasca Tar Sands are the major driver of the Mackenzie gas project. While Atomic Energy of Canada Limited has attempted to persuade the Alberta government that it needs nuclear reactors for the enormous energy appetite of the tar sands, the likely source of future energy will be the proposed natural gas production at the mouth of the Mackenzie River. The concerns of

Native people that led Mr. Justice Thomas Berger to recommend in the 1970s that a moratorium should be in place before allowing the Mackenzie gas pipeline to proceed have largely disappeared. At least at the level of Inuit, Dene and Gwich'in leadership and government, if not the elders and youth, the pipeline is being welcomed.

The Mackenzie River flows to the Arctic Ocean from its sources in northern Alberta, with a total watershed that is one-fifth the size of Canada. In the river's delta are reserves of natural gas. Current proposals from Imperial, Shell and Conoco Phillips are for three gas production facilities to be drilled in the delta, two inside the Kendall Bird Sanctuary. From there, the natural gas will travel under tremendous pressure through an underground pipeline. The pipeline will start through inconsistent permafrost and continue along the river valley all the way to a connecting pipe in northern Alberta. It is believed that most, if not all, of the gas will be used in the production of crude in the tar sands.

The impact on the boreal forest and the Mackenzie Valley wilderness will be devastating. The region is largely intact, with no roads or major industrial activity. Construction of the 1,200-kilometre pipeline will have a significant impact on the local environment. Well beyond the construction phase, however, the building of the pipeline will encourage other development in the region. Commercially unattractive reserves of oil and gas elsewhere along the Mackenzie River will become commercial. More roads will be built. More oil and gas exploration and development will take place. For Canada's frontier boreal forests in Alberta and the Northwest Territories, oil and gas is a much larger threat than the forest industry.

Part II
Once a Land of Trees

9 | THE LOST FORESTS

Four centuries ago, when Europeans first set foot on Canada's shores, forests spanned its entire territory. Since then the forest has been substantially diminished through settlement, agriculture, urbanization and industrial expansion; not only the size of Canada's forest, but also its biological characteristics have been altered. Species have been lost; forest ecosystems have been impoverished; what was complex and magnificent has been reduced to something far less diverse.

The process of change has been slow in human terms, but extremely rapid in geological, or even biological, ones. Forests are constantly shifting, never static. In the language of forest ecologists, "succession" is the natural advance of forest; "disturbance" reverses the movement toward a climax state. In the absence of major human disturbances, the composition, age and structure of a forest rolls and shifts over time. What several human generations can do to a forest may fall within the lifespan of a single long-lived tree.

By understanding the pace of human interference with the forest and the pattern of historical settlement, we can begin to comprehend why forest disputes are so intense in British Columbia, whereas environmentalists in Atlantic Canada are more likely to be concerned with controlling logging practices rather than stopping logging. Simply put, other than fragments of original stands found along steep ravines and valley bottoms, there is almost nothing of Atlantic Canada's pristine pre-contact forest left to save. Where New Brunswick environmentalists battle to preserve 50,000 hectares in the Christmas Mountains, B.C. activists struggle to protect intact watersheds of 250,000 hectares. Most of the forests of the Atlantic provinces have seen hundreds of years of logging; in coastal British Columbia, virtually all of the temperate old-growth forest is being logged for the first time.

As Paul Senez, past president of Sierra Club of Canada observed, "In the east, it has largely become a matter of protecting the public from a degraded environment, while in the west it's a matter of protecting the environment from a degraded public."[1]

When the economic exploitation of the forests is tracked from east to west, a consistent pattern emerges. Not only in biological terms, but in strictly economic ones, we wipe out our most valuable species, and then move on to the ones we considered worthless at the first cut. In the fishery, we moved down the food chain as we wiped out more valuable species, but the time frame has been briefer. Newfoundlanders recall the days of giant cod, redfish, American plaice and haddock, even as they listen to promotion efforts highlighting the potential in harvesting sea urchins now that the fish are gone. But the changes wrought on the forest cannot be experienced by the human observer. No one currently alive in Atlantic Canada actually participated in the building of the great tall ships. Those trees now live only in our imagination.

Forests at risk

Canada has a wide range of forest ecosystem types, from the stunted and scattered trees of the subalpine at the treeline, to the lush Carolinian forests of southern Ontario, to trees that outlived the last millennia in coastal British Columbia. Before the Earth Summit in Rio in 1992, there was a debate about what constitutes a forest. Mexico argued that areas where cactus predominate should be within the proposed forest convention. It is less complicated in Canada, but very nearly as varied.

Twelve different regions of forest types were mapped by the late Stan Rowe, one of Canada's foremost ecologists, refining the earlier work of W.E.D. Halliday. Generally, government forest services recognize eight distinct forest regions in Canada. However, even within the regions designated by Rowe, many sub-regions and species variations exist. The impacts of logging and other human encroachments have made a huge impact on the very survival of these ecological systems with their myriad elements. As the provincial reviews in the following chapters will establish, no forest type in Canada can be considered adequately protected.

THE CAROLINIAN

The most endangered of Canadian forests is the Carolinian forest of southern Ontario. It spans just 550 kilometres of the southernmost reaches of Canada, comprising a mere 0.1 per cent of the nation's total forested area. Although a tiny forest region in comparison with the vast boreal, which comprises 77 per cent of the nation's forests, the Carolinian forest holds more individual tree species than any other forest type in Canada. It has an incredible seventy different species of native trees, plus over two thousand types of plants, four hundred bird species, and nearly fifty different species of reptiles and amphibians.

The characteristic Carolinian species mix includes trees found nowhere else in Canada, such as the tulip tree, shellback hickory, Kentucky coffee tree, blue ash, common hoptree, eastern flowering dogwood and American sycamore, as well as species found in other regions: cottonwoods, black oak, maples, basswood, beech, Eastern white pine and cedar. Broadleaf hardwoods predominate; conifers are typically a small proportion of the Carolinian forest. Some of the tree species have already been listed as endangered or species of concern by the Committee on the Status of Endangered Wildlife in Canada.

The variety of plant life is astonishing, including many kinds of orchids, ginseng, prickly pear and cucumber magnolia. The call of the northern mockingbird is in the air, the flash of colour of the orchard oriole on the wing. There are even a few tall grass sites, more common in the prairies, and some savanna oak stands within the forest region. A few good examples of its old-growth state remain in provincial parks, such as the Backus Woods near Long Point, but much more needs to be done if this forest is to survive.

The Carolinian has become increasingly imperiled by the paving of southern Ontario. Less than 10 per cent of the original Carolinian forest remains. Urban sprawl is the main culprit. The Carolinian's original range, from the Windsor and Sarnia area in the west to Goderich in the east, is one of the most developed areas of Canada. Chemical refineries, highways, cities and agricultural areas have hemmed in the forest that remains. London, Ontario, in the heart of the Carolinian forest, prides itself on its claim to be the Forest City. Yet forest cover in London is being given up to shopping malls. London currently has more retail space per capita than any other Canadian city. Local efforts to replant the forest in indigenous species are hampered by the budget cuts of the Harris government era. It shut down the few government-run tree nurseries. Private nurseries have tried to fill the gap, but a lack of coordination in tree-planting efforts leaves nurseries unsure of how many tulip trees or Kentucky coffee trees to grow. Who will buy them? The Urban

League, the Upper Thames River Conservation Authority and other local groups remain committed to restoring London's Carolinian forest, but the task is daunting.

The survival of the Carolinian forest will depend on a combination of intensified actions: provincial action to set aside any Carolinian remnants that become available, accelerated efforts of stewardship by private landowners, arresting the threat of urban sprawl by removing the stranglehold that developers have on most municipal councils, plus enlightened corporate engagement.

THE ACADIAN

Unlike the Carolinian forest, the ecosystem known as the Acadian forest is found only in Canada. And although every species found within the Acadian forest is found somewhere else in Canada, it is the species assemblage that is unique in the world.

The Acadian forest region covered the original land mass of New Brunswick, Nova Scotia and Prince Edward Island, approximately 2.2 per cent of Canada's forests. It was a forest of massive hardwoods: oaks, maples, birch, beech, butternut and walnut. Conifers were also present, including magnificent hemlock, pine and spruce. Wildlife from lynx to caribou were indigenous in these forests. The caribou have been displaced by moose and deer; the lynx are rarely sighted and are listed as endangered. Fortunately, the raptors do well, with bald eagles abundant, scanning the river valleys and ocean waves for fish. Great blue herons stand stoically at the water's edge with Zen-like patience. Herons are also forest-dwellers, nesting in tree-top rookeries. Pine martens, river otters and other small mammals live in these forests, as do black bears, red foxes and snowshoe hares. Rare plants can be found below the branches, such as orchids, as well as witch hazel and staghorn sumac.

Centuries of human settlement, agriculture and logging have significantly changed the Acadian forest. Although it remains distinct to this day, the current Acadian forest is simplified. Many of the hardwood species have been virtually eliminated and softwoods—balsam fir and spruce—now predominate. Logging has moved the forest to a much younger, more even-aged condition. The original remnants of primary Acadian forest can be found on only about 5 per cent of the region.[2] True old-growth Acadian forest is vanishing, but mixed-aged forests with old growth in parts create unique old-growth features for wildlife and lichen. It is extremely important to protect such forests, but industry tends to deride any attempt at conservation of forests that are not pure old-growth.

Fortunately, five national parks and a number of smaller provincial parks contain at least some original Acadian forest. As most of the land base in the Maritimes is in private hands, the government's opportunity to set aside Crown lands as protected forests is vastly reduced. Sadly, the experience with the Nova Scotia and New Brunswick governments suggests that, even if the land were available, the political preference would be to further reduce its ecological value and biodiversity in the interests of pulp production.

The protection and restoration of the Acadian forest is a major conservation priority with a global imperative. What we have left is all that remains in the world. Forest departments should reorient themselves to the project of rebuilding the species mix that existed centuries ago. The reduction of the Acadian forest to a pulp plantation must be arrested and reversed.

ANCIENT TEMPERATE RAINFORESTS

The forests along the west coast of British Columbia are classified as coastal, but more usually described as temperate rainforests. The coastal rainforest ecosystem is found on every continent on earth except Africa and Antarctica. Once an abundant ecoregion, it has been reduced to less than half its former global range. Temperate coastal rainforests can now be found only in fragments in Chile, Tasmania, New Zealand, Norway, Alaska and Canada. Along the west coast of North America, the rainforest once stretched from northern Washington state to Alaska.

British Columbia has a full 20 per cent of all the world's surviving temperate rainforests within its borders.[3] The nearly 7.5 million hectares of coastal forest make up just 1.8 per cent of Canada's total forest base, yet it has produced a disproportionately large amount of forest products and wealth to the forest industry. This is because each tree can be enormous, producing more fibre than a hectare of logged forest elsewhere in Canada. More than half of the original coastal rainforest has already been clear-cut.

The coastal rainforest may not have the greatest species diversity in Canada, but it does have the heaviest forest, as much as 2,000 tons per hectare.[4] Its biodiversity weighs more due to the sheer mass of the ancient forest giants and the profusion of other life those trees support. The typical species in this predominantly coniferous forest are western red cedar, Sitka spruce, western hemlock and Douglas fir. An individual Sitka spruce, the tallest tree in Canada, can be over 95 metres tall, while western red cedar can measure 6 metres in diameter. Some of these forest giants can live well over one thousand years.

The coastal forest also has a profusion of smaller trees: western yew, Pacific willow, red and Sitka alders, Douglas maple, blueberry elder, western flowering bearberry (also known as kinnikinnick) and bitter cherry. The bark of the western yew is the source of the cancer treatment drug Taxol. Two tree species found nowhere else in Canada live in the coastal forest: the Garry oak and the arbutus. Seabirds form an intimate connection between forest floor and ocean wave, with ancient and marbled murrelets nesting in the cavities of trees and, urged on by frantic parents, running pell-mell to the ocean within days of birth. The spotted owl, the most endangered bird in Canada, relies on the old-growth forest for its needs. The Vancouver Island marmot is also endangered by logging.

The streams, cooled by the shade of huge tree limbs, with the occasional log deposited for nutrients, are the source of life for hundreds of distinct salmon stocks, 142 of which have already gone extinct due to habitat loss. Chum, chinook, pink, steelhead, coho and sockeye salmon begin and end their lives in the forest. Young salmon may remain for as long as three years in the fresh water of the streams and rivers before setting out to the depths of the salty ocean beyond. They return from the Pacific anywhere from one to five years later, unerringly finding the river and pebbly stream from which they emerged years before. The forest streams become a mass of reddish and decaying flesh, as the salmon, driven and desperate, swim upstream to lay their eggs before they die. The grizzly bears rely on salmon for their best seasonal feasts, depositing the skeletal salmon remains in and among the mosses and ferns of the forest floor, where they provide nutrients for the trees. The forest nourishes and protects the eggs and newly hatched salmon with nutrients and shade, and the intimate dance of forest, fish and bear begins once again.

Currently, only five of the eighty-four primary large (over 5,000 hectares) coastal watersheds on the south mainland coast remain unlogged. On Vancouver Island, only six out of ninety remain undeveloped. Protecting the salmon, the forest and all the life that depends upon them requires setting aside all of the intact, unlogged wilderness watersheds of the coastal giants.

The montane

In the southern interior of British Columbia, in the dry shadow of the coastal mountains, is a forest region known as the montane. Lodgepole pine is the most common species is this predominantly coniferous forest that covers 2.9 per cent of the forested land of Canada. Interior Douglas fir, also known as Rocky Mountain Douglas fir, is common too. Ponderosa pine is the third most dominant tree species, a tree not yet protected within any of Canada's national parks. Hardwoods do occur, especially after a fire disturbance, with trembling aspen a common species.

The montane stretches south to the Okanagan Valley and Canada's only true desert. A national park proposal, supported by Sierra Club of Canada and currently undergoing a feasibility study, would include some montane forest as well as desert, protecting a number of species at risk. The sagebrush ecosystem, the western rattlesnake and the American badger are found here and nowhere else in Canada. They are all listed as endangered.

The key challenges to conservation in the southern range of the montane are ranching and development. But in the more mountainous interior, the forest is fully committed to logging. The forests are home to deer mice, coyotes, American pine martens, mule deer and bighorn sheep along the mountainous ridges. The mountain pine beetle epidemic has taken hold of the montane forest's lodgepole pine on over 1.46 million hectares of forest. Both the beetle and the accelerated rate of logging created by salvage and pre-salvage efforts threaten the forest. Even before the beetle infestation—a crisis linked to climate change—the forest of the montane was being logged at an unsustainable rate.

The Columbia forest

The smallest of all the forest regions within British Columbia, the Columbia forest is found only in the southeastern part of the province, to the edge of the Alberta border, accounting for less than 1 per cent of the Canada's forests. The lush forests of the deep valleys benefit from long, warm summers and moisture from the heavy winter snows. The Columbia forest extends along the mountain slopes until it reaches the subalpine forest, and to the south and west, where it forms a transition zone to the montane and dry grasslands.

Its most common species are western red cedar, Douglas fir and western hemlock. Where rains are heavy, portions of the Columbia are known as temperate inland rainforest. The river valleys can become predominantly hardwood, with black cottonwood in leafy profusion. Much of the accessible Columbia forest has already been logged and is being scheduled for harvest as second growth.

THE SUBALPINE FOREST

The subalpine forest extends along the slopes of mountains in British Columbia and western Alberta. It starts at the very edges of glaciers and alpine meadows and connects the web of life to the Columbia, montane and coastal forests farther south. Its most common species are Engelmann spruce, subalpine fir and lodgepole pine. Although it is not found in one swath but scattered along the mountainous terrain, it makes up 4 per cent of the forested land of Canada.

It is home to grizzly bears, lynxes and coyotes, as well as mountain goats, mule deer, moose and hoary marmots. The climate at the forest's most northern reaches is harsh. This forest starts at the treeline with scattered and small forest stands. It occurs in patches, along the mountains of Haida Gwaii, along the central mountain range of Vancouver Island, and along the Rocky Mountains. Within these patches of subalpine forests there are significant species distinctions and variations. Each subalpine forest reflects echoes of the more productive forests found in less harsh conditions edging into its range.

THE GREAT LAKES–ST. LAWRENCE FOREST

As the name suggests, the forest of this region hugs the shores of the Great Lakes and St. Lawrence River, running in a broad swath from southeastern Manitoba all the way to the Gaspé of Quebec. It is a beautiful forest of deciduous and coniferous trees, where once towering white pine reached to the heavens. Its species mix typically includes sugar maple, red maple, birches, basswood, red oak, American beech, ironwood, aspen and ash. The coniferous species of eastern white pine, hemlock and eastern white cedar are also found in this forest. Over its entire range it occupies 6.6 per cent of Canada's forests. From this forest came the sawlogs that built early Canadian settlements, and the white pine that went to sea in a formidable navy.

The Great Lakes–St. Lawrence forest is as badly degraded as any in Canada, with a significant loss of diversity in age classes, a severe reduction in the most valuable species, such as white pine, and a consequent loss of biodiversity. The stands of old-growth pine that dwarfed early loggers are found only in faded photographs. It is the story across North America, where less than 1 per cent of the original old-growth red and white pine remain. Eastern hemlock was also decimated for the tannin in its bark valued by the tanning trade.

Below the forest canopy grow a wide variety of herbaceous plants—red trillium, snow trillium, wild leek, trailing arbutus, ram's head lady's slipper, dogtooth violet, winterberry and smooth blackberry. Red-shouldered hawks cut lazy circles overhead, while songbirds—chickadees and warblers—live in noisy profusion below. The northern goshawk lives in these woods, as does the ruffed grouse and pileated woodpecker, smashing the decaying wood of the dead and dying trees to feast on the insects within. Deer, porcupines, black bears and foxes all live in these forests.

Intact areas have been fragmented, except in parks. Long-lived trees such as white and red pine have been replaced with poplar and birch. As in every forest ecoregion of southern Canada, the time has come to shift our focus from saving remnant scraps of original forest to restoring the forest that once was.

THE BOREAL

The boreal forest of Canada is part of the largest of all planetary terrestrial ecosystems. Like the aurora borealis, the boreal forest draws its name from Boreas, the Greek god of the north wind. The boreal, or taiga, comprises the northernmost forest lands of Siberia, Alaska, Scandinavia and Canada, containing almost one-third of the planet's forests. Within the boreal region are the majority of the world's wetlands and lakes.

Too large to be endangered? Like the passenger pigeons that used to blacken the skies, these forests too could disappear. Despite its vastness, the special sub-committee of the Canadian Senate investigating the boreal concluded: "The world's boreal forest, a resource of which Canada is a major trustee, is under siege."[5]

Canada's boreal forest comprises nearly 80 per cent of all the forest land from coast to coast, a full 35 per cent of the planet's boreal region. It stretches into virtually every province, missing only the

Maritimes, but even there, in the northern parts of New Brunswick and the highlands of Cape Breton, the forest has boreal characteristics. Covering over 3.2 million square kilometres of Canada, the boreal performs essential ecological functions in protecting the carbon balance, creating fresh water and providing habitat for waterfowl in its huge wetlands, breeding areas for migratory songbirds and essential habitats for the woodland caribou, bear, wolf and beaver. The peat bogs, soils and trees of the planet's boreal hold more carbon out of the atmosphere than any other terrestrial ecosystem. While the Amazon is often called the lungs of the planet, the boreal has a more established claim to the term due to its key role in moderating climate. Without the boreal, we'd all fry.

As a seasonal home for songbirds, the boreal plays a crucial role. During breeding season, more than half of the population of about 40 different species of songbirds are nesting in Canada's boreal. As many as 3 billion land birds per year may hatch in boreal nests. Likewise is the boreal critical breeding ground for migratory waterfowl. In its expanse are approximately 1.5 million lakes and some of the country's largest river systems. Canada's boreal contains 35 per cent of the world's wetlands and has the largest coverage of peatlands in the world. Canada's boreal wetlands comprise over 40 per cent of the world's Wetlands of International Importance.[6] According to Ducks Unlimited, the boreal wetlands are second only to the prairie potholes in providing habitat to North America's ducks. Between 12 and 14 million ducks annually breed in the boreal wetlands of Canada, which also provide migratory habitat for as much as 75 per cent of all the continent's ducks during migration and molting periods.[7]

The Canadian Forest Service estimates that Canada's forests, most of which are boreal, contain approximately 140,000 kinds of living organisms, half of which are not yet classified. When we talk of forests, we talk of trees, and name those mammals and birds that live there. The boreal is home to black bears, beavers, caribou, moose and gray wolves. Yet, trees and vertebrates are a small component of overall species diversity. In fact, plants and vertebrates comprise only about 5 per cent of boreal species.[8] It is the beetles, insects, fungi and microbial organisms that make up the largest numbers of boreal species. In Finland, it was estimated that in 200 square kilometres of forest, over 4,000 to 5,000 saprophytic beetles alone and close to 900 beetle species could be found.[9]

Given the enormous extent of Canada's boreal forest, it has, not surprisingly, been further categorized into boreal sub-regions. In the transition zone from prairie to forest is a belt known as "forest and grass boreal," and north to the treeline lies a much larger band of forest and barrens known as the taiga.[10] The largest portion of the boreal zone is predominantly coniferous forest. The common species are balsam fir, white and black spruce, tamarack and jack pine, with a number of hardwood species, particularly in the south and in post-fire successional areas: trembling aspen, willow and white birch. The boreal forest is a fire-driven ecosystem. Huge fires have been part of the natural cycle for the last six thousand years. Fires consume thousands of square kilometres of boreal forest every year. Some fire cycles return to the same areas as quickly as within fifty to a hundred years; other forests may experience a three-hundred-year break between fires. All these cycles are within the range of normal.[11] Due to increased temperatures and changes in rainfall patterns, coupled in some cases with fire suppression efforts, the number of forest fires in the boreal is increasing. The average disturbance rate is a statistic encompassing losses due to both fire and insects. Between 1920 and 1969, the average disturbance rate was 1.7 million hectares per year. In the 1970s and 1980s, that figure increased dramatically to 3.9 million hectares per year.[12]

As forests in southern Canada become fully exploited, logging pressure has moved into the boreal. In the last fifteen years, over $7 billion worth of investment in the boreal region has resulted in forty-five new mills being built in the region. The rate of logging shot up. Much of the boreal, previously unallocated in long-term industrial leases, became committed to meet the new fibre demands. Nearly half of the southern boreal region was allocated by 2000, and industrial interests began to extend north of the 51st parallel.[13] In fact, Ontario adopted a land-use planning initiative to explore industrialization opportunities in the northern boreal. Currently, Canada's boreal is being logged at a rate of 2 hectares per minute.[14]

Already, in every province throughout its range, the boreal population of woodland caribou is at risk. The woodland caribou needs intact old-growth forest. Without the very old trees, the lichen that it prefers cannot be found. As a harbinger of unsustainable exploitation, the plight of the woodland caribou should be a wake-up call to those in provincial governments who continue to approve expanded logging. The forests are also threatened by hydroelectric development, mining and increasing oil and gas activity. The most devastating threat may be that of climate change, brought on by human activity and the profligate waste of fossil fuels.

The protection of Canada's boreal has become an increased focus for governmental and private concern. In 1999, Canada's Senate Sub-committee on the plight of the boreal made a number of radical recommendations. It called for provincial and federal government co-operation to create zones within the boreal: 20 per cent for intensive timber production, 20 per cent to be set aside in protected areas and the remaining 60 per cent managed less intensively, with "preservation of biodiversity as the primary objective."[15]

The Senate committee's call to action has been largely ignored. The logging pressures on the boreal forest have increased, as have other threats from industrial activity. Nearly three-quarters of the 15.4-per-cent increase in Canada's softwood sawmill capacity between 1995 and 2001 was for the boreal forests of the prairies, Ontario and Quebec.[16] The intact expanses of primary boreal forest give Canadians an opportunity to protect most of this forest. We cannot afford to drain our carbon sink. Our responsibility as global stewards of 35 per cent of the world's remaining boreal forest requires that we fundamentally alter our approach to forests. Without a change in mindset, we will set to the boreal with the same abandon with which our ancestors mowed through the last giant white pines, the oaks of the Acadian forest and the Douglas fir of the B.C. coast.

Newfoundland and Labrador

The forests of Newfoundland and Labrador are a study in contrasts. The province boasts a large expanse of never-logged forest in Labrador, while the island of Newfoundland has been subject to logging since 1550. It has now been so heavily logged that it is the first province to officially report that it is running out of wood to feed its mills.[1]

Newfoundland and Labrador was also the first place in Canada to experience extinctions. The Aboriginal people of Newfoundland, the Beothuk, were the only First Nation to be totally annihilated by the Europeans. The great auk, a flightless bird of the sea bird rookeries off Newfoundland's coast, was exterminated for its eggs, feathers and flesh.[2] Gone also are the Newfoundland wolf and the Labrador duck. And Newfoundland was the first place in Canada to convert forest land into permanent barrens. Some areas, particularly on the Avalon Peninsula, have never regenerated after logging. This is a relatively rare phenomenon in Canada, although not unknown. For example, the Magdalen Islands in Quebec have been deforested through logging. And large areas of Newfoundland's forests have been replaced with kalmia heaths or barrens. Kalmia (*Kalmia angustifolia*), commonly called "sheep laurel," currently covers 25 per cent of eastern Newfoundland, with most of that considered to be post-logging "unnatural" kalmia, replacing the boreal forest.[3] The few trees still found on these windswept heaths are of the stunted variety referred to as "krummholz" from the German words for "crooked wood."

The kalmia heaths also harbour a forest disease that has devastated the pines. The white pine blister rust attacks white pine trees, leaving them stunted and unable to reach maturity. Recovery of white and red pine has been hampered by the heaths and barrens, themselves created by deforestation.

This litany of extinctions is not meant to suggest that there is any particular anti-conservation animus within the heart of Newfoundlanders. But it was the place where European exploitation of Canada began in the 1500s, and the inhabitants have had a lot more time to damage their surroundings. As one of Newfoundland's many Royal Commissions on Forestry reported in 1955:

> One of the outstanding traits of the Anglo-Saxon race has always been its disregard of forests, both direct and indirect. The progress of the settlement of North America has been a story of forest destruction, wanton devastation by fire and heedless exploitation with no thought of the morrow.[4]

Fish and forests

What strikes a visitor to Newfoundland is the intimate connection between its people and the sea. Small fishing communities cling to the rocky shore like tenacious barnacles. The fishery was everything to the heart and culture of this province.

Even forestry in Newfoundland was ruled by the sea. The forests within 3 miles (5 kilometres) of the coast were reserved for the use of fishing communities. Trees were used for wharves, docks, boat building and settlements. Even the bark was used to cover the drying fish on the long tables called "fish flakes" in the days before refrigeration. This common-property approach to the coastal forests led to some serious overharvesting in areas where the population pressures were high.[5] Even so, the so-called three-mile-limit lands were judged to have a desirable amount of the quality spruce and fir required by the industry. In 1979, the three-mile limit was abolished.

Giving away Newfoundland and Labrador's forests

The granting of large leases in Newfoundland and Labrador forests and outright land giveaways rivals anything anywhere in the world. The first land-grab dates back to the Reid Newfoundland Company in 1897. Reid had built the cross-province railroad and was granted ownership of vast areas of the island's forest in exchange. Reid was given more than 150 lots across the province, some as large as 259 square kilometres. Over the years, the company sold its forested land to the first pulp-mill builders in the province, Bowater and Price.[6]

In 1905, the first large timber lease was approved by the province's legislature. It granted the Anglo-Newfoundland Development Company a ninety-nine-year lease for 5,180 square kilometres (518,000 hectares). The lease conveyed not only rights to timber, but water and mineral rights as well. The inalienable private right to build dams and use hydropower was also granted. All of this for the astonishingly low compensation of $2 per square mile (2.6 km²) per year (or less than a third of a cent per acre), with a royalty of 50 cents per thousand board feet of lumber produced.[7] Pulpwood was subject to neither stumpage nor royalties based on production. With such extremely attractive arrangements, a newsprint mill had been built in Grand Falls by 1909, where it remains in production to this day.

Between 1875 and 1946 another form of contractual arrangement between the province and its forest companies was developed. Under these timber licences, exclusive rights to minerals, water and timber were granted for an area of over 18 million acres (7.3 million hectares). The same terms applied as in the 1905 timber-lease arrangements—minimal royalty charges for lumber, less than a third of a penny an acre in "rent" and no stumpage at all for pulp, and all conveyed for a ninety-nine-year period.

Even more remarkable is that the terms of the lease and licences applied until 2002. The licences had expiry dates spanning from 2002 to 2021. The government was prepared to quietly renew them for another ninety-nine years without any public review. Thanks in large measure to a Sierra Club of Canada public awareness campaign, citizens across the province demanded a full review of the licence terms and conditions. To accommodate public pressure, but still provide an immediate extension to Abitibi-Consolidated, the provincial government amended the Forestry Act to collapse all the licence renewals to a single date—2010—and committed to a full public consultation process prior to any further extensions. The terms of the 1903 leases will apply to Corner Brook Pulp and Paper and Abitibi until 2010.

Kruger operates the pulp mill in Corner Brook, obtaining 90 per cent of its electricity from its own hydroelectric facility as part of its leased water rights. As well, Kruger is exempt from most forms of taxation. Attempts by Kruger to extend its hydroelectric developments into the Upper Humber, with impacts into the watershed of Gros Morne National Park, were defeated due to local opposition. Abitibi-Consolidated flooded critical Newfoundland pine marten habitat in its hydroelectric development at Star Lake.[8] The massive siltation and soil disturbance of that impoundment now threatens a genetically unique species of trout. As well, the local fish have experienced the typical post-dam problem of increased mercury uptake, leading to government warnings to restrict consumption of Star Lake fish.

Newfoundland is the only province with zero stumpage for trees from its licenced lands.[9] Even the rent has not increased to reflect inflation. Current charges amount to 77 cents per square kilometre ($2/square mile).

Sawmill owners and independent pulpwood producers cutting on unalienated Crown land, that is, Crown land not within a timber lease, pay stumpage, although the fee is still quite low.[10] The disparity created by giving the large multinationals, with generous terms on ninety-nine-year leases, a bigger break on costs of the resource than that paid by smaller local operators is also part of a national pattern. Canadian governments seem unable to do enough to encourage large foreign-owned forest companies.

Logging in Newfoundland and Labrador's forests

No one really knows what the composition of the original forest of Newfoundland and Labrador was like, but one thing is certain—it was quite different from what is left today after several hundred years of logging. Clearing of land, including for the construction of the now defunct railway, logging and the spread of the white pine blister rust have had significant impacts on what was once a forested landscape.

Newfoundland and Labrador constitute the farthest eastern regions of the Canadian boreal. Recently discovered is an extraordinarily ancient region of boreal. Most softwood species of the boreal live only a hundred years, but in the mid-Peninsula of Newfoundland, along the valley of the Main River, grow the oldest documented boreal trees on the planet. Trees that are hundreds of years old live in an area relatively untouched by forest fire and insect cycles. This rare forest was discovered by a Jesuit priest working on his doctorate in forest ecology, Father John McCarthy. Other scientists followed, studying the region and finding species of insects and lichen never previously identified. The apparent "sameness" of the boreal disguised an extraordinary ecosystem.

While black spruce and balsam fir currently predominate, there would have been greater species diversity in the forest primeval. A mid-1800s account of touring the Bay of Islands area related: "One feature of this locality, and of the whole Bay of Islands, is the pre-dominance and luxuriance of deciduous timber. Birch, Beech, Poplar, and Ash in many places quite take the place of the Spruce and Fir, and lofty Pines over top of the other trees."[11]

According to historical data, white pine probably made up 7 to 10 per cent of Newfoundland's coniferous forest. These trees likely were "over top," as the pine are recorded at heights more than 70 feet (21 metres). The balsam fir and spruce would have been just fine crowning under the pines, both because fir and spruce are shade-tolerant species and because the white pine would have been scattered throughout the forest.

The "lofty Pines" are a thing of the past. Between 1875 and 1925, it is estimated that 6 million board feet of white pine were logged and processed *every year* in Newfoundland. Astonishing production levels in pine were achieved more than a hundred years ago, with 11.4 million board feet produced by fifty-five mills in 1884, and a staggering 45.2 million board feet in 1910 by a prodigious 347 mills.[12] As noted, recovery of these pine forests after logging was made even more difficult by the spread of pine rust.

Very little remains of the "pine clad hills" that are celebrated in Newfoundland and Labrador's provincial song. One of the last reserves, the Serpentine River Valley, was part of a National Park of the Dominion of Newfoundland (established in 1939, ten years before Newfoundland joined Canada). One of the conditions of Confederation called for the continuing protection of the area, and it was considered a Provincial Park Reserve. Bowater Ltd. (now Kruger Ltd.) relinquished the commercial forestry rights to Stagg Lake Provincial Park in favour of Serpentine River Valley. In the early 1990s, the Serpentine River Valley Provincial Park Reserve was deregulated. Between 1995 and 1997 the seventy-seven parks in the provincial protected areas system, including Stagg Lake Provincial Park, were largely dismantled.[13] In 1995, twenty-eight parks were completely privatized, and the recreational enclaves of another twenty-eight were partially privatized in 1997.

In 1991, then Premier Clyde Wells asked the Wilderness and Ecological Reserves Advisory Council to investigate the feasibility of establishing a reserve around 900 square kilometres of the Serpentine River Valley. After several years of studies and consultations, petroleum interests were given permission to explore the area; the area was protected as a Crown Land Reserve, which pro-hibits forestry but not mineral exploration. The area is now without any protection.[14]

Other disturbances have occurred that shift the natural forest bal-ance. By the 1930s, the province began an active program of fire suppression, which had the effect of maintaining certain species and shifting regeneration patterns. As well, various non-native species have had their impact on the forest. The introduction of snowshoe hare and moose, neither indigenous to the island, has caused a shift in the for-est understory, as these browsers have different eating habits than the native caribou. So, too, have non-native diseases posed threats to the forest. The white pine blister rust made its way to Newfoundland from England, worsening the pine's chances of survival.

Historically, Newfoundland logging required very few roads. In the winter months, tractors or horses would pull logs over the snow to wait on the frozen ice of a nearby river for spring. A network of rail-roads was also used. While driving logs down rivers was not environmentally appropriate, the type of damage shifted when Newfoundland began using the line skidder, a logging machine that could work year-round. Damage to the soil and the surrounding ecosystem was certainly increased by the shift from river and rail to road. Logging roads erode soil.[15] It is increasingly accepted that log-ging roads do substantial long-term damage to the ecosystem, both because of the immediate damage and because the wilderness is opened to hunters, anglers and other traffic.

While Newfoundland's boreal remains primarily a spruce/fir for-est, within that composition the relative proportion of black spruce has declined through clear-cut logging. Tracking the reduction of black spruce is difficult, as the province's forest service lumps these species together and only indicates densities by individual species if the volume is above 25 percent. But regeneration surveys show a wor-rying decrease in black spruce after logging, reflecting the greater ability of balsam fir to regrow after a logging disturbance. "Regeneration failure is a problem on black spruce cut-over sites," reported a government survey. Only 31.9 per cent of logged-over black spruce areas were adequately recovering in black spruce.[16]

NSR (not satisfactorily restocked) lands, where commercially valu-able trees have not regrown after logging, are generally priority areas for replanting. Nationally, 2.6 million hectares are in this category.[17]

As of 2001, Newfoundland has a particularly high percentage in NSR lands—19 per cent of its logged Crown lands.[18]

Within this degraded forest ecosystem, wildlife has diminished as well. The logging pressures of recent years have all but eliminated old-growth forest on the island of Newfoundland. Currently, only 5 per cent of the forest is in old growth. Critically impacted by this is the Newfoundland marten, a fur-bearing forest mammal. In 1996, the pine marten was added to the national endangered-species list in the most critical category for species in peril. There are fewer than three hundred individual animals of this Newfoundland species left.[19]

The pine marten's survival is affected in virtually every province as old-growth forest is removed, giving way to a younger, "more productive" forest. Recent research confirms that the Newfoundland marten is genetically distinct from other populations. Thus, proposed efforts to rebuild the population by importing martens from Maine were abandoned. The only way to protect the marten is to protect its habitat.

As wood-supply shortfalls loom—and as the pressure to feed the mills continues unabated—the rotations between harvests become shorter. Trees are felled long before the stage at which the forest is richly layered with dead standing trees, or "snags," decaying logs and old living members of the plant world. Cavities in the old-growth forest are believed to be essential to the marten. Windfalls in old-growth forest are particularly important in providing shelter and food in deep-snow conditions. But even these habitat requirements are not fully understood. The marten may be able to use other types of forest than old growth to meet its needs. While forest management guidelines have been established to minimize logging damage to the endangered Newfoundland marten habitat, they have not been followed by the large pulp-and-paper companies. In fact, few places considered candidate sites for protection of marten habitat are protected.[20] Fortunately, the Little Grand Lake area and Terra Nova forests, known habitats for Newfoundland marten, are protected. Creation of the Little Grand Lake Ecological Reserve, after nearly thirty years of interim protection and promises, is finally approaching reality. The Little Grand Lake protected network comprises 150,000 hectares and includes three forest ecoregions. Terra Nova is within a national park. But the marten habitat in the forests of the Main River watershed is still open for logging. Logging, particularly clear-cutting, which is virtually the *only* logging method used in the province, threatens the future of the marten. Without some intervention, the Newfoundland marten may go the way of the Newfoundland wolf or great auk.[21]

Over the last few years, public awareness of the plight of the marten has increased significantly throughout the province. Within the last few years, both the federal and provincial governments have adopted legislation to protect species at risk. The federal legislation is of little use to the pine marten, applying, with rare exceptions, only to federal lands.[22] The provincial act, the Endangered Species Act, was enacted in December 2001. Identification of critical and recovery habitat is a key component of the Act. A pine marten recovery effort has been undertaken through the collaboration of federal and provincial agencies and Corner Brook Pulp and Paper (a division of Kruger.)

The depletion of accessible wood for harvesting has also led to logging in areas previously considered off-limits as critical salmon habitat. Many watersheds, especially in western Newfoundland, such as the Upper Humber, Main River and Robinson's River, are being logged near sensitive spawning grounds for Atlantic salmon. Forest-dwelling species are also in decline, including the brown bat and the muskrat.

Unfortunately, provincial forest departments tend to focus exclusively on the issue of supplying timber to the mills. There has been little research into declining terrestrial biodiversity in Newfoundland, which is clearly threatened, but even the threat to wood supply appears likely to be ignored until it is too late.

Newfoundland and Labrador's wood supply

The provincial inventory includes the overcut forest of the island of Newfoundland as well as the virtually unlogged forests of Labrador. The lumping together of the wood supply from these very different forests, separated by an ocean crossing, and the corresponding calculation of an annual allowable cut based on the composite forest, can be quite misleading. In reviewing the current wood-supply crisis in Newfoundland, it is important to keep the Labrador situation separate from that on the island.

The forests of Labrador, when included in the AAC figure, create the illusion of surplus. In fact, Labrador's forests have always been commercially undesirable. They are physically remote. An early 1980s estimate put the cost of Labrador pulpwood delivered to the island's pulp mills at $102.60/cord, with local wood at $47.19/cord, and wood from Prince Edward Island, far more distant but with better marine transportation links, at \$64.02/cord.[23] Moreover, the trees of Labrador have traditionally been described as a lichen forest of very small conifers, growing very slowly. Only the desperate could see them as a likely wood supply.

Thus, while the national forest database reports that the province has 23.2 million hectares of forest land,[24] the relevant information is the 5.2 million hectares considered forest on the island of Newfoundland. Of that 5.2 million hectares, only 58.4 percent, or just over 3 million hectares, is considered productive.[25] It is from this land base that three pulp mills, 1,800 small sawmills and untold numbers of firewood gatherers have taken far more than the ecosystem can support.

The three pulp mills on the island of Newfoundland are unable, at this moment and well into the future, to find adequate wood supply within the companies' enormous leases, or even with the addition of the rest of the island's forest. The overharvesting and mill overcapacity on the island of Newfoundland are compelling Abitibi-Consolidated to plan the clear-cutting of remote northern Labrador.

The forest companies control the majority of the productive forest on insular Newfoundland—58.5 per cent or 1.779 million hectares.[26] The land controlled by Corner Brook Pulp and Paper (Kruger) and Abitibi-Consolidated, through a patchwork of large licences, smaller leases and industrial freehold, is the province's most productive forest. The 35 per cent that is unalienated Crown land is generally found in the coastal regions, where forests do not achieve the volumes of more-protected inland relatives.

Initially, it was believed that the huge areas controlled by the mills would never be fully exploited. Even as late as 1980, John Gray, author of one of the few books on Newfoundland's forests, *The Trees Behind the Shore*, wrote:

> The zero stumpage charges on pulpwood and the token charges on lumber produced created problems.... With virtually no revenue from the forest, the government had little incentive to engage in forest management, as the financial benefits would go to the companies. On the other hand, there is little incentive for the companies to engage in forest management, since they already have a sufficient or excess timber supply.[27]

Yet, by 1992, the Newfoundland government was struggling to come to terms with an immediate wood shortage; there was simply not enough accessible forest to feed the island's three mills. For the first time, the province had undertaken a twenty-year forestry planning exercise, reviewing the inventory and re-examining the assumptions that went into the AAC. The central reality was alarming: the requirements of the mills plus other local users outstripped what was available. Even increasing the AAC by crediting future speculative growth based on intensive silviculture did not erase shortfalls on insular Newfoundland. According to the 1996 provincial Forest Development Plan, the island had a 27 per cent deficit of demand in excess of supply.[28] By 2003, the shortfall persisted. With a total AAC of 2.7 million cubic metres, the province estimates a 776,600-cubic-metre gap between mill demand and supply.

In fact, even that dire news probably underestimated the extent of the gap. The figure was based on requirements of the three pulp-and-paper mills, sawmills, fuel wood for industrial chips and the cutting of domestic firewood on Crown lands. Newfoundland's forests are the only ones in Canada where logging pressure for domestic firewood is actually a significant factor. While far below the more than 2 million cubic metres required for pulp, fuel wood and firewood combined come to an estimated 964,000 cubic metres.[29] This figure includes wood chips used to heat hospitals and for other industrial fuel uses, but a large component is firewood. The Poole Royal Commission estimated that there is probably an equivalent amount of firewood cut from Crown land without permits, unreported. Even the national park at Gros Morne is not off-limits to local domestic fuel-wood logging.

Within the immediate- and longer-term available timber shortages, there is no doubt that Abitibi-Consolidated woodlands are the major problem. The Corner Brook Pulp and Paper mill, which now operates what used to be the Bowater pulp mill, claims a small surplus within its licence. It continues to benefit from the 1905 lease conditions, which give it free of charge 90 per cent of all its energy requirements from its own hydroelectric station. It is also exempt from most forms of taxation. Abitibi-Consolidated, on the other hand, with mills in Grand Falls and Stephenville, has only 64 per cent of its total wood requirements. While Abitibi looks to purchase more wood from the unalienated Crown land, those lands are already in a worse shortage position than Abitibi-Consolidated. Based on reported users, the Crown lands have a 38 per cent deficit of demand above supply.[30]

After two years of study and analysis, in February 2002, the provincial government announced a new AAC for the island forests, leaving Labrador out of the calculation. The new approach attempted to quantify what could be logged that was both accessible and economical. Immediately the island's AAC dropped by 12 per cent. However, once again, when the Labrador forests were added to the provincial AAC, and the province added back in the hard-to-access stands on the island, the combined cut was only 2 per cent less than the previous rate of logging.[31]

How did the island so overexploit its forests that it can now maintain its mills only through off-island imports? Part of the problem may stem from overgenerous terms—even by Newfoundland standards—for the sale of the Stephenville mill to Abitibi-Consolidated. Abitibi already owned the province's oldest mill, at Grand Falls, built in 1909. In 1978 it opened negotiations with the province to purchase a second mill in Stephenville—the Labrador linerboard mill. The deal, like all timber licences in Newfoundland, still included exclusive logging rights, as well as all mineral and water rights. The terms of the lease suggest that, despite a requirement to manage the lands on a "sustained yield basis," it is Abitibi-Consolidated's exclusive prerogative to decide how much it will cut.[32]

The only concession to the twentieth century was the inclusion of stumpage rates for pulp, on a scale from 85 cents to $3 per cubic metre.[33] But the company is entitled to rebates for any silviculture operations on its leased land that are approved by the province. The government also committed to assist in the building of primary roads and bridges.

The problem seems to have been that no one checked the timber supply before committing over 1 million cubic metres a year from the forests to Abitibi. The story goes that, the day after concluding the agreement to sell the Labrador linerboard mill and its timber lease to Abitibi, the government called in its foresters and told them to find the wood to keep the mill going for twenty years. While such colourful rumours are hard to prove, the story fits. Currently, the wood from Abitibi licences for the Stephenville mill is not recorded by the forest service. The 1970 Royal Commission, one of four commissions and task forces that have reported between 1955 and 1973, expressed concern that, with a possible new mill at Stephenville, the wood supply should be carefully re-examined. In particular, it pointed to potential weaknesses in the inventory and growth data.[34]

Problems with the inventory persist. In calculating the amount of wood on the island, unwarranted assumptions were made about potential wood supply. Even the confirmation of wood shortages in the *20 Year Forestry Development Plan 1990–2009* was based on wildly optimistic premises. For instance, the inventory analysis predicted the volume of a fifty-five-year-old stand of regenerated forest, after one thinning, at an unrealistic 300 cubic metres per hectare. The volume in particularly productive natural forests is actually 190 to 210 cubic metres per hectare.[35] The future wood supply was also based on the assumption that damage by fire and insects will never be above "salvageable levels." A wood-supply analysis that assumes 100 per cent effectiveness of its fire-suppression and insecticide program is assuming the impossible.

The working rule on regrowth was that "there was no regeneration time lag for any regenerating stand."[36] This assumption requires the forest to recover from clear-cutting with almost miraculous speed. But, in fact, Newfoundland has a particularly high percentage in NSR (not satisfactorily restocked) lands—19 per cent of its logged Crown lands.[37]

Another working assumption, to improve the overall bright picture, was that 90 per cent of the best forest would be available for harvest. As bulldozers for road building and skid trails have been calculated to take out 10 per cent of the land base in Newfoundland logging operations, this assumption leaves absolutely no room for buffer zones around streams, nor for any other impediment to total clear-cutting.[38]

Newfoundland is now in a wood-supply crisis. Logging pressure has increased dramatically in the last forty years. In 1955, approximately 1.6 million cubic metres were logged.[39] Currently, the AAC is nearly twice as high, at 2.6 million cubic metres. In fact, the rate of cut has actually increased since the province determined it was in a deficit situation. Kruger's plant at Corner Brook retooled in January 1996 in order to increase the output from one paper machine.

In the 1996 provincial forest development plans, it is acknowledged that

Demand, defined as desire for timber, currently exceeds supply by 27% for the Island [industry and Crown lands]. Actual timber consumption, controlled through limiting the allocation, is estimated at 12% greater than the 1995 AAC.[40]

Meanwhile, Abitibi-Consolidated and Kruger have set their sights on the forests of Labrador. With a projected annual cut of 600,000 cubic metres, there is now a desperate plan for clear-cut logging of the marginal forests edging up to the treeline.

The Innu struggle in Labrador

A beacon of hope for the forests of Newfoundland and Labrador, and indeed, all of Canada, is now shining from the Innu Nation of Labrador. As Newfoundland's forests are exhausted, eyes turned to the tiny northern trees of Labrador. Abitibi-Consolidated began clear-cutting in Labrador in forested areas within the "land claim" of the Innu Nation. Starting in 1999, barges loaded with pulp from Labrador have been shipped to Newfoundland to help meet the demand from mills on the island. In spite of the higher costs of operating in Labrador and shipping the wood, Abitibi-Consolidated has been cutting in the remote forests across the water to the north. In 2003, approximately ten barge loads, each with 6,000 cubic metres, were shipped down the coast from Goose Bay, Cartwright and Port Hope Simpson. All told, since Abitibi-Consolidated logging began in Labrador, roughly 200,000 cubic metres has been delivered to the Stephenville mill from Labrador forests.

And so it seemed that the wholesale destruction of Labrador's forests had begun. But the Innu Nation, in partnership with the provincial Department of Forest Resources, created an alternate scenario.

The only indigenous peoples of the island of Newfoundland, the Beothuk, were exterminated over a century ago with the encroachment of European settlement, warfare and disease. Currently there are Mi'kmaq on the island, who have put forward claims that they, too, are indigenous to Newfoundland. Meanwhile, in Labrador, politically part of Newfoundland but geographically an extension of Quebec, two First Nations live—the more southerly Innu, and, toward the Arctic, the Inuit. The Innu have lived in Nitassinan, "Our Land" in the Innu language, for at least two thousand years. It is one of the last large roadless areas on earth.

The Innu people are dependent on the huge caribou herds that thunder across the rugged wilderness, less like animals than like a pulsating river of fur and hooves. The Innu also hunt geese and fish the clear streams. But all of that is under assault from an intimidating array of military and industrial developments.

The Innu have been subjected to low-flying fighter-bomber training from the former U.S. army base at Goose Bay. Every year, fifteen-thousand ear-shattering low flights take place in training exercises for the British, Dutch, German, French, Italian and Belgian bomber forces. Innu protests, arrests on airstrips and complaints that the flights are ruining their traditional life in the bush have been to no avail.

Now Labrador is the site of one of the richest mineral-deposit finds in history, and governments are doing whatever is necessary to truncate the proper environmental hearing process so the nickel riches of Voisey's Bay can move from the ground into bank accounts around the world.

In an atmosphere of rampant resource extraction and violation of the traditional rights of the Aboriginal people of Newfoundland, the Innu asked Herb Hammond, a nationally respected ecological forester from British Columbia, to assess the wood supply in Labrador and Abitibi-Consolidated's logging plans. His report confirmed that clearcut logging was completely inappropriate for the fragile and slow-growing forest of Labrador. The forest of Labrador is at the far northern reaches of the boreal. Essentially a lichen forest of small trees on fragile soils, it would never be considered commercially viable if not for the desperation engendered by wood shortages for the ever-hungry mills to the south. Moreover, Abitibi's logging plans were for 100 per cent heavily mechanized, low-labour clear-cutting. Hammond doubted that, once clear-cut, such a forest would be capable of recovery at all. The Innu have in the past blockaded clear-cutting near Goose Bay. They demanded an environmental assessment and resolution of their land claims before Abitibi was given the go-ahead.

In December 1993, the provincial Environment Minister registered the proposed logging plans for one-third of what Abitibi ultimately intended to log in Labrador for a "mini-assessment" to develop an "adaptive management" strategy. The Innu and island environmentalists feared this would be too little too late once clear-cutting was approved. In April 1995, members of the Innu Nation asked the Environmental Assessment Committee's chair why a full environmental-assessment process, including a complete environmental impact statement (EIS), had not been required. The chair replied, "If an EIS had been required, it would have been exempted by Cabinet. With the pressure from Interwood and Labrador Forest Resources [two industrial logging firms planning to set up operations in Nitassinan], we had to try a new approach or end up with nothing."[41]

In response, Innu Nation Environmental Advisor Larry Innes pointed out, "In resilient and contextually limited situations, adaptive management may be a useful approach. But Nitassinan forests are neither. There is very little room for 'error' in a fragile, climate-limited forest, and it is the Innu who will have to live with the mistakes. The proposed management plan contains no provisions which would suggest that 'adaptive management' is anything other than 'business as usual': it outlines an aggressive road-building program and slates 500,000 cubic metres for cutting in the first five years of the plan. At this rate, by the time Forestry 'adapts,' there will be nothing left to 'manage.'"[42]

Despite the bleak prospects, the Innu Nation persisted. In March 2003, the Innu and the Forest Resource Branch of the provincial Ministry of Natural Resources published a forest management plan covering most of the forested and traditional lands of the Innu people, an area referred to in the provincial forest plans as District 19. The plan is already winning accolades from ecological silviculture experts across Canada. The plan will protect key ecological features and habitats for endangered species, as well as extend a network of protected areas throughout their lands. The direct involvement of members of the Innu Nation in the plan and its implementation is an important step in demonstrating their ability to manage their lands sustainably. The provincial Forest Research Branch's role in the partnership is also significant. The new willingness of the province to work toward progressive solutions is encouraging.

Public relations versus wood shortages
In the face of the forest crisis in Newfoundland, politicians maintain that the situation is under control. A February 1, 1996, news release from the premier's office expressed buoyant optimism. Newly elected Premier Brian Tobin announced $41.7 million in new silviculture investments, primarily from federal and provincial government sources. Although the release conceded that the estimated wood-supply deficit would hold at 25 per cent (500,000 cubic metres/year) for the next

ten to fifteen years, the announcement created the impression that pumping new money into the forests would somehow avert the crisis.

"The $41.7 million worth of initiatives announced here today will significantly address the major issue facing the forest sector, which is the availability and security of short-term wood supplies," said Premier Tobin. "Today's announcements will secure current jobs in the forest industry and create new ones in the process, which is exactly what the new Liberal Government is all about."

Previous federal-provincial investments in silviculture had not prevented a wood-supply crisis. In fact, between 1974 and 1992, $180 million had been spent in Newfoundland through the federal-provincial Forest Development Agreements—a direct subsidy to an industry that was, for the most part, not even paying stumpage.[43] These figures do not include loans made available from another federal pocket, the Atlantic Canada Opportunities Agency (ACOA), for assistance to companies wanting to buy feller-bunchers, thereby reducing labour costs.

Conservative Premier Danny Williams was elected in 2003 on a platform with significant sustainable development commitments. His commitment to a comprehensive review of the province's forests and a "scientifically based plan for forest management" has not yet had any impact on the persistent overcutting in the province's forests.[44]

The province has opportunities to protect key ecosystems. The first step is to recognize that the persistent wood shortages are a symptom of failure. While demand for commercially available wood for the mills exceeds supply, some parts of Newfoundland and Labrador's overexploited forests are more at risk than others. As is the case across Canada, the most threatened forest type is the old growth. The province's unique ancient boreal remnants are not protected. They occur primarily on the east side of the Great Northern Peninsula. The conservation challenge is huge. Despite years of effort, the designation of the Main River as a National Heritage River and a voluntary moratorium on logging, the logging of the Main River watershed has resumed.

Corner Brook Pulp and Paper entered into an agreement with Sierra Club of Canada to conduct an independent scientific review of the ecological significance of the Main River boreal. Although logging plans have been modified based on the conclusions of that review, the fact that there is any logging at all in such an ecological treasure is disheartening. Recent research suggests that the ecological conditions that allowed the ancient boreal of the Main River to develop are also found in other river valleys along the Great Northern Peninsula. Yet these are also slated for clear-cutting. The area is one of high unemployment following the collapse of the cod fishery. It has suffered the highest level of emigration of any region of the province. A desperate local population wants employment opportunities, creating pressures against conservation of the oldest known boreal trees found anywhere on the planet.

No amount of press releases and silviculture subsidies can create forests. The threats to jobs and "security of short-term wood supply" are the result of overcutting, building too many mills and using logging methods that create large areas where nothing grows back. So long as industry and government use terms like "the wood supply is tight," when they mean "we've run out of wood for our mills," so long as they excuse present overcutting on the false premise of increased growth through future intensive silviculture, Newfoundland is destined to be a land of no fish and soon, vanishing forests.

Newfoundland

Forest and other wooded land in million hectares	20.1
Stocked harvested Crown land in hectares	360,000
Area logged in hectares (2002)	22,207
Volume logged in million cubic metres (2002)	2.1
Annual allowable cut in million cubic metres (2001)	2.6

Source: Natural Resources Canada, Canadian Forest Service, *The State of Canada's Forests 2003–2004* (Ottawa, 2004). These are federal government summaries, based on provincial government data. The figures are not necessarily accurate.

Newfoundland and Labrador Corporate Players

Abitibi-Consolidated
Corner Brook Pulp and Paper, a subsidiary of Kruger (Montreal)

Nova Scotia

Nova Scotia is a gentle province of pastoral valleys, breathtaking ocean views and forests that are a pale reflection of their former glory. Its forests were once part of the Acadian Forest Ecoregion, encompassing the original forests of Nova Scotia, Prince Edward Island and New Brunswick. Agricultural land clearing, coupled with the impacts of imported browsing deer, led to massive species conversion, while centuries of high-grading (taking the most valuable and preferred trees) led to a steady erosion of the quality of the forest. In much of Nova Scotia, one would be hard pressed to distinguish the spruce-fir softwood forests from those of the boreal.

The first trees felled by Europeans were used to construct the fort at Port Royal in 1605. Early settlers described a forest where hemlock, white pine and northern hardwood predominated, where elms, oak and ash were common in the deciduous forest.

According to historical accounts, the northern plateau of Cape Breton was boreal forest, spruce and fir, while along the lowlands, coastal areas and river valleys a luxuriant mixed-wood forest provided timber for shipbuilding and masts. As long ago as the early 1700s, sawmills in Cape Breton were supplying timbers for the construction of the thriving walled city of Louisbourg, built with no expense spared by King Louis XVI. Logging and clearing land for settlement and agriculture were removing the highest-quality species from within the forest. After the American revolution, grants to British officers accelerated the export of high-quality timber to Britain.

Nova Scotia was the first province to take a scientific interest in estimating the amount of timber available in its territory. An inventory was undertaken in 1801 by Titus Smith, who was known as Nova Scotia's "first scientific naturalist."[1] His descriptive work on the nature of the provincial forests would hardly be called an inventory by today's standards.

"Forests grow and are grown to be cut to furnish valuable material to man." So wrote Bernard Fenow in 1909. The Lumberman's Association of Western Nova Scotia had persuaded the government to undertake "a forest reconnaissance of the Province."[2] To do so, the province recruited, for the munificent sum of $2,000 dollars, one of North America's new league of professional foresters. Bernard Fernow, trained in Germany, had come to North America in 1876; like Gifford

Pinchot, he was an advocate of "sustained yield forestry." Although he argued for the preservation of natural forests as a crucial aspect of water conservation, he had a utilitarian view of forest resources, believing that their "influence, climatic and hydraulic, is by no means destroyed or checked by a well-conducted, systematic forestry which utilizes ripe timber, taking care for its immediate regeneration for the continuity of the forest as well as the timber supply."[3]

By 1907, Fernow had become the first dean of the newly established school of forestry at the University of Toronto. He trained virtually all of Canada's early foresters in the utilitarian view. He was one of the first foresters to believe old growth was an obstacle to sustained yield, and his legacy remains a powerful force. Fernow realized that the pattern of land ownership in Nova Scotia would make it extremely difficult for the government to influence forest policy. Nova Scotia was an anomaly in the development of forest-land tenure across Canada. In an exception to the rule that Canadian forests are primarily publicly owned as Crown land, Nova Scotia sold off large parts of its public forest land to private companies. By the turn of the century, only 600,000 hectares of Crown forest remained—and it was considered of poor quality and relatively inaccessible.

Turn-of-the-century Nova Scotia politicians looked longingly to New Brunswick, where a lease system covering large tracts of Crown land had been providing forest revenue since the late 1800s. Despite the small amount of remaining Crown land, Nova Scotia changed its Lease Act in 1899 in an attempt to make the most of its public forest resources. The new legislation allowed for the lease of Crown land for twenty-year periods, for a rental fee of 16 cents per hectare. No stumpage fees were included, and logging was limited to trees at least 25 centimetres in diameter.[4]

When Fernow came to survey the forests of Nova Scotia, he was hoping that Nova Scotia's experience would persuade the government of Ontario to begin its own forest inventory, with Fernow at the helm.[5] Fernow's work, while it was broad in intention, zeroed in on key issues of forest degradation: "each year sees changes from virgin into culled, from culled into stripped, from stripped into burnt forest or into new young growth..."[6] A decade later, in 1922, the process of species conversion by logging was documented by the provincial entomologist, Dr. J.D. Tothill:

There has been a great increase of balsam fir in our eastern forests in the past century and especially in the latter part of it. The big pines were the first to go from the forest, and the gaps were filled by spruce and fir, whose seed trees were undisturbed. Then the market demanded spruce and the big spruce were cut, leaving the large fir trees to reproduce. Thus there has gradually resulted a greatly increased percentage of fir in our softwood stands.[7]

At around the same time, the government initiated a review of the impact of the 1899 changes to the Lease Act. Nova Scotia's Chief Forester reviewed the situation and found that, despite the giveaway terms of the lease, leaseholders were generally ignoring the rules against logging immature trees, and that the rent collected was "ridiculously small." In fact, the revenue from Christmas-tree sales in some years surpassed the total rent collected for leasing the Crown forests.[8]

The largest single area of Crown land, the "Big Lease," was on Cape Breton Island. Fernow identified the fir of Cape Breton as ideal for the pulp-and-paper industry in his 1909–1910 survey, and the province began the search for a pulp mill. The Big Lease proved to be a gold mine for speculators, some of whom gained more in commissions from buying and reselling the lease than the province earned in rent. After one such speculative trade, in 1917, the original "purchaser" walked away with over $1 million in profits, and the Oxford Paper Company of New England ended up with the lease.

Portions of the highlands of Cape Breton were logged for the Oxford mill in Rumford, Maine. At the height of the logging in the 1920s, nearly one thousand men were working in the Cape Breton woods, using long saws and axes, and horses to pull logs to the road. The highlands provided nearly half of all the softwood used by the Maine mill, boosting its production. While Oxford held on to the Big Lease in Cape Breton, it also bought forest land throughout Nova Scotia and New Brunswick, as well as a controlling interest in a pulp mill in Fairville, New Brunswick, and the Crown lands that went with it.

Where multinationals rule

Early in its history, Nova Scotia sold most of its Crown forest land to private timber interests, and by 1926 the rest of its forests were in the hands of foreign and out-of-province pulp companies. Nova

Scotia's Chief Forester, Otto Schierbeck, commented on "the alarming rate at which American pulp and paper producers are buying Nova Scotia freehold land for the export of pulpwood. Over 810,000 hectares of the best timberlands in the Province are in the hands of American pulp and paper companies who have no manufacturing plans in the Province and are only concerned with the export of pulpwood."[9]

As well, a major British firm moved into Nova Scotia. In 1928, the Mersey Paper Company built a pulp mill in Liverpool, Nova Scotia, supplying all of its pulp from lands leased from the Crown on generous stumpage of $1 per cord as well as promised low power rates. The province began a program of expanding its Crown-land base in the 1930s, trying to rectify the loss of so much forest to large private landowners. At the same time, it negotiated the buyback of one-third of the Big Lease, the last large chunk of Crown forest land, for the creation of Cape Breton Highlands National Park in 1940, with compensation to the U.S.-based Oxford Paper of nearly $400,000. But the provincial government grew increasingly unhappy with the bulk of Crown forest lands being tied up by Oxford, which, since closing its small operation in Cape Breton in 1931, had done almost no logging on the lease.

In the mid-1950s, the Conservative government of Robert Stanfield took over a province with a depressed economy. The steel-and-coal industry of Cape Breton was on the ropes, and no pulp mill was yet in place to log the Big Lease. Stanfield's government set its sights on attracting a major Swedish pulp-and-paper company, Stora Kopparberg, to Nova Scotia. To do that, they needed more forest. Since the buyback effort of the 1930s began, the province had increased Crown-owned forest to nearly one-quarter of the province. But, so long as Oxford Paper Company had the Big Lease, there would not be enough uncommitted forest to attract Stora. Oxford's speculative exploitation of the Cape Breton forests paid off when the provincial government bought Oxford out at rates far above what it had received seventeen years earlier in the park settlement. With seventeen fewer years on the lease, the value of the ownership interest should have gone down, but Oxford received more than twice per acre what they had in 1940, for a total buyout of nearly $4 million!

Selling out Nova Scotia's forests

Once free of Oxford, the province set about wooing Stora Kopparberg. Stora is the oldest incorporated firm in the world, with articles of incorporation dating back to the year 1288. Stora had discussed the Big Lease with the previous provincial government, and Stanfield's government was prepared to offer nearly anything to get Stora to locate in Nova Scotia.

What Stanfield offered was a 405,000-hectare lease over the Crown-owned forest of Cape Breton Island, and the eastern mainland counties of Guysborough, Pictou and Antigonish, coupled with low electricity rates, grants in lieu of taxes and cut-rate stumpage. In fact, Stora's lease guaranteed stumpage at $1 per cord—the same rate Mersey had secured thirty years earlier. Research by L.A. Sandberg, published in his book *Trouble in the Woods*, confirmed that Stora would have been willing to pay three times as much if the province had negotiated instead of begged. The province also gave Stora the building site for a mill at the Strait of Canso and paid for the survey work. For all this, Stora did not even commit to building a mill until July 1959, when the firm officially took over its negotiated instrument for doing business in Nova Scotia—Nova Scotia Pulp, a wholly owned subsidiary of Stora.

Attracting Stora to Nova Scotia also coincided with the province's first serious effort at an inventory. Between 1953 and 1957, the province undertook a series of aerial photographs of the forests. Data derived from the analysis of these photos and from ground cruising of sample plots were compiled and released in 1958.

The 1958 inventory quoted Fernow's view of the province's forest: "It is now largely in poor condition, and is being annually further deteriorated by abuse and injudicious use, because those owning it are mostly not concerned in its future, or do not realize its potentialities."[10]

The report noted that "Fernow's remarks of 1910 are no less apt in 1958. The forest conditions have deteriorated considerably since, making the 'conservative' and 'recuperative measures' even more imperative now."[11] The 1958 survey found that the proportion of balsam fir had increased, while species prevalent in the 1800s, such as ash and oak, had all but disappeared. The amount of overmature fir forests was a cause for concern, as it provided ideal conditions for the spruce budworm. The inventory also took note that immature forests had been logged, contributing to regeneration problems.

The forestry advice from the 1958 inventory conflicted with the political direction toward pulp. The inventory was concerned with maintaining the sawlog industry, which had been the mainstay of the provincial forest industry since shipbuilding had ended. It warned that the province was already overcutting its forests:

> One immediate corrective measure for the present overcutting is a reduction in production. It is clear that any such reduction must be applied primarily to the sawmill industry. In order that the present inventory be maintained a reduction of about 50 per cent in sawlog harvest is required. If this is not accomplished, the growing stock will be reduced in size to material which will bring about a pulpwood economy, exclusively.... If the pulp industry expanded on the basis of the total inventory of pulpwood resources, there could be no future sawlog industry.[12]

This was to be the last government report that predicted shortages and recommended less logging. In the new era of industrial forests, the prescription for shortages was to be more intensive management and increased logging.

The political preference for large multinational pulp-and-paper companies over small, locally based sawmills was conspicuous. Pressure from the new corporate clients, Stora and Scott Paper, undermined the province's own foresters, who were advocating long-rotation sawlog forestry. Pulp was soon to rule the roost. As the head of the Halifax Power and Pulp Company put it in 1961, "We see that the forests of Nova Scotia, in general, are destined to become pulpwood producing forests."[13]

Beating the forests to a pulp

By 1962, the production of pulpwood overtook the sawmill industry, beginning the process of closing down small mills and expanding the pulpwood forests.

The sawmill industry had traditionally provided jobs throughout the province. Small family-owned businesses, such as the Prest Brothers Mill in the Musquodoboit River Valley, sold quality hardwood and softwood lumber to markets in the United States, the Caribbean and abroad, as well as providing for local building.

The shift to pulp was brought about by more than market pressure. It was legislated. In 1965, some of the best forests of mainland Nova Scotia were turned over to Scott Paper, based in Philadelphia, through the Scott Maritime Pulp Agreement Act. Under this legislation, Scott was given a lease for 100,000 hectares of the best forest and standing timber in the province. To sweeten the pot, Scott was given a five-year income-tax holiday and a twenty-year tax break on all land owned or leased by the company as well as on its new mill site in Pictou County. The government also kicked in a $5-million donation to Scott's new operation. Scott opened a bleached-kraft pulp-and-paper mill at Abercrombie Point, midway along the mainland's north shore. As a further concession, Scott's waste-treatment facility was owned and run by the provincial Department of the Environment, all the while dumping 25 million U.S. gallons of effluent every day into Boat Harbour on the Mi'kmaq reserve.

Murray Prest, owner of the Prest Brothers Mill and active spokesperson for the sawmill industry, rues the day Scott Paper came to Nova Scotia. "We were kind of having a love affair with industry at any cost," recalls Prest. "That's when we started looking for whatever we could give away to business to buy industry. The forest was one of those things."[14]

Concurrent with the Scott Act was legislative "reform" of the forest management legislation. The Stanfield government repealed the Small Tree Act, which had banned the logging of immature trees. In its stead, the government brought in the Forest Practices Improvement Act. While the new act was a forward-looking piece of legislation, it was not proclaimed for more than ten years, during which time, in the absence of any law, the field was wide open for clear-cutting small trees. Murray Prest described the results of the Scott Act and the repeal of the Small Tree Act as a "full-scale blitzkrieg—twenty years of the most destructive methods of forest harvesting in Nova Scotia's history."[15]

For Murray Prest and many sawmill owners like him, the shift to clear-cutting to feed the pulp mills spelled the end of an era. Quality trees were lost. Regeneration was compromised, and businesses like his, once prosperous and sustainable, went under.

The provincial government, against the advice of its forestry professionals, embarked on a deliberate program of forest degradation. By design, the forests, already degraded, were to be converted from a source of multiple ecological and economic values, from sawlogs *and* pulp, into virtually exclusive pulp production.

Pulp-and-paper domination

By the early 1970s three major pulp-and-paper companies were established in Nova Scotia—all of them foreign-owned. The largest pulp-and-paper operation, Sweden's Stora, managed to purchase a freehold of more than 20,000 hectares of forest land, supplementing the large lease of Crown land. The next largest was Scott Paper, based in the United States. The largest forest landowner in the province, it owned 520,000 hectares, over 1 million acres, outright, and held leases on more than 100,000 hectares. Kimberley-Clarke now owns Scott's mill and forest lands. A U.S.-based firm, Bowater, runs the mill originally built by Mersey in Liverpool. Bowater, which is 49 per cent controlled by the *Washington Post*, owns its whole wood-supply area, over 300,000 hectares in the western part of the province.

As well, J.D. Irving Ltd. of New Brunswick has been buying Nova Scotia's forests as a cushion against predicted wood-supply shortages in its home province. No one knows how much land Irving actually owns in Nova Scotia, but in one sale alone the company bought over 42,000 hectares in Cumberland County, close to the New Brunswick border. Cumberland County is one of the last places in the province where logging had not completed several cycles in the last several hundred years. In 1998, J.D. Irving Ltd. purchased land from Bowater and from private land that had been within the Tobeatic wilderness area in Yarmouth County.

The company's clear-cuts on the 80,000-hectare woodlot drove out a Carmelite order of monks who had lived year-round in the Nova Scotia hinterlands for over twenty-six years. Their order observes a vow of silence and offered retreats for those also seeking silence. In deference to the religious retreat's requirement for peace and quiet, Bowater had kept logging well away. But J.D. Irving Ltd. had no such compunction. The constant scream of the feller-bunchers, operating twenty-four hours a day, drove the monks to speak out. Sadly, despite huge levels of public support and media coverage across Canada, the Nova Nada monastery was unsuccessful in reaching any agreement with J.D. Irving Ltd. The monks sold the property in 2002 and dispersed to retreats in Ireland and Colorado maintained by their order.[16]

Two smaller pulp-and-paper companies, Canexel Hardboard of East River and Minas Basin at Hantsport, have large undisclosed holdings. Meanwhile, a sawmilling operation in Musquodoboit, MacTara, has become a significant drain on wood supply, with an appetite for 100 million board feet a year, purchased from Crown and private lands in the province. The previously little-known operation began to achieve industry dominance when it added a new log line in late 1996, becoming the largest sawmill in the province. New industry players in the last few years are drawing on the hardwood chip market. The Northern Fibre Terminal and Louisiana Pacific in East River are new drains on the existing forest resource, cutting hardwood solely to ship the chips offshore.

Power struggles and politics

Even though the large corporate interests own over 22 per cent of the province's forests and control another 27 per cent through Crown leases, nearly half of the forests of Nova Scotia are in the hands of private woodlot owners, each holding 400 hectares or less. From the 1960s on, there have been intense political struggles in Nova Scotia to allow these thirty thousand woodlot owners and pulp producers to establish collective-bargaining rights against the big companies. The price paid by mills in Nova Scotia for wood cut on private land and hauled to the roadside has historically—and notoriously—been substantially less than that paid for identical wood in New Brunswick or Maine.

Most woodlot owners were juggling several types of activities to make a living for their families. Cutting pulp off the family woodlot and selling it to the mill was one source of income, farming another, as well as fishing or other seasonal employment. This pattern of logging—a little bit in every year—had the added advantage of maintaining healthy forests. (In contrast to some of the Crown lands, private woodlots have had a greater age mix and species diversity.) The work was difficult and, at the prices being paid by the large mills, woodlot owners figured that either they were donating their labour to the pulp mills, or they were being paid for their time and giving their wood away. But there was no way to make a profit cutting and hauling wood to the roadside for $10 to $12 per cubic metre. In fact, the mills realized that, even with the bargain-basement stumpage prices, it was still cheaper to buy wood from private woodlot owners than to log it from land owned or leased by the company—but only so long as the private woodlot owners did not have any bargaining power.[17]

In the 1970s, when the Nova Scotia Woodlot Owners and Operators Association (NSWOOA) finally succeeded in being certified as a bargaining agent by a legislated Pulpwood Marketing Board, Stora played hardball. First it simply refused to bargain. Then it challenged the whole process in the Nova Scotia courts. The judicial system of Nova Scotia has always been kind to Stora. Nova Scotia board members in the shell company, Nova Scotia Pulp, have been drawn from the ranks of one of Halifax's oldest and most conservative law firms—McInnis, Cooper and Robertson. There has never been a shortage of legal tricks of the trade in Stora's strategic arsenal. After tying the small producers up in court over several years, the Nova Scotia Supreme Court decision was issued in June 1975. Stora won and the court quashed the certification of the NSWOOA over procedural errors of the Pulpwood Marketing Board. The legislation had to be reworked, and the movement for collective-bargaining rights was set back by years.[18]

But ecological impacts of the different types of forest management on large industrial and small private lands have also played a major role in Nova Scotia's forest politics. As the Crown land on the Cape Breton highlands became increasingly dominated by the spruce budworm's favourite food, balsam fir, and the fir became older and (in forester's language) "decadent"—conditions were ripe for a major budworm outbreak in the mid-1970s. Private woodlots, in contrast, held sufficient sources of supply to meet shortfalls should the budworm outbreak cause significant mortality in the highland softwood. But for Stora, the costs of becoming dependent on small woodlot owners were too high. In 1976, as the budworm outbreak reached epidemic proportions, Stora demanded that the province undertake, at taxpayers' expense, an aerial insecticide spray program over 40,000 hectares of Cape Breton Island. Initially, the Department of Lands and Forests recommended against a spray program. It noted that New Brunswick had been spraying annually since 1952, and still had a budworm outbreak, whereas Nova Scotia had not sprayed in the early 1950s at the point of the last outbreak and the epidemic had run its course and died out. The provincial entomologist in the 1950s had prophesied this outcome when he recommended against toxic chemicals, saying they would be "a vain attempt to offset a natural trend."[19]

Spray wars

The provincial Cabinet, under pressure from Stora, overruled the Department of Lands and Forests and approved a spray program with the organophosphate insecticide fenitrothion, which has since been banned. And thus one of the great forest debates of Nova Scotia was sparked. Grass-roots opposition to the spray mobilized throughout rural Cape Breton. News reports publicized research in Halifax linking the spray in New Brunswick with children's deaths from a rare disease, Reye's syndrome. Within months of approving the spray program, the Cabinet reversed its decision on the advice of the Minister of Health.

The following year, with higher budworm-population counts, Stora pulled out the big guns. Its president and CEO, Erik Sunbladt, flew in from Sweden to issue an ultimatum: either Nova Scotia agreed to a much larger spray program, covering all of Cape Breton Island, both Crown and private lands, or the company would close its mill within five years and put two thousand people out of work. Mr. Sunbladt told the local television news: "Nova Scotia is sick. It must take the medicine."[20]

In fact, the costs of the spray program would have exceeded the value of the annual harvest from the Cape Breton forest, but Stora wanted to maintain its control over its source of supply. Stora issued a massive report, arguing that, without spraying, half of its wood supply on Crown lands would be lost. It claimed that the remaining wood would not provide more than a five-year supply, thus justifying the threat to close the mill by 1981. But independent assessments, even using the company's worst estimates of softwood mortality, reported that there would be adequate wood supplies from Crown and private land for at least forty years, with no provision for growth. Stora was never able to back up the five-year shutdown calculation.

The campaign against the spray made local woodlot owners and executives of the Woodlot Owners' Association into active environmentalists. (It was my personal introduction to fighting forest companies.) A loose coalition of beekeepers, woodlot owners, schoolteachers and local concerned citizens formed, calling themselves Cape Breton Landowners Against the Spray. In all, the battle was restaged every year until the outbreak collapsed of natural causes, as predicted, in 1981. The Liberal government of Premier Gerry Regan and Lands and Forests Minister Vince MacLean held firm despite mountains of propaganda and personal invective directed at them by Stora, with the full support of Scott and Bowater. The budworm issue was a landmark in Nova Scotia, being the first time that a major pulp-and-paper company had not extracted exactly what it wanted from the government. It was also the last time.

The empire strikes back

When, against all odds, the environmentalists won the budworm spray wars, I came to think of the experience as "Star Wars." The next brutal contest, which we lost, I referred to as "The Empire Strikes Back."

In the next provincial election, all three major political parties had a firm "no spray" position. But when the Conservative government of Premier John Buchanan had its first taste of Stora pressure, it turned out their position had a loophole. They never said they would not allow *herbicide* spraying. With a new program of government subsidies, in 1982, Stora, Scott and Bowater received permits to spray vast areas—nearly one hundred different locations, ranging in size from several hectares to several thousand. The spraying was to be from the air, with 2,4-D and 2,4,5-T, the phenoxy herbicide mixture known as Agent Orange. The announcement of the spray permits came without warning or prior public discussion, the day after the provincial legislature broke for the 1982 summer recess.

Already banned in Sweden and the United States, as well as in Saskatchewan, Quebec and Ontario, 2,4,5-T had never before been used on Nova Scotia's forests. The rationale for its use was that following clear-cutting, the small herbaceous shrubs, the pioneer species of pin cherry and birch, were "competing" with coniferous growth. Overcutting softwoods could now be approved by the Forest Department, as long as "intensive" silviculture methods offered the possibility of accelerated growth in the future. And the companies would receive reimbursement through the federal-provincial subsidy program. Once again, the pulp companies in Nova Scotia were demonstrating political muscle.

The Mi'kmaq Nation was one of the first to become actively opposed to the planned defoliation. Their reserve at Whycocomagh was just below a spray site on Skye Mountain, which was also the source of the community's drinking water. Chief Ryan Googoo led a dawn protest of men, women and children up the mountain, where they uprooted seedlings planted by Stora, the planned beneficiaries of the toxic spray. As publicity mounted, the Cabinet announced that the spray permits had been cancelled.

Within a month, however, notices appeared in newspapers across the province that herbicide spraying was to take place with 2,4-D and 2,4,5-T. Having phoned the Nova Scotia Department of the Environment every day to ensure that no new applications for spray permits had been received, I was convinced that any herbicide spraying by the big three pulp companies must be illegal. When I phoned the usually friendly information officer with whom I had spoken every day for over a month, he put me through to the Deputy Minister of Environment. Mr. E.L.L. Rowe explained that the permits had never been cancelled. "The Minister may have said the permits were cancelled, but what he meant was, they were *varied*."

In fact, the permits had merely been altered from approved aerial spraying to approved ground spraying. Same chemicals, same spray sites—only now spraying was to begin within the week. With no time and fewer options, communities throughout Cape Breton and eastern Nova Scotia opted to seek a court injunction. In what became known as the Herbicide Case, seventeen plaintiffs, their families and local support groups saw nearly two years of their lives vacuumed up in a brutal court battle. Stora's lawyers resorted to every procedural obstacle imaginable to force the plaintiffs into bankruptcy before the trial could begin. In one round of threats that involved sending the sheriff around to collect on a collateral bill of costs from an effort to stop spraying on the Scott Paper lands, my family lost 80 acres. In all, the plaintiffs— Cape Breton activists and their families—were able to raise nearly a quarter of a million dollars for their own legal costs. As the social activist June Callwood commented at the time, "It was a David and Goliath struggle, only this time Goliath had the sling shot."[21]

The injunction, granted on an emergency basis in August 1982, prevented any spraying on Stora's holdings in Cape Breton and most of what it had planned to spray on the mainland. We ran the legal marathon of appeals against our injunction, court orders for costs and a month-long trial, in which the company successfully argued that we be denied access to a jury. After hearing from dozens of expert witnesses, following the second season during which our injunction held off the spraying, Mr. Justice Merlin Nunn, in his first major trial, ruled that the chemicals were safe. He went so far as to find, as a matter of fact, that 2,4,-D and 2,4,5-T had not caused any ill effects in Vietnam, nor had dioxin been of lasting harm in Sevesco, Italy. Then he ruled that the plaintiffs owed Stora for all of their court costs. While Stora's press relations people speculated that the plaintiffs owed over a million dollars, nerves were frayed, spirits flagged and, ultimately, the plaintiffs accepted an out-of-court settlement rather than take the issue to appeal.

Ironically, it turned out that Stora could not spray 2,4,5-T, even after Judge Nunn ruled that it was safe. The U.S. Environmental Protection Agency and the herbicide's manufacturer, Dow Chemical, agreed to allow no more old stock of banned 2,4,5,-T to be exported. Meanwhile, Stora had sold the Agent Orange it planned to spray on Nova Scotia. It was sprayed in New Brunswick instead.

Stora continues to benefit from government largesse. It has milked the decision of the Nova Scotia government in the mid-1970s to allow the budworm outbreak to run its natural course. Although at the time Stora had bluffed and threatened to close the mill by 1981 if the provincial government did not conduct a spray program for the company, Stora has expanded operations since that time. It gained government subsidies for the salvaging of budworm-killed wood. Later, the provincial government put $10 million into a new on-site electrical generator running on wood waste. Stora also received extensions so that new federal pollution standards would not have to be met during an economic downturn, even though it had reported profits of $1.5 billion between 1983 and 1993.

In another grandstanding ploy in 1993, Stora threatened to close the mill in light of new pollution laws coupled with the recession. Responding to the threat, the government provided a $15.4-million loan, and Stora's workforce accepted pay cuts amounting to $1.5 million, with the company committing to no new increases. The cited rationale was Stora's reported losses in the early 1990s.

Yet a close reading of Stora's financial statement for 1993 suggests a different picture. The main purchaser of Stora's Nova Scotia pulp was another arm of the Swedish conglomerate, Stora Feldmuhle. Stora reported the market rate for pulp as averaging $430 (U.S.) per ton for bleached long-fibre pulp. But the company's annual report indicates the Nova Scotia mill was selling its bleached long-fibre pulp for approximately $330 (U.S.) per ton.[22] By discounting sales of pulp, Stora would have been able to transfer as much as $17 million (Can) in revenues to other divisions within the company. While Nova Scotia workers and wood suppliers took significant pay cuts, Stora CEOs and directors rewarded themselves with a 10 per cent increase in salaries and bonuses.

In December 1995, Stora announced a major expansion in order to produce a more finished paper product suitable for magazines, integrated with its existing newsprint and pulp lines.[23] This is the same company that claimed there was an inadequate wood supply to see it through 1981 without massive chemical spraying. But accountability is unknown in forest management. Other than the chemical insecticide-spray program that Stora demanded, Stora, Scott (now owned by Kimberly Clark) and Bowater have received whatever they wanted from a compliant provincial government.

Industrial forestry and loss of species

Over centuries, previously common and valuable long-lived tree species have been mined out of Nova Scotia's forest. With them have gone the woodland caribou and the timber wolf.

Environmentalists of the twenty-first century must be grateful for the foresight of the government in 1940 in setting aside part of the Big Lease in Cape Breton Highlands National Park. Of course, Oxford Paper of Maine received a windfall in compensation for its forest lease on the Highlands, but one of the largest, intact old-growth Acadian forests anywhere in the province was spared logging when the national park was created. And it is by no means the only Acadian old-growth forest remaining.

Significant Acadian forest in a pristine state can still be found on the steep slopes, as well as north of the park, and in pockets throughout the province. In 2002, local residents in the Chester area banded together to protect 1,200 hectares of Acadian forest with important old-growth characteristics on Bowater land. The area, known as Kaizer Meadow Brook, became a province-wide concern as Bowater denied it was old growth. Ecological foresters and scientists toured the area. Dr. Wolfgang Maass discovered a rare lichen, confirming the significance of the area's old-growth features. The company agreed to a one-year logging moratorium in 2002, explaining the cessation in logging was to "avoid unnecessary confusion and misinformation among the public."[24] The following year, the company announced its logging plans. Bowater agreed that the area was ecologically important and committed to more sensitive logging. The area will not be clear-cut, approximately 160 hectares of wetland will be protected and the Bog Lakes area, within the Kaizer Meadow Brook, is a potential candidate for the company's Unique Areas Program, due to the discovery of the rare lichen. The local Friends of Nature, led by one of the province's most respected conservationists, Martin Rudy Haase, and the Kaizer Meadow Preservation Group continue to push for higher levels of protection.[25]

There is inadequate protection for forest biodiversity, as witnessed by the brouhaha over clear-cutting hardwood for export to the United States, Germany, Great Britain, the Middle East and Sweden. When Stora, with a mill and cutting rights throughout eastern Nova Scotia, clear-cut an area of Acadian hardwood forest in the Keppoch Highlands of Cape Breton in 1990, a raging controversy ensued. Local environmentalists claimed the area had been predominantly birch and maple, some as much as 170 years old.

The clear-cut hardwood was shipped to Sweden for Stora to pulp there. Stora's initial response was to deny that the area had been a hardwood forest. Television news crews toured the site with foresters and environmentalists who pointed out the hardwood stumps and branches. Stora admitted the clear-cut had some hardwood, but maintained it had to be logged due to the dead-softwood component. Stora president Tom Hall ridiculed the environmentalists' claims, insisting that only an "infinitesimal" amount of maple had been shipped to Sweden.[26] A campaign was launched to set aside the remaining original Acadian forest in the 6,000-hectare watershed of Trout River on the Keppoch Plateau. Meanwhile, the provincial Department of Lands and Forests representative, Ed Bailey, defended the continuing conversion of the forest from hardwood to softwood: "A lot of softwoods were killed by the budworm and we had to have replanting to restore the forest.... The industry we have here utilizes softwood species. If we are not able to supply these, the industry will fold."[27]

One of Cape Breton's leading forest activists, Charlie Restino, put it differently: "They're trading in Rolls-Royces and Cadillacs for Volkswagens and Chevrolets."[28]

For the Tourism Industry Association of Nova Scotia, the concern was different. Expanding clear-cuts were beginning to be noticed by tourists. The tourism group joined environmentalists in asking for action to protect the wilderness characteristics that draw visitors from around the world.[29]

In response to growing public concern over loss of habitat for species and inadequate protected areas, in December 1998 the provincial legislature passed two key pieces of legislation. After years of interim protection for thirty-one protected areas, punctuated by the removal and subsequent re-protection of Jim Campbells Barrens, the province finally passed its Wilderness Areas Protection Act. The act increased the percentage of province within protected areas from 2.9 per cent to 8 percent.

The second milestone legislation to be passed in the same month was the Endangered Species Act. The Nova Scotia government approach, with its emphasis on stewardship and partnerships, was well received across Canada. Unlike the federal act, the Nova Scotia Endangered Species Act ensures that scientists make the determination of which species are listed. Six species currently listed are primarily at risk due to loss of forest habitat. The mainland moose, Canada lynx, Bicknell's thrush and southern flying squirrel and the Cape Breton population of American pine marten and wood turtle are the animals at risk. The boreal felt lichen is the only listed lichen endangered through loss of forest.[30]

While progress has been made in setting aside a few areas, overall the rate of logging continues to rise in Nova Scotia. Listing species alone does not help their recovery. Only protecting habitat can do that.

Nova Scotia's wood supply

Nova Scotia has probably the most intensively harvested forest in Canada. With only 1.3 per cent of Canada's productive forest land base, Nova Scotia forests produce nearly twice that—2.4 per cent— of total roundwood (a term for logs and pulp) for Canada.[31] In addition, an unreported amount of Nova Scotian forests is exported to New Brunswick and Maine by private woodlot owners.

A government Forest Management Strategy produced in 1994 recognized the historic damage done to the province's forests:

> The practice of removing the best and largest trees (high-grading) over centuries has reduced the physical and genetic quality of our forests. Natural events such as wildfires, insect infestations, hurricanes, land clearing and abandonment in many instances created overmature stands. Over 40 per cent of Nova Scotia's forests are more than sixty years old.[32]

The Royal Commission on Forestry public hearings in the early 1980s examined a range of options for the future of Nova Scotia's forests. It found that, at predicted rates of logging, by 2025 the demand for wood would exceed supply by 44 per cent and the annual allowable cut would drop by 33 per cent. The commission then examined the "basic silviculture" option, but found the supply of wood would still fall short of demand by 28 per cent by 1994, and by 36 per cent by 2025.

Last, the commission looked at an "intensive management" option. This approach involved a full array of silviculture treatments over Crown and private lands: thinning, planting, herbiciding and use of faster-growing seedlings, called "plus trees." Backlogged NSR areas, after years of neglect, would receive special attention to reclaim them as viable productive forest. Under this option, the coming shortage was re-engineered into a *doubling* of wood supply.

It will likely strike those uninitiated in the mumbo-jumbo of forest regulation as silvicultural alchemy that a province facing shortages should be treated as one on the verge of doubling supply. This is how it was done.

In determining the annual allowable cut, Nova Scotia has, in recent years, relied on a simulation model called SAWS (Strategic Analysis of Wood Supply). Every province has its own system of projecting wood supply, each using a different modelling approach. The only thing they seem to have in common is clever acronyms: while Nova Scotia SAWS, B.C. foresters listen to the sound of MUSYC (Multiple-Use Sustained-Yield Calculation).

The SAWS model is applicable only to even-aged management. Moreover, it essentially treats all the forest as though it were softwood, without differentiating between softwood species. Hardwood is dealt with through an adjustment to the overall softwood assumption. Like all computer models, everything in the result is determined by the initial assumptions. Recent forest reviews have cast doubt on the accuracy and reliability of the SAWS model: because so much is aggregated in terms of species, growth projections are likely unreliable.

Using the SAWS model, adjusted to the appropriate level, it was possible to project a doubling in wood supply. All the industry needed was a compliant bureaucracy and a pile of dubious assumptions. It also needed government subsidies.

The goal of doubling the wood supply by 2025 was adopted during the peak years of federal-provincial silvicultural subsidy agreements. Between 1977 and 1993, a total of $416.4 million was spent in Nova Scotia's forests. Government funds reimbursed landowners and the pulp companies for road building, silviculture and fire and insect protection. Much of this was applied to privately owned small woodlots.

The land-ownership patterns in Nova Scotia have had a major impact on Nova Scotia's efforts to stabilize its wood supply. With nearly 70 per cent of the forest privately owned, and most of that in small woodlots, implementing intensive forest management across the province has been a major government preoccupation since the mid-1970s. Small woodlot owners are responsible for 59 per cent of the wood supplied to mills, with 29 per cent coming from industry-owned forests and 12 per cent from Crown land.[33] In the wake of the budworm outbreak, the province created funding to assist independent wood co-operatives, known as "group or joint ventures." The idea was to combine small woodlots into units sufficiently large that management plans could be drawn up. Landowners would be reimbursed for building logging roads, planting seedlings, herbiciding and thinning their forests.

The government paid for a great deal of environmental damage. Poorly built roads ruined stream quality. Defoliation spraying took place in areas where, even by industry standards, there was no excuse for it. But the intensive silviculture option was fulfilling its primary objective: justifying overcutting, premised on improved and speculative future growth. In 1988, the area harvested was 42,000 hectares, with a 3.5-million-cubic-metre demand for wood to the mills.[34] By 1994, that figure had increased to 49,968 hectares, and the total volume logged to 5.2 million cubic metres.[35] And in 2003, the total logged had increased once more, with 54,433 hectares cut, yielding 6.2 million cubic metres.[36]

Various audits of performance under federal-provincial silviculture agreements should have given the super-charged industrial forest modellers cause for concern. In 1987, an evaluation of one round of spending concluded:

> The problems created by the existing age distribution are evident from the small area in younger stands; *in twenty years there will be insufficient mature forest available to meet the*

needs of the forest products industry. The age distribution problem stems from the lack of adequate forest management over the last fifty years.

Low density stocking, less than 60 per cent stocking on over 53 per cent of the forest land, is also a serious problem.... Some of this land lacks natural regeneration, and some has sparsely stocked, poor-quality, older forest. The net result is a large area of non-commercial forest.

Taken together, the consequences of these problems are a *serious deficit in the volume of harvestable wood relative to current levels of use beginning in about twenty years* [emphasis added].[37]

In March 1995, another consulting firm was hired to project the success of a further round of subsidies. The goal for spending up to 1995 was to achieve an immediate increase in the AAC of 3.75 million cubic metres for softwood and 1.5 million cubic metres for hardwood, working toward the ultimate goal of a combined hardwood and softwood annual allowable cut of 7.3 million cubic metres by 2025.

The audit report found that the target had not been met at either end of the equation. First, the AAC was an overcut, going 5 per cent above allowable levels. This was possible because, although Nova Scotia includes private lands in the AAC, it cannot regulate the cut on those lands. The cut may well have been more than 5 per cent above the AAC, as private forest landowners had been lured by sky-high pulp prices in the mid-1990s into clear-cutting entire woodlots. Contractors sought out economically desperate landowners, particularly in forest-rich Cumberland County, close to the New Brunswick border, with offers of $30,000 to clear-cut a standard family woodlot. The wood generally was trucked to New Brunswick, or through to Maine. But even as pulp prices plummeted, overcutting of small private woodlots was increasing, with no regulation or monitoring.[38] Moreover, private woodlot owners were also overcutting preferred species, even when those trees were too young for harvest.[39]

Second, the targets were not met because levels of silviculture upon which the AAC was calculated were not met. The effort faltered on two promised goals—there was less planting and less thinning of trees prior to their commercially valuable state. On the other hand, there was overharvesting by thinning in merchantable stands. This trend has continued with some operators thinning thirty- to forty-year-old trees, and returning to complete the logging by age sixty.[40] The failure to meet planting targets was primarily due to a drop in subsidies. Of course, the targets were hardly scientific. Overall, the program encouraged widespread clear-cutting.

The auditors flunked the province: "The market demand study... concludes that from 1994 to at least 1999, *the demand for softwood will exceed the AAC*.... We conclude that the Agreement has not met the AAC's objectives specified in CAFD 2 due to a combination of lower than expected budget approvals (and, therefore underachieved silvicultural treatment targets) and harvests that exceeded the AAC in the latter part of the 1991–1995 period [emphasis added]."[41]

The consultants expressed concern that, even with subsidies, small-landowner participation was lagging. Small woodlot owners are being asked to turn their forests into a fibre farm for the pulp-and-paper industry. Some object. For instance, the audit report noted that the Mi'kmaq participants found the subsidy program incompatible with their own land-use priorities:

> The Mi'kmaq participants...did not believe that the overall management plan allowed for multiple uses of their land. They wanted to conduct multiple species plantings, but these were not supported by the Agreement...we concluded that the *Mi'kmaq Bands were less committed to the goal of total growth than they were to the development of a broad species forest base* [emphasis added].[42]

In other words, the Mi'kmaq did not want to sacrifice biological diversity in the drive to produce more pulp. The Pictou Landing First Nation's success with their woodlot further demonstrates the cultural gap between the Mi'kmaq approach and the industry approach to forests in Nova Scotia. In 2000, they received the first Forest Stewardship Council certification of any woodlot in Nova Scotia, the fifth woodlot to be FSC-certified in Canada and the first certification of forest managed by a Canadian First Nation. The 384-hectare woodlot is managed with the goal of restoring its ecological health to pre-colonization conditions.[43] No even-aged, softwood plantation for the Pictou Landing First Nation.

New regulations

The wood-supply crisis in Nova Scotia has reached the point where industry is raising concerns. As mentioned in Part I, the head of the Forest Group Ventures Association of Nova Scotia, John Roblee, told a legislative committee in 1997, "We don't have the data of what is leaving the province by rail, by truck and by boat. It's going on twenty-four hours a day.... It's just clear-cutting."[44]

Nova Scotia's AAC is still being set as though wood supply is increasing due to the intensive silviculture model. Despite reports from the province's own auditors that silvicultural targets have not been met, the overcutting continues. Nova Scotia has even increased the number of mills since becoming aware it was headed for wood shortages. Chip mills, in Sheet Harbour and Weymouth, heighten the pressure on the province's forests. The Sheet Harbour hardwood chip mill sends 250,000 tons of hardwood chips every year to Mitsubishi's operation in Japan.

Recognizing the credibility problem with unregulated logging on private woodlots and increased allowable logging by the major Crown lease holders—based on imaginary aggressive silviculture—the provincial government made some changes. In 1999, Nova Scotia announced its Interim Old Forest Policy to identify areas of old growth for preservation.[45] The policy has not made much of a dent in the dramatic decline of old growth. A 2002 report by the Nova Scotia think tank GPI Atlantic noted that in 1958, 25 per cent of Nova Scotia's forests were more than eighty years old. Today, just over 1 per cent is over eighty years old.[46] The GPI report had a significant impact in Nova Scotia. Dr. Ron Coleman, an ecological economist, presented the decline in ecological health for what it really is—depreciating capital—by evaluating Nova Scotia's forests as loss of value to the "owners," the people of Nova Scotia. "This is bad accounting," Coleman explained, "like a factory owner selling off his machinery and counting it as profit."[47]

In April 2000, new provincial regulations came into force to attempt to control the clear-cutting of private lands. The Forest Sustainability Regulations focus on the buyer of wood from private lands. Everyone who purchases 5,000 cubic metres of wood or more must either contribute $3 for every cubic metre of wood purchased to a Sustainable Forestry Fund or carry out a silviculture program worth the same amount somewhere in Nova Scotia.[48] A registry of buyers was established by law in 1998 to get a handle on how much wood was being logged and how much was being trucked out of the province. Each buyer must now submit Wood Acquisition Plans, setting out their planned silviculture based on wood acquired the previous year.

The Forest Sustainability Regulations have as their stated goal the sustainability of fibre—not of the forest ecosystem. The silviculture options qualifying for reimbursement from the new fund range from the ecologically sensitive—tree pruning and selection management—to the more conventional forestry treatments to establish and maintain softwood plantations (site preparation, planting, herbiciding and "weeding"). The vast majority of silviculture dollars are flowing to these industrial activities. Of the $16.4 million spent in 2002, less than $10,000 went to ecological silviculture (0.04 per cent of the total), while over $11 million went to softwood plantations (over 69 per cent).[49] The reason the spending is skewed toward non-ecological treatments is that the program is run by the buyers and the mills. Anyone seeking to conduct silviculture on private land, whether a contractor or landowner, must seek assistance from the registered buyers—generally mills—or from the Association for Sustainable Forestry (ASF). The ASF offices are located with the group that oversees its activities, the Forest Products Association of Nova Scotia. The conversion of mixed-age Acadian forest to even-aged softwood plantations is aided by the silviculture program, even if some headway may be made in avoiding a drastic fibre shortfall.

Another effort to meet public concern about the crisis in Nova Scotia's forest was the 2002 Wildlife Habitat and Watercourses Protection Regulations. These regulations apply on all forested land in the province. There are three elements: ensuring that in any cut a clump of at least thirty representative trees remains on any logged area more than 3 hectares, or at least ten trees per hectare; establishing a 20-metre "special management zone" along fresh or salt watercourses; and ensuring that dead trees and coarse woody debris are left on the site for use by wildlife.

The regulations have been criticized as inadequate to protect key ecosystem features. Forest ecologist Bob Bancroft has found convincing evidence that the 20-metre special management zones along waterways will not be sufficient to protect most Acadian forest wildlife. He cites research on fur bearers, small mammals, songbirds, raptors, amphibians and trout suggesting that a 100-metre riparian buffer zone would be required to ensure habitat opportunities for most species.[50]

Others have criticized the ten-tree clump per hectare rule as wholly inadequate. Most forests have between two thousand and ten thousand trees per hectare. A pathetic clump of ten trees is vulnerable to drying out in summertime and blowing down in the strong fall winds. Contractors may be prepared to leave ten trees behind, but few will ensure the selected trees are representative of what was there before logging. As for leaving standing dead wood, few contractors understand the benefits to cavity-feeding and nesting birds of standing snags and of coarse woody debris to small mammals like the marten. They generally see the salvage value of more fibre. These provisions are subject to blatant violation.

But perhaps the most telling criticism is that there are, in effect, no penalties for ignoring the regulation. In the fall of 2003, residents near the community of Baxter's Harbour reported to the Department of Natural Resources that J.D. Irving Ltd.'s contractors were clearcutting everything—no dead trees left standing, no small clumps of representative trees. Although the residents informed the provincial DNR staff soon after logging had begun, DNR waited a full month before visiting the site of the logging to investigate the complaint. By then, the whole area was clear-cut. The Minister of Natural Resources confirmed in a letter to residents that "full compliance with the Wildlife Habitat and Watercourses Protection Regulations [had] not been achieved."[51] However, there were no penalties. The contractor was offered the chance to attend a one-day technical training session. J.D. Irving Ltd. was not required to do anything.

The last piece contemplated in an expanded tool kit for improved provincial regulation of forests is a Code of Forest Practice, released in October 2004.

In 2003, more than 6.2 million cubic metres was logged. The AAC has been increased to 6.7 million cubic metres so this rate of logging will not appear to be alarming. Since Nova Scotia first realized it faced a looming shortage of available wood to feed its mills, rates of logging have steadily increased. Logging rates have not declined in order to compensate for the overcutting.

A growing network of Nova Scotians are concerned about the future of the province's forests. There is greater awareness that the remnant old-growth Acadian forests are globally significant and must be protected. At a 1998 forum on the sustainability of Nova Scotia's forests, a group of environmentalists and academics heard from a former Deputy Minister of Forests. Dr. Wilfred Creighton, who had retired in 1969, delivered an electrifying critique of current forest policy in Nova Scotia. He characterized the merging of responsibility for both mines and forests as creating a situation in which the government "couldn't have a deputy minister that knew about both mines and forests, so they appointed a deputy that knew nothing about either." Creighton recalled that when he was deputy, the maximum amount of sawlogs that could be harvested in any year was topped at 150 million cubic metres. The previous year, 600 million cubic metres had been logged. And he found fault with the clear-cutting, especially along stream banks: "We're clear-cutting on steep hillsides that cause erosion...in the summer, there's not enough water, the salmon get sunburned." Creighton was worried the province was headed for mill closures: "Our forests are in danger," he warned. "Not pulp and paper, but the sawmill industry. We're over-cutting, seriously overcutting."[52]

Nova Scotia is now grappling with an extremely perilous wood supply. By choosing maximum industrial silviculture options, it has allowed increased levels of harvest even as a wood shortage looms. Everything is based on the accuracy of the models and on achieving the level of required silviculture. Of course, even if the intensive silviculture is performed, the expected levels of forest productivity remain entirely speculative. Even hard-line advocates of the "forests on steroids" model are now faced with the stark reality of ravaged forests.

When past targets have been missed, the AAC went up anyway. Between 1982 and 1989, $88 million of taxpayers' funds was spent in silviculture. Despite finding that less than 70 per cent of the required treatments had actually been performed in that period, the AAC kept climbing. The Forest Department merely recalculated and decided these essential treatments were not needed after all.[53]

There is no question that the province has taken steps to increase its ability to know what is being logged and to regulate the worst of bad logging practices on Crown and now on private lands. Previous bad actors, such as Stora, have improved enormously. In fall 2004, an unprecedented dialogue between forest industry representatives and environmentalists took place, in a forum dedicated to the memory of the great activist Colin Stewart. The climate for respectful communication is growing. But the scope of the problem requires far more than small steps toward better logging. The rate of logging is too high. More areas must be set aside if old-growth Acadian forest characteristics, and the wildlife that depend on them, are to survive.

Nova Scotia

Forest and other wooded land in million hectares*	4.3
Stocked harvested Crown land in hectares (2001)	203,000
Area logged in hectares (2002)	49,959
Volume logged in million cubic metres (2001)	6.0
Annual allowable cut in million cubic metres (2001)	6.7

Source: Natural Resources Canada, Canadian Forest Service, *The State of Canada's Forests 2003–2004* (Ottawa, 2004). These are federal government summaries, based on provincial government data. The figures are not necessarily accurate.
* Still based on the 1991 inventory, revised in 1994.

Nova Scotia Corporate Players

Bowater Mersey Paper Company Limited
Harry Freeman and Son Ltd.
J.D. Irving Ltd.
Keywood Recovery Inc.
Kimberly Clark
Ledgwidge Lumber Company
MacTara Ltd.
Northern Fibre Terminal Inc.
Port Hawkesbury Limited
Stora Enso
Truro Lumber Ltd.

New Brunswick

New Brunswick's forests are still described as predominantly of the Acadian forest type, and classed as a single ecoregion along with the forests of Nova Scotia and Prince Edward Island. These forests were once unique in the world.

The original forests of New Brunswick were described in 1847 in a report for *Simmonds Colonial Magazine*. The author, M.H. Perley, an early timber surveyor, was overwhelmed by the great diversity of deciduous species—"tall, durable oaks," butternut trees "plentiful and abundant" along the Saint John River Valley, five different species of maple and three beech. As for softwood, Perley recorded, "In New Brunswick, hemlock forms a large proportion of the evergreen forests"—with hemlock reaching heights of 80 feet.[1]

As early as 1849, leaders of the Mi'kmaq people made this heart-breaking appeal to the New Brunswick House of Assembly:

> In old times, our wigwams stood in pleasant places along the river sides. These are now all taken away from us; and we are told to go away. Upon our old camping grounds you have built towns, and the graves of our fathers are broken up by the ploughs and the barrow. Even the Ash and the Maple are growing scarce. The lands you have given us are ruined or taken away.[2]

The Acadian forest of towering white pine, strong hardwoods, ancient hemlock and red spruce was substantially diminished. In fact, the 1986 inventory for the province placed the percentage of hemlock at about 1 per cent of the total softwood.[3] Anyone hoping to see the magnificent stands of old-growth hemlock need not waste time searching the province's hinterlands. One of the best examples can be found in Odell Park in the provincial capital, Fredericton.

No other province in Canada has so completely brought its forests into full industrial production. For modern foresters in New Brunswick, it is a source of considerable pride that the province's forests are all accessible by a network of logging roads—more than 50,000 kilometres of logging roads on Crown land alone. No forested area is farther than 200 kilometres from a mill.[4] True wilderness, out-side of parks, is rarer than a non-Irving gas station. Of all of New

Brunswick's forests, only 3.4 per cent of the land base is within a provincial protected area or national park.[5] And those forests outside national parks are entirely spoken for. As Max Cater, former head of the New Brunswick Forest Products Association, put it, "Every tree has a company's name on it, and a destination."[6]

How New Brunswick's forests became a fibre farm

The social and economic factors that have led to the colonization of New Brunswick by its pulp-and-paper industry go back to the earliest days of the province's history. Since the 1800s, the province allowed large tracts of its forests to be controlled by a few large sawmill owners. Profits from the forest washed through the province until the large trees of the highest value were gone. The high-grading process allowed the faster-growing and commercially undesirable species of balsam fir to become predominant.

By the 1920s, the sawmill kings of the nineteenth century were losing their political foothold. The Great Depression sharply reduced profits, but the decline began earlier. What had been a 46 per cent share of total provincial revenue in 1920 dropped to 22 per cent by 1922.[7] The first pulp mill in the province was built in 1915 by Bathurst Lumber. Where the sawmill industry was experiencing more difficulty finding quality logs, the forest was virtually perfect for the pulp-and-paper industry, for which fast-growing small trees are ideal. Both the government and the banks set policies that favoured the rise of pulp mills. After the Depression the banks were unwilling to risk loans to the sawmill industry. And the government seemed eager to grant generous licences to large pulp-and-paper companies.

By 1930, the two largest pulp companies, Fraser Company and International Paper, had been granted long-term licences on very attractive tax and royalty terms for over 70 per cent of the province's Crown land. Six years later, the pulp companies also owned 36 per cent of the province's privately held forest land.[8] What high-quality trees still existed were now increasingly hard for the sawmill industry to access. Cutting for the sawmills became restricted to smaller private lands, with overcutting the result.[9]

The pulp-and-paper industry's control over vast areas of the province as well as the pulp mills themselves created an economic stranglehold that exists to this day. The small private woodlot owner or pulp cutter had little economic leverage. Moreover, the pulp-and-paper industry follows boom-and-bust cycles in which the international price of pulp and newsprint is subject to wide fluctuations. When the economic conditions were bad for the industry as a whole, it was the small private landowners who suffered the most. Not only could the large pulp-and-paper companies dictate prices through control of the market, in the period from 1948 to 1954 they were actually meeting regularly and setting prices for the farmers and woodlot owners in Ontario, Quebec and New Brunswick. This price-fixing was uncovered in a government commission, but without guaranteed access to markets, the independent small producers were bound to comply with whatever conditions the pulp companies dictated.[10]

By the early 1960s, in the wake of one of the cycles of depressed demand and low prices, the woodlot owners and independent pulpwood suppliers began to organize themselves to take on the pulp-and-paper industry. In what looked like class warfare, the woodlot owners' associations pointed out that the province was losing not only quality sawlogs but also farmland to the pulp-and-paper industry. The Acadian Federation of Northern New Brunswick argued that the people of New Brunswick would not "tolerate the existence of a private industry which enriches itself at the expense of tar paper shacks, wasted minds and bodies, impoverished, badly educated children, despairing fathers, despondent mothers and ruined communities."[11]

Although the first woodlot owner marketing board was established in 1962, it was not until the 1970s that wood marketing boards covered the whole province. They allowed for region-by-region negotiation among the large mills, the sawmill owners and the small producers. But they still lacked the power to set prices or to dictate what proportion of wood should come from private woodlots. It was not until 1982 and the massive reforms of the Crown Lands and Forests Act that the marketing boards were given teeth. The new legislation established the overriding directive that the industry's primary source of fibre must be the private woodlots. This concession to the economic interests of the private woodlot owners was more than balanced by a sweeping shift in Crown licences, consolidating all Crown land in ten licences to be held by pulp mills. The pulp mills themselves were given the responsibility of managing the forests within their licences to ensure supply, not only for themselves, but for the roughly one hundred smaller sawmills operating in the province. Still, industry objected to the new power of the marketing boards.

In the wake of the recession in the early 1990s, the provincial government brought in amendments to the Crown Lands and Forests Act as part of a larger group of measures known as the Pulp and Paper Rescue Plan. The 1992 amendments, which included such provisions as deferred stumpage, abolished many of the marketing boards' powers.[12] The private woodlot owners lost their legislated position as primary suppliers, although the pulp companies were urged to continue to buy from them.[13] There are no controls on the level of harvest on private lands.[14]

New Brunswick's war on the budworm

For decades, the provincial government seemed to define its role in forest policy as doing the bidding of large industry. In 1952, the New Brunswick forests were hit with a serious infestation of spruce budworm. This indigenous forest pest is perfectly suited to balsam fir. The appearance of the fir's tender buds in springtime is exquisitely timed to the emergence of the budworm in its larval state. While always present at low levels, the spruce budworm has reached epidemic proportions every forty years or so, for thousands of years. But the logging patterns of the last 150 years had, as if by design, created vast expanses of the budworm's favourite food.

New Brunswick had been warned of the risks it faced by allowing the forest to go to fir. In the 1920s, during a previous period of high budworm infestation, entomologist Dr. J.D. Tothill wrote:

> In the primeval forest bequeathed by our forefathers there were no important outbreaks of insects because Nature had established a natural balance that prevented any one insect becoming too abundant. There were no pure stands of fir... on a large scale, there were great numbers of insectivorous birds, and insect parasites were uniformly distributed and destroyed vast quantities of spruce budworm.... For a century we have been working in direct opposition to Nature and in the course of our ordinary lumbering methods have finally succeeded in destroying this delicately adjusted balance.[15]

From what he observed, Tothill recommended that the province begin an immediate silvicultural program to "budworm-proof" the forest. In essence, he was advocating a return to the natural Acadian-forest mix. He urged that more hardwood be present, with more trees in mixed-age stands. While the original forest had always included a large portion of spruce, it was generally red spruce, which is less susceptible to budworm. Logging was increasing the proportions of balsam fir. Unless the natural species mix was restored, he argued, the next budworm epidemic would come sooner and with greater severity.[16]

Rather than heed the warnings, the pulp-and-paper industry went about converting the forest to spruce and fir. When faced with the serious budworm outbreak Tothill had predicted, the provincial government did not address the root cause of the problem, the unnaturally high proportion of fir. Rather, the province armed itself to fight the symptoms. New Brunswick declared war on the spruce budworm.

In order to fight the budworm outbreak, the province began a massive insecticide-spray program at public expense. It began in 1952 as a 100,000-hectare spray program with DDT, with the stated objective of eradicating the budworm. The following year, the spray program was extended to an area four times as large. It created an artificial state of permanent epidemic. Rather than collapsing from natural causes within four to five years, as would normally have occurred, the outbreak lasted for more then forty years. The insecticide had the unintended effect of knocking out the budworm's natural predators, birds and other parasitic insects, while maintaining the food supply, thus preventing conditions for natural collapse. While significant short-term mortality in balsam fir was averted, the province experienced continual losses to budworm for over forty years.

In the course of the war against budworm, the province created a Crown corporation, Forest Protection Ltd., and bought a squadron of Second World War Grumman Avenger bombers, supplying them with millions of litres of chemicals. Rachel Carson related the early years of the spray program in *Silent Spring*, with a chapter on the Miramichi called "Rivers of Death." From DDT to phosphamidon to fenitrothion, the chemical arsenal the province used against budworm has since been banned. Songbird mortality was huge. Depending on the chemical, the province lost its fish or its birds or both. Blueberry growers had to be compensated for crops that failed because pollinating bees had been eradicated by spray drift. The province lost a court case launched by a local family after spray drift affected their health. In order to avoid that problem in the future, the province changed the law to allow insecticide spraying over private property, with or without the landowners' consent, through the right of eminent domain. In several painful years, 1976–1978, the insecticide's emulsifier was linked to a cluster of children's deaths from Reye's syndrome, an otherwise rare disease.[17]

The Minister of Natural Resources at the time, Roland Boudreau, said: "I don't like to see people dying. This is one of those things I wouldn't really like to see. But, at the same time, knowing the forest as it is, my decision will have to be with the forest and the future of New Brunswick."[18]

By 1994, the budworm was in decline. Use of a biological alternative, Bt, had allowed natural predators to rebound from the effects of chemical spraying. In the early 1990s, fenitrothion was deemed "environmentally unacceptable" by the federal Environment Department. In 1995, the federal government announced that fenitrothion would be banned, phasing out the chemical by 1998.[19] While the provincial government stopped spraying it, Irving continued to use fenitrothion on its privately held lands.[20]

By the time the government stopped its annual chemical dousing of the province in 1994, in total over 39 million hectares of forest had been sprayed since 1952—the equivalent of spraying the entire forested land base of the province nearly seven times over![21]

Nothing has ever been allowed to interfere with the business of making pulp and paper. In describing the pulp-and-paper empire that is New Brunswick, it is hard to avoid the word "feudal."

Impact on forest biodiversity

The dominant view of forests from the New Brunswick government and its industry is that the forest is like a garden. It grows a crop. The crop must be tended, sprayed, thinned and harvested. The industry can walk the visitor through vast stands of plantations. Irving was the first company to engage in extensive tree planting. It actually calls itself "The Tree Growing Company" and boasts of planting nearly 400 million seedlings in the last thirty years.

But the New Brunswick vision of the forest is a dark one indeed if you value a forest for anything other than fibre production. Past logging regulations had little regard for the maintenance of old-growth forests. Now there are policies to maintain 12 per cent of older trees in a cutblock (although this policy is limited to six forest ecosystems). Foresters are finding that there are not enough older trees to meet the requirements.

In New Brunswick, 20 per cent of Crown lands are targeted for plantations (to date, 8.9 per cent of the land has been commercially thinned, and 8 per cent is in plantations). For these managed areas, even middle-growth classes will be reached only because relatively short-lived trees are planted. Every stick is to be harvested on a rotation of forty to sixty years, or even earlier due to commercial thinning. Even the steep slopes of the Appalachians that had been left unlogged are now being cut with the cable-logging system common in British Columbia.

It is clear that the pattern of human exploitation of the New Brunswick forest has fundamentally altered the richness of its ecosystems—from both a biological and economic point of view. For example, a single unprocessed bird's-eye maple can command between $5,000 and $10,000 in today's marketplace. This tree, which is a sugar maple, has a genetic defect that creates a unique pattern in its grain. Conversion of the forest has reduced its abundance, while those few trees that remain are likely ending up in pulp or veneer mills.[22] The same would hold true for other high-value fine furniture woods. They are increasingly rare.

As logging has impoverished the forest, shifting the species mix and age classes, New Brunswick has also lost plant and animal species. The big predators, the cougar and wolf, have all but disappeared from the province's forests, and the Canada lynx is on the provincial endangered species list. Woodland caribou was extirpated in the 1930s. The bald eagle, peregrine falcon and eastern cougar are regionally endangered. Species relying on dead trees for cavity habitat, food and shelter are also disappearing. Old forest habitat is in decline everywhere. There has been very little research on the impacts of logging on amphibians and reptiles, but one study on the red newt demonstrated that clear-cuts prevent it from migrating from its upland habitat to wetland habitat to breed.[23] As well, at least forty-five species of forest plants are endangered or threatened.[24]

As watersheds are affected by clear-cuts, stream life is damaged.

Studies in New Brunswick show significant decreases in brook trout and invertebrates in clear-cut watersheds.[25] Studies in the Maritimes show that while songbirds will live in a forest after it has been clearcut, they are not the same species as found in the original forest. Once abundant in the mature hardwood forest, the least flycatcher, hermit thrush, ovenbird, red-eyed vireo, a number of warbler species and others were totally absent from the clear-cut forest five years after harvest. Trees and shrubs created new habitat and a completely new set of species moved in.[26] Simple counting or wandering around with an untrained eye to look for birds might lead to the false conclusion that all was well.

Biodiversity is inevitably lost when old growth is removed. While this holds true for almost all of Canada's forests, the situation in New Brunswick is particularly troubling because of the inadequate protection of old-growth forest within parks. With only 3.4 per cent of the province within protected areas, and not all of that in forested areas, the amount of old growth actually set aside from logging is minuscule. Moreover, clear-cutting and the conversion of forest to plantations *outside* of parks is taking its toll on ecological integrity *within* parks. The forests around Fundy National Park have been clear-cut right up to the park's borders.[27] The impact is to effectively shrink the national park, reducing usable habitat to such an extent that it may not be possible to maintain viable populations of all its native species.

In recent years, the government has become more sensitive to its critics. The vast majority of New Brunswick's forestry production is destined for export, mostly to the United States. *National Geographic* magazine is published on glossy paper that was once fir and spruce in the Miramichi, while pulp from Nexfor's Edmundston mill goes to phone books in Europe, and poplar and white birch in the Saint John River Valley become photographic paper for Kodak and Fuji.[28]

Concern for markets, coupled with strong citizen action and public pressure within New Brunswick, has resulted in the formulation of new rules to protect non-timber values. Since the late 1980s, clearcut size has been restricted to 100 hectares. Since 1992, the forest management plans for Crown land, now drawn up every five years, must include protection for certain commercially valuable wildlife, with deer yards in place. Buffer zones along streams are now mandatory.[29] Habitat targets for species dependent on deciduous and mixed-growth forest habitats were set in 1999. A total of sixteen different vertebrate species are known to be dependent on old deciduous, mixed-wood and old pine habitat. Companies are not yet required under licences to provide special management for these types of habitat.[30]

The deer-yard areas ensure the proliferation of a valuable game species. The white-tailed deer increased in numbers as the indigenous woodland caribou disappeared. Generally, deer can do well in clear-cuts, which increase the area for browse. But large clear-cuts create difficult winter conditions for deer. They dislike venturing out into large openings at any time, and in winter, clear-cuts accumulate much deeper snow than does a forest. The obvious fact that the forest canopy intercepts a lot of snow has implications for the soil hydrology and climatic conditions year-round. But, for the immediate object of maintaining deer populations, the licences require maintaining winter deer yards with areas of standing forest near the clear-cuts. The areas set aside as winter deer yards often overlap with the requirement for mature-conifer habitat, but the total acreage is added up as though these requirements were cumulative.[31] The industry points to these commitments, and the AAC to allow for them, and claims to have done enough to protect non-timber values.

Initially, the New Brunswick government had committed itself to the Endangered Spaces campaign. The campaign goal is a network of parks and protected areas, comprising a minimum of 12 per cent of Canada's land base in a network of adequately represented ecosystems. However, there was no real progress until after the hard-fought battle to protect wilderness in the Christmas Mountains was launched by the Conservation Council of New Brunswick and the New Brunswick Wildlife Federation in 1993.

The Christmas Mountains are part of the Appalachians in the north-central part of the province, so called as each mountain is named for one of Santa's reindeer. Still largely road-less, the announcement by Repap, the licence holder in the area, that it planned to carry out extensive clear-cutting in the area propelled provincial groups into action. Within a matter of months a province-wide coalition among environmentalists, conservation organizations, students, hunters, anglers and trappers was formed. Soon the Union of New Brunswick Indians entered the fray in support of wilderness protection.

Despite the public outcry that ensued, the government of the day rejected even a temporary moratorium on logging the area to examine the potential for wilderness protection. Instead, it announced it was going to establish some small protected areas north and south of the Christmas Mountains in an attempt to suggest that it was willing to compromise. As Donner and Blitzen were clear-cut, protesters began to organize. Students from Mount Allison University and Université de Moncton set up a wintry blockade in November 1994. The following year individual Mi'kmaq and Malisset people joined student protesters in the woods and on the steps of the provincial legislature. The company responded with an injunction and a threatened lawsuit.

The Christmas Mountains protest was one of the true wilderness struggles in recent times in New Brunswick. The campaign received support from environmental groups across Canada. Sadly, the calls for protection were unsuccessful. Still, the Christmas Mountains campaign must be seen as pivotal in pushing the New Brunswick government to finally begin to honour its 1990 commitment to protect Endangered Spaces. Following on its heels, the New Brunswick Protected Areas Coalition was successful in its efforts to have the province move forward in establishing a network of large protected areas.

In 1997, the provincial government commissioned a Université de Moncton professor, Louis Lapierre, to develop a protected areas strategy and propose the candidate sites. The public consultation process on the proposals was launched in late 1999. On May 24, 2001, the Conservative government of Premier Bernard Lord announced ten new protected areas covering nearly 150,000 hectares. Five areas were larger than 20,000 hectares, including Loch Alva, Kennedy Lakes, the Spednic Lakes, Canaan Bog and the Jacquet River Gorge. More than 11,000 hectares was added to Mount Carleton Provincial Park, for a total of 32,000 hectares protected in the Appalachians. Still, even after more than doubling the amount of land with protected-area status in New Brunswick, the total area protected is the smallest of any province in Canada—3.1 per cent of the whole province, and 6.5 per cent of all Crown lands.

The government has not met its commitment to the Endangered Spaces campaign. The province has no plans to create any large parks for protection of old-growth or other ecosystems. In fact, in 2002, the government announced that no new protected areas on Crown land larger than 5,000 hectares would be created again—ever. In three of the new large protected areas, some logging will be permitted until 2012. The companies would like to count the winter deer yards, mature conifer habitat and buffer zones around streams as meeting protected-area requirements.

The provincial government has made serious strides toward large protected areas of forests. The public has been engaged. With support from a broad cross-section of New Brunswickers—woodsworkers, First Nations people and environmentalists—forests in New Brunswick are being valued for more than pulp.

New Brunswick's wood supply

Since the early 1970s, there has been concern that New Brunswick was running out of wood. The efforts to revise the Crown licence systems in 1982 through a substantial overhaul of forest legislation, The Crown Lands Forest Act, was largely in response to supply concerns. The Deputy Minister for Forests of that day, Dr. Gordon Baskerville, recalled, "There was pretty severe denial among most people about the seriousness of the problem.... All of the computer forestry models forecast a problem. None of them showed a sustainable harvest forty or fifty years in the future."[32]

In response to the coming supply crunch, 483 parcels of Crown land were consolidated into ten. The prerequisite for a licence was simple: you had to own a mill. As a result, there are currently six pulp-and-paper conglomerates controlling half of New Brunswick's forests through licences. All of its Crown land, 51 per cent of the land base, is controlled by the pulp companies. Two large companies, J.D. Irving Ltd. and newcomer Helsinki-based UPM Kymmene, control over two-thirds of all the Crown land in the province. Of the remaining forests in private hands, 18 per cent is classified "industrial freehold," which means the industry owns that too. Another 29 per cent of forest is in smaller privately owned woodlots.[33]

The annual allowable cut has decreased only slightly in anticipation of the potential shortfall. The AAC set in 1992 was 18 per cent lower than the AAC in 1987,[34] largely to accommodate new guidelines for deer yards and mature habitat. But while the AAC has fallen, the rate of cut has not. In fact, it has gone up. In 1993, New Brunswick cut 8.8 million cubic metres from a total AAC of 10.9 million cubic metres. By 1994, the rate of cut increased to 9.2 million cubic metres.[35] In 2000, 11.9 million cubic metres was logged, above the current AAC of 11.1 million cubic metres.[36] Compared with the levels of cut in 1960, New Brunswick's annual harvest has more than doubled.[37]

New Brunswick's AAC is 35 per cent too high on the basis of natural rates of growth. Only through faith in the benefits of intensive silviculture and voodoo forestry is the level sustainable. Even then, the rate could be considered sustainable only if ecological values and biodiversity were excluded from the equation. Nevertheless, even by industry and government estimates, the current timber supply in softwood is fully utilized. There is no margin for error. Everything depends on the accuracy of the inventory, the reliability of computer models, and the wonders of modern industrial forestry. No variables are permitted. No new budworm outbreaks, or fires, or reductions in tree growth resulting from climate change or air pollution are allowed—and certainly, no new parks.

The last published inventory was completed in 1986. A more recent digital inventory has not yet been published, but the 1986 inventory was clearly progressive for its day. In contrast to those conducted in most provinces, it was fairly thorough and was entered into geographic information system (GIS) software. Soon thereafter the accuracy of the 1986 inventory was called into question. In the 1992 Crown licence granted to J.D. Irving Ltd. for the Queens–Charlotte County areas, the Forest Management Plan noted a number of problems. In particular, Irving found "a large discrepancy between what was assumed to be available for harvest according to our wood-supply model; and what our foresters (and their reconnaissance) think is operationally available."[38]

Revising the inventory became an ongoing effort in 1992. It is currently anticipated that every ten years the province will have a complete picture of its forests. However, even with the newer inventory information, many species are still merely lumped together. Further, the inventory relies on the private companies to report the status of industrial freehold lands. In the meantime, there is no question that AAC levels are being allocated before the inventory is complete.

What the current inventory shows is that the softwood supply is optimistically "tight," or realistically falling far below demand. The age classes of the standing softwood are unevenly distributed. Much wood is in older age classes, bearing in mind that an eighty-year-old balsam fir is considered "overmature" or "decadent" in foresters' language. There are also a lot of trees in the younger age classes. What is in short supply are the trees that should be ready for harvest twenty to thirty years from now.

To avoid the anticipated shortfall, New Brunswick is trying to defy time and nature; first by making younger trees grow faster, and second by hoping old trees will not die. The AAC not only expands to take advantage of potential future growth through intensive silviculture, but also stretches out the life span of old trees to cover the coming shortfall in wood supply. Having converted the province to short-lived, low-quality species, it is not surprising that companies are concerned that the predicted yields from these older stands may not hold up. The stands will likely die before the pulp companies get to them.[39]

J.D. Irving Ltd. addresses the risk directly in its Forest Management Plan: "Since the 1982 photography, we have noticed an almost complete mortality of the remaining balsam fir component on the Licence as well as a significant and accelerating spruce deterioration.... It may indicate that our natural unmanaged stand yields may be somewhat optimistic."[40] But the problems do not end there. Inventory information suggests that the individual tree size will continue to decline. The sawlog industry has already adapted its equipment to handle smaller logs, as the anticipated "harvested piece size," or log, is going to get much smaller quite quickly. Maintaining a forest where high-quality logs become a priority has not been suggested. This is again reminiscent of the collapse of the cod fishery. As the large cod disappeared off Newfoundland, fish plants brought in new equipment to process increasingly small fish. As an ecosystem warning sign, it was ignored.

In the late 1990s, bad news emerged from the private woodlots, comprising 29 per cent of the forest land base. For the first time in the province's history, overcutting these smaller private forests was becoming a serious problem. Traditionally, a family farmer with a woodlot treated the forest like money in the bank. He would fell a certain amount of his forest every year, with sales to the sawmills or pulp mills, depending on quality. The stewardship of private lands was always something of an ideal for conservationists. The best species diversity and age mix tended to occur on these gentle valley lands. But several factors have conspired to change that picture. First, after depressed global pulp prices in the early 1990s, the price shot through the roof. Second, the workforce on Crown lands had been reduced. Many of these independent contractors had purchased expensive mechanized harvesters that can cost hundreds of thousands of dollars, and needed to find somewhere to clear-cut to generate income to pay the interest on loans for their mortgaged machines. The increasing mechanization of logging inevitably leads to greater clear-cuts, as machines like feller-forwarders and feller-bunchers are good for nothing else.[41] These pressures, coupled with high unemployment and favourable federal tax treatment of clearing forest land, have led to a new phenomenon in the Maritime private woodlot—"the liquidation cut." It is the next step in the industrialization of the forest: extending the liquidation clear-cut from Crown to private land.

Contractors were literally going door to door in New Brunswick asking owners of 100-hectare woodlots if they would consider clear-cutting the entire area for a quick profit. It was encouraging that, according to the president of the New Brunswick Federation of Woodlot Owners, Peter deMarsh, contractors had to approach several dozen landowners before they could find one ready to liquidate a forest.[42] But, in the absence of the power of marketing boards to regulate the harvest, a power abolished in 1992, there was no way for the province to regulate or even monitor the rate of cut. Some of the harvest was shipped to Maine and was not reported. For purposes of the AAC, the government estimated the unreported softwood export at 300,000 cubic metres a year, but admitted that it could easily be much higher.[43] Even as pulp prices tumbled in the late 1990s, the pressures to liquidate family woodlots remained high.

As the problem of liquidation cuts worsened, the issue became a political concern. The National Round Table on Environment and the Economy held meetings throughout the Atlantic provinces, after which New Brunswick Premier Frank McKenna addressed the forum and promised reforms.[44]

In May 1996, the province announced plans to levy higher property taxes against landowners who clear-cut more than 10 per cent of their woodlots in any given year. This scheme was subsequently abandoned. The province instituted a system to keep track of the wood trucked off private woodlots, addressing both the problem of private woodlot liquidation and wood theft from private lots. Any vehicle trucking wood on public highways is now required to have a transportation certificate from the forest marketing board.[45] The province's motivation in acting to discourage liquidation cuts is clear. It was likely not a concern based on the ecological unacceptability of clear-cutting. An estimated 70 per cent of New Brunswick's logging on Crown lands is by clear-cutting. The driving motivation to restrict liquidation cuts on private lands is that, with an impending shortage of softwood, the last thing the New Brunswick–based mills want to see is wholesale cutting for export. Every stick of wood in the province will be needed if mills are not to start closing for lack of supply in the next fifteen to twenty years. It appears that the overcutting on private woodlots is now in decline.[46]

Meanwhile, the "underutilized" component of hardwood in the province is feeling increasing logging pressure. Pulp mills are adapting processes to make use of intolerant hardwood species, such as poplar and birch. New Brunswick has also expanded its forest industrial sector to include oriented strand board. A laudatory story in the Saint John *Telegraph-Journal*, heralding the opening of an OSB plant at a once-bankrupt Miramichi pulp, and then waferboard, mill, noted, "As big trees and old-growth forests get harder to find in North America, OSB is becoming a cheaper, more popular construction material. It is expected to outpace plywood as North America's building panel of choice by the turn of the century."[47]

The reality that there is no margin for error, coupled with inaccurate inventory information, and a likelihood that old trees cannot be forced to stretch out their life span to accommodate industry harvesting plans, spelled a shortage of softwood by the year 2015. Meanwhile, the New Brunswick courts dealt with a series of challenges by Mi'kmaq, Malisset and Passamaquoddy First Nations, challenging the stranglehold on Crown forests by the large mills. The New Brunswick Court of Appeal has decided in favour of the First Nations right to cut trees on Crown land for personal use and, in a separate case, their right to harvest trees to derive a "moderate livelihood."[48] The provincial government has appealed the "moderate livelihood" decision to the Supreme Court of Canada, and may appeal the other. Meanwhile the three bands in the Miramichi have filed a comprehensive land claim to the entire northwest Miramichi watershed. The case, currently before the courts, is the first such land claim anywhere in Atlantic Canada. In addition to a shrinking wood supply due to overcutting, the large mills see First Nations logging as another threat to their control over Crown lands.

Power grab

The forest industry examined its narrowing options. Wood supply was dwindling, the AAC had been slightly reduced to accommodate

special management areas for old spruce and fir and habitat requirements, First Nations were demanding their rights, and pressure was
building at a grassroots level across the province for community
forestry. In 2001, the New Brunswick Forest Products Association
jointly commissioned and funded with the provincial Natural
Resources Department a review of management options, conducted
by Finnish consultants Jaakko Pöyry.[49] Its report, released in
November 2002, noted, "the tightening softwood fibre supply has
prompted" the review.[50] The recommendations ignited the biggest
debate on the future of its forests in New Brunswick history.

The report proposed a modern industry solution to shortages:
doubling the rate of cut. It argued for increases in silviculture spending from the 2001 level of $23 million a year to $50 million, and then
back down to $34 million within thirty-five years. In a blatant power
grab by the forest industry, the report went well beyond the usual
voodoo forestry calculations to increase logging while the forest dwin-
dled. In essence, the forest industry wanted to tie the hands of any
future government that might reduce the AAC. The Jaakko Pöyry
report recommended that "timber supply objectives should be set for
each licence area binding for the government and the licensee."[51]

The implications of this recommendation were staggering. The
forest industry wanted the government to pay compensation to industry if government policy reduced any access to fibre. The industry
wanted to avoid any more special management areas to protect habitat, prevent any new parks and be protected against future court
decisions on Aboriginal land claims. Its ambitions went beyond the
binding targets. In an industry document leaked to the Conservation
Council of New Brunswick on the eve of the hearings, the industry
proposed that independent arbitration be established to resolve
instances when the government and licence holder could not agree.[52]

The industry attempted to paint itself as a victim. It complained
that protected areas and special management areas were denying it
needed fibre. Clearly, the small proportion of protected areas did not
anger the industry as much as the special management areas. All told,
the Jaakko Pöyry report estimated the total amount of both at 32 per
cent of Crown land. At the press conference, industry made the case
that it was at the mercy of public policy. The industry, casting itself as
victimized by government, sought to wrestle absolute guarantees to
tie the hands of future governments.

Referencing the demise of other industries in New Brunswick, Jim Irving, CEO of J.D. Irving Ltd., asked, "Can it happen to the pulp and paper business and the forest industry in this province? Absolutely, make no mistake." Irving added, "Someone will say, 'Mr. Irving, you're trying to make people fearful.' But I'm just stating a fact."[53] Irving was clear. New Brunswick should double its cut, and also double the number of mills. "The fundamentals are if we can double the wood supply and, more importantly, double the manufacturing base in this province, then I think we're going someplace."[54]

To review the recommendations, the government established hearings under a Select Committee of the New Brunswick Legislature. To their astonishment, hundreds of people and groups wanted to appear to oppose the recommendations. The demand to be heard was so high that the number of hearing days had to be doubled, from November and into December 2003, and even then, the committee could not accommodate all the people who wanted to be heard.

The public sentiment was summed up in the frequent refrain "Give us back our forest!" That it was given away two hundred years ago did not matter. When the licence holders had not demanded every tree, every stick, every inch of forest; when utilization of wood for jobs and the economy still left room for wildlife and recreation; when there were more jobs and fewer mechanical harvesters—then, the people of New Brunswick did not feel that they had lost their forest. In 2003, the people of New Brunswick woke up, rejected the industry power grab and demanded a say in forest policy.

On September 15, 2004, the Select Committee on Wood Supply tabled its report in response to the public hearings. The Committee rejected the majority of the Jaakko Pöyry recommendations, and instead endorsed managing the forests for greater diversity, thereby "creating greater benefits for people over the long term."[55] Environmentalists applauded the Select Committee report, praising the recommendations to reduce clear-cutting and expand value-added industries. The Committee called for forest management to protect the natural diversity and ecological features of the Acadian forest.[56]

There is much left to fight for in New Brunswick's forests, but substantial progress is being made. Recognition of non-timber values is beginning to take root in the bureaucracy, and is firmly embraced by the citizens.

New Brunswick

Forest and other wooded land in million hectares	6.2
Stocked harvested Crown land in hectares	638,000
Area logged in hectares (2002)	105,834
Volume logged in million cubic metres (2002)	10.1
Annual allowable cut in million cubic metres	11.0

Source: Natural Resources Canada, Canadian Forest Service, *The State of Canada's Forests 2003–2004* (Ottawa, 2004). These are federal government summaries, based on provincial government data. The figures are not necessarily accurate.

New Brunswick Corporate Players

Bowater
J.D. Irving Ltd.
Nexfor (Fraser Papers)
Parsons and Whittemore (St. Anne Nackawic)
UPM-Kymmene
Weyerhaeuser

Prince Edward Island

Prince Edward Island and its forests are unique in Canada. Almost none of the generalities about forests in other provinces apply here. The island has no pulp mills, and virtually no annual allowable cut is set; almost 90 per cent of the island is in private hands; there are no large-scale leases. But it one respect it is no different from any other province in Canada: the forest has been substantially degraded by centuries of human exploitation.

This little jewel of green in the Atlantic, with the Northumberland Strait separating it from the mainland, is Canada's smallest province. With a population of 140,000 and a land base of only half a million hectares, Prince Edward Island is smaller than any number of parks found across the country.[1] Most Canadians would be surprised to hear that Prince Edward Island even has a forest industry. But prior to European contact, the island was 98 per cent forested in the species and composition typical of the original Acadian forest. As in its neighbouring provinces, Nova Scotia and New Brunswick, the character of the forest has been wholly altered. Shipbuilding and sawmills took the best wood in the nineteenth century, but it was the clearing of land for agriculture that removed most of the original forest. By the early 1900s, only 20 per cent of the island remained forested as the industrious settlers established the pastoral and well-manicured landscape made famous by Lucy Maud Montgomery in *Anne of Green Gables*.

During the Great Depression, islanders left the farm in droves. This population shift escalated after the Second World War. Abandoned fields returned to forest, but as in New Brunswick and Nova Scotia, they regenerated in the early successional species. In Prince Edward Island, this led to a predominance of white spruce, with a small component of hardwoods—white birch, grey birch, poplars, red maple and pin cherry.

Although nearly half of the island is now classed as forestland, none of it is the original forest. There is no area of productive forestland that has avoided the axe, chainsaw or harvester, *including* land within national and provincial parks.

Having discussed the impact on biodiversity of the cutting down of the original forest in other provinces, it is not necessary to dwell on the same impact here. But the list of species that have become extinct in Prince Edward Island is longer than that of its neighbours. The lynx, black bear, pine marten, fisher, river otter, moose and other forest dwellers disappeared from Prince Edward Island long ago. Certain songbirds have likely been affected by the clear-cuts, but no specific studies have been done.

Of particular concern to Prince Edward Island ecologists is the disappearance of the rare indigenous forest trees and shrubs. The few remnants containing rare species such as ironwood, witch hazel and hobblebush have insufficient protection. In 1995, a large area of witch hazel (one of the island's rarest shrubs) was cleared by a work crew *within* a protected Natural Area.[2]

Despite Prince Edward Island's small role in the Canadian forest industry, it does have logging, clear-cutting and mills. PEI exports to pulp and sawmills, and logging also supplies island sawmills. Lately, some hardwood shipments have gone to Maine as the market for hardwood in pulp and paper increases. All told, in 1995, the island logged 188,000 cubic metres for the pulp mills of neighbouring provinces, 230,000 cubic metres for sawmills on the island and 190,000 cubic metres for domestic fuel wood, with smaller amounts for fuel chips and exported sawlogs.[3] Since almost all of this happens on private land, there is no set allowable cut and no legislated sustained yield. There is a weak provincial Forest Management Act, with little enforcement. The government instituted a Forest Renewal Fund, with $2 from every cord of wood sold being placed in a fund for silviculture.[4] Unfortunately, to date this has primarily funded more conifer plantations, brush burning and herbicide use.

As small as the island's forest industry is, it is still overexploiting the degraded forest that remains. While unwilling to regulate harvest levels, the province's Forestry Branch does attempt to monitor them. Harvest rates between 1990 and 2000 jumped from about 450,000 cubic metres to nearly 700,000 cubic metres. Over the same period, the area of forest also diminished substantially. *The State of Canada's Forests* in 2000 noted a 6-per-cent decrease in forested land, primarily due to agricultural conversion, not including clear-cuts. In a January 1996 press release, the department warned that cutting levels on the white spruce, mostly found in abandoned fields, was unsustainable. They reported, "this softwood resource will be gone in ten to fifteen years."[5]

Meanwhile, the traditional threats to the island's forests continue in the form of agricultural expansion. Of the 31,700 hectares of forest logged between 1990 and 2000, one third was converted to agriculture. Land continues to be cleared for agriculture. As well, the provincial agriculture branch had been actively promoting the conversion of marginal forest land to blueberry production.

The saga of forest plantations to blueberries should become a classic Canadian tale of battling subsidies. Through the 1980s, there was a federal-provincial program called the Forest Regional Development Agreements (FRDAs). In Prince Edward Island, the FRDAs led to a number of intensive forest management practices for the first time. Logging roads, herbiciding, thinning and planting were all subsidized on private land. The landowners, in turn, were contracted to maintain any plantations on their land for ten years or be forced to compensate the province for the forest improvement.

The FRDAs dried up after fiscal year 1993–1994. And along came the Agriculture Department with subsidies to convert woodland to blueberries. It turned out that many of the best sites for blueberries

were the previously subsidized forest plantations. They were accessible by road and easily cleared with a brush mower. So down came
some of the six- to ten-year-old trees. Thus far, a few landowners who
have failed to maintain their plantations have been sent bills by the
forest service, but no blueberry growers have been charged.

Logging pressures on Prince Edward Island are likely to increase
substantially due to upcoming shortages in its neighbouring
provinces, combined with increased accessibility to mills now that the
Confederation Bridge to the mainland is complete. In the absence of
regulations on clear-cutting private lands, the island will suffer even
more severe shortages than those projected on the basis of current
levels of cut.

The dream of restoring the Acadian forests

Like Camelot, there was one brief shining moment when it seemed
something magical might happen in Prince Edward Island's forests. It
was the mid-1970s, when Dr. Stephen Manley became the director of
the PEI Forestry Branch. With a doctorate from the Yale School of
Forestry, Dr. Manley had a vision for the future. He set about recre-
ating the original Acadian forest—to plant not the species immediately
required by the pulp-and-paper industry, but the original native
species: white pine, red oak, eastern hemlock, white ash, yellow
birch, butternut and beech. Many of these species are long-lived, representing the climax stage of the Acadian forest. Some live up to four
hundred years. Repeated clearing and conversions to lower-value
species had almost entirely removed them from the island landscape.
Early successional species of white spruce, white birch and red maple
had grown in dominance from an original 10 per cent of the forest to
approximately 90 per cent today.

For many Maritimers, the notion that their forests had once
harboured large and valuable species, fine-furniture wood and nut-
bearing trees was a revelation. Dr. Manley's vision was featured across
Canada, with a cover story in *Harrowsmith* magazine. He argued not
solely from an ecological viewpoint, but from an economic one as
well. The forests of the Maritime provinces, he said, should yield 50
to 80 cubic metres to the hectare, while our current "bastardized" forest provides only 15 cubic metres to the hectare. "We have literally
reduced by orders of magnitude the capacity of the landscape to produce a lot of valuable material," Manley explained.[6]

He created a wonderful dream. Instead of allowing current economic pressures to steadily degrade the forest, why not restore the ecological wealth of the forest for future generations? And, if there was anywhere in Canada where such a dream could be realized, it was Prince Edward Island.

Sadly, it was too bold a dream for the modern world. By 1979, the provincial government decided to shift its forest policy toward the production of softwood for pulpwood and sawlogs. Dr. Manley left the provincial government. As he later said, somewhat ruefully, "I don't think anyone wants to take the chance on having a vision... vision takes a long time."[7]

But the dream had taken root. Local environmentalists continue to work toward the restoration of the forest. The Environmental Coalition of Prince Edward Island has converted what had been planned as a historic preservation of a 175-year-old house and homestead into an Acadian-forest rehabilitation project.

The Macphail Woods Ecological Forestry Project now boasts not only historic house tours, but a major Acadian-forest restoration project in the Macphail Woods. After conducting a biological inventory of the forests on the 57-hectare property, the local environmentalists collected seeds from thirty-five representative species for the Macphail nursery. They have been successful in growing thousands of seedlings of such original species as red oak, white ash, beaked hazelnut, ironwood, yellow birch and butternut. They have also worked to preserve the rare shrub species and other woodland plants. The nursery is now providing seedlings not only within the Macphail Woods, but to schoolyards and other properties across the province. They have helped individuals and communities set up small nurseries to cultivate native trees and shrubs. Biodiversity within the site is carefully monitored, particularly within the area of neotropical migratory songbirds that are declining in eastern North America.

The focus of island environmentalists on restoring the forest that once blanketed 98 per cent of the province is inspiring. The province recently launched a review of forest values, and has hired one of the province's leading environmentalists, Kate MacQuarrie, former head of Island Nature Trust to head up its Forest Department.[8]

We need a similar vision for the rest of Canada. In the face of the vast forest conversions to lower-value species that are occurring across Canada, the enthusiasm for working to achieve ecosystem health a hundred years hence suggests that this is a necessary dream. As Stephen Manley said, "Vision takes a long time."

Prince Edward Island

Forest and other wooded land in million hectares	0.3
Stocked harvested Crown land in hectares	54,800
Area logged in hectares (2002)	4,903
Volume logged in million cubic metres (2002)	0.4
Annual allowable cut in million cubic metres	0.5

Source: Natural Resources Canada, Canadian Forest Service, *The State of Canada's Forests 2003–2004* (Ottawa, 2004). These are federal government summaries, based on provincial government data. The figures are not necessarily accurate.

Prince Edward Island Corporate Players

Arsenault's Saw Mill (family business)
J.D. Irving Ltd.

11 | QUEBEC

Alberta may claim to be the Canadian cultural equivalent of Texas, but geographically, Quebec has them beaten hands down. In terms of land mass, Quebec is approximately twice the size of Texas; it is Canada's largest province, with an enormous territory of 1.5 million square kilometres (154 million hectares).[1] Northwestern Quebec embraces the entire east coast of Hudson Bay, while its smaller relative, James Bay, juts toward Quebec's population centres. Still, the urban dwellers of Montreal are as remote from the source of Quebec's massive hydroelectric facilities as New Yorkers are from Newfoundland.

Quebec's forests cover 84 million hectares, about half of the province. The taiga, or far northern forest, which reaches up to the treeline, is typified by open forests and bog. Farther south is the Quebec portion of the transcontinental boreal forest ecoregion. The boreal within the province extends from the shore of southern James Bay all the way east to the Atlantic coast—the Gaspé to the south and the Labrador border to the north. The boreal of Quebec is predominantly a dense black spruce forest, interspersed with balsam fir and jack pine. Along the river valleys farther south is the mixed-wood Great Lakes–St. Lawrence ecoregion. Within Quebec, this ecoregion is luxuriantly covered in the sugar maples that provide Quebec with maple syrup.

Historically, European settlers established themselves in the rich river valleys of southern Quebec—the St. Lawrence, the Ottawa and the St. Maurice. And it was in these valleys of the Great Lakes–St. Lawrence forest that the logging of white pine began in the 1700s. The pattern found in the Maritime provinces was repeated here. One Quebec observer reported in 1808 the logging of pine trees that were 120 feet (37 metres) long and four feet (1 metre) in diameter.[2] These giant pines were first logged for the British Navy. By the 1800s the prime use had shifted to sawmills and lumber. Quebec brought in its first forest regulations in 1849 and began to benefit from some revenue from stumpage fees—despite the minimal amount charged.[3] Early in the 1900s, the economic forest power shifted to the pulp-and-paper industry as Quebec became a major exporter of pulp to the United States and Great Britain.[4]

For centuries, Quebec's forests have been heavily exploited, so much so that it is estimated that south of the 49th parallel, a mere 10 per cent of the forest remains untouched.[5] Traditionally, large timber companies logged Quebec's largely Crown-owned forests, covering 85 per cent of the productive forest area through twenty-year procurement contracts and large "evergreen" forest concessions.

While the Crown owns almost all of Quebec's forests, private woodlot owners are by far the most productive forest workers on the Quebec scene. Even though they hold only 11 per cent of the forest, they produce 24 per cent of the total volume of wood annually in the province, primarily because their lots are in the warmer, more fertile southern regions of the province.[6] Private owners are also the backbone of the province's lucrative maple syrup industry. Sales of Quebec maple syrup totalled $134 million in 1999.[7] The forest has been threatened by environmental stress, acid rain and airborne toxic chemicals, implicated in a frightening crown dieback in the late 1980s. That particular maple dieback is now believed to have been part of a natural disturbance pattern related to drought and insect epidemics, with environmental stresses playing a relatively minor role. Research continues into the ongoing damage to forests caused by the combined stresses of increased UV exposure, ground-level ozone, acid rain and climate change.

Quebec boasts a highly productive forest co-operative sector—businesses in which the workers are both the employees and the owners. Some of these worker co-operatives own their own sawmills, as well as running logging operations. There are over fifty co-operatives, with approximately six thousand workers. All told, they account for almost 15 per cent of the total volume, with 5.8 million cubic metres harvested.[8] Co-operatives have argued that they have a better forest-stewardship record than the large corporate interests.

As the Quebec forests were mowed down, the province experienced local supply shortages and Quebec, at least for the sawlog industry, became an importer of wood. With fewer and fewer high-value trees available, Quebec mills were forced to look to Maine for a source of supply. While today only 13 per cent of wood milled in Quebec comes from out of province, historically the volume was greater.[9] In the early 1980s, two-thirds of Maine's sawlog spruce-fir lumber and half of its softwood lumber was exported to over forty hungry mills north of the border. As U.S. forest critic Mitch Lansky noted:

> The main reasons large landowners give to explain why they export sawlogs to Canada are that the markets are handy.... *The Quebec mills lack a local sustainable supply and are willing to pay far more than the Maine mills.* Researchers have cited other reasons why the Canadian mills can afford the higher prices: the Quebec mills have the advantage of better exchange rates, experienced managers, cheap power, government-sponsored training, state-of-the-art equipment, export assistance, cheap Canadian wood (but shipped in from a distance), lower rates for workers' compensation, and subsidies for new mills or mill expansion [emphasis added].[10]

In the early 1970s, the Quebec government realized that it was not benefiting from the overly generous terms given to the large companies. There had been widespread and careless "cut and run" logging, with precious little silviculture investment to offset it.[11] Future wood supply began to look threatened, especially after a spruce budworm outbreak in the mid-1980s that affected large areas of eastern Quebec. At taxpayers' expense, in 1976, the province conducted an aerial insecticide-spray program over 4.5 million hectares of forest.[12] While public opposition focused on the widespread deleterious effects of dumping poison on the forest, the policy-makers were more concerned about reform of the tenure system.[13]

The province's large industrial players, of course, wanted no change at all. But a serious recession in the mid-1970s created an opening for a political review of the whole forest management system for the province.[14] At the same time, the health of the forests was in doubt. As one forestry official said, "Quebec's forests are in such a pitiful state, we are facing shortages in many regions."[15]

The government blamed the impending wood shortages not on fundamental flaws in the industrial forest model, but on their antiquated tenure system. As a first step toward change, initially by policy in 1985, and subsequently by legislation in April 1987, all existing timber tenures were extinguished, with the promise that tenure-holders could either obtain compensation or be entitled to an agreement under the new system.[16] In anticipation of the new system, many large-scale pulp-and-paper firms bought out smaller sawmills. This gave them greater access to supply, as well as more effective vertical integration. The pulp mill could send good-quality roundwood to its own sawmills, while using the wood chips, a by-product of the sawmills, as raw material for the pulp mill. There were so many buy-outs in the mid-1980s that 60 per cent of the province's sawmill production was purchased by the pulp-and-paper industry.[17]

The pulp-and-paper mills received another boost in the lead-up to tenure reorganization. Massive federal-provincial subsidies poured into the pulp-and-paper sector for mill modernization in Quebec. Between 1983 and 1996, federal support came to over $456 million, with funding matched by the province.[18] These subsidies were, of course, additional to the subsidized lower power rates provided by the Crown-owned company, Hydro-Quebec, until 1988. In that year, Hydro-Quebec began to raise rates, prompting industry lawsuits against the government. Now the mills were about to be granted long-term tenure on virtually all of the province's forests.

By 1987, all the forested land in the province—the entire committed annual allowable cut (AAC)—had been consolidated into a series of contract agreements established by the Quebec Forest Act, passed in 1986. Called CAAFs (*Contrats d'approvisionnement et d'aménagement forestier*) or Timber Supply and Forest Management Agreements, the contracts tied up all of the productive forest base in twenty-five-year leases, with five-year renewal terms.

About ten major pulp-and-paper companies and fifteen independent mills control virtually all of the CAAFs; about two hundred contracts cover the AAC for the province. In 1996, five pulp-and-paper companies controlled 80 per cent of production; the companies are mostly Canadian-based, with Daishowa of Japan being the only completely foreign-controlled company. In February 1997, Chicago-based Stone-Consolidated merged with Quebec-based Abitibi-Price. Abitibi-Price already had four Quebec paper mills, churning out some of what ends up covered with "all the news that's fit to print" in the *New York Times*. It also has operations in Georgia and Alabama.[19] The conglomerate created by the merger, Abitibi-Consolidated, had become the world's largest newsprint manufacturer.[20] In 1998, Abitibi-Consolidated grew once again, merging with another of

Quebec's major companies, Donahue Inc. Donahue had had 1996 sales of 1.6 billion from operations in Quebec, Ontario and British Columbia. Tembec also expanded in Quebec, purchasing two Nexfor sawmills in 2003.

The other Canadian companies are also international. Kruger has three pulp mills in Quebec as well as mills in the United States and Britain, and ownership interests in tissue mills in Venezuela, Colombia and Italy. Repap, Avenor, Alliance Uniforêt, Cascades, Noranda-Maclaren, Cartons St. Laurent and Domtar are also present in the Quebec woods. Domtar, while not a Crown corporation, is 45 per cent owned by the Quebec government.

The system is criticized by various groups within Quebec, including the Grand Council of the Cree, for the government's conflict of interest, being both "shareholder in industry and protector of the forest." Quebec has long dabbled in government investments in logging operations.[21] In the post-recession period, the government bought out failing mills to protect jobs in remote areas. Its first forest Crown corporation, Rexfor, was established in the late 1950s to assist Quebec forest companies in financial trouble. Once a company is bailed out, Rexfor moves on.

The CAAFs prohibit the processing of Quebec wood outside the province and compel contract holders to conduct sufficient silviculture to regenerate logged areas. CAAF holders are expected to abide by management guidelines, which include public consultation on management plans and incorporating respect for wildlife habitats, other non-timber values and recreational areas. The Minister of Forests is empowered to terminate any CAAF for non-compliance, without compensation.[22] The Quebec government proclaimed its new legislation as a remedy to past forest practices and the legacy of clearcutting, depleted ecosystems and diminished soil and water quality. "With this act, Quebec enters a new forestry era, in which public forests will not only be more productive (based on long-term sustained yield), but also more versatile, permanent and better protected, for the greatest benefit of industrialists and outdoor recreation enthusiasts."[23]

There is no doubt the 1986 Forest Act had an impact. In the first ten years under the new regime, the average cost of wood increased from $2 a cubic metre to $12, and total stumpage fees increased from a 1987 level of $53 million to a 1997 level of $400 million—a 600-per-cent increase.[24] While the provincial government prided itself on the CAAF system as a great step forward in sustainable development, many environmental groups were appalled that the province had gone the route of long-term licences—committing the best lands to huge forest companies. Indigenous peoples throughout Quebec have always opposed large-scale industrial forestry as they are only too familiar with its impacts on their traditional lands. They were outraged that the government had committed virtually the entire productive forest for the long term without consulting them.

Another view was expressed by respected Quebec ecologist Jules Dufour:

> The new silvicultural system is a veritable windfall for the forest industry, which will benefit from minimal cutting rights, disguised development subsidies, and exemption from paying the cost of restarting production in previously non-regenerated areas.... The new system will contribute to the development of industrial silviculture, transforming the forest into a plantation consisting solely of species that are desirable from a commercial viewpoint.[25]

Another Quebec commentator, D. Vanier, in an article in French titled *"Cadeau pour l'industrie forestière"* (A gift for the forest industry), wrote: "Whether it is called 'forest concession' or 'timber supply and forest management agreement,' nothing has changed. Industry will continue to dominate forest use."[26]

The CAAF system gave control of Quebec's forests to centralized corporate powers, under contracts that will run for decades. But public awareness of forest practices would soon result in tougher environmental protections.

First Nations of Quebec defend the forest

The Algonquin of Barrière Lake, a small indigenous community 200 kilometres north of Ottawa, have taken *Our Common Future*, the report of the Brundtland Commission (the United Nations World Commission on Environment and Development) as their inspiration and guiding document in efforts to reverse the tide of industrial domination of the landscape. They have a reserve located within the La Vérendrye Wildlife Reserve. It sounds perfect—a First Nations community surrounded by a wildlife reserve, with Aboriginal rights of hunting, trapping and fishing intact. But unfortunately, nothing in Quebec law says that a wildlife reserve cannot be logged.

When half of the land areas of the wildlife park had been clear-cut, and after much of the area around their community had been treated with toxic herbicides, the community decided to take a stand. Blockades were erected along logging roads, and a long siege began. The Algonquins' intention was always clear. They did not want all logging stopped, but they wanted the principles of sustainable development, as laid out in the Bruntland Report, instituted on their lands.

Chief Jean Maurice Matchewan took a copy of *Our Common Future* to government officials, asking them to incorporate its principles into any further logging of their reserve. Nothing changed. Clear-cutting, herbiciding and destructive road-building continued. After the blockades, the forest contractor obtained an injunction, and arrests were made by the Quebec provincial police. The SQ (Sûreté du Québec) have a reputation for shooting first and asking questions later. Even though Chief Matchewan's arrest was being filmed by a National Film Board crew, he was man-handled, thrown against a truck and treated like a violent criminal, all while urging his people to practise Gandhian non-violence.[27]

When the case came to trial, their lawyer urged them to advance land claims as a defence. To that point, the community had not seen the conflict as an ownership issue; for them, it was a question of the future of the land: the ecological sustainability of logging practices. It was about traplines being destroyed and traditional hunting and fishing areas devastated. It was about the rights of local communities to have a voice in decisions that affect them. That was what had drawn them to the Brundtland Report, which specifically recommended that indigenous people and other traditional communities have a "decisive voice in the decisions about resource use in their area."[28]

But acting for ecological sustainability is not an accepted defence to charges of violating an injunction, so the defence was based on a land claim. In the past, the Quebec government had been unyielding, even dismissive, in relations with its First Nations communities. The Cree opposition to the dams at James Bay in the early 1970s had taught them about political confrontation. That conflict had pitted a government that believed it had an absolute right to every drop of water flowing to James Bay against an Aboriginal people who refused to accept the inundation of their traditional lands by enormous reservoirs.

Part of the problem for indigenous peoples was the historic jurisdiction of the federal government. In a country defined as a bilingual society of French and English founding nations, the federal system ensured that—because they were not French—Aboriginal peoples in Quebec received public education in English. They could speak their own languages, and English as a second language, but very few indigenous peoples of Quebec could speak French. In a political climate of separatism, nothing is more sensitive than the survival of a distinct Québécois culture. Language is a political powder keg. Moreover, the province's First Nations communities were seen as sympathetic to federal jurisdiction within Quebec.

The height of the Quebec–First Nations conflicts occurred in the summer of 1990 in a Quebec town called Oka. Sûreté du Quebec forces had attempted to storm a Mohawk barricade erected to preserve the old-growth pine forest near their reserve. The threat was not from logging in this case, but from a golf course. One police officer died in the crossfire. The press reported that the Mohawk were viewed locally as "Anglos with feathers."

It was, to put it mildly, not an auspicious time for the Algonquin to negotiate with the provincial government. But on August 22, 1991, they accomplished something truly remarkable—an unprecedented agreement between the provincial and federal governments and the Algonquin of Barrière Lake. The Trilateral Agreement called for sustainable development of the lands in the traditional territories of the Algonquin. All told, it covered more than 10,000 square kilometres. The goal of the plan was to develop an integrated resource management plan, reconciling traditional indigenous concerns for wildlife, the collection of medicinal plants, respect for spiritual values and the preservation of the forest itself.[29]

As an immediate measure, the Algonquin were to identify "sensitive zones," areas likely to receive special treatment once the plan was completed; these zones would be given interim protection. The identification of sensitive zones was a community effort, with elders assisting younger community members in locating spiritual sites, hunters helping to delineate crucial moose habitat, and contracted ecologists and foresters helping to defend the highest principles for ecologically sustainable practice in the short term.

However, this remarkably peaceful solution to years of blockades was jeopardized on a nearly daily basis. The key difficulty was that neither the logging contractor nor the largest wood purchaser in the area, Domtar, was a party to the agreement. Although the entire Quebec government was bound by the document, it had been negotiated and signed by the Indian Affairs Minister only. The Forest Minister and the ground-level forest service bureaucracy were largely hostile to the effort, allowing the new rules to be broken time after time. In other words, one branch of government would guarantee that critical, sensitive habitat was under interim protection, and within days, the area would be logged. Provincial forest service employees would shrug their shoulders and admit that the contractor still had valid cutting rights for the whole area.[30] The Algonquin began posting community members as observers around all sensitive zones. They rushed to scene after scene of logging, but there was little they could do but lodge complaints and issue reports.

Meanwhile, the five-year process of developing the integrated resource management plan for 10,000 square kilometres was underway. The Algonquin set about mapping the entire territory, drawing on traditional knowledge and providing detailed overlays of the biological diversity and historical uses of the area, in far greater depth than any university team could have hoped to achieve. The Algonquin did not shun technology; they had the entire database entered into a GIS (Geographic Information System) that community members were being trained to use. The mapping exercise led to many fascinating exchanges between the forest service staff, who had done many maps and logging plans, and the Algonquin, whose maps conveyed a completely different picture of the landscape. In one memorable exchange, the forest service representative on a planning committee was heard to say, "But this map can't be right. Why would anyone put a graveyard next to a highway?"

Forest industry forces gained the upper hand in Barrière Lake when the whole community was destabilized through internal factional disputes. In January 1996, the federal Minister of Indian Affairs and Northern Development, the Honourable Ron Irwin, stepped in and appointed an interim band council. The next few months saw the closing of the school, suspension of basic services to the community and the derailment of the Trilateral Agreement. Chief Matchewan and his supporters smelled a rat. It seemed that legal advice proffered to the anti-Matchewan faction had come from a Winnipeg lawyer who, coincidentally, also represented Domtar.

In early 1997, after nearly a year of rule by the interim council, the Algonquin defenders of the forest returned to the blockades, concerned that clear-cut logging was compromising the integrity of the future resource management plan.[31] In the spring of 1997, the Minister of Indian Affairs relented and appointed another interim band council that was satisfactory to the majority of the community. The Trilateral Agreement remains in place, and a draft Resource Management Plan is now ready for approval.

Cree protests and the Peace of the Braves

As prime forest land in southern Quebec was degraded, logging pressure was increasing in the remote areas to the north. In the 1990s, massive clear-cutting was taking place on traditional Cree lands, so far distant from population centres that they are invisible to the Quebec public and the media. Having successfully dealt a knockout punch to the planned massive Great Whale hydroelectric project on Hudson Bay, the Grand Chief of the James Bay Cree, Matthew Coon Come, set his sights on the forest industry.

The rate of logging increased substantially in the area the Cree call Eeyou Astchee ("Our Land"). In 1974, the total amount of forested land in Cree traditional territory was 24,000 square kilometres. By 1994, the CAAFs covered an area more than twice as large—52,000 square kilometres. These forest management agreements, each for a renewable period of twenty-five years, were held by seven non-Native companies, supplying twenty-eight different mills. The Cree identified significant differences between the CAAFs on their territory and others in the rest of Quebec. The average CAAF in the rest of Quebec is 1,600 square kilometres, while the average area in Eeyou Astchee was more than twice that, at 3,471 square kilometres. One lease alone, to Barrette-Chapais, covers an area of 17,000 square kilometres, or an area 4,000 square kilometres larger than the state of Connecticut. The wood from that lease feeds the largest sawmill in Quebec, also owned by Barrette-Chapais. Although the mill was in the heart of Cree territory, not one of the 400 to 450 people employed there was Cree.

The Cree estimated that since 1975 over 5,000 square kilometres of their lands have been clear-cut. Huge volumes of primarily softwood for sawmills and pulp mills are logged annually. In 1995, more than 5 million cubic metres of wood were taken from Cree lands.[32]

The Cree connected the increased rate of cutting and road-building with the drastic decline in moose throughout their lands. Moose form an important part of the Cree diet, and hunting moose is an integral part of their culture. In 1985, the moose population was estimated at 1,200. After increased logging and road construction in this most affected area, there are now fewer than 400 animals. The Cree identified unsustainable levels of hunting and poaching as the main culprit, made possible with the easy access provided by the hundreds of kilometres of logging roads built in the 1990s. Clearcuts destroyed habitat for fur-bearing mammals. Logging itself led to loss of stream quality. Downed trees across streams made canoe travel impossible.

The Cree took their case to the world, just as they did to halt the devastation of their lands by flooding for hydroelectric power. They toured Europe and asked for market pressure to force Quebec's forestry companies into more ecologically appropriate methods of logging. In a book prepared to enlist public support, Crees and Trees, they make the following plea:

> Preserving the integrity of the boreal forest environment is
> imperative not only for the economic needs of our people, but
> also for the survival of our culture. It is not just a question of
> too many trees being cut by the forest industry but rather an
> issue of cultural survival and fundamental human rights. That
> is why the destructive practices of the forest products industry
> and the policies of Quebec's government must change.[33]

The Cree effort to raise public awareness about the threat to Quebec's boreal forest was given a major boost in 1999. One of Quebec's most popular singers, Richard Desjardins, released a damning documentary on the clear-cutting of the boreal.[34] L'erreur boréale was a sensation within Quebec on the scale that Michael Moore's Fahrenheit 911 was in the United States. For the first time in Quebec, clear-cutting was becoming a hot political issue, as it had been in British Columbia for more than a decade. The documentary brought the clear-cutting of Quebec's boreal forest, with shocking footage of the denuded landscape, into living rooms across the province. It also uncovered the political coziness between industry and government regulators, denouncing the "intellectual prostitution" of forest engineers and the appointment of the former Assistant Deputy Minister of Forests to the head of the Forest Industry Association. Beyond the ecological issues, the filmmakers also took on the complicated software program that sets the AAC, denouncing the computer-modelled approach to overcutting in the short-term.

Following the airing of *L'erreur boréale*, a poll conducted for *Le Devoir* revealed that three-quarters of Quebecers believed that "the big forestry companies are pillaging forests in northern Quebec."[35] The province, in the midst of its ten-year review of the 1986 Forest Act, had to respond to the concerns of its urban population, outraged by the devastating images of *L'erreur boréale*, as well as the protests of First Nations.

In 2002, Quebec reached a stunning agreement with the Cree— stunning in its scope and price tag. The agreement, called the "Peace of the Braves," spans fifty years, with a total of $3.5 billion in revenue to be transferred to the Cree, as well as a share in the benefits from the natural resources in their territories. In exchange, the Cree agreed not to block planned expansions of the province's hydroelectric facilities. While the province committed to leave the Great Whale River alone, the Rupert and Eastmain Rivers would be dammed. Many individual Cree activists who had opposed the James Bay and Great Whale developments were outraged by this concession, and others in Quebec remain mobilized to oppose the dams. The ecological impact on the forests, however, was far more positive.

The new forestry regime over Cree lands requires any logging to accommodate the Cree traditional activities of hunting, trapping and fishing. As well, sites of particular significance to the Cree will be removed from harvest plans. Wildlife conservation measures will be increased. Buffer zones around rivers more than 5 metres wide are to be increased to 200 metres—a ten-fold increase. This will necessitate a reduced rate of cut of as much as 2 million cubic metres—approximately one-quarter of the AAC for the area—as well as a re-allocation of 350,000 cubic metres to the Cree through their own forest management agreement. A Cree-Quebec Forestry Board has been created to ensure Cree participation in forest management decisions.

The agreement has led to a sea change in Quebec relations with First Nations. Former Grand Chief Ted Moses, a leader in opposition to the Bourassa government and to the first James Bay projects, was reported to have endorsed the separatist Parti Québécois in the

2003 provincial election. In any event, the victorious Liberal Premier, Jean Charest, pledged to honour the Peace of the Braves.[36]

At this writing, the Quebec government is in negotiations with the Innu, the Atikamekw, and the Abitibi-Temiscamingue Algonquins. Twelve First Nations communities and corporations have allocated portions of the provincial annual allowable cut, totalling 651,000 cubic metres, through various forest management agreements.[37]

A number of these operations came about through partnerships between corporate forestry giants, Aboriginal communities and government. In 1999, a sawmill opened in the Atikamekw community of Obedjiwan, 350 kilometres northwest of La Tuque. It was the result of co-operation between the community, Abitibi-Consolidated and both the federal and provincial governments. The mill is meeting needs for local employment with sixty-five new jobs, all but ten of which are held by Aboriginals, plus sixty more seasonal jobs in silviculture, all held by members of the Atikamekw community. A similar partnership between the Waswanipi Mishtuk Corporation and Domtar led to the opening of the Nabakatuk sawmill in June 1997. The sawmill has transformed life in the region, with $2 million worth of salaries injected into the remote region.

More mills and fewer trees has never been an ecological solution, but creative First Nations partnerships with the private sector and government can be both a boon to desperate communities and a way of enforcing sustainable cut levels. So long as Aboriginal people value traditional non-timber aspects of their forest land, there will be a counterweight to valuing forests only for their fibre. In the last decade, First Nation agreements with the province have profoundly improved the prospects for Quebec's boreal forest.

Ecological forest reform

While First Nations made progress with the provincial government, so too did conservationists. In 1998, when this book was first published, Quebec had the worst record in Canada for protected areas. Only 3.7 per cent of Quebec's land base had any protected status, and the amount that represents forested ecosystems was far lower.[38] Almost half of the areas protected were in the tundra. Even the 3.7-per-cent figure exaggerated the amount of protected land; as under World Conservation Union classifications, only 1 per cent would have been considered adequately protected.

In 2003, the Parti Québécois government of Bernard Landry, at long last, created new protected areas. Of particular significance was the expanded protection of boreal forest. Nearly 19,000 square kilometres of boreal forest was added to the protected areas network. Most of this protection occurred along the north shore, with eleven separate protected areas, ranging in size from 32 square kilometres (Collines de Brador) to over 4,000 square kilometres (Vallée de la Rivière Natashquan).[39] All told, the new protected areas total 3 per cent of Quebec's land base, using international protected areas criteria, while Quebec claims it has reached 5.3 per cent in protected status.[40] The Quebec government has adopted a goal of 8 per cent and is continuing to work toward protecting new areas from development. But, as in other provinces, the allocation of virtually all of the forested land base south of the 52nd parallel to logging is a large obstacle to new protected areas. Any new park means less wood for the mills, as there are virtually no unallocated areas. This creates local pressure in forestry-dependent communities to oppose new parks.

Many of Quebec's forested ecoregions have lost diversity through selection logging of valuable species going back to the 1700s, and more recently through species transitions following clear-cuts. Quebec was one of the first Canadian provinces with legislation to protect endangered species. Twelve species have been listed as endangered, and sixty-seven others are under consideration for listing, but most of these are not forest-dwelling species.[41] The pressures of logging and settlement have led to population declines in the eastern cougar, while the woodland caribou are included on both the federal and provincial lists.[42]

As the wood-supply problem worsens in southern Quebec, logging roads are being pushed farther into the north, opening up, and ending, the wilderness south of the 52nd parallel. The pressures on wildlife populations needing a large range, such as the caribou and wolverine, will increase owing to wilderness fragmentation created by logging roads. The roads also mean that hunters will now have access to areas where moose and caribou previously lived undisturbed.

Public pressure has made a difference, however, as the Quebec government continues to revise its 1986 legislation. In 2001, it adopted new requirements that increased public participation in forest decisions, increased controls and fines, with increased monitoring of the environmental performance of the industry. The revised rules also created a new approach to potential conservation. Forests of high significance for biodiversity can be classified as "exceptional forest ecosystems (EFE)." The three categories of exceptional forest ecosystems are rare forests, old forests and wildlife refuges. Once an EFE is identified, it is submitted to public consultation. EFEs granted full status are not only removed from the total harvestable area, they are also excluded from mining development.

Quebec's response to environmentalists' criticism of its logging practices has—in some ways—been progressive. Quebec is the only province that has banned the use of chemical herbicides and insecticides. In the early 1980s, Quebec was one of the first provinces to ban the use of the phenoxy herbicide 2,4,5-T at a time when the Canadian government still registered it for use. While the New Brunswick and Nova Scotia forests were slated for spraying with the same chemicals used in Agent Orange, Quebec's position was a sharp contrast.[43] Quebec has also, in response to public opposition to toxic chemical spraying against budworm, instituted a "no chemical insecticides" approach. While budworm spraying continued, Quebec approved only the biological insecticide Bt. Although there are also problems with Bt use, Quebec is nevertheless progressive in having outlawed such toxic chemicals as fenitrothion (when it was still federally registered), carbaryl and matacil.

The Quebec Forest Protection Strategy guards vulnerable forest lands, threatened ecosystems such as wetlands and forests on thin soils or steep slopes. Since 1996, the Quebec government has introduced numerous new forest policies that they claim spell the end of clear-cutting in the province.

The government claimed that by requiring "cutting with soil and regeneration protection," clear-cutting had become a thing of the past. The Algonquin of Barrière Lake quickly became familiar with the various euphemistic phrases used by the forest companies: clear-cutting and its new and improved successors "cutting with regeneration and soil protection," "regeneration cut" and "improved cutting." For the most part, these methods, particularly cutting with regeneration and soil protection and regeneration cut, are nothing more than repackaged clear-cuts. Cutting with regeneration and soil protection, for instance, still involves the complete clearing of all trees from sites as large as 150 hectares. The only innovation to make the practice "careful" is that the logging equipment is required to reuse the same route leaving as it used coming in to log an area, thus reducing some of the impact on the soil and on existing regeneration. The ecological differences are minimal. The Cree described the new logging as "new names, old policies." In their territory they found that, "in reality, these reduced clear-cuts are made adjacent to one another with thin tree buffers so that over time these clear-cuts add up to massive deforestation."[44]

At the World Forestry Congress in Quebec City in the fall of 2003, Minister of Forests Pierre Corbeil trumpeted his claim that clear-cutting had not been practised in Quebec for over three years. In a press release, Greenpeace Canada campaigner Richard Brooks proved the minister wrong. The National Forestry Database Program reported that 260,000 hectares was clear-cut annually in Quebec. "All the figures given came from public government sources," said Brooks. "Clearly, the government is using fancy language to deceive the citizens of Quebec and Canada. They understand how negative an image clear-cutting has."[45]

The government's 2003 commitment to adopt the "mosaic cut" for 60 per cent of its harvest areas has been met with mixed reviews. The cuts are more aesthetically pleasing, satisfying demands from recreational users of the forest. Although supported by some conservationists, since they require the retention of at least 30 per cent of the forest within each cutblock and place upper limits on the size of cuts, mosaic cuts are criticized by others. They increase fragmentation, ensure only temporary retention of a percentage of forest and can end up covering a large area.

Research in Quebec's southern boreal forest confirms that "one size does not fit all." Depending on understory conditions, age classes and many other factors, silviculture treatments should be adjusted. "Nature itself behaves with considerable variation and should inspire different silvicultural interventions," noted researchers Yves Bergeron and Brian Harvey.[46]

Perhaps the most significant of Quebec's reforms is the 2001 law protecting the boreal forest north of the 52nd parallel. No timber extraction will be allowed in the currently unallocated northern boreal. As noted earlier, these forests may be subject to losses from non-timber activities, such as hydro and mining. But with this 2001 law, Quebec placed itself firmly in the forefront of protection of Canada's boreal forests.

Quebec's wood supply

Quebec's wood supply is still arguably huge, with the province allowing logging of less than 1 per cent of available wood supply each year. With a published AAC of 58 million cubic metres and an annual harvest level of 39.6 million cubic metres, comparisons with Newfoundland or New Brunswick could lead to the conclusion that, while Quebec forest practice is damaging environmentally, the industry itself is not at risk of supply shortfalls.[47]

However, of Quebec's productive forest lands, it is estimated that over 180,000 square kilometres are inaccessible. As pressure builds for new logging roads to open up remote areas, the individual tree size will decline. Trees growing farther north just naturally grow smaller. In fact, many of the new mill developments on Cree territory are specifically designed to handle the small trees found in the northern fringes of the commercial boreal forest. The industry will be paying more to truck smaller trees from greater distances. The volume on the ground is likely to be less than the estimates in provincial inventories, and, due to climatic conditions, regeneration will be more difficult.

As is the case across Canada, the wood supply is tight; there is no margin for error. Everything depends on the accuracy of forest inventories, the efficacy of silviculture and the legitimacy of the AAC calculation. In 2002, all of these factors were questioned by a critic the government could not ignore—its own provincial Auditor General. In his annual report to the provincial legislature, the Auditor General took aim at provincial forest management, finding "shortcomings in the oversight work done by the Ministry concerning forest management activities."[48] Specifically, the Auditor General found "flaws in the information from the ten-year inventory.... As a result, the Ministry is not able to determine if the allowable annual cut calculations are over-evaluated and consequently, if there is an overcut of timber in public forests."[49]

On October 23, 2003, Minister Corbeil announced a public inquiry to review forest management in the province. The eight-person commission was specifically asked to review the AAC methodology and forest management practices and develop an overall vision for sustainable development in Quebec's forests. Once again, industry pushed for more intensive forest management as a means of maintaining current mill supply. As in New Brunswick, public response was strong. Many criticized the short mandate with only one year to examine all forest issues. Action Boréale, a Quebec citizens' group, criticized the government's decision to withhold the results of its AAC calculation until 2006.

Released in December 2004, the results of the Commission were a mixed bag of progressive elements within business-as-usual recommendations. Echoing the National Forest Strategy, the Commission recommended that ecosystem-based management be applied within the province's forests, but it did not outline what this management system would entail on the ground. Specific recommendations to restore degraded hardwood forests, reduce the harvest volume for commercial fir, spruce, jack pine and larch by 10 per cent, and move toward an AAC calculation for each forest management unit without the yield effect of the silvicultural strategy are all positive steps. The Commission also identified serious deficiencies in the methods currently used to assess the state of forests and to evaluate the maximum sustainable yield in a particular area, recommending that corrective action be taken. The goal of the protection of 8 per cent by 2006 was reinforced, with a recommendation for 12 per cent protection in the boreal zone by 2010.[50]

Still, some of the recommendations cast a cloud over the future of Quebec's remaining intact forests. The Commission recommended building more roads to make it possible to harvest a higher number of presently inaccessible stands in the northern boreal forest. The road-building is especially alarming as the boreal population of Quebec's woodland caribou is in decline primarily due to habitat fragmentation. The Commission responded to industry's demands for more intensive forest management, recommending increasing wood production to new levels, including intensive silvicultural projects, "where appropriate."[51]

The urban forest

One encouraging sign that could lead to reduced pressures on the forests is the move to produce recycled paper. Driven by consumer demands primarily from U.S. customers, a number of Quebec mills are installing de-inking facilities in order to process newspapers into paper. Some U.S. states have legislated a required recycled content. For instance, 40 per cent of paper used in New York must be recycled.[52] Abitibi-Consolidated installed a $20-million de-inking facility at its Alma plant, while Kruger's board mill in Montreal produces 100 per cent recycled-content linerboard as well as other products.

Unlike mills in more remote parts of Canada, the Quebec mills are sufficiently close to the urban forests of New York to make processing recycled paper an immediately viable proposition. Having clear-cut Quebec to run off the *New York Times*, Quebec mills may be able to turn the tables by harvesting the mountains of used newspapers from New York. In fact, Kruger has established a facility in Albany, New York, as a "harvesting" operation for the curbside collections in upper New York state, eventually planning to purchase used newsprint from as far as Boston and Baltimore. Abitibi-Consolidated seems to be pursuing a different strategy, locating its new recycled-content mills in the United States. Relatively speaking, they have put a far larger investment into their recycled-content mills south of the border than they have in Quebec.

Recycled paper *should* reduce logging pressure, but there is as yet no indication that it is doing so. The area and volume logged continue to increase. As in other provinces, Quebec's AAC is still set on the basis of projected future growth from silviculture rather than a sustainable yield based on natural growth rates. If the recommendations of the Coulombe commission are fully implemented, Quebec may end its reliance on the perverse annual cut effect.

Between 1986 and 1995, when the subsidies were in place, Quebec replanted 2.1 billion trees on public and private lands. Between 1992 and 1996, subsidies for private lands alone came to $136 million.[53] However, in 1990, the government announced its preference for natural regeneration. In 2004, it is estimated that 80 per cent of cut-over areas regenerate naturally. The federal subsidies for replanting have ended. The companies still receive a 40-per-cent rebate on stumpage fees for silviculture performed on harvested lands; in 1994–1995, this amount came to $58.4 million. But, as the Auditor General noted, the province does not adequately ensure that silviculture treatments, on which it relies for AAC calculations, actually take place.

While natural regeneration is clearly preferable to plantations, with attendant herbicide use and regeneration problems, the success rate of natural regeneration is improved when logging methods do not ravage the site, as clear-cutting does. Natural regeneration should be allowed to take place, as the term implies, *naturally*. It is completely consistent with Quebec's herbicide ban to get out of planting and to allow for the forest to recover from logging in the natural successional fashion of a pre-industrial forest. But the AAC calculations should then follow suit and remove the voodoo projections of impossible gains from intensive silviculture.

Quebec's wood supply information remains harder to access than that of other provinces. Political posturing has led to Quebec's absence from many of the national forest review processes. For example, Quebec contributed no data to the national timber-supply survey conducted by the federal forest service.[54]

Quebec's evolving forest vision

In the last decade, tremendous change has occurred in Quebec's forest management. First Nations now have a genuine role to play. The Quebec public no longer assumes that the vast northland is pristine. And they are demanding an end to clear-cutting. Greater protection of ecosystems has taken place, more than doubling the land base in parks.

Costs to the forest industry have increased. While stumpage fees of $12 per cubic metre are hardly astronomical, they represent a significant increase in what had been a virtual give-away.

Non-timber values are increasingly important. With restrictions on exports during the softwood lumber quota system, forest industries in Quebec became more adept at greater secondary processing of forest products. More can be done with less. Non-timber products such as Christmas trees and maple syrup had always been valued, but now even medicinal plants from the forest are being valued.

The next decade is critical. The loss of old-growth forest in the Great Lakes–St. Lawrence forest and the southern boreal must be further reduced with logging practices designed to ensure survival of critical habitat for species, the way of life of indigenous peoples and the protection of jobs in remote communities. It may seem daunting, but it must be done.

Quebec

Forest and other wooded land in million hectares	84.6
Stocked harvested Crown land in hectares	5.9 million
Area logged in hectares (2002)	309,195
Volume logged in million cubic metres (2002)	39.6
Annual allowable cut in million cubic metres (2001)	55.9

Source: Natural Resources Canada, Canadian Forest Service, *The State of Canada's Forests 2003–2004* (Ottawa, 2004). These are federal government summaries, based on provincial government data. The figures are not necessarily accurate

Quebec Corporate Players

Abitibi-Consolidated
Alliance Uniforêt
Avenor
Bowater
Canadian Pacific Forest Products
Cartons St. Laurent
Cascades
Commonwealth Plywood
Daishowa
Domtar
Kruger
Louisiana Pacific
Noranda-Maclaren
Tembec

Ontario is Canada's most populous province, with 90 per cent of its 11 million residents in communities that hug the southern border in and around the Great Lakes. Torontonians, stuck in bumper-to-bumper traffic on Highway 401, harbour the comfortable thought that once outside the stretches of Metro, there is a vast expanse of wilderness all the way to Hudson Bay. But as someone's teddy bear once said, "If you go down to the woods today, you're in for a big surprise."[1]

Ontario is huge—110 million hectares of land and water. It encompasses four distinct forest ecoregions, covering 58 million hectares of the province:[2] the poorly drained area bordering Hudson and James Bays, described by provincial forest officials as the Hudson Bay Lowlands; the boreal; the Great Lakes–St. Lawrence forest shared with Quebec; and the most threatened of all Canada's forests, the southern deciduous or Carolinian forest.

The far northern part of the boreal forest and the Hudson Bay Lowlands have been too remote and the forests too uneconomical to have been the object of commercial logging, but every other forest ecosystem has been significantly altered by logging. In recent years, even those vast forests north of the 51st parallel, currently unlogged and without roads, are under threat. Both the federal and Ontario governments are committed to industrial expansion in the northern boreal.[3]

The Carolinian forest ecoregion has been reduced to a tiny fragment of its original range. This southernmost of Canada's forest ecoregions is rich in biological diversity, sheltering 2,200 different herbs, 70 tree species, over 400 different types of bird, and other mammals, reptiles and amphibians unique in Canada.[4] But the Carolinian forest has been reduced to less than 10 per cent of its pre-settlement range. Land clearing for agriculture and settlement accounts for most of the deforestation. In some municipalities, forest cover is only 3 per cent of the land base.[5] As a result, over 40 per cent of Canada's rare, threatened and endangered species are found in this small area.[6]

The other two major ecoregions are the sites of Ontario's booming forest industry. Wood from the more productive southern boreal and the Great Lakes–St. Lawrence forest currently supply more than one hundred pulp mills, sawmills and other forest product operations. Historically, the areas that have been logged—some having a two-hundred-year history of commercial exploitation—are within these regions. The result has been a steady decline in high-value species and a transition to new, early successional, lower-quality trees.

Logging the Great Lakes–St. Lawrence forest

As European settlers established themselves, the pattern of logging experienced in the Atlantic provinces repeated itself in Ontario. The forest was immense, lush and overwhelming. As one early settler wrote, the forest of Kent County, Ontario, was "so thick with overhanging foliage that it not only shut out the sunshine, but almost the daylight."[7]

Logging spread west, to the Great Lakes–St. Lawrence ecosystem of Ontario and Quebec, where vast areas of forest were cut to make way for human settlement and agriculture. Settlers had the first choice of high-value timber. Prior to European settlement, the forest covered 90 per cent of the land base. In the early twenty-first century, it has been reduced to 30 per cent in Ontario, and logging and clearing have replaced fire as the major disturbance factor.[8]

The forests of this ecoregion boasted sixty different tree species. Dominant ones included red and white pine, red and white oak, eastern white cedar, hemlock, black spruce, sugar maple, basswood, aspen and white and yellow birch. The original forest was 30 to 40 per cent old-growth pine.[9] So dominant was the white pine in Ontario's history that it was chosen in 1984 as the provincial tree.

The same pressures to supply the British Navy that launched the forest industry in the Maritimes led to the logging of the southern Ontario and Quebec Great Lakes–St. Lawrence forest as well. Huge pine trees from the Ottawa Valley disappeared onto the high seas. In Barrie, Ontario, logged red pine was recorded at 60 metres in height and 8 metres around.[10] Currently, between as little as 3 and 9 per cent of the Great Lakes–St. Lawrence forest is red or white pine, and much less than that is old growth.[11] Even so, the tiny fragments of remaining old-growth pine in Ontario represent 95 per cent of that ecosystem for Canada and 60 per cent of what remains worldwide.[12]

By 1835, most of the watershed of the lower Ottawa Valley had been denuded of its valuable pine, and the timber barons moved on to its upper reaches. Once the entire 12 million hectares of the Ottawa Valley had been scoured, substantial timber interests moved westward, felling the tallest, straightest and most valuable trees. Through the watersheds of the Trent, Lake Simcoe, the Kawarthas and the Muskokas, logging virtually eradicated the pine. Timber barons such as E.B. Eddy, J.R. Booth and F.H. Bronson employed thousands of people, built their own railways and began the steady process of industrial control over public forests. The province began to grant "timber limits" to the companies, guaranteeing access in exchange for a token licence fee and duty on the wood actually cut.

In the late nineteenth century, an industry sprang up in hemlock bark, which was used in leather tanning; ultimately, overcutting succeeded in reducing hemlock to a regionally rare species. In 1868, a government inquiry was launched to address the threat. The commission was doubly concerned when it discovered that much of the hemlock bark was being exported to U.S. tanneries, thus threatening not only Canada's hemlock, but Canada's tannery jobs as well. The inquiry concluded that an export duty should be placed on hemlock bark, "with a view to checking the wholesale destruction of our forests now going on."[13] In the end, however, no export duty was levied, and the hemlock-bark trade continued unabated.

By mid-century, the prime use of forests had shifted to sawmills and lumber. The forest had been fundamentally altered. White and red pines were disappearing, and sawmills had sprung up to use the shorter timbers. But no one seemed to notice. The Ottawa Valley was described in the 1850s as having "timber enough here to supply the world for thousands of years."[14] The forest appeared unending, its riches there for the taking.

Canada's first Prime Minister, Sir John A. Macdonald, was one of the first to express concern over the disappearing forests. It was not some government commission that alerted him to a threat. It was the view from his window. Both his home and his office were perched on the banks of the Ottawa River, which in those days was the liquid highway that carried tons of logs past his window. In 1871, he wrote to a friend: "The sight of immense masses of timber passing my windows every morning constantly suggests to my mind the absolute necessity there is for looking into the future of this great trade."

The forests of the Ottawa Valley were literally disappearing before his eyes. "We are recklessly destroying the timber of Canada, and there is scarcely a possibility of replacing it. The quantity of timber reaching Quebec is annually decreasing, and the fires in the woods are periodically destroying many millions of money." Unlike the observer who thought the Ottawa Valley alone had enough timber for thousands of years, Sir John A. was worried. "What is to become of the Ottawa region generally, after the timber is cut away, one cannot foresee."[15]

Dr. Bernard Fernow, the first dean of forestry at the University of Toronto, was also distressed by the rapacious pace of logging in Ontario. Between 1867 and 1913, he estimated, Ontario had logged an astronomical 25 billion board feet of white pine. "As yet," he wrote, "the forests are viewed solely as a source of current revenue, not as capital, and the rights of people and of posterity are sacrificed."[16]

The threat to biodiversity

The liquidation of old-growth pine has had significant impacts on the Great Lakes–St. Lawrence ecoregion of Ontario and Quebec. Only 1 per cent remains of the white pine forests that once blanketed almost half the region. And of that 1 per cent, only 37 per cent is within protected areas.[17] Not only old growth, but even young trees are rare; regardless of age, pine is a disappearing species in Ontario's forests, and the forest itself is degraded through the removal of such a key species.

Like a domino effect, that degradation moves through the ecosystem. Without old-growth pine, wildlife dependent upon it for habitat are driven out, and other plant and animal species dependent on that wildlife vanish with them. Of course, this forest is not a moonscape. Something will grow back to replace the species that logging has depleted, and as these early successional species move in, their compatible fauna move with them. The entire forest composition is altered. And while one makes no subjective value judgements—that one type of fern, for instance, is "better" than another—there is no question that global biodiversity is diminished when a particular ecosystem, rare or unique in the world, is vastly reduced or disappears.

Old-growth white pine is necessary to many of the inhabitants of the forest. Female black bears prefer leaving their cubs near old white pine, so the cubs can more easily escape predators by climbing the ridged bark of the pine.[18] Black bears will even use dead trees for hibernation. The pileated woodpecker prefers old-growth pine, making large cavities in its search for food. The cavity left behind may then be used for nesting by a saw-whet owl, or, if near a wetland, by a wood duck.[19]

Old-growth pine forests are the preferred habitat for the lynx, pine marten, three-toed woodpecker and white-winged cross-bill. Both ospreys and bald eagles prefer old-growth pine for their treetop nests. Even when old white pines comprise less than 1 per cent of the forest's larger trees, 77 per cent of the osprey nests and 80 per cent of the bald eagle nests were found in these few old pine trees.[20]

In addition to loss of biodiversity in both the landscape and species, the genetic diversity of the trees themselves is reduced. Old-growth pine forests lose between 25 and 80 per cent of their genetic variability, even after partial logging.[21] In contrast to clear-cutting, a forest fire would leave behind the adult, fire-resistant trees, allowing them to reproduce before succumbing to old age, thus maintaining natural genetic variability. Recent forest policy for white pine logging is attempting to better mimic fire by requiring "thinning from below," leaving mature trees to contribute to regeneration of the forest.[22] The government has taken some steps by shifting to selection logging and shelterwood techniques in the Great Lakes–St. Lawrence region. However, restoring the white pine of southern Ontario to its original grandeur would take centuries.

The boreal forest

The great swath of northern forest, known in Europe as the taiga and in North America as the boreal, covers an area twice the size of Great Britain. The boreal forest accounts for the vast majority of Ontario's forested lands—49.8 million hectares of the province.[23] The most productive boreal forest has been exploited at an ever-increasing rate. The original forest of this northern region was dominated by white and black spruce, jack pine, balsam fir, trembling aspen and white birch. It was not subject to heavy commercial logging until the 1940s, when the white pine of the more southerly ecoregions was gone; but then, logging began in earnest.

In recent years, the effects of widespread clear-cutting in the boreal are being felt. Although efforts to suppress natural fires have had an effect on the forest composition in certain areas, clear-cutting is having a more significant impact. Unlike the reversible disturbances caused by natural fires, removing all the trees through clear-cutting is leading to a sweeping species conversion, right across the landscape. A 1992 government-commissioned study, which examined more than one thousand clear-cuts in Ontario's boreal, found that softwoods were being replaced by lower-value small hardwoods. In fact, regenerating spruce had dropped by 77 per cent, while the proportion of lower-value hardwoods had increased by over 200 per cent.[24]

The "green rush" for Canada's northern boreal is on. The area being logged quadrupled between the 1940s and the 1980s. In the forties, 2,000 square kilometres a decade were logged. Forty years later, the figure was 8,000 square kilometres.[25] Not surprisingly, it is the most productive areas that have been logged first. The boreal has varying topographic features, some very poorly drained, others quite rocky and unproductive. The geological features of outwash plains and eskers support the best forests. Since 1940, virtually all of the forests on outwash plains and 70 per cent of those on eskers have been logged at least once.[26]

In 1994 the provincial NDP government gave permission for the cut to increase by up to 50 per cent. Eighteen months later, new mills had increased the total annual harvest by about 12 per cent. The increased harvest was largely in the birches and poplars that grew in abundance due to logging practices. These hardwoods were now of value for oriented strand board. In 1990, the actual amount of wood cut was 20 million cubic metres; by 2000 it was over 28 million.[27]

The steady erosion of old-growth habitat in the boreal has had an impact on biodiversity. The woodland caribou is threatened through loss of its preferred old-growth habitat, as it is right across Canada. Many other species of mammals and birds face an uncertain future with the steady loss of older pine and mixed-wood conifer forests in the boreal.

But north of the 51st parallel, the boreal forest in Ontario has yet to be allocated to the forest industry. Responding to the interest in economic opportunities expressed by Aboriginal communities living in the boreal, the provincial government has initiated a planning process called the Northern Boreal Initiative. Ontario has a tremendous opportunity to do the right thing in the northern boreal: ensure that logging supports local communities and that enough intact forest is maintained for wildlife such as the woodland caribou.

The battle for Temagami

The most high profile of logging disputes in Ontario history, complete with clashes on the logging roads and arrests, was the fight for the old-growth pine of Temagami, near North Bay. The Temagami forests have been the subject of a long campaign for wilderness protection and for the rights of the Teme-augama Anishnabai, the traditional owners and occupiers of the forest. The Teme-augama Anishnabai call their ancestral homeland N'Daki Menan. It is a vast territory of more than 10,000 square kilometres. N'Daki Menan stretches from just north of the northern reaches of Georgian Bay almost to the height of land dividing the Arctic and Great Lakes watershed. In 1877, Chief Tonene travelled south to Lake Nipissing to stop activities by the lumber companies in Teme-augama Anishnabai territory. His nation had never signed the 1850 Robinson-Huron treaty, Chief Tonene told the Indian agent, and the lumber companies had no right to log in N'Daki Menan in the absence of a signed treaty.

Nearly one hundred years later, in 1973, Chief Gary Potts filed "cautions" under the provincial land titles act to stop incursions by forest companies and the Ontario government. In 1978, the provincial government, having failed to have the cautions removed, brought an action in the Supreme Court of Canada against the Teme-augama Anishnabai. Eighteen years later, the highest court in the land ruled that the Teme-augama Anishnabai had an Aboriginal right, but that it had been lost through adherence to the Robinson-Huron treaty— which they had never signed. The court did find, however, that the government had a responsibility, a fiduciary duty, to the First Nation. Negotiations began in 1990 to resolve the outstanding obligations to the Teme-augama Anishnabai.

Since the turn of the twentieth century, the Temagami district has been a tourism destination for urban dwellers. It has been logged for at least as long. Tourism and logging do not always mix, and conflicts between the forestry companies and tourists have occurred for over a century. Lumbermen worried that careless canoeists would start fires, while tourists complained that the water was discoloured from use as a floating-log highway.[28]

The history of recent battles over Temagami began in the 1980s. Decades of logging had degraded the Temagami forests and reduced the old-growth pine. Nevertheless, in 1983 the government proposed significant increases in the cutting rates for the Temagami district.

The government, having what they called an "over-supply of over-mature" spruce and jack pine, required a substantial increase in logging to meet market demand as well as to maintain the desired age classes in the forest. As a result, the softwood harvest was to shoot up by nearly 200 per cent by the year 2000—from 93,000 cubic metres to 255,000. Logging of hardwood species, such as poplar, was to increase even more drastically—from 24,000 to 125,000 cubic metres.[29]

But even before the huge logging increases were announced, a forest management analysis by C.A. Benson, a Lakehead University forestry professor, had revealed that cutting rates were already too high. He argued that the Ministry of Natural Resources (MNR) calculations had been based on "a low intensity provincial ground survey."[30] As is the case across Canada, the methodology of forest mensuration, or the measurement of both standing and harvested timber, is notoriously unreliable. In this case, Benson alleged, it had led to unjustifiably high estimates of the volume per hectare. Moreover, the MNR had underestimated the age at which pine became "overmature," a mistake that, once again, had the impact of increasing the cut. It was, in the view of Temagami experts Bruce Hodgins and Jamie Benidickson, "overly optimistic and outdated in its views on natural regeneration without fire, and was determining the size of the allowable cut to suit the perceived needs of the local industry rather than considering the ecological reality."[31]

To provide access to the forest for increased logging, an extension of the Red Squirrel Lake Forest Access road was proposed, linking an existing road—the Liskeard Lumber Road—with another provincial highway. This would create a route right through the heart of the Temagami wilderness. Mills in one part of the district would gain access to timber in other areas, increasing logging pressure and threatening a newly created park, the Lady Evelyn-Smoothwater Wilderness, and the recreational paradise provided by a large system of interconnected canoe routes around and through the wilderness park. The corridor for the Red Squirrel Road was quickly approved—before any of the legal requirements for public review and planning were fulfilled.

Opposition to the extended road was intense, with environmental groups and cottager and recreational organizations supporting the Teme-augama Anishnabai in demanding that the permits be rescinded. As work crews began to extend Red Squirrel Road, they were met with blockades. Hundreds of people were arrested in blockades that ran continuously from September 17 to December 19, 1989, including Ontario's New Democratic Party leader Bob Rae. The protests ended only after the Ministry of Natural Resources informed Chief Potts that road construction was completed.

Once Mr. Rae became Ontario Premier, hopes were high for permanent protection of the site. Instead, the government began a plethora of consultation processes with some interim protection attached. A multi-stakeholder local committee, the Comprehensive Planning Council, was created, a memorandum of understanding was signed to restart treaty negotiations, and a legal caution was put in place. But no permanent protection was afforded the area, nor were the rights of the Teme-augama Anishnabai resolved. In June 1996, the Progressive Conservative government of Mike Harris, elected one year before, substantially altered a compromise package of protection measures recommended by the Comprehensive Planning Council. The court lifted the legal caution, and the government opened the land for logging and mineral staking.[32]

In 1997, based on the Comprehensive Planning Council compromise, the Harris government announced a series of land-use designations for the area. Some of Temagami would be protected in conservation reserves, or special management areas. Logging and other resource extraction activities could take place in the integrated management and development areas.[33]

While representing some level of progress in conserving Temagami's forests, the land-use designations were hardly adequate. Moreover, due to the ineffective nature of government enforcement of the designations, violations occurred frequently. One 2003 study by the Wildlands League found that at least 45 to 55 per cent of the access controls designed to protect remote areas had been violated at least once.[34]

Meanwhile, a dozen years after land claim negotiations began, with talks periodically breaking down and resuming, on December 18, 2002, the Ontario government and the Temagami First Nation announced a proposed settlement. If approved, a new Indian Reserve of 330 square kilometres will be created for settlement purposes, with protection of 77 per cent of the shoreline of Lake Temagami.[35] The remainder of the shoreline would be open to potential mining or cottage development. But it did not prevent the reopening of the Red Squirrel Road.

In 2002, the Red Squirrel Road was reopened. With a new conservation reserve adjacent to the Obabika River Waterway Park along the road, provincial guidelines would ordinarily not have allowed any new road building. Moreover, the conservation reserve had actually been approved and mapped in 1996, before the approval of the forest management plan containing the Red Squirrel Road extension. Complaints fell on deaf ears. The road had been approved in the old forest management plan before the reserve was officially regulated.[36]

The conflict continues between ecological values and the rare old-growth pines of Temagami and the area's role as a supplier to Ontario mills. In spring 2004, one of the stalwart groups in defence of Temagami, Earthroots, filed a request for a full environmental assessment of the Temagami forest management plan.

Meanwhile, a logging blockade by another First Nations community has been in place since December 2002. It is the action of the Grassy Narrows First Nation, the Ojibway community devastated by mercury contamination in the 1970s by the Reed Paper Company's mill at Dryden, Ontario. That horror story was documented by one of the earliest environmental books in Canada, *No Safe Place*, by the late Warner Troyer.[37] Now the Grassy Narrows community was back at the barricades, protesting the damage done by Abitibi-Consolidated clear-cuts on their traditional lands.[38]

As B.C. ecologist Bristol Foster once observed, "In wilderness campaigns, the victories are temporary. Only the defeats are permanent."[39]

Biodiversity and protected areas

Biodiversity is eroded through the fragmentation of wilderness. Obviously, human settlements in southern Ontario are significant disturbances, amounting to permanent deforestation. But throughout the remote forested hinterlands, areas as narrow as hydro corridors and roads can lead to loss of usable wilderness for wildlife. "A band of about 400 hundred metres on either side of the route is effectively lost," according to research into the impact of roads and other corridors on normal forest life.[40]

The presence and use of logging roads leads to permanent disturbance. Not only are the roads themselves damaging to the ecosystem, particularly if they are poorly built, but the access to previously remote areas increases hunting and can stress wildlife. A 1976 study in the forest management area around Temagami found that moose populations were significantly lower within 2 miles (3 kilometres)of logging roads, whether or not the forest had been logged,[41] while a study in 1997 found serious declines in moose populations over a larger area.[42] Although primarily due to loss of old-growth habitat through logging, the plight of the woodland caribou is also linked to roads. Not only has the woodland caribou's habitat been fragmented by roads, more and more are killed by hunters and vehicle collisions.[43]

As Ontario loses biodiversity through logging, it has set aside areas within provincial and national parks. As part of the nationwide Endangered Spaces campaign, led by World Wildlife Fund, conservation groups across Ontario pressed for expansion of the province's network of protected areas. Prior to 1999, just 6.3 million hectares of Ontario was protected within provincial parks and much of that did nothing for forest conservation. In fact, fully half of that protected area, the Polar Bear Provincial Park, had no timber with any commercial value. Existing parks were not fully protected. Algonquin Provincial Park, for example, was created to provide for ongoing logging. Although the park is one of the province's jewels, and serves as a key habitat for wolves—being the southernmost habitat for the eastern wolf in Ontario—only a quarter of the park is off-limits to logging.[44]

The Ontario government had signed on to the commitment of the Endangered Spaces program, so hopes were high when NDP Premier Bob Rae came to office. But instead of slowing the rate of clearcutting, the provincial government increased the annual allowable cut by up to 50 per cent. Discouraged environmentalists received some good news in the last hours of the Rae government when a major expansion of the Wabakimi Provincial Park in the northwestern part of the province was announced. This boreal wilderness is key habitat for the woodland caribou. As logging fragments and destroys their favoured old-growth habitat, the additional 900,000 hectares of protection in expanded parkland was essential. However, the full establishment and regulation of the park was left to the future government.

The breakthrough in protected areas came through a controversial initiative by the Conservative government of Mike Harris. In February 1997, the government launched a land-use planning process, called "Lands for Life." Its goals were to complete the protected areas system, increase certainty for industries such as forestry and mining, consider the needs of nature-based tourism and, announced subsequently, expand opportunities for hunting and fishing.

Many in the environmental community were dubious. Harris was unsympathetic to environmental goals. The 1996 "omnibus bill" overhauled many regulations, including the Public Lands Act and the Mining Act, reducing requirements for permits for road-building, quarries and other activities on public land. His government slashed funding to the Environment Department by 36 per cent, cut regulations protecting the air and water and reduced the budget to the province's Forest Department.[45] In April 1996, the government announced an astonishing 45 per cent staffing decrease in its Ministry of Natural Resources.[46] Forest regulation would be significantly curtailed; industry self-regulation was to increase. The Temagami District Office closed, just as logging pressure increased in one of Ontario's most significant forest wilderness areas.[47]

Coming from the Harris government, the term Lands for Life had an Orwellian flavour. Certainly, it appeared that the cards were stacked against conservation. The consultation process was based on three regional round tables that excluded voices from outside the resource-rich areas. Communities dependent on the forest industry were seen as least likely to support more habitat for endangered wildlife. A number of conservation groups organized a campaign under the banner Partnership for Public Lands.[48] Local organizations urged their members to let the government know they wanted to protect more Ontario wilderness. Polls showed interesting splits. While men in northern Ontario tended to favour industrialization over conservation, support for protected areas among northern Ontario women was on the same level as Toronto residents.[49]

Over the eighteen-month consultation period, pressure for protected areas grew. There were complaints that the consultation process and the consolidated report emerging from it did not meet the goals of protected areas. A record fourteen thousand letters demanding greater protection were submitted to Natural Resources Minister John Snobelen.

When public reaction became loud and angry, the government shifted gears and moved into closed-door negotiations with the forest industry and the Partnership for Public Lands groups. The result was the single largest expansion of protected areas in Ontario history. On March 29, 1999, the government announced the "Ontario Living

Legacy," 378 new protected areas, covering 2.4 million hectares of public land. Full protection remains slow: the areas received interim protection, gaining full protection only after detailed consultations. As of the summer of 2004, 67 per cent of the areas set out in the Living Legacy had been protected by regulation.[50]

Of particular concern are a number of the so-called Signature Sites, including the Kawartha Highlands, parts of the Great Lakes Heritage Coast, Killarney Provincial Park additions, Woodland Caribou and the Nagagamisis. The majority of these were still not regulated by early 2005.

One of the best examples of Great Lakes–St. Lawrence forest remaining in Ontario has been protected in the 50,000-hectare Algoma Headwaters Provincial Park. Old-growth pines are still found at higher elevation, while the valleys contain the lush hardwood growth that used to typify the region. Its old-growth forest provides habitat for moose, bald eagle, lynx, otter, bear, osprey and lake and brook trout. A series of smaller parks in the same watershed along the Goulais and Aubinadong rivers expand the conservation opportunities.

One of the groups that had worked the longest to secure protection for the Algoma headwaters, the CPAWS-Wildlands League, decided to "walk the talk" about conservation providing economic opportunities for remote communities. In 1998, it set up an office in the little town of Searchmont, located about 45 kilometres northeast of Sault Ste. Marie, with the goal of developing economic development projects linked to the protected wilderness.

Searchmont was a town in serious economic trouble. About a decade earlier, the sawmill had closed. As the workers and their families moved on to other mills, the church closed, the train station closed, and the school was to be next. The community was suspicious of the newcomers. Local coordinator Andrea Maenza recalls: "There was a strong impression, for instance, that all environmentalists spike trees."[51] She was referring to the extreme tactic of driving metal spikes into trees, creating a serious hazard to loggers.

Following initial distrust, the local people began to accept that the Wildlands League was committed to helping the community benefit from the protected areas nearby. Ecotourism and bed and breakfast businesses are opening up. More people are discovering the beauty of canoeing the Goulais, and while the effort to build the community's economic base is just beginning, there is new hope.

Although Ontario's land base is now 9.2 per cent protected, the network is not yet complete. Environmentalists were encouraged when the Ontario government of Conservative Premier Ernie Eves confirmed that the 387 new parks in the Living Legacy program were not to be the province's last parks. The "Room to Grow" framework, the product of tireless effort by Ontario's conservation organizations, is designed to address gaps in the current system—identifying conservation opportunities in central and northern Ontario. In addition, the province established the Northern Boreal Initiative, a community land-use planning process in the northern boreal region.[52]

The creation of parks, their protection with a new Parks Act, and the protection of species at risk remain commitments of the Liberal government of Dalton McGuinty. But McGuinty says he will go further and "end the [previous government's] policy of allowing unlimited size clear-cuts in Ontario. These massive clear-cuts cause irreparable damage to our forests."[53] A look at the province's forest management history will confirm that such a promise, though welcome, will be hard to keep.

Forest management and sustainability

Over the last two decades, as logging has increased, so too have the studies, commissions, environmental assessments and audits of the province's forests. Many people have joked that the province's pulp-and-paper industry had to boost production just to provide enough paper for all the studies.

The forests of Ontario cover 58 million hectares out of the province's 89-million hectare landbase. Of the forested land, 88 per cent is Crown land, managed by the province for the people of Ontario. Only 11 per cent is in private hands, and a mere 1 per cent is federal.[54] For forest management purposes, the Ontario MNR excludes the far northern boreal and the Hudson Bay Lowlands, and concentrates on the productive forest occupying the lower two-thirds of the province, excluding the southern Great Lakes–St. Lawrence and Carolinian forests. It is from within this area that the annual allowable cut (AAC) is derived and to which all forest management decisions relate.

The inventory of the productive forest lands of Ontario was developed in the 1940s, and the province conducts updates on a continual basis. The province's inventory is ongoing; that is, every area must be reassessed once every twenty years. Inventories on Forest Management Plans are updated once every five years, relying on regeneration, assessments of silviculture and any depletions of forest cover.[55] Aerial photographs with some ground sampling were used both to develop and update the information. Since 1986, some of the information has been entered into GIS. The inventory covered the lower two-thirds of the province. Of this area, 46 million hectares was classified as forest—both productive and unproductive —with 7 million hectares excluded as non-forest.[56] Eighty per cent of the logging in these areas takes place on Crown land.[57]

Almost from the beginning, the reliability of the inventory was attacked. No one questioned its general accuracy as a broad-brush estimate, but its use to generate volume figures and, based on those figures, to set logging rates, was widely considered unwise. In 1974, an internal study by the provincial government concluded that the inventory was significantly overestimating the amount of available wood. In fact, the inventory exaggerated volume by as much as one-third.[58]

A similar finding was made by an independent audit conducted ten years later by Dr. Gordon Baskerville, the former Deputy Minister of Forests for New Brunswick. He noted that the inventory had not been designed for the use to which it was now being put, but was meant simply to "provide an average representation of an area in the order of 200,000 hectares." It was not intended to predict volume within a single stand of 200,000 hectares.[59]

Relying on a shaky inventory, the wood-supply picture was further muddied through use of an "acceleration factor" in calculating the annual allowable cut. In order to equalize the age classes within the forest, the MNR compared the average age of the existing forest with that of an ideal "normalized" forest, as described by Bernard Fernow, the first dean of Forestry at the University of Toronto, back in 1907. (That "normal" forest is still much sought-after by foresters across Canada!) In such a forest, there is an equal area within each age class. Where forests have been heavily logged and poorly regenerated, there is a lack of young forest. The process of accelerating the AAC hastens the removal of older trees to make room for young age classes. That is, trees are cut down in order to allow trees to grow. That, at least, is the theory. Several independent government reports and audits have drawn attention to the fact that use of the acceleration factor, coupled with poor regeneration of forests after clear-cutting, will lead to shortages in the wood needed to maintain overinflated mill capacity.[60]

Ontario has its own language and set of acronyms for calculating each year's allowable cut. The forest planners use a concept called Maximum Allowable Depletion (MAD). The MAD concept is used "to identify the area available for depletion from all sources (harvest, fire, insects, disease, management reserves and others)."[61] Within that area, a planned harvest volume is derived, with the actual harvest usually somewhat lower. In recent years the MAD model has been supplemented with more sophisticated computer models: the Strategic Forest Management Model, to allow different strategies to accommodate different goals; and the Ontario Timber Demand Model, which uses an econometric model to project information through time for long-term forest management plans.[62] The federal government's national forest database uses MAD as equivalent to what other provinces call an AAC.

The cut in Ontario has been slowly, but steadily, increasing. As noted above, in 1994 the Rae government gave permission for the cut to increase by up to 50 per cent. Eighteen months later, the new mills had increased the total annual harvest rate by about 12 per cent. In 1990, the actual amount of forest logged was 20 million cubic metres; by 2000, it was 28.1 million cubic metres.

The area of Ontario Crown land under long-term licence to forest companies has increased dramatically. In Ontario, the first legislation to deal with the management of forests on Crown land was the 1849 Crown Timber Act. By 1929, with the Pulpwood Conservation Act, pulp companies were required to manage Crown forests within their lease on a sustained yield basis. Concern that the province's forests were not being sustainably managed led to significant changes in the 1947 Forest Management Act. Under the new regime, timber management plans were required. Forest companies gained rights to harvest and were given responsibility for forest regeneration. Any Crown lands not licenced to forest companies were the responsibility of provincial foresters.

Between 1952 and 1990, there were a dozen attempts to enforce sustainability of forest on Crown land through amendments to the Crown Timber Act. The most significant was in 1979, when for the first time the Ontario government was authorized to enter into long-term (twenty-year) lease arrangements with private companies for control of Crown land. The Forest Management Agreements (FMAs) transferred the majority of forest management responsibilities to the companies. In 1985, 58 per cent of Ontario's Crown land was licenced to the industry. By 1993, this figure had increased to 70 per cent.[63] In 1998, the Harris government created Sustainable Forest Licences, similar to FMAs, for all Crown land forests licenced to industry.[64] By 2004, out of forty-eight forest management units, all but four are controlled by forest companies either directly or through industry-controlled shareholder companies.[65] Two of these, Temagami and Cochrane-Moose River, are managed by the MNR directly, one through a Crown agency (Algonquin Forest Authority), and French Severn Forest through a community-based co-operative (Westwind Forest Stewardship).

In exchange for exclusive rights to log Crown forests, the companies were obliged to reforest (with seed and seedlings provided for free by the government), maintain logging roads (with subsidies of over $40,000 per kilometre for primary roads, $12,000 a kilometre for secondary roads and $471 per kilometre for annual maintenance) and pay a stumpage fee.[66] As in every province, the stumpage is far lower than the cost of wood south of the border, in the United States. Ontario's stumpage rates in 1990 were $7 per cubic metre for softwood; and between $1.20 and $5.75 per cubic metre for hardwood.[67]

Reforms to the stumpage system were initiated by the NDP government. It established a market-based system in which stumpage is calculated in three separate charges: a base stumpage, a residual stumpage and a forest renewal charge. The base rate for fiscal 1995–96 was set at $1.25 per cubic metre for all species. The forest renewal charge varies depending on the kind of tree harvested and the anticipated costs of regeneration.[68] Residual stumpage is tied to the average market price for a particular forest product. Whenever it appears that the industry has received a profit in excess of production costs and beyond a reasonable rate of return, the government takes a 29 per cent share of the increased profit as "residual stumpage."[69] When the profits reach the "windfall" level, the province's share drops to 10 per cent.

Out of this stumpage system, both the base stumpage and the residual charge are applied to the province's consolidated revenue fund; only the forest renewal component of stumpage collected is placed in a Forest Renewal Trust Fund.

The Rae stumpage system is still in place, although in 1998 the base rate increased to $2.85 per cubic metre. In 1999, the forest renewal charge was further refined to account for volume differences by region and forest management, as well as species.[70] While the average annual stumpage revenue between 1990 and 1992 in Ontario had totalled $67 million—with provincial expenditures in forest management nearly four times that amount[71]—the total stumpage charged in 1999–2000 was over $155 million, with $104 million paid out for forest renewal activities.[72]

In the past, before the major reductions in MNR staffing, violations of logging guidelines were rampant. Many documented cases of non-compliance and non-enforcement were cited, but dismissed by governments as unfortunate exceptions to the general rule.[73] The thought of the forest industry policing its own clear-cuts as forestry staff were laid off to meet budget constraints did not inspire confidence.

The evidence of the last decade confirms that concern. Under the 1994 Crown Forest Sustainability Act, the safeguard over industry self-regulation is a third-party audit every five years. The consequences of failing such an audit are hardly intimidating. If recommended, the licence is extended for another five years. However, if the licence is not renewed, it does not constitute a revocation. It simply means that the licence is valid for only fifteen years, instead of the twenty years of the original term. As there is an audit every five years, a forest company has three chances to successfully clear an audit and have its licence renewed. In the decade since the act came into force, no company has ever had its licence revoked.[74]

Legal watersheds

Two legal watersheds—the Class Environmental Assessment for Timber Management on Crown Lands in Ontario and the 1994 Crown Forest Sustainability Act—are essential to understanding the current and future management of Ontario's forests.

The Class Environmental Assessment (EA) of timber management in Ontario was the hearing to end all hearings. The process for examining the environmental impacts of timber management in Ontario remains a classic case of how *not* to involve the public in decision-making. The hearings themselves took four and a half years. It was more than a full year into the hearings before the Ontario Ministry of Natural Resources had entered its case in evidence. After 70,000 pages of recorded transcripts and 2,300 exhibits were presented by over 500 witnesses, it took a further year and a half for the board to render its decision. As a "class" environmental assessment, it dealt not with ecosystem-specific cases, but rather with the whole class of forest planning and decision processes. Many were frustrated that the mandate for the board excluded specific land-use decisions or the formulation of a vision for the future forest.

In April 1994, the Environmental Assessment Board issued its 561-page decision. In large measure, it rejected the case put forward by environmental groups, dismissing their calls for alternative management approaches as impractical or untested. The Board further found that "land-use guidelines are only guidelines...not binding land-use decisions."[75] But it did promulgate a new series of legally binding requirements for forest operations. Among the 115 new requirements were the creation of citizen advisory committees at the local level, the development of a strategy for the conservation of old-growth forests and research on the environmental impact of logging.[76]

A decade later, the province still has not developed a comprehensive old-growth strategy. And while citizen committees were created, their role was one of passive advice. The EA ruled that "a guiding force in the Board's ruling was the public's right to be a partner in the decision-making processes that affect Crown forest resources."[77] While the province has improved opportunities for the public to some degree, opportunities for meaningful engagement in forest management are still lacking.

While ignoring key ecological aspects of the Class EA ruling, government claimed to be responding through the passage of new forestry legislation, the Crown Forest Sustainability Act (CFSA). The act shifted the object of timber management from providing a continuous supply of timber to the economy to providing "for the sustainability of Crown forests."[78] "Sustainability" is defined as "long-term forest health." But before concluding that ecological principles reign, check the definition of "forest health": "the condition of the forest ecosystem that sustains the ecosystem's complexity *while providing for the needs of the people of Ontario*" [emphasis added]. Thus the legal requirement for timber production remained at the heart of the new act.

Under the act, Forest Management Agreements (FMAs) became Sustainable Forest Licences (SFLs), and the government rewrote its timber manuals into a Forest Management Planning Manual. Non-timber values, such as biodiversity, are supposed to be weighed in making management decisions. Most environmental groups in Ontario have been disappointed with the legislation, finding the act unnecessarily vague and discretionary. Concerns were exacerbated when the Harris government transferred responsibility for the act's implementation to the forest industry. The Forest Management Business Plan placed virtually all Crown land in Sustainable Forest Licences. This includes all of the unallocated Crown land, previously managed by provincial foresters as Crown Management Units (CMUs). Thus, the entire productive Crown land forest within the area covered by the Class EA was to be managed by the forest indus-try for the first time in the province's history.

In 2003, the Timber Class Environmental Assessment Approval was replaced by the Ontario government when it issued a "declaration order." The order renewed the authority of the MNR to approve log-ging on 365,000 square kilometres of public land. But it did not complete key outstanding requirements set down when the Environmental Assessment Board first issued its decision in 1994. In particular, it failed to incorporate the draft old-growth policy. There are no requirements that an old-growth policy include specific plans and targets for protecting old-growth forests.

The new rulebook further reduced public control over forest com-panies by enshrining automatic renewal of the Class EA ruling, thus allowing logging on Crown land with no fixed expiry date. With no requirement or opportunity for review of forest policy, public lands appear to be destined to status quo forest practices. And even the ini-tial EA has been weakened. While the Class EA had required the government to develop a policy to maintain roadless wild areas and a strategy to reduce the impact of motorized travel through the forests, this was abandoned. The MNR claimed it had met that requirement through the creation of parks.[79]

The 2003 order also opened up the province's forests to unlimited clear-cuts. The new rules confirmed a 2001 guide premised on the notion that logging should mimic "natural disturbance patterns."[80] While the guidelines do have some progressive elements, such as requiring forest managers to maintain forested islands and peninsulas within cutblocks, previous limits on the size of clear-cuts were repudiated. The government argued that, in order to emulate natural conditions, such as forest fire, it was preferable to have no limits on the size of clear-cuts. The MNR did limit the number of clear-cuts, but there is no upper limit on the size of the individual cuts. Internally inconsistent, at times the guidelines state that monitoring should take place to ensure that logging considers the habitat needs of wildlife. Elsewhere, the guide states that the natural disturbance pattern should be altered to accommodate wildlife only "if absolutely necessary to prevent significant habitat loss."[81]

In the public consultation to review the natural disturbance emulation guidelines, the government received 1,500 letters and petitions opposing the removal of limits on clear-cutting, and only seven in favour.[82] Even the forest industry opposed the change, although for different reasons than those of the environmental groups. The industry argued that not enough was known about how this change would impact wood supply.

The whole approach came in for close scrutiny in the 2002 report of Ontario's Environment Commissioner, who termed it "an experiment on a massive scale."[83] Mimicking fire may sound scientific, but the Commissioner observed that even the MNR's guideline document noted that clear-cutting is a physical process, while fire is a chemical one. Moreover, fires continue to occur, and many burn out of control. Thus, he argued, the ministry would have to account for both logging that imitates forest fire and the real thing, and the cumulative impact on wood supply. Observing that it is well documented that boreal forests are undergoing significant species conversion, with clear-cutting and inadequate regeneration the main causes, the Commissioner warned that "the continued commitment to clear-cutting large areas of the original forest seems to run a great risk that conversion will continue."[84]

The Liberal government of Dalton McGuinty has pledged to review logging rules and end unrestricted clear-cutting. The province has progressive policies for maintaining intact forested areas within a cutblock for forest-dwelling wildlife, such as the marten and caribou. In early 2005, these guidelines call for retaining core areas of older trees that are 30 to 50 square kilometres for marten and 100 square kilometres for caribou. However, government has suggested that these guidelines might be revised, and the thresholds for intact areas decreased.

Ontario's wood supply

There is a general consensus that the province is running out of quality softwood, particularly for sawlogs, and that absolute shortages will appear within twenty to thirty years. Government publications have speculated about how to increase silviculture investments as "a remedy for wood shortages in the 2020–2040 period."[85] Senior industry representatives have described the "reality" of "long-term wood supply...decreasing; quality...decreasing."[86] A review for the Ministry of Natural Resources concluded that "Ontario's softwood sawtimber harvest has been held above sustainable levels in the past, and will have to be reduced in the coming decades as sawlog inventories are depleted."[87]

In 1994, the Minister of Natural Resources referred to current localized "acute shortages of good softwood logs" in northern Ontario and went on to predict "a wood supply shortage or a scarcity of certain types of fibre within the next twenty years."[88]

In addition, Ontario's 2001 *State of the Forests Report* detailed that the habitat of the American marten is predicted to decrease by 28 per cent over the next 120 years. This is a major cause for concern, for the marten and for other forest dwelling species, as marten are used by the MNR for landscape planning for core areas of mature, contiguous conifer. The anticipated decline in marten habitat will result from a decrease in core habitat areas and a decline in the age class of the forests in Ontario.[89]

What is happening to Ontario's softwood supplies is no secret. In 1970 about 70 per cent of everything that was logged was clear-cut. Today, the figure is 90 per cent.[90] Massive clear-cutting leads to species conversion on a large scale in the boreal, from spruce to small hardwoods. The softwood that remains is predominantly in older age classes. One exception within the boreal is logging of jack pine, which can be regenerated in jack pine plantations. Species conversion also occurs in the Great Lakes–St. Lawrence forest.

Ontario has surplus industrial capacity, and forest managers are faced with the challenge of not being able to find enough accessible wood to meet mill demand. As the first forest is logged off, the second-growth trees lack the volume of the first. Thus, the quality of individual sawlogs is decreasing, as logs keep getting smaller. The end of the sawlog industry is in sight, although government publications in the 1990s announced the news in muted tones:

"Supply of suitable timber products from Ontario's forests will limit expansion in this sector, which can expect a contraction after the turn of the century"[91]; "Softwood supplies will tighten throughout the province and mitigative measures will be needed to overcome this deficit."[92]

The growth in the forest industry is predicted through shifts to trees that were previously considered worthless. The small hardwood, poplar and birch, are being targeted for massive expansion through oriented strand board and fibre board mills. In 1995, the government committed an additional 2.3 million cubic metres a year in hardwood logging. That amounts to a 10 per cent increase in the annual harvest, without any opportunity for public review or comment.[93]

The government's econometric models forecast a tripling of the hardwood harvest by the year 2020. So as softwood harvests in the boreal go down, hardwood will go up. With OSB fever gripping the province, Ontario now leads the country in new forest-industry investments, with $800 million in new investments in 1994 and $1 billion in 1995.[94] Five OSB mills in 1997 consumed over 1.5 million cubic metres of wood.[95]

The bulk of these investments are for the production of oriented strand board and medium density fibreboard (MDF). Like OSB, MDF is made of wood fibres and glue, pressed together in an attempt to imitate real wood. The opening of an OSB mill should be seen as a neon sign glowing in the dark above an ecosystem: "Going Out of Business! Everything Must Go!"

An OSB mill does not take trees to make forest products, in the sense that shipbuilding, sawmills and, at a lower level, pulp mills do. It takes trees to make flakes. The flakes are then "oriented," or lined up perpendicular to each other. Add glue, press and—voila! You've got oriented strand board for use in construction. Given the processing method, it is fairly obvious why OSB mills are on the increase. Literally any small tree, particularly small hardwood, can be flaked and converted to OSB.

Industry apologists point out that the use of these less economically valuable trees is an opportunity to use what was once wasted and take pressure off mature forests. However, the tendency in Ontario has been to use OSB mills as a means of increasing forest harvesting, not decreasing it.

But concerns are already being raised that the "underutilized" hard-wood is being overallocated. The *Logging and Sawmilling Journal*, of all places, reported that "according to [Martin] Kaiser (Policy Manager for the Ontario Forest Products Association), the [poplar] inventory was not particularly accurate. Now there is a question of whether or not the amount of poplar the government says is there actually exists. *There is concern in some quarters that the government may have over-committed the hardwood supply*" [emphasis added].[96]

The article also quotes Mr. Kaiser as saying, "From the standpoint of using the productive land base, [the Ministry of Natural Resources] is trying to get every last stick of wood out there into the mills."[97]

Another government publication is blunt on the subject of hard-wood supply. Referring to the vast northeast forest planning region, the report notes: "The demand for hardwood fiber in this region will exceed supply within twenty years."[98]

Ontario will be experiencing shortages of softwood to feed its mills within five years. Current government projections anticipate serious shortages from 2010 until 2065.[99] Forest-dependent communities will suffer, with the probability of mill closures. The pulp mill sector is also over-capacity and will likely close mills as well. The new OSB and MDF investments are likely to cause shortages of poplar and birch. In the meantime, the province's forests are losing critical ecosystems, while clear-cut logging practices will be subjected to industry self-regulation.

Ontario will not run out of trees in the sense that it will lose for-est cover. What are most at risk are the diversity of the forest, the presence of old-growth forests, the species mix and the habitat for species, from the woodland caribou to the red-shouldered hawk. How can any forest policy be described as sustainable when it can neither ensure the supply of wood to the mills nor the wildlands for its creatures?

Ontario

Forest and other wooded land in million hectares	58
Stocked harvested Crown land in hectares (cumulative since 1975)	4.3 million
Area logged in hectares (2002)	184,322
Volume logged in million cubic metres (2002)	26.3
Annual allowable cut in hectares (2001)	293,288

Source: Natural Resources Canada, Canadian Forest Service, *The State of Canada's Forests 2003–2004* (Ottawa, 2004). These are federal government summaries, based on provincial government data. The figures are not necessarily accurate.

Ontario Corporate Players

Abitibi-Consolidated

Bowater

Buchanan Group: Aitikokan Forest Products, Dubreuil Forest Products, Great West Timber, Long Lake Forest Products, Mackenzie Forest Products

Columbia Forest Products

Domtar Group: Domtar Inc., Norampac Inc., Pineland Timber Co. Ltd.

Elk Lake Planing

Kimberly-Clark

Norbord Industries

Tembec Group: Tembec Industries, Spruce Falls Inc.

Weyerhaeuser Company Ltd.

Manitoba

A vast province, Manitoba encompasses such a large chunk of the northern hemisphere that the polar bear and the prairie burrowing owl are both residents. The frigid waters of Hudson Bay force the treeline farther south than in neighbouring Saskatchewan. While all the forests of the province are classed as boreal, there are substantial differences in both species composition and ecology between the various sub-categories of the Manitoba woodlands. The boreal within Manitoba is, however, hugely significant as part of the last intact primary boreal forest in the world. What has been dubbed the "Heart of the Boreal" is found in the untouched boreal forests shared between Manitoba and Ontario.

Manitoba's farthest northern forests are not considered commercially viable. They are in the transition zone to tundra and are wholly excluded from the forest inventory. The "commercial" forest includes the stunted trees that cling to existence in the thin soil and acidic bogs of the Precambrian boreal, along the northern edge of productive forest. The soils of the Precambrian shield were sheared off by glaciers thousands of years ago. The work of millennia in rebuilding soils through the actions of mosses and lichens allows coniferous trees to survive, but they grow slowly. Controversy about the definitions of "productive forest," growth cycles and regeneration time following fires persists in decision-making about Manitoba's boreal forest regions.

The boreal plain forests are dominated by conifers—black spruce and jack pine. This vast dark green northern forest gives way, closer to the prairie, to the mixed-wood boreal, a transition zone forest leading into the original tall grass prairie. The mixed-wood boreal of Manitoba moves from the southeastern corner of the province west in a swath of predominantly deciduous forest of aspen and poplar. Much of Manitoba's agricultural land was created by clearing these forests.

European settlement left the forests largely untouched by logging well into the twentieth century. Early settlers cleared land for agriculture, destroyed forests in the search for minerals and allowed forest fires to escape, but the vast forests of the province were unattractive to the huge commercial interests that were busy removing the most economically viable trees from eastern Canada and from coastal British Columbia. The primary forest users were the Aboriginal peoples— Ojibway, Cree and, farther north, the Dene. The First Nations communities relied on the forest for food, fuel and shelter. The forest mammals were hunted for clothing and food, while the waters of the forest provided fish. Although the first white man travelled through what is now Manitoba in 1690, the forests were little disturbed by human intervention until the first large-scale paper mill was built in 1925 near the southeast corner of the province at Pine Falls.

Scandals, politics and pulp

Manitoba's colourful approach to giving away its forests spans four decades—from building the mill at The Pas in the early 1960s to doubling the rate of cut to accommodate Louisiana-Pacific in the 1990s and licensing a new mill at Pine Falls with triple the capacity and no public review.

The history of the mill at The Pas—the scandal that erupted when the public found out the extent of taxpayer funding for the mill, with subsequent deals and subsidies to keep the mill in production—warrants a book of its own.

It dates back to the Conservative government of Duff Roblin, who came to power in Manitoba in 1957. The province searched for years for an entrepreneur willing to open a pulp mill at The Pas, midway to the province's northern border, along the Saskatchewan border. The project was not an easy sell. The province's own feasibility studies estimated the surrounding forests to have "timber...spread out over a large area, generally of small diameter and young growth. Over 80 per cent of the timber volume is less than 10 inches in diameter."[1]

To sweeten the deal, the province decided to offer substantially reduced stumpage rates; cut-rate hydropower at lower-than-normal costs for a long term; fire protection and other costs to be covered by the government; and, of course, access to a long-term lease on a vast chunk of territory, as much as 15,000 square kilometres. Even this proved insufficient for the innovative and shrewd businessman who ultimately opened the Churchill Forest Industries complex at The Pas. By the time Dr. Kasser was done, the province had paid the entire cost of building the privately owned mill, nearly $100 million. Not only that, the developer had managed to funnel $24 million in provincial funds into Swiss bank accounts.[2]

Once elected, the New Democratic Party government of Premier Ed Schreyer ordered a full commission of inquiry into the tangled web of the mill at The Pas. Three years and $2 million later, the commission concluded its work, and in 1973 the province took over the Churchill Forest Industries mill to be run as a Crown corporation, called MANFOR.

Under the MANFOR regime, the mill complex was never a winning proposition. In good years it broke even. And no one wanted to know about the bad years. The government's economic strategy could take comfort in the fact that, whether or not the mill was profitable, it created employment. Still, the media tagline for the MANFOR mill became "the troubled mill at The Pas," and, in the late 1980s, the new Conservative government of Gary Filmon began looking for ways to get the public mill back into private hands.

It is ironic that the MANFOR complex actually began to make a profit in early 1989, just months before the closing of a sweetheart deal that rivalled the original development.[3] In secret negotiations, the province of Manitoba wooed Repap to take over the mill. The Montreal-based company was one of the few remaining forest giants to reverberate with the name of one man. Just as, in New Brunswick, J.D. Irving is Irving Pulp and Paper, so George Petty is Repap. From fairly humble beginnings, Repap ("paper" spelled backwards) had in its heyday in the 1980s become one of North America's leading producers of coated printing paper.[4] Its status as an industry giant was short-lived, but in 1989, the province of Manitoba was intent on getting Repap to take over the MANFOR operations at The Pas.

By March 1989, the province had confirmed its decision to sell the public company to Repap, but still the text of the agreement was kept secret. No public hearings were held while Manitoba negotiated the deal that would give Repap long-term leases covering almost one-fifth of the province—an area of nearly 11 million hectares, equivalent to 110,074 square kilometres![5] As George Petty bragged,

"It's probably the largest single remaining under-utilized softwood resource in Canada and probably the world for that matter, if you exclude the Soviet Union."[6]

Pressure from citizen's and environmental groups was mounting. What publicly owned resources and businesses were being traded away behind closed doors? When the agreement was made public in May 1989, it was not because the government had acceded to public demands to know what was going on, but because a group of Manitoba Cree were familiar with the secretive ways of the government. The Manitoba Keewatinowi Okimakanak (MKO), an organization that represents twenty-five Northern Cree First Nations, obtained a copy of the text from New York, where, by law, it had been filed with the U.S. Securities and Exchange Commission.[7] Once the MKO saw the agreement, they realized nothing in it would protect their treaty rights over the same territory.

Under both Churchill Forest and later MANFOR, the mill had the legal right to log within a forest area nearly as large as that leased to Repap. But Repap planned to *triple* the rate of logging within the area. Repap also committed to $1 billion in new investments—building a new bleached-pulp mill at The Pas, as well as a wood-chipping facility at Swan River, a community about 200 kilometres due south of The Pas that was owed something in political terms. While the provincial government was negotiating with Repap, however, the municipal leaders of Swan River had successfully interested another company in building an oriented strand board (OSB) plant in their town. The only problem was that the province had secretly negotiated away the wood needed for the Swan River venture to Repap. The province also committed a further $90 million to roads for Repap's use.

No environmental hearing took place to examine the impact of tripling the rate of cut. One unnamed official was quoted in the provincial press as saying, "No comprehensive ecological studies were made when MANFOR came into being in 1966 and none have been done since."[8]

The commercial softwood forest was close to wholly committed to pulp mills with the giant Repap agreement in 1989, and the trend toward rapid industrialization of Manitoba's forests increased in subsequent years under new forest management. Repap's interests were purchased by Tolko, a change in ownership without impact on the direction of forest management. Again, no public notification, hearings or review of the legal agreement—which created barriers to the establishment of protected areas and treaty land selection—was provided for Manitobans.

The oriented strand board boom

New technology in the manufacture of oriented strand board was creating increased interest in Manitoba's mixed-wood boreal forest at just the point that the Conservative government of Gary Filmon was looking for ways to expand the provincial forest industry. Hardwoods in the province had been considered "underutilized," and that rationalization was soon to form the basis for the clear-cutting of aspen throughout the southwestern portions of Manitoba's boreal. The aspen tree was suddenly commercially viable as raw material for OSB. A 1989 symposium in Minnesota concluded:

> Canada has five times as much aspen as the United States... [which] is widely dispersed from Ontario to British Columbia.... The last few years are proving that this increase in aspen utilization, particularly in western Canada, far exceeded our expectations. *What was considered a weed species before 1972 is now described as a champion species or the Queen of the North* [emphasis added].[9]

Suddenly, the Manitoba commercial forest expanded. Since estimates of what is commercially available are always premised on known technology, the emergence of a technology that prized not lumber but wood flakes substantially increased the volume of forest the government considered "available." The aspen forests of the mixed boreal could be used to lure a multinational giant to the province. Meanwhile, the Repap deal was proving disappointing, particularly for Swan River. A downturn in pulp prices through the end of the 1980s and early 1990s significantly reduced Repap's financial position. By 1995, Repap had not met the promised commitment of a $1-billion investment in the province. It had not built a new plant for bleached pulp at The Pas, nor had it proceeded with the wood-chipping plant at Swan River.

Enter Louisiana-Pacific—the giant pulp-and-paper firm that had once been part of Georgia Pacific. Louisiana-Pacific already had Canadian plants—a mill producing oriented strand board in Dawson

Creek, British Columbia, and a small fibre gypsum plant in Nova Scotia. The OSB industry was expanding everywhere. The price of OSB had more than doubled since 1990. Analysts did not believe the market was yet saturated. And Manitoba was about to make Louisiana-Pacific an offer they could not refuse.

Prior to any public hearings, Manitoba offered Louisiana-Pacific a long-term lease to log 900,000 cubic metres of hardwood annually from its mixed-wood aspen forests, both private and Crown lands. The province sets stumpage rates substantially lower than most provincial governments, and well below U.S. rates. The Manitoba rate would come to $1.17 per cubic metre, while the Ontario rate for comparable wood for OSB use was $6.00 per cubic metre.[10] With planned rates of logging, Louisiana-Pacific would be producing $180 million worth of OSB annually, while paying stumpage rates totalling only $1 million.[11] In return, Louisiana-Pacific would build an $80-million OSB plant near Swan River. The Forest Management Licence Area (FMLA) of some 5,863 square kilometres included cutting rights inside Duck Mountain Provincial Park and some of the last remaining stands of old-growth hardwoods in the province. In 1997, this park was expanded significantly. All the added lands were protected from development.[12]

The Louisiana-Pacific forest licence went up to the very boundary of Riding Mountain National Park. Predictably, the ecological integrity of the national park has been eroded by ten years of logging along its borders. And compounding the problems of unprecedented clear-cutting of the aspen forests is the fact that the business plan for this new mill and FMLA with Louisiana-Pacific included an assumption that much of its fibre would come from private lands, including those along the national park escarpment. Forest management standards for public land do not apply on private land, where harvesting is arranged with the owners. Manitoba does not have equivalent standards for forestry operations on private land.

To accomplish all this, the province had to renegotiate the Repap deal, since Repap's exclusive logging rights to 17 per cent of the province included areas now needed by Louisiana-Pacific. Fortunately for the province, it had some bargaining power. Repap was behind on its commitments. The Repap deal was announced again in November 1995. Louisiana-Pacific got the hardwood, Repap got comparable rights over the same areas in order to log softwood and the hardwood not already allocated. Repap reorganized its promised investment. Any plans for Repap to build in Swan River could now be safely scrapped, as Louisiana-Pacific would be building near there. And Repap committed to building a $250-million bleached chemithermal mechanical pulp (BCTMP) mill at The Pas. The BCTMP mill had been developed by Repap to manufacture bleached pulp without the environmental hazards of chlorine use. The plant also had the "advantage" that it, too, could utilize small hardwood species such as poplar.

The province got out of its promised $90-million commitment for road building for Repap, and it got Repap to pay $20 million for its outstanding preferred shares.[13] The long-term viability of the Repap mill at The Pas was in question. Repap's financial fortunes from coast to coast were substantially reduced when the shareholders of Avenor turned down a proposed purchase of Repap assets in early 1997.[14] Heavily in debt, Repap was flirting with going under. By August 1997, Repap Manitoba had been purchased by Tolko. The province did not open the FMLA to improve its provisions, especially in regard to First Nations entitlements and the establishment of protected areas. They simply signed over the agreement—the largest in North America. No public review was undertaken, and the Repap long-term forest management plan and environmental review were simply rolled over to Tolko. In 1998, the corporate landscape changed once again when the original Pine Falls mill was purchased by Tembec.

The First Nations of Manitoba were alarmed by the government forest leases. With 40 per cent of the province tied up under binding logging contracts, indigenous peoples in Manitoba escalated their organized opposition to logging. The MKO filed a statement of claim in federal court in July 1995, asking for a court review of the Louisiana-Pacific deal with Manitoba and potential abrogation of First Nations rights. The Grand Chief of the Assembly of Manitoba Chiefs, Phil Fontaine (now Chief of the Assembly of First Nations), asked for federal intervention in a full environmental assessment of the increase in clear-cutting that was authorized to accommodate Louisiana-Pacific. The federal Minister of Environment refused to conduct an environmental assessment. The MKO and the Swampy Cree Tribal Council, representing several Cree First Nations that would be affected by Louisiana-Pacific logging, have filed a request for judicial review of the minister's refusal.

Local communities turned to direct action. In April 1996, the Mathias Colomb First Nation blockaded a railcar, preventing Repap from unloading road-building equipment. The projected road was to open up First Nations traditional lands to logging, despite the fact that both the federal and the provincial government acknowledged that the First Nations of Manitoba, including the Mathias Colomb and Pukatawagan First Nations, had unresolved treaty entitlements. The province was failing to follow through on an agreement in principle regarding land selection, while doing business with Repap for expansion. To protect treaty land entitlement, the men, women and children of the small community of Pukatawagan, 710 kilometres north of Winnipeg, blockaded the railcars. Even after Repap had obtained a court injunction ordering them to suspend the blockade, the community remained adamant, and the blockade continued in defiance of the injunction.

The local RCMP Superintendent, George Watt, decided to take a cautious approach. Through an unlikely twist of fate, Watt was a veteran of forest blockades at Clayoquot Sound in British Columbia, where nearly one thousand people were arrested, and of blockades by the Lubicon Cree in Alberta against logging by the Japanese multinational Daishowa. Watt decided to avoid arrests in this case. Having initially insisted that failure to remove the blockade would result in a two-month shutdown at the mill, throwing 150 people out of work, Repap relented and removed the contested equipment from the area.[15]

Things did not change much when corporate control shifted from Repap to Tolko. The Pimacikamak Cree forced Tolko to remove its equipment from their traditional territory.

Environmentalists also worried about Louisiana-Pacific's arrival in the Manitoba woods. The company had a terrible reputation for pollution offenses in the United States. In fact, it had been levied the largest pollution-related fine in U.S. history—$11.1 million (U.S.) for toxic air emissions from one of its OSB plants.[16] Its then CEO, Harry Merlo, had been quoted as saying, "We need everything that's out there....We log to infinity. Because we need it all. It's ours. It's out there, and we need it all. Now."[17]

While Manitoba promised to submit the Louisiana-Pacific OSB mill to provincial environmental assessment, environmentalists and First Nations vigorously opposed the government's decision to split the assessment and licensing review. On a fast track to accommodate Louisiana-Pacific's building plans, the government first assessed the mill itself, concluding that the toxic effluents of the Louisiana-Pacific mill were within environmental standards and that they would not be subject to the same level of environmental regulation in Manitoba as in the United States. In response to public outrage, just before the conclusion of the environmental assessment hearings, Louisiana-Pacific agreed to install the same pollution-abatement technology required by the more stringent laws in the United States.

Once the mill was approved and under construction, the company's plans to log 900,000 cubic metres per year of hardwood—or more than 4 million trees per year—were subjected to a separate environmental review. The exercise had a sense of futility. The agreement signed with Louisiana-Pacific had already confirmed that the mill was to receive the 900,000 cubic metres of hardwood a year. The mill was being built to those specifications. The agreement further confirmed that, should the province decide to reduce the wood supply to the mill, it would either pay Louisiana-Pacific substantial compensation or find sources elsewhere at no greater cost to the company. The province was allowed to take back only 0.5 per cent of the land base every ten years. It was no surprise to anyone that the logging plans received provincial approval. As well, within several months of the licence being issued, the Filmon government relaxed the conditions for pollution abatement.[18]

Prior to any public review, Manitoba doubled the level of permissible hardwood logging in Louisiana-Pacific's licence.[19] The on-the-ground impact of doubling the rate of cut was complicated by a number of factors. The original AAC was intended only for large hardwoods, whereas OSB technology allowed for the use of smaller trees and trees of lower economic value. The impact to the forest would likely be similar. With the doubling of the AAC and the new chipboard technology, all of these trees could now be logged as well.

In announcing the Repap and Louisiana-Pacific deals, the Industry, Trade and Tourism Minister, the Honourable James Downey, claimed, "Our forestry sector, *which operates under the principles of sustainable development*, now has two strong companies producing four products, so these jobs will be less vulnerable to the ups and downs of the marketplace. This is great news for the people of northern Manitoba and for the Manitoba economy" [emphasis added].[20]

Are Manitoba's forest policies sustainable?

Manitoba stands out as a province deep in sustainable development rhetoric, if not practice. For instance, when Premier Gary Filmon joined Prime Minister Brian Mulroney in announcing the International Institute for Sustainable Development, based in Winnipeg, he enthused that henceforth, Winnipeg would be to sustainable development what Vienna is to opera. Premier Gary Doer has also developed a propensity for sustainable development flourishes to his speeches, while allowing intensive livestock production to grow rapidly and logging up to the boundaries of the national parks. The Doer government's forest policy, released in 2002, commits the province to sustainable forest management, but it has not been fulfilled.[21] With vast sections of the province allocated to just three companies, the province has an excellent opportunity to prove that the principles of sustainable development do indeed guide its forest policy.

Manitoba's first serious attempt at maintaining a forest inventory began in 1963, when the Churchill Forest Industries complex was under development at The Pas. As in all provincial inventories, the basic assessments were made from aerial photographs, with some ground "cruising" to determine if estimates from the air corresponded to what was actually in the forest. But, while no provincial inventory is without significant inaccuracies, Manitoba's system still lags behind that of other provinces. The province did not establish permanent sample plots to assess changes over time until 1979.[22] Thus, the database for average rates of growth is extremely limited. Growth data are only available since 1979 and only for mature timber and two density classes. Moreover, there are only 284 active permanent sample plots, reducing the value of the information for decision-makers.[23]

The inventory itself was also limited in area. The province surveyed only those areas believed to be valuable to the forest industry; thus inventories of the southwestern part of the province began only in 1986–1987. Manitoba Natural Resources (which became the Manitoba Department of Conservation, Forestry Branch, in 1999) acknowledged that its information was accurate only to within plus or minus 27.9 per cent. As a research goal, the Branch hopes to reduce the margin of error for any particular Forest Management Unit (FMU) to below 20 per cent.[24] Several FMUs in the Mountain Forest Section have been updated, particularly critical as the initial inventories did not include hardwood species such as aspen.

While periodic updates of the inventory have been undertaken, they are, as in other provinces, increasingly the responsibility of the forest companies, creating issues of access to data that is the property of the companies. Concerned environmental groups are unable to access some information at all, and are frustrated by the lack of historic data. For example, as soon as an area is logged, the existence of the logging roads is erased from the map.

From one of the worst records in Canada in 1995, Premier Filmon managed to substantially increase Manitoba's network of protected areas by the end of his government in 1999. In 1990, the province had only 300,000 hectares of protected land. By the close of the millennium, the province had 5.5 million hectares protected from industrial development, as well as a new Parks Act, a process for First Nations protected areas creation and 3.6 million hectares approved by the mining sector as protected from industrial activity.[25] These sites were among the over one hundred design areas the Manitoba government has mapped for future protected areas.

Interim protection was extended to 3 million hectares as of 2000. Parks established prior to 1986 were open to various resource extraction activities, including clear-cutting. Parks established during the 1990s and since 2000 have been off-limits to forestry, hydro development, oil and gas, and mining.

A review of the older parks resulted in a concept found only in Manitoba—"protected zones" within parks, with prohibitions on forestry and other industrial activities. Forestry continues to be allowed in portions of the Grass River, Whiteshell, Nopiming, Clearwater Lake and Duck Mountain parks. Whiteshell experiences logging over nearly half of its area, while 62 per cent of Nopiming Provincial Park is zoned for resource extraction. Nopiming has been heavily clear-cut and was the site of protests. Resource extraction is allowed in 61 per cent of Duck Mountain Provincial Park. Much of Duck Mountain has already been logged and is now plantation or failed plantation, or was never replanted. Some of Louisiana-Pacific's wood chips come from the aspen forests of the park. Moreover, Louisiana-Pacific's licence gives the company cutting rights along the northern, eastern and western boundaries of Riding Mountain National Park. This permission violates the United Nations Convention for the Conservation of Biological Diversity, which specifically requires a transition zone as a buffer between protected areas and industrial activity. Requests for a federal environmental assessment of the impact of clear-cutting on the national park have been rejected, despite the fact that this clearly falls under federal environmental assessment law.

In 1999, the long-serving Conservative government of Gary Filmon was defeated and the province reverted to New Democratic Party control. Premier Gary Doer promised to conduct land-use planning over key Crown land regions, such as the east side of Lake Winnipeg, and do more to establish protected areas and conserve wildlife.[26] If anyone thought the shift from the political right wing to the social democrats would create dramatic shifts in forest management, they were sorely disappointed. Logging under the NDP is business as usual.

Doer has made some small steps, trumpeted announcements of parks protected under the previous government and further padded his record by announcing interim protection as though it was permanent. The first step was a minor expansion of the protected areas network in April 2000. Three new park reserves were added, plus twenty-one wildlife management areas.[27] In 2002, Doer announced the permanent protection of 7,640 square kilometres in the Caribou River Provincial Park—an area protected in 1995. In 2004, the long-awaited Lowlands National Park moved toward completion with the signing of a memorandum of understanding (MOU) between the provincial and federal governments, replacing the last MOU, signed for the same purpose ten years before. Key to creating Lowlands National Park, however, is the decision-making of affected local communities. The Doer government would do well to ensure that appropriate consultations and participation by these communities form the basis for interim protection and national park establishment.

Regulations to protect 11,310 hectares in the Porcupine Provincial Forest were also brought forward in 2004. At the end of 2004, Premier Doer's government protected the Manigotogan River corridor. In the same month, Doer and his Conservation Minister publicly indicated support for the 4.3-million-hectare boreal forest World Heritage Site proposed for the east side of Lake Winnipeg. Five First Nations initiated nomination of their traditional territories, from Manitoba extending into Ontario, for World Heritage Site inclusion in 2002. The next step the Manitoba government must take is to provide interim protection for two Aboriginal communities that have been waiting since 1999: the Pauingassi First Nation and the Little

Grand Rapids First Nation. All told, Premier Doer's government claims to have brought the land base of Manitoba within protected areas to 8.5 per cent, a figure including both permanently protected areas and those with only interim protection.[28] Loss of two park reserves during the tenure of the Doer government means the amount of protected land in the province has actually fallen since 1999. The province's protected areas network is one-third complete.

Particularly troubling is the lack of protected land within large forest licences. One of Doer's 1999 election promises had been to establish protected areas within all forest licences. But the Tolko FMLA, for example, has only about 0.2 per cent of its area fully protected and less than 1.35 per cent with interim protection.[29] This 11-million hectare FMLA is the largest in North America.

The need to move more aggressively to protect ecosystems is intimately connected to the expansion of industrial forestry. Logging roads, in particular, ignited controversy, making Doer's promise to act on land-use planning on the east side of Lake Winnipeg even more critical. The threat to the area dated from the mid-1990s, when the government approved an all-weather road, opening up vast tracts of roadless wilderness along the east side of the province's largest lake. In fact, the building of roads into the area, especially roads in preparation for a potential provincial highway through the east side, had been expanding slowly for some time. Pine Falls Paper wanted access to more northern forest within its existing FMLA to supply the new 1,200-ton-per-day paper mill, even though the mill operates at one-third capacity.[30] The initial logging road, started in the 1980s, went 77 kilometres up the east side of the lake, but major expansions of the road would be necessary to meet Pine Falls' logging plans. The licensing process for this road was done incrementally, as part of an annual forestry operations licence, and with no assessment of the expected or cumulative impacts on the environment.

Pine Falls Paper was given environmental licences by the province of Manitoba to begin roadwork and build bridges without waiting for all necessary federal approvals. In 1997, one of Canada's most diligent volunteer conservation activists, Alice Chambers, exposed the fact that the bridge over the Manigotagan River had not received the required approvals under the federal Navigable Waters Protection Act (NWPA). Adding insult to injury, the Manigotagan River is inside Nopiming Provincial Park. Citizen complaints were filed with the responsible authority under that act, the Canadian Coast Guard. In 1998, Ontario forest giant Tembec purchased Pine Falls. Among Ontario forest activists, Tembec has a reputation as one of that province's more environmentally progressive forest companies. It is one of the national leaders in seeking third-party certification of the environmental standards of its forest operations. Tembec is pursuing Forest Stewardship Council certification for all of its holdings in Manitoba.

But Manitoba conservationists did not detect much difference between Tembec and Pine Falls. Tembec applied for late authorization under the NWPA to build a bridge that had already been built, and its plans for the region were no less ambitious than those of Pine Falls. It wanted to more than double the intake of wood from 360,000 to 750,000 cubic metres to meet the needs of a proposed new sawmill. All of this would require hundreds of kilometres of new roads. Pine Falls planning documents from 1995 revealed it wanted to build a bridge over the Bloodvein, a National Heritage River. The Bloodvein is a popular river for canoeists and has never been crossed by a permanent bridge. The threat of a bridge across the Bloodvein cut right to the heart of Manitoba's commitment to ecological integrity.

Alice Chambers kept on digging through approvals and forest-management plans. Cancer didn't stop her, although from time to time it slowed her down. She'd show up at government offices, seeking more documentation, a red bandanna covering her hair loss from chemotherapy. Alice Chambers uncovered more illegal bridge building, but she did not live to see her work validated by the Coast Guard review. The conservation movement lost one of its heroes when she died in 2000. In 2001, the Coast Guard and the Department of Fisheries and Oceans completed its environmental review of the 1998 Tembec request triggered by Alice Chambers' dauntless research. To no one's surprise it approved *post facto* the building of the bridge that had already been built. But it also confirmed that twenty-six other company bridges had been built without proper authorization. Fourteen of them require NWPA review and approval.

The building and licensing of a new thermal mechanical mill at Pine Falls was done without public notification, environmental assessment, public comments or hearings. Federal responsibilities under the Canadian Environmental Assessment Act were ignored. The "grandfathered" licence for the existing mill, parts of which dated from the 1930s, was simply rolled over to a licence for the new mill during the final months of the Filmon government. In the summer of 1999, Tembec attempted to file a two-year operating plan and environmental application during the provincial election. The application again contained altered boundaries and changes to provincial forest designations. At the last minute, as a change of government for Manitoba appeared imminent, the closing date for review of the application was moved up by the company. Several First Nation leaders and environmentalists worked together to make sure that the dying Filmon government did not approve Tembec's expansion plan in 1999.

Meanwhile, by 2000 Premier Doer's election commitment to "ensure land-use planning on the east side of Lake Winnipeg" had still not been delivered.[31] In the summer of 2000, the government launched public participation in "wide-area planning." The east side of Lake Winnipeg is the only area in the province subjected to such planning. The planning exercise would impact over 12 per cent of the province, an area larger than 8 million hectares. The process engaged representatives from industry, First Nations, trappers, outfitters, academics and northern affairs community councils in its Round Table. Several other advisory groups were also created in 2002. Except for one appointment to the Round Table, environmental groups were relegated to secondary committees. The role of First Nations in any land-use plan would be key. Sixteen different First Nations live within the planning area. When it came time to sign a memorandum of understanding with the province over the exercise, at first only half signed. The eight First Nations communities who refused cited the flawed process, the need for more time and the lack of clarity. More First Nations signed a year into the consultation, but a protocol for the role of First Nations was not established.[32] In the end, the Round Table could not complete the land-use plan in the time allowed. Rather than extend the deadline, the government gave permission to file an interim report with recommendations. The original completion target of June 2004 proved unrealistic, and at this writing it is unclear if the draft will receive more work, if the Round Table will remain in place and whether the process will end in triumph or failure.[33] Confusion over how to achieve its goals still prevails, with some recommendations of the draft report actually contradicting the original terms of reference.[34]

The concern over the fate of the boreal forest region on the east side of Lake Winnipeg became more intense with the confirmation in 2000 by the international Global Forest Watch that the area is part of the largest intact piece of boreal forest anywhere in the world.[35] Work at the international level verified the arguments of local conservationists that the boreal forest on the east side of Lake Winnipeg is a significant primary forest by global standards. Manitoba Wildlands and the Boreal Forest Network won the support of the Washington-based Natural Resources Defence Council for the protection of the intact forests of the region under the banner "Heart of the Boreal." With the support of these organizations, the communities of the First Nations Protected Areas Accord have nominated their lands to be included with one Manitoba park and one Ontario park in the Woodland Caribou/Atikaki/First Nations World Heritage Site nomination, now on Canada's official tentative World Heritage List.

With increased logging on the horizon, it appears that development continues to trump conservation in Manitoba. Even at existing rates of logging, many forest species are already at risk. The woodland caribou west of the Ontario border has been listed as a species at risk by the Committee on the Status of Endangered Wildlife in Canada (COSEWIC) for five years now. Although Manitoba has not acted to list the woodland caribou under the provincial Endangered Species Act, in 2000 it did bring forward a conservation strategy for the woodland caribou. The strategy's stated goal is to maintain the present numbers and distribution of the species through the province. This is an odd goal for a species at risk. Generally, action plans for a species like the woodland caribou, in trouble throughout Canada due to logging pressures, aim to restore the population through larger numbers. Nevertheless, even the goal of maintaining present levels of caribou is undermined by government actions such as allowing Tembec to log in prime woodland caribou habitat, as it did in 2004 in Owl Lake.[36] New roads and radically increased clear-cutting will only make matters worse. Tolko's annual plan, which covers 2004–2006, totals 250 kilometres of both winter and all-weather roads.[37] Tolko's forest management area includes several provincial parks, including Grass River Park, with only 2 per cent of its total area protected from industry. The woodland caribou is endemic to all three FMLAs. Its habitat on both sides of the Ontario-Manitoba border is under assault. The wolverine, black bear and elk are also suffering from the effects of logging.[38]

Is Manitoba running out of wood to feed its mills?

Manitoba has the greatest gap between its AAC and its harvested volume of any province in Canada. With an AAC pegged at 9.6 million cubic metres and an actual logged volume of 2.0 million in 2002, theoretically, Manitoba has lots of forest to meet the needs of its mills and should have no problem in expanding conservation opportunities. This picture is misleading, as some of Manitoba's forests are substantially more attractive to industry than others. The primary reason is access. Some forest regions with large AACs are presently inaccessible. As elsewhere in Canada, confidence depends on the methodology and quality of data used to calculate the AAC. In Manitoba's case, one of the most deceptive aspects of the FMLA is the calculation of total forest within the AAC as "net merchantable." Logging does not occur at the net-merchantable level for softwoods. Logging for softwood generally occurs for what is termed "level 1" quality softwood. The impact of logging level 1 softwood is minimized when the AAC is based on the far larger categorization of forest as "net merchantable." As well, the AAC figure is based on inventory combining recent and not-so-recent data. There are few permanent sample plots and burn areas are being put back into inventory.

Using a dated information base, the Forest Branch has set rising annual allowable cut rates over the years. While it may stretch credulity, apparently as the number of industries increases so does the number of trees! This alchemy is not all that difficult to explain, although it is far more difficult to defend.

Manitoba estimates that 14.8 million hectares or 43 per cent of the forested land of the province is "productive forest."[39] Yet in the Louisiana-Pacific and Tolko long-term Forest Management Plans and environmental impact statements, the productive forest is estimated to be far lower, closer to one-third of the forest. The vast majority of this land base—94 per cent—is Crown land, publicly owned and managed by the province. Most of it is open and available to logging. Manitoba began the practice of long-term leases only in fairly recent times.

The first such licence was included in a Forest Management Licence (FML), granted in 1989 to Repap for the famous mill at The Pas. Everything derives from the FML; it is the agreement that establishes access to fibre. The FML defines the area to be logged, sets stumpage rates and stipulates the agreed-upon volume to be cut; all of this is based on the AAC calculations at the time the lease was granted. Negotiations for the FML are done in private. The public process that follows, including any environmental assessment, cannot change anything about the FML. In Manitoba, other than First Nations rights at some future date, it is difficult to imagine changes to the FML commitments.

The first mill in the province, the Pine Falls mill, was established in 1925. The wood for its first lease came from a local First Nations reserve, as well as from large tracts of land running north of the Winnipeg River. The viability of the mill was enhanced by cheap power from the hydroelectric dams upstream. Under the management of the Spanish River Pulp and Paper Company, the mill was producing 258 tons of paper a day by 1929. Eventually Abitibi-Price took it over and operated it from the 1930s until 1994, when it was sold to the employees. At the time of sale, the mill was still using some of its original 1920s equipment. The new Pine Falls Paper Company was given the 1979 FML, with lease rights until 2008, and a $30-million provincial loan guarantee—and the local community presented a Browning Citori Grand Lightning shotgun to the new CEO.[40]

A separate FML was negotiated with Louisiana-Pacific. Tembec is operating within the 1979 FML as well. The Tolko and Louisiana-Pacific FMLs are quite different from those extended to Pine Falls and Tembec. Terms vary from licence to licence, but, in general, Manitoba demands very little from licensees. While increasingly companies must conduct inventories, the government remains responsible for collecting much of the data to develop the annual allowable cut, seedlings are provided to the industry, and the stumpage rates remain very low. Stumpage was recently increased to $3.15 per cubic metre.[41]

In any event, Manitoba has clearly demonstrated that it does not recognize the importance of regenerating the forest on ecological principles. While its official policy document on sustainable forestry practices states that "reforestation shall maintain the natural species diversity found within the forest ecosystem," the agreement with Louisiana-Pacific orients planting around "site-suitable species as good as, *or better than* the present forest" [emphasis added].[42]

A total of 40 per cent of the productive forest AAC is locked up in three large FMLs. In addition, smaller forest companies buy timber quotas and other short-term agreements for forest access. Tembec is still seeking an additional $70 million to build its new sawmill, which when completed will increase the pressure for more fibre. The province's twenty-year plan, developed under the Filmon government, forecasts a rate of cut more than three times the current level at 8.27 million cubic metres.[43] In recent years, hardwood logged in Manitoba has been exported as raw chips to OSB mills in northern Minnesota. Some aspen from as far north as the Swan River area has been trucked south of the border.

The Forest Management Sections with the highest rate of cut, described by the Forest Branch as the Mountain, Highrock, Interlake, and Saskatchewan River Regions, are almost completely committed to long-term logging of softwood. In fact, these regions all stand at over 97 per cent of their softwood AAC. The section for which the AAC is fully committed for both hardwood and softwood is the Mountain Forest Section. While many forest companies are not utilizing the AAC to the full extent permitted, in terms of available timber supply, Manitoba is arguably short of softwood. As early as 1986, *The First Five-Year Review of Manitoba's Forest Royalty System* concluded that local industry was already approaching total utilization of available softwood.[44] A major government-sponsored report concluded in 1995: "Given current AACs, regional allocations of coniferous timber are tight, particularly after allowances are made for Crown timber that is considered inaccessible."[45]

The hardwood, of course, is considered "underutilized" and now forms the basis of the bonanza for clear-cutting aspen through the southern portions of Manitoba's mixed-wood boreal. As a deal with Louisiana-Pacific came into focus, Manitoba doubled the hardwood AAC in the area of Louisiana-Pacific's licence. The AAC for hardwood logging in the Mountain Forest Region surrounding Swan River went from 578,290 cubic metres to 1,100,000 cubic metres, excluding private lands. Since Louisiana-Pacific had stated its intention to log 900,000 cubic metres a year, the government believed that it would not have been possible to lure the OSB development to the province with the original hardwood AAC. The government defended its decision as being premised on the technological innovation of OSB. Where previously only forest stands capable of producing more than 40 cubic metres of sawlogs to the hectare had been included in the AAC, now all hardwood was included, with a mere 10 per cent reduction for decay.[46]

A provincial biologist who criticized the ease with which this conversion was computed was quickly fired. Dan Soprovich had been with the Department of Natural Resources for fifteen years. Having sat through the environmental review hearings, he realized that the government's guarantee of a 900,000 cubic metre AAC to Louisiana-Pacific was based on a fundamental misconception. In setting levels to meet Louisiana-Pacific's requirements, the government was assuming all hardwoods were interchangeable. But in the hearings, Louisiana-Pacific representatives made it clear that they would need 80 per cent aspen and only 20 per cent birch or balsam poplar. Dan Soprovich became convinced that this would inevitably lead to "drastically over-harvesting the aspen."[47]

As a wildlife biologist, Soprovich knew that aspen forests are essential habitat for neotropical migratory songbirds. A wide array of birds migrate annually, wintering in South America and spending the summer in Canada. The hardwood forests of southern Manitoba are key habitat for many of them, from hummingbirds to warblers. These forests had never been subject to widespread clear-cutting, and no one seemed to be looking at the biodiversity implications of Louisiana-Pacific's plans. Even the federal scientists from the Canadian Wildlife Service expressed concern that Louisiana-Pacific's logging plans could prove disastrous for biodiversity. In testimony before the environmental hearing, they urged Louisiana-Pacific to avoid logging the aspen altogether and sharply criticized "the lack of baseline data, which includes...breeding bird surveys, community and habitat work."[48] They urged Louisiana-Pacific to undertake this essential work prior to logging. When they discovered that Louisiana-Pacific planned to "selectively log" even in the buffer zone areas around streams, federal wildlife scientists and federal fisheries biologists lodged an official objection.

But only Dan Soprovich was fired. Following his presentation to the hearings, he received a letter of dismissal, citing his public criticism of the Louisiana-Pacific logging plans. He told the media, "I have absolutely no regrets. I honestly believe I did the right thing."[49]

The Manitoba District Office of the federal forest service also objected to the province's calculation of the AAC for Louisiana-Pacific. Jim Ball, the director, was caustic about the approach the province's Forestry Branch had used. For one thing, as Dan Soprovich had noted, the Forestry Branch treated one type of hardwood as interchangeable with another. In a strongly worded letter, Jim Ball wrote, "Lumping aspen and balsam poplar together will obfuscate 'forest inventory' now and into the future...how will one know whether balsam poplar is being overcut or undercut? Combining two species in one height/diameter equation is really pretty sloppy forest mensuration."[50]

One reason for Mr. Ball's concern was that balsam poplar and aspen respond very differently to logging. Balsam poplar will do better than aspen in wet soils, and its regeneration improves with mineral disturbance. Logging creates somewhat wetter sites compared to naturally disturbed areas. Thus, treating them as the same is ecologically flawed. Given Louisiana-Pacific's desire to log 80 per cent aspen, it is also bad business and environmentally disastrous.

Mr. Ball noted in a document presented during the environmental assessment hearings that the proportion of balsam poplar had been "trivialized" to 2 per cent of the total volume. In fact, Manitoba's own inventory for the area in question had shown the average balsam poplar densities in Manitoba to be at least 10 per cent of total hardwood. Mr. Ball speculated that perhaps the sample plots had been chosen on drier sites, creating a bias in the data in favour of aspen and against accurate reporting of balsam poplar.[51] The sample plots were nearly all near roads, suggesting a selection based on convenience rather than ecological representation. The implications of this were indeed significant. It meant that the entire forest inventory for the Louisiana-Pacific FML was premised on a superabundance of aspen, 98 per cent of all hardwood. Mr. Ball concluded that "data showing 98 per cent aspen for an area the size of FML3 are seriously flawed."[52] But if there was less aspen, then the AAC could be out of whack. Overcutting of aspen will be unavoidable if Louisiana-Pacific meets the production targets guaranteed by its agreement with the province.

Jim Ball also took issue with the magical doubling of wood supply. The remarkably low "cull" rate of 10 per cent, the estimate of wood unavailable due to decay, was not justified in the view of the federal forest service. Mr. Ball asked, "How was the [Forest Resource Inventory] massaged to double the hardwood AAC? The magnitude of the AAC increase...is provocative...[and] requires explanation beyond an unstated increase in utilization standards for OSB using smaller diameter trees."[53] It is likely that the province also exaggerates the AAC by underestimating the amount of decay and "cull" that should be excluded from the anticipated volume per hectare.

Clearly, testimony from the federal forest service would have been of use to the environmental hearing on Louisiana-Pacific's wood supply. But Mr. Ball did not testify. The morning he was to appear, he was instructed to stay away.[54] Since then, the Manitoba office of the federal forestry service has been shut down, lost in budget cuts. The closest federal forestry scientists are now in Edmonton.

The future of Manitoba's forests

With the AAC increases, Manitoba is poised for an assault on its forest without historical precedent. The committed volumes for softwood and hardwood resources are arguably already unsustainable, and new mills are being contemplated. What is certain is that the inventory is faulty and the AAC is designed to meet industry demand rather than ecological capacity. Funding for the forestry branch continues to decline, with a smaller budget and lower morale compared to the late 1990s.[55] Efforts to increase funding to improve the forest inventory have failed in recent years. The Doer government gives no indication of caring about the forest inventory.

The Manitoba government continues to act as a co-sponsor of industrial forest expansion. The process of negotiating in private and presenting final deals to the public virtually eliminates meaningful public participation. The province has ignored the advice of its environmental commission—that logging in parks be reviewed and that logging be stopped in Nopiming Provincial Park. More recently, the North American Commission for Environmental Cooperation came to much the same conclusion in its review of Tolko's forest management.[56] Woodland caribou, in particular, continue to be at risk from logging. New protected areas throughout Manitoba's boreal forests are essential for the future.

Underscoring all of the problems is the consistent undervaluing of the forest. Manitoba subsidizes industrial expansion through cheap stumpage, road construction, incentives and tax expenditures. Even if the forest amounted to a pile of sticks, Manitoba is undervaluing that resource. But a forest is much more than a source of raw material for mills. The value of the Manitoba forest lies in its ecological bonuses: providing clean air, water and a cushion in global climate change. In fact, its huge intact areas of boreal forest may have their highest value as a carbon reservoir. The forest has immeasurable value as the habitat for a wide range of creatures whose interrelationships are, as yet, little understood. Moreover, the Manitoba government consistently ignores the value of the forests to First Nations communities, and their constitutional and treaty entitlement to use the forest.

Nevertheless, Manitoba has an opportunity to become a leader in integrated land-use planning. With over 8 million hectares to work with on the east side of Lake Winnipeg, the government could demonstrate co-operative planning, recognizing the rights of First Nations, the global imperative for conservation of the boreal and, with help from Tembec, sustainable approaches to forest management. The plans for the rest of the province require at least the same level of consultation and broad area planning. Manitoba still has a chance to change course.

Manitoba

Forest and other wooded land in million hectares	36.3
Stocked harvested Crown land in hectares (2001)	308,000
Area logged in hectares (2002)	15,042
Volume logged in million cubic metres (2002)	2.0
Annual allowable cut in million cubic metres (2001)	9.6

Source: Natural Resources Canada, Canadian Forest Service, *The State of Canada's Forests 2003–2004* (Ottawa, 2004). These are federal government summaries, based on provincial government data. The figures are not necessarily accurate.

Manitoba Corporate Players

Louisiana-Pacific Canada Ltd.
Mountain Quota Holders (taking over parts of the Louisiana-Pacific and Tolko leases)
Tembec
Tolko

Saskatchewan

Ask the average Canadian to describe Saskatchewan, and forests are not likely to come to mind. Vast, undulating fields of grain, open prairie skies and unending horizons are the hallmark images of this prairie province. Yet forests cover more than half of the province and, as logging has intensified, so too have controversies and conflicts. It is Saskatchewan that holds the national record for the longest-running forest blockade—one and a half years of camping by First Nations people on a remote logging road near Canoe Lake. There is little of the original forest left on the boreal plain and in the aspen parkland. Old-timers can still recall the days of huge trees, but there are few such specimens today.

Prior to European settlement, the forests of Saskatchewan were home to Aboriginal peoples. The forests provided for their needs in a variety of ways—from berries and game to wood for shelter and firewood. But European contact changed the forest, even as it also colonized and oppressed the Aboriginal residents of what was to become Saskatchewan. By 1774 the first trading post had been established, and the trapping of fur-bearing animals drastically increased. For the first time, the land was asked to do more than provide for the needs of the people. It was to create wealth and profit for the Hudson's Bay Company.

Once the white pine was gone from the eastern forests, the market turned to the white spruce, a prominent part of the southern boreal ecoregion, growing along the valleys and near lakes. It grew well with the other prevalent deciduous species—willow and alder.[1] With a strong demand for white spruce, the predictable high grading followed, and the government of Saskatchewan introduced logging quotas in response.[2]

Logging the big spruce

The province's first sawmill opened in Prince Albert in the winter of 1878, years before Saskatchewan existed as a province. Other large mills followed, but as local timber resources were exhausted, the larger facilities closed. By 1920, smaller, portable sawmills were in operation. Although the province of Saskatchewan was created in 1905, it did not have control over its natural resources and Crown lands until 1930. In 1931, the province firmly established its control over the forests by passing the Forest Act. The object of the legislation was to ensure the perpetual growth of timber on lands reserved as provincial forests. Yet after the Depression, market pressure on the forest increased and, without effective regulation, there was rampant overcutting of white spruce and jack pine. At that time in Saskatchewan, there was no inventory, no annual allowable cut (AAC), no fees or stumpage.

Nearly all of Saskatchewan's forests—88 per cent—are Crown land. The Crown owns 100 per cent of the commercially allocated timberlands. Management of this publicly held resource left a lot to be desired. As the public became increasingly alarmed about disappearing forests, the government appointed the Royal Commission on the Forest Resources and Industries of Saskatchewan in 1945. Its recommendations set the stage for the norms of a modern, regulated forestry industry. It took nine years to complete the first inventory, but by the mid-1950s, Saskatchewan's forest service was trying to reduce the logging of white spruce, while setting AAC levels for the commercial forest. As the best sawlogs had already been removed through high grading, the government began to look to pulp-and-paper, as well as to new sawmill technologies capable of utilizing smaller trees. By the mid-1970s, seven new sawmills had been established; the pulp mill that had opened in the late 1960s was still in operation.[3]

The industry went into a brief decline in the 1980s and early 1990s. Due to the effects of decades of overcutting combined with the impacts of a severe forest fire that destroyed a ten-year supply of timber, one mill was forced to close in 1990 for lack of wood.[4] But while the steadily increasing level of exploitation took a slight dip in those years, the overwhelming trend was to increase logging. In the 1990s, Saskatchewan's forests were three times more heavily logged than they had been thirty years earlier.[5]

Prairie aspen and multinationals

While most Canadians would hardly identify Saskatchewan as a logging province, in the 1990s large multinationals like MacMillan Bloedel and Weyerhaeuser expanded production in the aspen forests of this prairie province.

MacMillan Bloedel, one of the largest forest companies at the time (with $3.9 billion in sales in 1994) was the first major industry giant in the forests of Saskatchewan. In 1965, it bought a waferboard plant in the town of Hudson Bay, a community virtually on the Manitoba border and far south of its marine namesake. It was expanded and ultimately converted to the production of oriented strand board (OSB). In corporate promotions for new OSB plants, MacMillan Bloedel claimed its Saskatchewan plant "was the base from which the multibillion-dollar commodity OSB industry has grown."[6]

The provincial government also tried its hand at running forest companies—hardly surprising in the heartland of the CCF and the wellspring of social-democratic politics. In 1949, it established the Saskatchewan Forest Products Corporation (Saskfor), a Crown corporation. It produced a range of forest products over the years—from railroad ties to fence posts and pulpwood. Saskfor had no pulp mill, but another Crown corporation, PapCo, operated one, originally built by Parsons and Whittemore. In 1973, Saskfor built the province's only plywood mill at Hudson Bay. It also operated a sawmill at Carrot River.

Saskfor ultimately formed an alliance with MacMillan Bloedel, Saskfor-MacMillan, which was created to bring in a new OSB plant on the Saskatchewan-Manitoba border. While MacMillan Bloedel's plant required 316,000 cubic metres of wood annually, the new mill required an additional 860,000 cubic metres, in a district already supporting the Saskfor sawmill, the plywood plant and thirty smaller sawmills. Logging would occur in the same ecoregion supplying the Louisiana-Pacific OSB plant on the Manitoba side of the border. Despite repeated attempts by First Nations and environmentalists to initiate an environmental review, the notion of looking at the *cumulative* impacts of logging the same ecoregion on two sides of an interprovincial border seemed to be beyond the grasp of any government. In September 1996, then federal Minister of Environment, Sergio Marchi, refused to undertake an environmental assessment of the OSB logging boom along the Saskatchewan-Manitoba border.

Provincial government involvement as an owner ended when it sold its interest in the Saskfor-MacMillan operations. Shortly afterwards, MacMillan Bloedel sold its entire Saskatchewan complex of operations to Weyerhaeuser.

Today, the dominant multinational forest corporation in Saskatchewan is Weyerhaeuser. Based in Tacoma, Washington, it is one of North America's largest forest-product companies. In 1986, it purchased the province's first pulp mill at Prince Albert, which had originally opened in 1969, as well as a chemical plant in Saskatoon (which it no longer owns), a sawmill and their related woodlands in Big River, in the middle of the province. Weyerhaeuser substantially expanded the facilities, constructing a 200,000-ton-per-year paper mill adjacent to the older pulp mill.[7] Weyerhaeuser's dominance was firmly established when in 1999 it bought out MacMillan Bloedel, including the operations that had been Saskfor-MacMillan.[8]

The government reduced the size of the Forest Management Agreement covering the original Weyerhaeuser logging by a third, but allowed the AAC to *double*. In 2001, the Saskatchewan government approved a twenty-year logging plan for the modified Weyerhaeuser holdings, while logging on the lands previously controlled by MacMillan Bloedel continued under a separate FMA. The multinational had control over 3 million hectares of the province.

Two private companies based in the province have substantial leases. Mistik Management is jointly owned by Millar Western Pulp and NorSask. Since 1999, NorSask has been completely owned by the Meadow Lake Tribal Council. The third big player in Saskatchewan's forest industry is also based in the province, L & M Wood Products Ltd. Founded in 1985, L & M has an FMA of nearly 71,000 hectares. All told, these three companies (Weyerhaeuser, Mistik and L & M) have leases covering nearly 100,000 square kilometres and are responsible for logging 20,000 hectares of forest annually.

Opposition to clear-cutting

In Saskatchewan, pressures to log the boreal led to more blockades and protests. In the Hudson Bay area in the east of the province, and in Meadow Lake to the west, there has been substantial and rapid expansion of the forest industry. The Meadow Lake blockade was organized by First Nations residents around Canoe Lake, calling themselves the "Protectors of Mother Earth." The irony is that the mill they were blockading, NorSask, was 40 per cent owned by the Meadow Lake Tribal Council.

The NorSask sawmill in western Saskatchewan had a complicated ownership structure. At the time, the Meadow Lake Tribal Council was only a partial owner, with a 40 per cent interest in the company. A corporation representing the workers (Techfor Sask) owned 40 per cent and the remaining 20 per cent was held by Millar Western, an Alberta-based pulp-and-paper company. The Meadow Lake pulp mill was 49 per cent owned by a government investment corporation, which had no management role in the mill, and 51 per cent controlled by various holding companies related to the only private corporation in the structure: Millar Western. The financing of the Meadow Lake pulp mill, arranged through an agreement in 1990, suggests a rather friendly brand of socialism. The government put up $60 million in direct investment, and a further $186 million in loans, under terms that called for repayment only after the company produced its first net profit. Millar Western bought its 51 per cent share in a $180-million, zero-effluent aspen pulp mill for $10.2 million. Meanwhile, the forest-management operations for NorSask's sawmill and the Meadow Lake pulp mill were looked after by Mistik.[9]

To attract greater levels of investment and increase production, the Saskatchewan government made favourable arrangements for long-term tenure through Forest Management Licence Agreements (FMLAs). The agreements ranged from 100,000 to in excess of 2 million cubic metres per year.[10] In all, nearly 8 million hectares of provincial forests are committed under FMLAs. As is the norm in other provinces, holders of FMLAs must be owners of forest-products processing facilities. Industries operating in Saskatchewan get the benefit of very low stumpage fees. In 2004, Weyerhaeuser, for example, paid a total of $9.86 per cubic metre of hardwood logged and $6.00 for softwood. Saskfor and the Mistik Management Group paid only $0.50 per cubic metre of hardwood and $5.20 for softwood.[11]

The trouble with the NorSask FMLA for the Meadow Lake area began almost from the minute the agreement was signed. In 1988, the government conveyed an FMLA to Mistik to provide raw material for NorSask's sawmill and the Millar Western pulp mill, granting rights for a twenty-year period to over 3.3 million hectares of forest—with an AAC of over 2 million cubic metres of combined hardwood and softwood per year.[12] Approval and financial support were given to Millar Western to build and operate the pulp mill before the completion of an environmental-impact statement on the wood supply. The same approach—approvals first, environmental-impact study later—was followed for the building of a new OSB plant in the Hudson Bay area.

Following protests by Cree and Métis residents in the Meadow Lake area and provincial environmentalists, the Environment Minister conceded that the twenty-year management plan did need an environmental assessment. But Mistik was given six years—until 1994—to prepare the plan and environmental assessment; in any event, the plan was not available for public review until August 1996. In the meantime, logging had been underway for years under the authority of the FMLA. The Protectors of Mother Earth (POME) pointed out that, by the time the assessment was complete, over 60,000 hectares of their traditional lands would have been clear-cut.

The situation became more confusing when it developed that the indigenous community of Green Lake had actually been owners of a sawmill, which the government, mistakenly believing it to be Crown-owned, had conveyed to NorSask. The conveyance of the sawmill had to be reversed. The value of the sawmill went from $84,000 when NorSask "bought" it two years earlier to $445,000 in compensation to NorSask when it turned out it could not properly be conveyed. As well, the FMLA included the traditional lands of the Cree and Métis people. Meanwhile, both POME and the Green Lake community alleged that cutting took place without prior legal authority, and that the mill had been operating without the required licence under the Clean Air Act. Underlying this whole mess was a morass of conflict of interest: the government was part owner of several entities that it was required to review and consider for approval.

In May 1992, as allegations of illegalities swirled around the government, the indigenous men, women and children of the communities around Canoe Lake, dissenting from the management of the Meadow Lake Tribal Council, set up their blockade. Community divisions ran deep, with the Meadow Lake Tribal Council pointing to the 80 per cent unemployment rate on the reserve and the need for development to save dispirited communities. The leadership had become convinced that their economic interests lay in industrial development. Once the NorSask sawmill and the Meadow Lake pulp mill were up and running, the Tribal Council entered into discussions with Atomic Energy of Canada Ltd. about becoming a high-level nuclear-waste repository, disassociating themselves entirely from the protesters, whom they characterized as lazy community members addicted to welfare.[13]

Led by the Meadow Lake elders, the protesters included local Cree and Métis people. On June 30, 1992, the RCMP decided that an injunction should be enforced. As one of the POME leaders put it, there was "an onslaught of close to one hundred uniformed

RCMP, a SWAT team with heavy weapons, shields and dogs."[14] The unarmed POME protesters refused to budge, so the Mounties moved to the clear-cut to allow NorSask contractors to remove logs felled before the blockade had been erected. When elders sat on the logs, they were arrested and taken away. In all, thirty people, including elders and pregnant women, were charged with intimidation—a charge subsequently amended to "obstruction" and eventually stayed.

The blockade continued, despite arrests, despite the sacrifices and hardship involved, through the winter and into the spring. There were more conflicts with the RCMP and more arrests. The provincial Minister of Resources at the time, Eldon Lautermilch, was asked by the news media if it was not hypocritical to enforce laws against the protesters when so many outstanding questions remained about the granting of the FMLA and the operations of the pulp mill. The minister replied, "I can't just pick and choose the laws which I'll enforce."[15]

There were good reasons for the Protectors of Mother Earth to oppose the rapid expansion of industrial forestry in their territory. Many indigenous people in Saskatchewan are dependent on the forest, returning to the bush to escape the grim social problems of the reserves, to hunt and fish and trap. Others make their living from the non-timber resources of the forest. There is a $5-million-a-year industry in wild rice in the Saskatchewan forest, and a smaller but growing business selling wild berries, both fresh and made into jams and jellies. Still others are seasonal mushroom pickers. The wild chanterelles, morels and pine mushrooms of the Saskatchewan forest are prized locally and as far away as Japan. About 4,500 kilograms of mushrooms are collected from Saskatchewan's forests each year, earning mushroom pickers $1 million annually.[16] Development in non-timber products from the forests has the potential to include native plants for use in herbal teas, oils and extracts and medicinal plants, as well as branches, twigs, cones and berries for crafts, floral arrangements and seasonal wreaths.

More traditional forest occupations bring benefits to the provincial economy, with tens of millions of dollars in revenue from commercial fishing, outfitting, big game hunting and trapping. Meanwhile, camping and tourism are estimated to bring $1.1 billion annually into the province,[17] with wildlife-viewing activities in 1996 amounting to another nearly $40 million.[18]

But for the Protectors of Mother Earth, what was at stake was not easily reduced to dollars and cents. They were protesting the loss of something sacred. Whether or not they succeeded is an open question. The government did, in 1999, create the opportunity for First Nations to more directly control their resources—an opportunity that is still more theoretical than real.

First Nations and the boreal

Since the end of the Canoe Lake blockade more than a decade ago, Saskatchewan First Nations have played a larger role in forest policy. As noted, Mistik is co-owned by the Meadow Lake Tribal Council, which in turn holds the largest FMA of any First Nation in Canada. Moreover, Mistik significantly increased the numbers of Aboriginal community members employed in its operations. Mistik is 50 per cent First Nations owned (Meadow Lake Tribal Council 50 per cent, Millar Western Pulp 50 per cent).[19] Other First Nations communities have entered into partnership arrangements with smaller forest companies. In November 2002, the Métis communities of Beauval, Buffalo Narrows, Green Lake, Ile-a-la-Crosse, La Loche, Patuanak and Pinehouse Lake created a partnership called Northwest Communities Wood Products Inc. The new Métis partnership was granted a five-year Timber Supply Licence (TSL) over nearly 800,000 hectares of forest. In October 2003, the Lac La Ronge Indian Band joined with Zelensky Brothers Forest Products and were granted a TSL for nearly 600,000 hectares, with an allowable annual cut of 350,000 cubic metres.[20] The Peter Ballantyne Band also has a forestry arm, Mee-Toos, with a timber permit allowing 60,000 cubic metres of logging every year.

Saskatchewan forest laws require integrated land-use planning for each management unit of its forest. This progressive requirement has engaged First Nations across the province in planning decisions. In the vast northern boreal, where unallocated forest still remains, a land-use process with the Athabasca Denesuline, the Dene of northern Saskatchewan, will make decisions that impact 12 million hectares. The Athabasca Planning Area process is the largest land-use planning exercise in Saskatchewan history, covering over 15 per cent of the province.[21] Although incomplete at this writing, the exercise could protect a large part of the land base from forestry and mining.

The Athabasca Denesuline are dependent on the Barren Grounds caribou herds, around which their lives and culture revolve. While roads and mines have already intruded on their territory, this huge tract of wilderness is primarily undisturbed. What makes the Athabasca Denesuline planning process hugely significant is its emphasis on traditional knowledge. The Dene First Nations are accumulating and mapping a huge amount of data about non-timber values. The comprehensive Traditional Land Use and Occupancy Mapping has pulled together information from over six hundred elders and traditional users of the land, creating about 70,000 data points for mapping. If this approach was taken in every FMA, it would mark a paradigm shift in land-use decisions.

Protecting the northern boreal forest is increasingly a preoccupation of Canadian environmental groups. While the value of fibre to the mills is calculable, it is the loss of economically less quantifiable values that strikes at the heart of biodiversity—the forest margin habitats, gone with clear-cutting, the loss of hardwood habitat for neotropical migratory songbirds, and the vanishing of old-growth forest habitat. As ecologist Michael Fitzsimmons observed: "Boreal forests do not have the popular appeal of rainforests, and they contain no high-profile endangered species. However, in Saskatchewan terms, forests such as these are rich ecosystems."[22]

The recent booms in hardwood logging for oriented strand board mills pose a serious threat to the biodiversity of the mixed-wood boreal. Saskatchewan's forests are being transformed, with hardwood on a rotation schedule of clear-cuts every seventy years and softwoods every ninety. The characteristics of old growth will disappear. The Saskatchewan government has estimated that, of the rare plants in the province, 29 per cent are found in the commercial forest region.[23]

The drastic increase in forestry led to a renewed push for logging roads into previously untouched areas. By 1987, there were 42,000 kilometres of logging roads, which cumulatively removed 65,874 hectares of the forest land base. The impact of roads on forest biodiversity is significant and lasts well past initial logging.

In April 1999, then Premier Roy Romanow announced even more ambitious plans to expand logging and mills in the province. Calling it the "single biggest announcement of private-sector job creation in the history of the province," Romanow unveiled plans to double the rate of logging and the number of mills.[24]

As logging increased, it was critical that adequate representative ecosystem areas be given protected status. Despite significant announcements in the last five years, less than 4 per cent of Saskatchewan's land base has strictly protected status, although a further 4 per cent is protected with some tourism, fishing and hunting allowed.[25] Since the late 1990s a number of new protected areas have been created in Saskatchewan's boreal forest, but the province is still far behind the rest of the country in achieving adequate levels of protection for its ecosystems.

Forested ecosystems in Saskatchewan require protection from more than logging. In the southern regions, deforestation occurs as forested lands are converted to agriculture, while, in the far northern forests, widespread uranium mining and potential hydroelectric development on the Churchill River threaten ecosystems for miles around.

Legislative reform

In 1996, Saskatchewan was the scene of battles between the industry and reformers who wanted to create a new sustainable forest policy. The provincial government had introduced a Forest Management Act to remedy weaknesses in its forest regulations. The draft act, by doubling stumpage fees, would have generated far more revenue for the province, which could have helped with the costs of an accurate inventory and seedling nurseries for reforestation. Where the province received $3.5 million for all its major mills and clear-cut forests, under the new law the government would have received $7 million. As well, individual companies would be hit with new fees to cover silviculture, fire-fighting and insecticides.[26]

Looking at the new costs, the industry went ballistic. Ray Cariou of NorSask complained that "They're just making the situation in the north untenable. Jobs that would be created in the north would be cancelled."[27] Weyerhaeuser announced that it had been contemplating plans to double the size of its pulp-and-paper mill in Prince Albert as well as its sawmill in Big River. All told, the company claimed that the new law could kill $1 billion worth of expansion. Steve Smith, Weyerhaeuser's vice-president, said, "This is not what we would consider fertile ground for growth and investment."[28] And Saskfor-MacMillan CEO John Robillard began to express doubts about restarting its postponed Hudson Bay oriented strand board project: "We couldn't survive as a company, with all the downloading of government and the doubling of stumpage."[29]

Interestingly, no one in the Saskatchewan media compared what the companies were paying with the competition in other provinces, much less what was being spent south of the border. Even doubled, the Saskatchewan stumpage rate would only equal Ontario's hardwood stumpage. Inadequate inventories don't trouble the industry. As long as it can get virtually free wood, subsidized mills and lax environmental enforcement, the industry will stay in business—until it runs out of wood to feed its hungry mills.

The industry's relentless lobbying paid off. Between the first and second reading of the legislation, the act was substantially weakened. Stumpage fees were not raised—that was left to future negotiation—and the industry will not have to finance insect, fire and disease protection. The industry also succeeded in protecting the favourable terms it enjoys under lease agreements. And any changes to the FMLA will have to go through the legislature, instead of the proposed, more accessible route of a change by regulation.[30] The Forest Management Act came into force in 1999. Subsequent amendments have not overturned the industry win while the legislation was under development. Amendments in 2003 were designed to improve Saskatchewan's position in the ongoing softwood trade wars with the United States. As a result, the amendments open up the possibility of selling logs on the open market, adjusting the fees charged and increasing the flexibility around the cancellation of harvesting rights for companies that do not maximize their AAC allocations.

Is Saskatchewan running out of wood to feed its mills?

Of Saskatchewan's 24.3 million hectares of forest, half are classified as commercial.[31] It is from this area that the AAC is calculated, even though the forest leases are primarily the 8 million hectares in the middle to southern zones of the provincial forests.

Ever since Saskatchewan's first provincial inventory was completed, there have been concerns about its reliability. But recently the doubts about the inventory have become even more pronounced. Cutbacks have forced the government forest service to abandon rudimentary ground checks and permanent plot sampling, and the quality of the aerial photography, used as the basis for the inventory, has been compromised.

Saskatchewan's 1993 *State of the Resource Report* provided a surprisingly candid and blunt appraisal of the inventory and its limitations. The inventory was criticized for out-of-date information and low-quality aerial photography (photographers were hired on "short annual contracts, based on selection criteria stressing the lowest bids"). It was also cited for widely varying standards of accuracy and detail from one part of the forest to another, weaknesses in the stand classification system and areas where "inventory coverage is lacking." All in all, the inventory was summarized as having "weak areas, inefficiencies, and limitations and...some serious deficiencies brought about by recent cutbacks. The shortcomings will become more critical if the forest resource management is expanded."[32]

Forest exploitation *is* being expanded and intensified. Huge areas are being committed, in the absence of either environmental assessment or an accurate inventory. The twenty-year logging plan for Weyerhaeuser, completed in 2001, allows overall harvesting rates in its lease areas to increase by 26 per cent. The provincial government admitted that the plan was "logging-based," not "ecosystem-based."[33] The plan also allows the logging of much younger trees, gradually reducing the age at harvest from 120 years to 65 years. With the enlarged wood allocations, Weyerhaeuser doubled production at its Big River sawmill, making it one of the largest mills in Canada.

The 1999 provincial government promise to double the size of its forest industry came complete with a list of new mills to be delivered by the private sector. Ten new projects were highlighted in then Premier Romanow's announcement, of which four never came about due to a lack of financing or failed partnership efforts. Despite some non-starters, most of what the provincial government touted as its biggest-ever job creation announcement were at least built, even if two mills are not operating. Weyerhaeuser took over the Saskfor-MacMillan OSB mill in Hudson Bay and built a mill in partnership with several First Nations in Prince Albert. The completed mill has not been able to open due to supply problems created by the softwood tariffs. The softwood tariffs are also blamed for reduced job creation at the new sawmill built by the partnership between the Lac La Ronge First Nation and Zelensky Brothers. A new OSB plant was built in Meadow Lake by a group that includes Tolko, Meadow Lake Tribal Council and a Métis partnership—the Northwest Communities.

Much of the new development was made possible by Weyerhaeuser reallocating wood volume surplus within its Forest

Management Agreement. Still, a commitment to double the forest industry carries significant environmental consequences. The impacts of expanded industrial operations are becoming apparent. The new Tolko OSB mill has placed serious pressures on the forests managed by Mistik logging. Old-growth forest in the Weyerhaeuser FMA is being liquidated. Other than in the Mistik forest area, the Aboriginal communities are not effectively engaged in forest management. The protected areas strategy is still incomplete, and may come too late for some critical areas.

There is no doubt that areas in the middle to southern reaches of the boreal and aspen parkland, referred to by the forest service as the "Commercial Zone," are being overcut.[34] As in other provinces across the country, as softwood is overcut and supplies dwindle, the government and industry look to "underutilized" hardwood. Of course, the birds and animals that live in those forests utilize them quite nicely. But, for industry purposes, the aspen and mixed-wood boreal represent only an opportunity for expansion at a time when industry would otherwise be forced to reduce logging operations.

Logging rates for hardwood are catching up with softwood. In 1992, 2 million cubic metres of softwood were logged, as well as 1.4 million cubic metres of hardwood. But the new and proposed mills are moving toward hardwood. The Millar Western pulp mill at Meadow Lake runs entirely on hardwood—825,000 cubic metres annually. And further large increases in hardwood use will come from OSB manufacture.

As more hardwood is logged, some forest operations have shifted from taking only the softwood and leaving the mixed wood behind, to a 100 per cent clear-cut to remove all the trees of all species from the site.[35] About 80 per cent of the logging in Saskatchewan is by clear-cutting, and the forest service is actively promoting increased reliance on clear-cuts, claiming problems with regeneration success after selective cutting.[36]

With the recent addition of twelve new OSB plants, Canada had twenty-two operating plants in 1997. The quick increase in supply led to a glut in the market between 1995 and 1996. Prices fell from $300 (U.S.) for 1,000 square feet (305 square metres) in September 1995 to $190 (U.S.) in February 1996.

The "Green Rush" has hit Saskatchewan. While the numbers for timber supply may look healthy, the reality is far different. The best forest areas are already substantially overcut. The reserves are currently unavailable, and their inventories are inexact and unreliable. A particularly worrying trend is the failure of regeneration on logged-over areas. According to data from the most recent year for which statistics are available, Saskatchewan's percentage of not satisfactorily restocked (NSR) lands is the highest in Canada—64 per cent.[37] The problem is alarming. According to a report from Global Forest Watch, "two-thirds of the forests logged in Saskatchewan since 1975 cannot be considered stocked."[38]

Prior to 1986, FMAs granted in Saskatchewan did not contain any requirements for renewal. For example, a Seattle-based company, Simpson Timber, granted an FMA in 1965, cleaned out mature stands of white spruce, ignored the government demands that replanting take place, and, after twenty-five years, closed its mill and moved away. Approximately one-quarter of the NSR lands in the province is on the logged-over lands left by Simpson Timber.[39] Still, research shows that logging in the boreal is leading to a steady increase in the proportion of NSR lands. One government analysis suggests that the rate of increasing deforestation as determined in 1993, over the next ninety years, would lead to a 34 per cent reduction in the AAC.[40]

As every province overbuilds its processing capacity, as every province overcuts, all the elements of an ecosystem disaster are in place. In the words of former World Bank economist Herman Daly, "There is something fundamentally wrong in treating the Earth as if it were a business in liquidation."[41]

Saskatchewan

Forest and other wooded land in million hectares	24.3
Stocked harvested Crown land in hectares (2000)	150,000*
Area logged in hectares (2002)	23,222
Volume logged in million cubic metres (2002)	4.3
Annual allowable cut in million cubic metres (2001)	8.9

Source: Natural Resources Canada, Canadian Forest Service, *The State of Canada's Forests 2003–2004* (Ottawa, 2004). These are federal government summaries, based on provincial government data. The figures are not necessarily accurate.
* The stocked harvested Crown land figure comes from the previous year's *State of Canada's Forests*. The most recent report lists as "unavailable" both the stocked and unstocked figures.

Saskatchewan Corporate Players

L & M Wood Products Ltd.
Millar Western
Mistik Management
Tolko
Weyerhaeuser Canada Ltd.

Alberta

Alberta is oil and cattle country, where business barons are heroes, and the annual Calgary Stampede is its most famous cultural icon.

But Alberta also has a long tradition of ecotourism, if you can call Victorian travellers relaxing at a spa-like hotel at Banff, "ecotourism." The first national park in Canada was established in Banff, Alberta, in 1886. The Rocky Mountains provide a rich habitat for a wealth of biological diversity. A second Rockies National Park followed in Jasper. And countless other areas of Alberta's complex landscape, from flat prairie to mountainous peaks, to forests and unique habitats such as the Whaleback, are magnificent ecological treasures and essential parts of another Alberta identity. But the Alberta business ethic is a threat to them all.

Wood Buffalo National Park, for example, is designated a World Heritage Site by the United Nations, yet it took a court case to stop logging there. Subjected to clear-cut logging since the end of the Second World War, this national park has been stripped of virtually all its old-growth boreal.[1]

Hotels and ski resorts, sprawling developments, golf courses and highways are hemming in the wildlife in Banff, while open-pit coal mining has been approved within 3 kilometres of Jasper National Park, threatening critical ecosystems even within Canada's strictest protection designation.

Unlike the eastern provinces, Alberta did not experience early surges in logging followed by a gradual transition to the kind of full-throttle exploitation endured by, for example, New Brunswick. Alberta has a very short history of forestry, with exploitation moving into high gear in the mid-1980s. During the Alberta "green rush," huge areas of the province have been offered up to multinationals. Large investors, primarily from Japan and the United States, moved in on Alberta's boreal. It was the last big land grab. The boreal forest in Alberta was auctioned off at the lowest prices anywhere—Premier Ralph Klein, receiver in a classic case of bankruptcy, presiding: Everything must go.

Early forests

Alberta's fire history created forests that were even-aged and dominated by few species. The government estimates that 47.4 per cent of the forest is composed of pure coniferous stands and 32.8 per cent of pure deciduous trees.[2] The use of the term "pure stands" is not accurate ecologically, but an instrument of measurement for forest allocation purposes. Alberta's forests are more commonly mixed stands of white and black spruce, jack pine, aspen, poplar and birch. Pure stands are less common. Fire typically removes the climax species of white spruce, and replaces it with invading pioneer species, such as aspen. In the Alberta foothills, the pattern is slightly different, with conifer forests of lodgepole pine dominant.

Into this naturally driven engine of change, death and rebirth, came the first settlers. As town sites sprang up in the late nineteenth century, large sawmills began to provide for Calgary, Edmonton, Red Deer and Crowsnest Pass. But the forest did not inspire huge levels of trade, as it had in the east (and to the west, where British Columbia's timber trade was burgeoning in the mid-1800s). Alberta's forest industry primarily served local needs until the first plywood mill was built in 1953. Located in Grande Prairie, the mill processed only hardwood species. A few years later, a pulp mill followed in Hinton, northwest of Edmonton. By 1970, the forest industry was cutting over 4 million cubic metres a year to feed its mills.[3]

Forests for sale

In the mid-1980s, the Alberta government adopted a deliberate industrial forest strategy. Unlike most Canadian provinces, where land-use decisions were constrained by existing agreements with the forest industry, Alberta was still in a position to decide where logging could go, where oil and gas would be allowed and where tourism would be encouraged.[4]

With the goal of diversification of the provincial economy, federal and provincial governments provided research and development funding to adapt Japanese technology to the pulping of aspen. As aspen dominated large areas of Alberta's post-fire successional ecosystem, technological innovation could provide a commercial value to a previously "worthless" tree. Once the technology had been perfected, Alberta's Forest Minister hit the road, hoping to lure Japanese- and U.S.-based corporations to northern Alberta.[5] With 87 per cent of the forest in Crown land, controlled by the provincial government, Alberta could promise investors huge tracts of forest, low stumpage rates and a cookie jar of other subsidies.

As an industrial strategy, it was a smashing success. Between 1986, when the venture was launched, and 1994, over $3.7 billion in new investments were made in Alberta's forest industry—moving forests up to the rank of the province's fourth-largest business, after oil and gas, agriculture and tourism.[6] In fact, the bulk of the aggressive marketing and new mill commitments was packed into the short space of eighteen months, between September 1987 and March 1989. By the time Forest Minister Leroy Fjordbotten was through with the marketing blitz of the century, Alberta and the federal government had committed $1 billion in loans and subsidies and thousands of square kilometres of forest to the industry, in seven new and two renegotiated Forest Management Agreements (FMAs), each with a twenty-year renewable licence.[7]

Alberta's big forest giveaway covered 136,120 square kilometres, or roughly one-fifth of the province. The FMAs required the companies to do any road building not specifically subsidized through other agreements, but left the province responsible for all fire and insect protection. The FMA holder also committed to being financially responsible for the regeneration of the site. But the subsidy that continues is the cheap stumpage rate. After the first round of negotiations, Alberta doubled its stumpage, which was embarrassingly low, even by Alberta standards of corporate charity. Softwood stumpage for pulp mills ranged from $1.50 to $2.50 per cubic metre, dropping as low as $0.25 per cubic metre for aspen.

Even with the doubling of stumpage and with nearly $5 billion invested in mills, in the year 2001–2002 Alberta collected $64 million in timber royalties and fees, spent $25 million on forest management, $306 million on forest fire suppression (although much of this was for reasons of public safety) and an undisclosed amount on road maintenance.[8] For all its devotion to commercial goals, not only did the province fail to make money on its new forestry industrial base, it lost money and exported jobs.

In the wake of the great forest sell-off, a number of forest giants had settled in the province. The Al-Pac mill, owned by Mitsubishi and Oji Paper of Japan, has the largest FMA in the province, a territory of a single block of 58,000 square kilometres. The other Japanese firm, Daishowa-Marubeni, also secured a single huge block of territory— 29,000 square kilometres under a single FMA. Tolko has several FMAs, totalling 39,400 square kilometres. Weyerhaeuser is also established in Alberta, with nearly 30,000 square kilometres of forest in several FMAs. Lastly, International Paper, having purchased Weldwood with its mill in Hinton as well as Sunpine, has a number of FMAs, totalling nearly 17,000 square kilometres. In addition to these five largest companies, another five play a significant role. All of these companies log as well as operate mills, primarily pulp mills, both kraft and chemical thermal mechanical pulp processing, sawmills and OSB mills.

The approval process for Al-Pac's mill on the Athabasca River was highly controversial. The Athabasca is a major tributary to the enormous Mackenzie River Basin, which covers 570,000 square kilometres of Canada's north. In 1990, a joint federal-provincial environmental assessment pointed to existing high levels of dioxin and furans in the Athabasca, raising concerns for the safety of fish for human consumption downstream in the Northwest Territories. The sheer size of the mill and the cumulative impact of so many mills led the panel to recommend that it not proceed. In response, Alberta convened its own "independent" assessment of the scientific data, angering many who felt the environmental assessment process was being undermined. Meanwhile, Al-Pac realized that its corporate interests coincided with a higher environmental standard. It revised its proposal, reducing organochlorine emissions by a factor of five. The province issued the approval, and the mill went into production.[9]

The Al-Pac mill is the largest single-line bleached kraft pulp mill in North America, but all the secondary paper processing is done elsewhere. The economics of transforming cheap Alberta wood into expensive Japanese paper go something like this: the stumpage rates charged by Alberta when it first negotiated the deal would total $90 for a stand of sixteen aspen trees, fifty feet (15 metres) tall. Once converted into pulp, they would fetch $590. After finishing and paper processing in Japan, the end product is worth $1,250.[10]

The Daishowa mill also benefited from generous provincial government assistance, and also received a federal subsidy from the Western Diversification Office for road building to the mill. However, neither government gave much thought to the rights of local First Nations residents of the area; Daishowa's Forest Management Agreement covered much of the traditional lands of the Lubicon Cree.

The Lubicon had already been subjected to serial abuses from the combined impacts of oil and gas development and logging. Within a two-year period in the early 1980s, more than four hundred oil wells were drilled within a 24-kilometre radius of the Lubicon village of Little Buffalo. UNOCAL, a California-based oil and gas company, built a sour gas battery plant within 5 kilometres of the same community. Sour gas is exactly what it sounds like, with the rotten-egg smell of hydrogen-sulfide emissions posing health problems for the Lubicon. The oil and gas sector did not discriminate against the Lubicon; its gas wells were located across the province near ranches and farms and homes, prompting the only campaign of eco-sabotage in Canadian history, culminating in the trial of Weibo Ludwig.[11]

The health of the Lubicon was also being compromised by logging. As traditional sources of food in the bush become unavailable, they relied increasingly on store-bought food. The rate of diabetes has soared, as have suicides, still-births and other social problems. What was once a healthy, self-sustaining community has been devastated. Currently, 95 per cent of the population is on welfare, and 35 per cent have health problems ranging from tuberculosis to respiratory problems and cancer—at rates that exceed the national average.[12]

When the Lubicon Cree discovered that the giant forest deals with Japanese multinationals had taken place in their traditional territory, they mounted blockades and appeals across Canada and around the world for help. A "Boycott Daishowa" campaign followed, featuring consumer boycotts that caused some of Daishowa's customers, such as Pizza Pizza, to switch suppliers. Daishowa initially tried intimidation, suing a number of young people in Toronto, known as "Friends of the Lubicon," for millions of dollars in business losses.

The Japanese investors had already used intimidation to good effect in silencing an Alberta critic. The late John McInnis, Associate Director of the University of Alberta Environmental Resource Studies

Center, had attended a conference in Japan, where he was critical of the giant giveaway of Alberta's forests to Mitsubishi, Honshu Paper and Daishowa-Marubeni. Shortly after he returned to Canada, his job at the University of Alberta was gone. Something had been said to the university about a promised multimillion-dollar commitment to research that could be in jeopardy under the circumstances. Despite lawsuits, he was never reinstated.

Daishowa modified logging and began to deal more directly with the Lubicon, instituting a temporary moratorium on logging Lubicon land. But Japanese investors were heard to complain that, when the government was courting them, no mention was made of disputed land titles with Alberta's indigenous peoples. In fact, many of the FMAs, negotiated without consultation with Alberta First Nations, are for unceded traditional lands. The Grand Chief of Treaty 8, Johnson Seewepegaham, stated his position that the FMAs are inconsistent with existing First Nations rights pursuant to treaty entitlements.[13] A Cree elder spoke eloquently of what these developments mean to his people:

> This you must know: this land, these forests and waters, are
> not just resources to be harvested and managed. They were
> given to us to take care of and treat with respect, the way our
> grandfathers have always done. We are responsible for taking
> care of Mother Earth because she takes care of us. These
> pulp mills will take those things away from them. The land
> won't be the same after they take away the trees. This destruc-
> tion weighs heavily on us, like a war. You don't need a war to
> destroy a native person. Just take away the bush, just take
> away the trees. That will destroy us. The money will be all
> that is left.[14]

Still, the current conservative government of Premier Ralph Klein, like that of his predecessor, Don Getty, remains unwilling to address issues of First Nations rights and resolution of land claims. What is more curious is that the federal government, with a constitutional obligation to protect First Nations rights, has been willing not only to turn a blind eye to the Alberta development boom on First Nations land, but even to subsidize it through the Western Diversification Office, a regional development fund. While across Canada the trend has been toward increasing engagement of First Nations in partnerships with the private sector, or in managing forest licences, there are no First Nations–owned mills in Alberta.

The large expansion in the production capacity in Alberta's forests led to a drastic increase in clear-cut logging. Twenty years before, Alberta was cutting about 4 million cubic metres of wood a year. By 2002 that amount had increased six-fold, to 24.6 million cubic metres logged.[15] The Forest Management Agreements and long-term leases issued in the 1980s and 1990s have basically allocated all of Alberta's forests—99.6 per cent of all estimated coniferous forest and 88.6 per cent of the deciduous trees.[16] Many people, even within the industry, are wondering if there is enough wood to go around.

The myth of the endless forest

Alberta invested heavily in the technology to pulp aspen and laid the groundwork for a massive marketing campaign aimed at the world's forest companies. One would imagine that the province had conducted a careful inventory of its forest to determine how much wood was available for the "green rush." One would be wrong.

The forest inventory in place when Alberta handed out eleven FMAs, covering one-fifth of the province, was completed using aerial photography taken between 1970 and 1982. Unlike other provinces' efforts to continuously update the inventory with permanent plot sampling and new photography, Alberta's updates consist of removing areas of inventory known to have been devastated by fire or logging.[17] Relying on photos creates real problems in differentiating hardwood species, such as aspen and balsam poplar. Moreover, while such a rough cut at the inventory stage provides guidance as to the broad generalities of forest age and composition, it is notoriously unreliable as a basis for making specific assessments of volume.

Before 1966, record-keeping was spotty. No one really knows for sure what areas were cut in the past, and so regeneration success on those lands is hard to judge. Meanwhile, with the recent surge in clear-cut logging, it is likely that 95 per cent of what is being logged has never been logged before.

In 1991, the forest service itself called on the government to provide the necessary funds to establish another three thousand permanent sample plots, so that the work of verifying estimates based on aerial photography could begin.[18] In fact, the forest service study

came to the conclusion that significant budgetary increases were necessary if the forest service was to cope with the runaway increase in
logging. Without an increase of $40 million by the 1992–1993
budget, the report warned that "the Alberta Forest Service will be
unable to monitor and enforce the environmental standards promised
by the Government of Alberta to its citizens...[and that] insufficient
staffing will prevent the division from protecting forests from large-
scale environmental damage."[19] But no such increases were made. In
fact, the budget has continually been reduced.

From this doubtful inventory, the province estimated its annual
allowable cut (AAC). The government's own view is that "the
approach used to determine the AACs must be flexible and sensitive
to a wide range of users...the selected AAC was a management decision and not strictly a calculation."[20] There is a remarkable degree of
candour in the Al-Pac Forest Management Plan as to what factors
directed the level of permissible cutting. "The proposed annual allowable cut (AAC) on the deciduous land base was *calculated based on
the mill requirements*, plus an 11 per cent allowance for stand structure, fire losses and local timber permits, less the volume of
deciduous wood that is expected from the coniferous land base"
[emphasis added].[21]

Alberta adopted an intensive forest management regime in the
early 1970s, and like the other provinces, it used the allowable-cut
effect to authorize more logging in the short term, based on speculative future growth as a result of promised silviculture.[22] In short,
every effort was being made to exaggerate the wood supply.

Alberta has already run into problems in overestimating the forest.
In a general overview of the most recent inventory, an Expert Review
Panel on Forest Management in Alberta concluded: "In at least one
volume sampling region, the stand volumes associated with the...
inventory types appears to be too high by as much as 30 per cent."[23]
The FMA for the Alberta Newsprint Company, producing a partly
recycled newsprint and holding one of the province's smaller FMAs
for 500,000 cubic metres a year, also overestimated the available
wood by as much as 30 per cent. Leaked briefing notes from the forest service in April 1993 argued that the AAC for the FMA should be
reduced by the same amount.[24]

Another problem emerged when the province was courting Procter
& Gamble to come to the Manning area. Having offered the company

an area with a 675,000 cubic metre AAC, the forest service discovered that, in reality, the wood supply was nowhere near that volume. Chief Forester Ken Higginbotham was quoted as saying, "The timber supplies are very young and there is virtually no timber that is harvestable at present."[25] Fortunately for the province, it was in the rare position of not having executed the FMA in advance. Procter & Gamble backed out, and the AAC was reduced to 300,000 cubic metres. In the case of Al-Pac, the timber inventories were done *after* the FMAs were signed.

The provincial government did not improve the forest inventory. The forest companies themselves did. Under the 1999 Forest Act, the holders of FMAs were put in charge of conducting updated inventories to a new high-resolution Alberta Vegetation standard. The quality of the information is far better, but it is no longer publicly available; the inventories of public forest are now the proprietary information of the forest industry.

The Forest Act was not prescriptive. Other than establishing that the purpose of forest management is to provide a perpetual sustained yield, the act was minimal in its powers. Most of the guidance for forest policy was relegated to policy directives.[26] Increasingly in Alberta, individual forest companies were responsible for conservation innovations. Given the nature of the Klein government, companies such as Al-Pac were easily more environmentally sensitive than the government.

Part of the reason for Alberta's casual attitude toward its wood supply is that its bureaucrats suffered from the same misconception as the early loggers of the Ottawa Valley a century before; they believed that Alberta enjoyed inexhaustible timber resources. Back in 1970, when total logging came to 4.1 million cubic metres, the AAC was set at 26 million cubic metres. The wood supply had a healthy margin for error. The margin is shrinking. Now, the AAC is set at 26.2 million cubic metres and the volume logged is nearly 24.6 million cubic metres.[27] In fact, shrinking the gap between the AAC and the volume harvested is the explicit target of the provincial government. The Forest Industry Development Target is described: "Increase the timber cut and reduce the gap between the harvest and the Annual Allowable Cut (AAC) cap."[28] Looking at logging pressures from the forest industry does not tell the full story.

The situation is made worse by logging on private land, none of which is regulated or inventoried. While many provinces make an effort to include private lands in their AAC, Alberta does not.[29] Although only 4 per cent of Alberta's forests are privately owned, since the 1990s they have been heavily overcut.[30] Many farmers still clear their land for grazing. Conversion of forest for agriculture is not the only problem. When pulp prices were sky-high in the mid-1990s, and British Columbia, just over the mountains, began running out of wood for its mills, large-scale clear-cutting of private land became a serious environmental threat. No one knows how much wood left Alberta during this period, unprocessed, for mills to the west and in Montana to the south. In 1994–1995, the amount of wood cut from private lands was estimated at approximately 2.3 million cubic metres, but it could be more.[31] In the first half of 1995, $3 million worth of timber crossed the border into British Columbia *every two days*.[32]

Even after nearly doubling stumpage rates in 1994, the province of Alberta collected only $10 to $12 per cubic metre in stumpage for its coniferous wood, whereas B.C. mills were offering $48.75 per cubic metre, *at the stump*.[33] Cheap wood from private land in Alberta was a windfall for the B.C. forest industry. Even after the costs of transportation, it was cheaper than logging locally.

In response, a 1995 federal-provincial government study urged caution regarding any further FMAs: "Further allocations of the few remaining uncommitted public forests in Alberta is inadvisable and not consistent with the current national and international directions in forest stewardship."[34] Ty Lund, provincial Environment Minister at the time, dismissed the study as one man's opinion. In fact, it was the work of twenty-one scientists.[35]

The reality is that new forestry allocations are extremely unlikely. The forest has been fully allocated to existing forest industries. The last wilderness areas in the province are under assault from industrial activity, and time is running out.

For example, two of Alberta's remaining wild spaces, Castle Wilderness and Bighorn Country, are threatened by forestry and oil and gas. Located in west-central Alberta, they are home to grizzly bears, elk, and gray wolves. Sierra Club of Canada, with a coalition of other local, national and international groups, has been pushing for the protection of Bighorn Country as a 7,000-square-kilometre conservation area. Bighorn Country is sufficient in size to provide habitat for predators that require a large range.

In 2004, Castle Wilderness was selected as a "biogem," an endangered wild place, by the National Resources Defence Council (NRDC), an American-based environmental organization. The NRDC noted that the wilderness area was under significant threat from the oil and gas industry, which has proposed a plan to build up to six new sour gas wells in an area considered critical habitat for grizzly bears.

The Alberta government has shown scant regard for endangered species. The province's draft Recovery Plan for Woodland Caribou, released in 2004, contained graphs of declining caribou populations and details on the increased level of industrial activity within their habitat. While some on the recovery team pushed to protect habitat, pressure from industry won out. Logging and oil and gas exploration continue at present within areas critical for caribou survival, while range teams explore options for the individual caribou populations.

The footprint of oil and gas

The forests leased to the forest companies under FMAs are not exclusively the domain of those industries. They are also open to oil and gas development. Even though they are operating over the same land base, the forestry companies and the oil and gas companies do not generally engage in integrated planning. The impact of oil and gas in Alberta is not inconsequential. In fact, the annual amount of forest removal by oil and gas companies for seismic lines, pipelines, roads and transmission lines can be nearly as much as a forest company's annual harvest.

The amount of forest disappearing as the Athabasca Tar Sands operations multiply is staggering. When one thinks of petroleum development, an oil well usually comes to mind. In the Athabasca region, don't think of oil wells; visualize open-pit mining on a gargantuan scale. Each bitumen mining operation involves the removal of all forest and surface soils and often streams and wetlands from an area as large as 10,000 hectares. No one has a current accurate figure for the total amount of forest removed in the oil sands operations, but it is easily over 100,000 hectares.[36] And no end is in sight for petroleum expansion. Another $50 billion in new investment in the Athabasca region has already been announced.[37]

The issue of the wood supply impacts of the oil and gas industry gained public attention in Alberta thanks to the actions of the forest giant, Al-Pac. Al-Pac became concerned about the cumulative impact of the activities the Alberta government had permitted over the same land base. With the largest FMA in the province, over 58,000 square kilometres in the northeastern part of the province, entirely within the hydrocarbon-rich Western Canadian Sedimentary Basin and covering most oil sands development, Al-Pac's territory made an ideal case study. The company commissioned scientists from the University of Alberta as well as independent consultants to attempt to quantify the combined impact of all disturbances over its FMA. The study developed a computer model to predict the changes in the FMA over a hundred-year period.

The results, published in the journal *Conservation Ecology* in 2003, were startling.[38] Alberta news media condensed the science with the headline: "Energy, Forestry on collision course in northern Alberta."[39] The *Edmonton Journal* made the study the subject of an editorial:

> The provincial government prefers to manage the forest by voluntary cooperation between the two industries. But clearly, that's not good enough.... This report is another wake-up call for government.[40]

The researchers found that while Al-Pac and other small operators in the region logged 16,000 hectares per year, the combined activity of the petroleum sector cleared nearly as much forest—11,000 hectares.[41] For each well drilled, Al-Pac's GIS data suggested 3 kilometres of seismic lines had been cleared. As the oil and gas business left permanent structures and often replaced forest with replanted grasses, its activities constituted permanent deforestation. None of this forest removal made its way into the AAC calculation. Neither did the losses from fire. The study estimated that 0.65 per cent of northern Alberta was lost every year to fire, and that this amount was increasing.

All told, the study concluded that if the conflicting resource use continued unabated, within sixty years the forest industry would face wood shortages to maintain the fibre flow to mills. The model anticipated significant shifts in the age classes and structure of the forest, with old-growth softwood virtually disappearing within twenty years, and old-growth hardwood being eliminated within sixty-five years. Forest fragmentation would also increase dramatically. At current rates of disturbance, every square kilometre of forest logged results in 1.8 kilometres of fragmented habitat. Over the one hundred years of the study, the researchers saw the cumulative impact from all industries increase that edge to 8 kilometres. Without a significant change in direction, wildlife will be severely affected. The woodland caribou, already in trouble throughout the boreal and listed as "threatened" in Alberta, will be particularly impacted with its available habitat shrinking from its current 43 per cent of the study area to just 6 per cent.

"Although the boreal forest presents a seemingly endless expanse," the article concluded, "it does in fact have limits and they are now being reached."[42]

Voluntary efforts to better coordinate activities across the landscape to reduce the cumulative impact have not proven effective. To Al-Pac's credit, it did propose an environmentally sensitive approach to the Liege watershed, asking the petroleum industry to join with the forest industry in applying ecological benchmarks. Not only did the oil and gas industry rebuff the offer, it actually increased activities in the watershed, accelerating disturbance of the forest ecosystem.[43]

The Alberta government is committed to a massive industrialization strategy. Unfortunately for the various industries—whether forestry, mining, oil and gas or ranching—the province has not bothered to consider the cumulative impacts. Caught in the crossfire between competing interests is the environment itself.

Caught in the crossfire

Environmental damage has already begun. Biodiversity is threatened, with plants and animals dependent on the boreal becoming rare or endangered. In Alberta's forests, the yellow Indian tansy and the cypripedium orchid, rare plants of the boreal, are threatened.[44] The wood bison is currently found only in national parks or in captivity in Alberta, with other jurisdictions, such as the Northwest Territories, reintroducing wood bison to the wild. Its once thundering masses have been reduced to a captive herd in Elk Island National Park and the wild bison of Wood Buffalo National Park. The grizzly bear, woodland caribou, bobcat and Canada lynx are in trouble; so, too, are the trumpeter swan, whooping crane and wolverine.

Currently, no provincial legislation is in force to protect endangered species in Alberta, and the federal act applies only on federal lands. On September 8, 1995, Premier Ralph Klein met with environmental groups and promised that Alberta would bring in its own endangered species legislation. The Premier specifically assured the environmental groups that the legislation would protect not only endangered species, but their habitat as well. But the amendments to the Alberta Wildlife Act will not protect anything. They merely require that the minister establish an advisory committee on endangered species, with its own subsidiary scientific advisory body. Advisory committees have been established for a number of species, but work is slow and political will is absent. Initial drafts of caribou recovery strategies are far too weak to accomplish anything beyond slowing the rate at which the situation deteriorates.

Alberta does claim to have fulfilled its promise to protect 12 per cent of its representative ecoregions through its Special Places 2000 program. While Alberta did reach the percentage target, it has failed to achieve the requisite ecological representation. The ecological zones described as Foothills, Parkland and Grasslands each have less than 2 per cent levels of protection. As well, protected areas have been undermined as standards are relaxed to allow resource development within the parks. Legislative reform is necessary; existing parks legislation does not prohibit industrial development. Roads and five wells have gone into Dinosaur Provincial Park. A controversial road has been permitted through the Wood Buffalo National Park. Off-road vehicle use is occurring in Lakeland Provincial Park, and logging is being considered. Cypress Hills Provincial Park is also facing threats of logging and intensified agriculture.[45] Tourism threats include additional lodges at Jasper, a new ski lift at the Marmot ski hill and huge buses to take tourists to the Columbia icefields. On the good news side of the ledger, the creation of Caribou Mountains Wildland Park, adjacent to Wood Buffalo National Park, was a significant conservation achievement.

The commitment to logging virtually all of Alberta's forests on a rotational basis will ultimately eliminate all old-growth aspen and coniferous ecosystems. A Canadian Wildlife Service study concluded that "intensive forest harvest (e.g., clear-cut logging of sixty to seventy year rotations) in mixed-wood boreal forests, by simplifying the structure of young stands and reducing the frequency of old stands, will not maintain the abundance of flora and fauna at levels found in unmanaged forests."[46]

The rich habitat along streams and rivers is particularly at risk. Scientists have found that old-growth habitat is steadily being eliminated along waterways, known as riparian zones.[47]

But the environmental damage of which the forest service warned is not only damage affecting what the industry calls "non-timber values." It is affecting the ability of the forest to grow new trees. There are huge areas of not satisfactorily restocked (NSR) land. The most recent available federal statistics for unstocked harvested Crown land lists Alberta at 33 per cent or 332,000 hectares, and this statistic excludes those areas denuded, more or less permanently, by the oil and gas industry.[48] Moreover, Alberta has a regeneration problem, similar to that of the Newfoundland kalmia barrens. A native grass called "calamagrotis," or bluejoint reed grass, is extremely invasive, growing in sites after clear-cutting. A 1984 study found that 33 per cent of the second-growth conifers were having serious difficulty as a result of the spread of calamagrotis.[49] The grass produces a thick mulch and lowers the temperature of the soil, making it less hospitable to conifer seedlings. Interestingly, foresters speculate that the grass, like certain insects and disease, does not do well after fires, but it thrives after clear-cuts.

The provincial policy of replacing conifer forests with new conifer forests is constantly undermined by the natural process of succession, which government foresters are desperate to avoid. According to one forest service spokesman: "The profuse regeneration capabilities of many deciduous species...can limit successful regeneration and a return to pure coniferous areas following harvest."[50] In other words, just as in every other province, clear-cut logging leads to species conversion. Mixed-wood forests, the most typical stands of Alberta's boreal forest, are also not regenerated in their original composition.

Even in simple economic terms, maintaining a timber supply on publicly owned land requires strict government regulation. But any notion of effective regulation is the stuff of pipe dreams. The 1996 provincial budget cut six hundred staff positions and $123 million from the Environmental Protection budget over a three-year period. The forest service, far from getting the increased resources it had insisted were necessary, has been reduced by $42 million, with a 13 per cent cut in staffing.

Even before the cuts, the will to enforce the law had been doubtful. Of twenty-three enforcement actions for pollution violations by mills between January 1989 and April 1996, only four resulted in prosecutions. The provincial registry of pollution offenses fails even to mention twenty-two violations of effluent guidelines by Millar

Western's Whitecourt pulp mill. Procter & Gamble's bleached kraft pulp mill accumulated 167 complaints before any charges were laid. But even though $140,000 in fines were levied, the government happily renewed Procter & Gamble's licence, just in time for them to sell to Weyerhaeuser.[51]

The cuts were not accidental side effects of fiscal restraint; Alberta was not short of cash. The prevailing political ideology favoured shifting regulation and control over public resources from the government to the companies. The 1995 Regulatory Reform Report set out plans for the delegation of enforcement activity to the forest industry, for streamlining the approval process for a range of industrial activities and, of course, for cutting enforcement costs.

Under Regulatory Reform, the industry is in charge of timber production audits, FMA planning, the establishment of seeding standards and other silviculture decisions. The industry monitors itself, keeps its own records and reports from its own data.

The deregulation of the pollution-control requirements through reduced enforcement has been defended by the government with the suggestion that citizen watchdogs will replace government regulators. But according to one Alberta environmental group, relaying public complaints to the government is useless. When the Pembina Institute followed up on previously filed complaints, they were told that no one had investigated them because there was no staff to do the work.[52] Similarly, the Minister of Environmental Protection admitted that, of seventy calls received between March 1995 and May 1996 reporting poor logging practices on private lands, only five had been investigated.[53]

Alberta's largest forest companies have management plans that are based on ecological forest management principles. The two companies based in Japan, Al-Pac and Daishowa-Marubeni, have attempted to better understand the ecosystem in which they operate, with the goal of emulating natural forest structure. Dr. Richard Schneider of the Alberta Center for Boreal Studies, a researcher with frequent good words for Al-Pac's efforts, still concluded that "Al-Pac's management plan amounts to a grand experiment—that may or may not have a favorable outcome."[54]

Weyerhaeuser also claims to have embraced ecological forest management, but is still wedded to sustained yield management. Although these are large operators, the vast majority of the forest base is controlled by all the other companies combined, with little or no effort to accept more ecological practices.

Some hope is being held out for the provincial system of biodiversity monitoring. After years of effort, a small pilot program for biodiversity monitoring was recently initiated. Its success depends entirely on industry leadership—or a change in government.

Industry self-regulation has led to predictable self-congratulatory efforts. ForestCARE was established by the Alberta Forest Products Association to aim for a higher standard than government regulations. Over thirty Alberta companies have joined in ForestCARE's program of self-assessment. The international Global Forest Watch conducted a reality check on ForestCARE's members. It compared ForestCARE's membership with the list of companies fined by Alberta Environmental Protection for breaking forest-related laws in 1997 and 1998. It found that half of the companies fined were members of ForestCARE, and that "half of all ForestCARE members were fined at least once for breaking the law in those two years."[55] This lack of environmental care is even more stunning when one considers how lax Alberta's laws are, how few staff remain to enforce them and how difficult it must be to be caught, charged and fined in a system that values corporate wealth over ecosystem health.

Alberta's current political agenda is geared toward industry self-regulation. And what does that finally mean, in plain language? That decisions about whether Alberta's public forests are to be sustainably managed will be made in Japan.

Alberta

Forest and other wooded land in million hectares	36.4
Stocked harvested Crown land in hectares (2000)	662,000*
Area logged in hectares (2002)	68,430
Volume logged in million cubic metres (2002)	24.6
Annual allowable cut in million cubic metres (2001)	26.2

Source: Natural Resources Canada, Canadian Forest Service, *The State of Canada's Forests 2002–2003* (Ottawa, 2003). These are federal government summaries, based on provincial government data. The figures are not necessarily accurate.
* This statistic was unavailable in the 2003–2004 report and comes from the last available year, *The State of Canada's Forests 2000–2001*.

Alberta Corporate Players

Alberta Newsprint Company
Al-Pac (Mitsubishi and Oji Paper Company)
Canfor
Daishowa-Marubeni
International Paper (Weldwood and Sunpine; sold to West Fraser
   in July 2004)
Millar Western
Sundance
Tolko
West Fraser (Slave Lake Pulp; Blue Ridge Lumber)
Weyerhaeuser

---

14 | BRITISH COLUMBIA

British Columbia is a land of superlatives: the most magnificent mountain ranges, the greatest seismic action, the tallest and oldest trees and the greatest biodiversity in Canada. British Columbia has more distinct ecosystems than any other province, embracing Canada's only true desert in the south and glaciers in the mountains.[1] It is the only province where can you ski one day and sail the next. As the tourist ads proclaim, it is "Super Natural British Columbia."

The ancient coastal rainforests are luxuriant with cedar, spruce, creepers, ferns and lichens. Mosses cover fallen trees in these lush forests, and new trees sprout from the fallen trunks of the old giants. British Columbia has record-setting biomass, the heaviest in the world: rare Garry oak forests, boreal forest to the north and montane in the interior. But British Columbia also sets another kind of record: the only evidence of human activity visible from outer space—along with the Great Wall of China and the burning Amazon—is the scarred landscape of British Columbia clear-cuts.

B.C. forests have been the site of record-setting protests, too. Twelve thousand people at Clayoquot Sound, with more than eight hundred arrests. More flashpoints per square kilometre than any other Canadian province. The names read like a mantra: Carmanah, Meares Island, Gwaii Haanas (South Moresby) and Lyell Island, Slocan Valley, the Stein, the Kitlope, Khutzeymateen, the Walbran. That all but Meares and part of the Walbran have now been saved seems almost a miracle, certainly a tribute to public pressure and political will. But the industry cry goes out that the environmentalists' agenda is unending. How many forests have to be "saved?" Where are they supposed to log? Environmentalists feel beleaguered. We have won so many battles. Why do we still feel we are losing the war?

Because we *are* losing the war. And under the current Liberal government, industry is now in firm control of our public forests. So long as the question of survival of ecosystems rests on setting aside fragments of the original forest, the forest loses. As long as everything outside those fragments is viewed as actual or potential industrial forest, to be managed as fibre farms for a second-growth timber supply, then British Columbia's never-logged forests will experience the same degradation and decline as has been seen across Canada.

In the beginning

Only a few hundred years ago, the forests of British Columbia were home to thriving communities of indigenous peoples. There were sea people and forest people. The coastal First Nations plied the ocean waters in huge, intricately carved and ornamented war canoes, each made from a single giant cedar tree. Materials for longhouses were taken from the forest by these Aboriginal coastal dwellers. The tribes of the interior also found their needs met by the vast expanses of forest, its wildlife and fish.

The first settlers and explorers gained riches through the exploitation of fur, opening trading posts in the eighteenth century. The first sawmill followed, built by the Hudson's Bay Company in 1848. The forests of New Brunswick and Nova Scotia were felled to build ships for the British Navy, but the first logging boom on the West Coast was driven by the gold rush. San Francisco's nearly insatiable appetite for building materials demanded imports from as far away as Maine.[2]

Other mills followed and, with them, legendary stories of the West Coast giants. The first commercially valuable tree was Douglas fir, the tallest tree in Canada. One ancient Douglas fir, well over 1,100 years old, was measured after it finally fell to the forest floor in the 1990s. It was 300 feet (90 metres) tall and was 45 feet (14 metres) around at its base. Douglas fir produced excellent lumber, as well as masts and planking for shipbuilding. Today, less than 1 per cent of the original coastal old-growth Douglas fir ecosystems remain.

Production levels of the early B.C. forest industry were astonishing. One of the first large lumber camps at English Bay, built within the shadows of what are now the highrises of downtown Vancouver, produced 9 million board feet of Douglas fir from only 80 acres (32 hectares). The forests that used to ring English Bay became the panelling and stairs of English churches and the beams of the Imperial Palace in Peking.[3]

Regulating the timber boom

With 94 per cent of the forest owned by the Crown, the government instituted a timber licence system in the mid-1880s. The first stumpage rate in British Columbia was 15 cents per tree. Some government reports were unhappy with how the benefits from logging were being distributed. In 1905, one such report noted: "In a sense, the lumber industry in British Columbia has not been a prosperous one, though owners of mills and timber limits, as a rule, have grown into wealth."[4]

The timber licences were easy to obtain, and as the shortages of wood elsewhere, particularly in the United States, became pronounced, the B.C. forests were not only staked by mills, they were claimed by timber speculators. By 1910, the bonanza in "timber prospecting" was out of control, warranting the province's first Royal Commission on Forests. Foresters in the province warned that if speculative timber staking and uncontrolled logging were allowed to continue, British Columbia could run out of wood.[5]

The report of the Royal Commission resulted in the province's first Forest Act in 1912. Timber Sale Licences were legislated, based on a process of competitive bidding for small- to medium-sized blocks of timber.[6] In advance of putting a parcel of forest up for sale, it had to be surveyed. All costs of classifying, surveying and advertising the Timber Sale Licences were paid by the winning bidder. The licences were for only three to four years, so the forest was not tied up in long-term commitments. Other than a grandfathering provision for hand-loggers, working small areas along the coast, Timber Sale Licences became the province's only form of tenure.[7]

All of that changed in 1945 with the recommendations of the next B.C. Royal Commission, chaired by Mr. Justice Gordon Sloan. It largely reflected the vision of the provincial Chief Forester, C.D. Orchard, who was a proponent of sustained yield forest management in the tradition of Pinchot and Fernow. He favoured long-term leases, to be called Forest Management Licences (FMLs), over the 1912 Timber Sale Licences. What Orchard envisioned was a system that distributed several long-term forest management licences fairly among the applicants who qualified for them.[8] Instead, the opportunity to gain access in perpetuity over huge areas of the province was seized by the companies with the political and financial wherewithal to make a killing. Large corporations saw the FMLs as a way to raise capital to build pulp and lumber complexes. And, as the new legislation made the granting of FMLs a matter purely within the discretion of the Minister of Forests, the whole system was virtually designed to reward corruption.

By the time the first round of major FMLs had been issued, the Minister of Forests, R.E. Sommers ("Honest Bob"), had been jailed. Sommers was convicted of accepting bribes to grant an FML to B.C. Forest Products. Provincial Chief Forester C.D. Orchard had opposed issuing the FML on the grounds that it would constitute "a dangerous overcut...a timber grab and legalized liquidation."[9] But the minister had overruled his Chief Forester, granting B.C. Forest Products the desired FML. Several years later, evidence of a $30,000 payment from B.C. Forest Products to Sommers finally came to light. The minister went to jail, but B.C. Forest Products was acquitted, and all of the FMLs issued by Minister Sommers remained valid.

In the 1958 Forest Act amendments, Tree Farm Licences (TFLs) replaced Forest Management Licences, and the standard term changed from in perpetuity to a fixed period of twenty-one years. Substantial licences were granted to large companies, often based and financed from outside the province, and thus the forest industry eventually shifted to multinationals.

Corporate windfalls in British Columbia

In an atmosphere of political payoffs and scandals, the granting of British Columbia's forests to private interests has always been a high-stakes game. And no wonder: nearly half of all the wood logged in Canada comes from B.C. forests.[10] In the 1990s and the early part of the first decade of the current century, anywhere from 160,000 to 204,000 hectares were logged every year, and depending on the year, 86 to 98 per cent by clear-cutting.[11]

Rates of cut have increased dramatically from pre-1970 levels. The cut rate doubled between 1950 and 1975, rising to about 50 million cubic metres annually. By the late 1970s, it had grown by another 40 per cent to approximately 70 million cubic metres. The B.C. government allows the industry to overcut the annual allowable cut in any given year, so long as the averages over a five-year period fall within AAC limits, which means that in some years, B.C. Crown land forests have experienced rates of cut above 80 million cubic metres.[12] The private tenures have consistently, since 1950, provided another 10 to 14 million cubic metres annually. The 2000 AAC was set at 74 million cubic metres—more than the total logged in Quebec, Ontario and Manitoba combined.[13]

British Columbia, with a total area of nearly 95 million hectares, has roughly 64 million hectares of forest "and other wooded areas," as the new federal inventory describes it. That forested area runs the gamut from the coastal temperate rainforest, containing some of the world's most valuable timber, to the northern boreal and open sub-alpine forest of stunted small trees on rocky and boggy soil, to inaccessible forests on steep slopes and otherwise uncommercial forest. Of the 60 million hectares, only 47 million hectares are actually productive forest. Protected areas are supposed to be removed from calculations of the forest land base before the process of establishing cut levels begins (so the AAC is set only on "net," not "gross" holdings).

Of all the provinces of Canada, British Columbia has the largest percentage of its territory in protected areas—13 per cent. However, this represents only 41 per cent of the area required to protect its key ecosystems, according to the World Wildlife Fund of Canada.[14] The total area of protected forest is inadequate—approximately 10 per cent of forest and a further 19 per cent of open forest and parkland.[15] Nearly 69 per cent of the protected areas are not forested or contain high-elevation forests—primarily alpine, rock and ice. According to forest ecologist Dr. Reed Noss, "Most estimates of the area needed in reserves to attain well-accepted conservation goals range from 25 to 75 per cent of a region."[16]

Even within British Columbia's protected areas of forest, much is in bogs and rocky zones that were never commercially viable in any event. Of the 10.5 per cent of the coastal western hemlock zone that has been protected on Vancouver Island, much is of the bog variety, with stunted trees, not the towering old-growth Sitka spruce and western red cedar.[17] Only 7 per cent of the protected areas are low-elevation forests, although low-elevation forests account for 70 per cent of all forests in the province.[18]

It is not hard to see why it is easier to create parks in the areas dominated by rock and ice than in forested areas. Most valuable forest ecosystems are already locked up in long-term leases to forest companies. While historically the fees companies paid for the right to cut forests did not approach market value, the province has at times in the past interpreted the leases as requiring compensation to forest companies for areas converted to parks. When South Moresby in the Queen Charlotte Islands was set aside as Gwaii Haanas National Park, Western Forest Products negotiated tens of millions of dollars in compensation for a lease they had bought for only tens of thousands. As the provincial and federal government neared successful completion of negotiations to protect the ancient forest giants of Gwaii Haanas, the logging contractor moved to triple shifts, logging around the clock, to clear-cut as much of Lyell Island as possible before the lease was revoked.[19] The logged areas of Lyell Island remain today as mute testimony to the destructive clear-cutting legacy of Western Forest Products.

A total of 96 per cent of the 95-million-hectare land base of the province is owned by the Crown, 3 per cent is owned by the forest industry, and 1 per cent is in private hands.[20] The 64-million-hectare forest area is "netted down" to determine the productive operable forest base. Once reductions have been made to allow for inoperable and inaccessible areas—the largest reductions—then protected areas are also subtracted. The remainder is the productive forest land base, estimated to be between 18 and 21 million hectares.[21]

By 1970, the corporate control of the forest was fairly well established. Most of the Crown forest had passed into the hands of powerful multinationals who have access to huge tracts of forest, on very easy terms. Since 1976, the twenty largest forest companies have increased their control of harvesting rights from 74 per cent to 86 per cent. The five biggest forest companies now control over 40 per cent of the cut in the B.C. interior.[22] Corporate concentration increased in the first half of this decade as Weyerhaeuser bought up MacMillan Bloedel, Slocan bought into Canadian Forest Products, Tembec bought Crestbrook, and Riverside Forest Products bought Lignum. The increasing corporate consolidation has been encouraged by the policies of the current Liberal provincial government.

By 1970, thirty-four Tree Farm Licences had been issued, covering approximately 4 million hectares of some of the most productive Crown land and providing 26 per cent of British Columbia's total forest cut. In the same period, between 1950 and 1975, logging more than doubled. The integrated companies producing both lumber and pulp and paper were able to use smaller, lower-quality logs. The result was that the cuts in some TFLs increased by as much as 600 per cent—all in the name of sustained yield forest management.[23]

Overall, the cut increased from 30 million cubic metres in 1960 to 90 million cubic metres by 1990, dropping to 73.6 million in 2002.[24]

The TFL system was once a social contract: corporations got access to public timber in exchange for obligations to mill wood locally. This was called appurtenancy, and the intention was to provide jobs and stability to communities throughout the province. The Campbell Liberals have ripped up that social contract, giving companies access to public timber but removing the obligation to provide local benefits. But Campbell is hardly the first Premier to give the B.C. forest industry what it wanted.

Concentration of corporate power came in for criticism by the fourth of British Columbia's royal commissions, a one-man inquiry by the respected resource economist Peter Pearse in 1975. The Commission was established by the left-wing government of Premier Dave Barrett and the New Democratic Party. In the wild world of B.C. politics, by the time Pearse issued his findings, the government was back in the hands of the far-right Social Credit party. His report highlighted the remarkable degree of power and control over the industry by a handful of companies.

On the B.C. coast, for example, the largest ten companies controlled 86 per cent of the AAC for their area. In the interior, the ten largest companies held rights to 53 per cent of the AAC. On a province-wide basis, nearly 100 per cent of the pulp industry, 94 per cent of the paper production capacity, 55 per cent of lumber, and 90 per cent of plywood was in the hands of the twenty-seven largest forestry companies. All told, these same twenty-seven firms had rights to 86 per cent of the provincial AAC.[25]

Pearse wrote: "The forest policies we have pursued have not... been neutral; while they have not been deliberately biased to the disadvantage of smaller, non-integrated firms and potential new firms, there can be little doubt that they have nevertheless accelerated the consolidation of the industry into fewer, larger, and more integrated enterprises."[26]

Pearse's solution was to break the stranglehold of the industry giants through competitive bidding for timber sales and rights, as well as making tenure less permanent. Two years after the report was issued, the Minister of Forests, Tom Waterland, introduced new forest legislation. Whereas Pearse had recommended reducing the term of TFLs to fifteen years, Waterland settled on twenty-five years, on renewable terms. TFLs remained a powerful form of tenure across the landscape, but they were not the only way in which British Columbia allocated rights over publicly held timber. British Columbia has more instruments for tenure arrangements over Crown land than any other Canadian province.[27] Volume-based forest licences are the most common form of tenure. There are also TFLs, timber sales and a few remaining Timber Licences as well. Other recommendations of the Pearse Commission to break up corporate concentration and to increase competition in the log market were defeated by industry opposition.

By 1986, Waterland was forced to resign from Cabinet following revelations that he held a $20,000 personal investment in Western Forest Products, a company to which he had issued TFLs and in whose favour he had made decisions as minister. Other Cabinet colleagues were also enmeshed in the scandal, having made personal investments in the province's forest industry. Stephen Rogers, later to rejoin Cabinet as Environment Minister, briefly resigned over his $100,000 Western Forest Products investment.[28]

The B.C. Socred government in the early 1980s gave wholehearted support to the industry. When an economic downturn adversely affected the corporate bottom line, forest service officials were instructed to turn a blind eye to logging infractions. Whole valleys and mountains were clear-cut. Excess slash, cutting through streams and waste levels above departmental guidelines were all allowed through a policy of "sympathetic administration," as the government referred to it. The policy was described as an "interim" approach to the economic difficulties of the industry. In other words, "Anything goes." And what went was the old-growth forest and any semblance of ecological non-timber values. The abusive clear-cuts in old-growth were described as "relaxed utilization of the over-mature."[29]

In this same period, the government laid off about one-third of its forest staff and combined ranger districts into larger forest districts. Many of British Columbia's current pressing forestry and ecological disasters can be laid at the door of "sympathetic administration." This period of wilful negligence resulted in significant areas of non-regenerating not satifactorily restocked (NSR) land, destroyed watersheds, overcutting, landslides and devastated fish habitat.

Subsequent governments created large *post facto* subsidies to remedy the wanton destruction and short-term profit of the Socred policies. The first of these programs was the Federal Regional Development Agreement funds, totalling $500 million in British Columbia, much of which went to planting the NSR lands. The NDP government that followed the Socreds created Forest Renewal BC to attempt rehabilitation of forested land and fish habitat. Up to $4 billion in tax revenue, largely generated by increased stumpage rates, was spent in a last-ditch effort to bring back ecosystems in which salmon once thrived. By 2001, 626,700 hectares or 18 per cent of the logged forest Crown land was still not fully regenerated.[30]

Efforts to enforce the few laws that existed were thwarted. Canada's strongest environmental law is the federal Fisheries Act. Under that law, destruction of fish habitat or placing nearly any substance in water in which fish live is a federal offence. One of the few times the federal Department of Fisheries and Oceans invoked the law in an attempt to protect a B.C. salmon stream from clear-cut damage was in 1977 when Queen Charlotte Timber, a wholly owned subsidiary of the Japanese corporation C. Itoh, was planning to clear-cut along Riley Creek on northern Graham Island within the Queen Charlotte Islands. Federal fisheries officials, recognizing that Riley Creek provided significant salmon spawning area with steep unstable slopes prone to slides, ordered a halt to logging. Queen Charlotte Timber ignored the order and began logging the creek's fragile slopes. In a rare display of federal muscle, possibly unique in Canadian history, the federal fisheries officers sent in the RCMP to halt the illegal logging. The forest industry in British Columbia rallied around the company to ensure that the Fisheries Act was never again used to protect salmon streams or interfere with logging. Loggers were flown in by helicopter to replace men arrested for ignoring the Fisheries order. Political pressure mounted and charges against Queen Charlotte Timber were stayed by the provincial Attorney General. Logging went ahead in Riley Creek. That fall, massive landslides—one of them was 600 metres long, 60 metres wide and 1.5 metres deep—destroyed the fish habitat of Riley Creek.[31]

But if governments were unwilling to protect the forest environment, public concern about the environmental impacts of logging was growing. Other resource users, including fishermen, guide outfitters, tourism operators and trappers, were worried that their economic base was being degraded by poor forestry practices. Loggers became concerned about the increased mechanization and resulting job losses, and, perhaps more fundamentally, Commissioner Pearse's report had drawn public attention to the fact that the current AAC actually exceeded the sustainable level. The term "fall-down effect"— the reduction of volume in a second-growth forest—came into more common parlance.

Some British Columbians began to realize that logging rates would have to be reduced once all the high-volume old growth was gone. As Ian Miller of the B.C. Forest Service described this period: "The physical and economic boundaries of timber supply were no longer on the horizon, they were already becoming limiting."[32] More fundamentally, British Columbians began to fight to protect the last remaining wilderness areas from the impacts of industrial forestry.

The vanishing wilderness

In British Columbia, substantially more forest has been protected than in other provinces. However, the total area of forests protected is still only 9.5 per cent of the forest land,[33] and not all of the protected forest area was commercially viable in any event, making protection much easier.[34]

Magnificent forest ecosystems of temperate rainforest, old-growth Douglas fir, interior montane and boreal have been eliminated in the last half-century. Using state-of-the-art satellite-mapping techniques, Sierra Club of Canada's chapter in British Columbia determined how much original forest remains on Vancouver Island. The results were startling. By 1990, nearly half of the ancient temperate rainforest extant on the island in 1954 had been logged.[35] Even those areas not completely logged have suffered serious fragmentation. Similar satellite mapping of Haida Gwaii (the Queen Charlotte Islands) shows the same pattern of lost old growth. As of 1992, most watersheds on Vancouver Island, the south mainland coast, the plains of northeast British Columbia east of the Rockies, and the interior plateaus from the U.S. border to two-thirds of the distance to the Yukon border were no longer undeveloped. The remaining untouched watersheds were largely confined to higher-elevation mountainous areas and the far north.[36]

Sierra Club of Canada mapping of the southern British Columbia coastal temperate rainforest, released in March 1997, demonstrated that over half of the ancient temperate rainforest along the B.C. coast had been cut.[37] The southwest corner of the province had been stripped of its exceptional old trees, including over 70 per cent of the forests on Vancouver Island.[38] All major salmon rivers have already been logged and the most productive forests are gone.

In the southern interior, there were once 208 undisturbed watersheds of 5,000 hectares or larger. Currently, only two of these remain undeveloped.[39] The situation is not much better along the south coast. The rich primary coastal watersheds, those where the land mass is completely within the watershed of a stream draining to the ocean, were prime targets for logging. The volumes that can be logged from temperate rainforests are beyond anything found in the rest of the country. These wet coastal forests have little fire history. Disturbances occur chiefly through the actions of strong storms, or through the process of old giants keeling over, creating openings of sunlight for the young growth below. Currently, only five of the eighty-four large (over 5,000 hectare) coastal watersheds on the south mainland coast remain unlogged. On Vancouver Island, only six out of ninety remain undeveloped.[40]

The B.C. chapter's mapping exercise focused attention on the last major intact area of coastal temperate rainforest. Located on the remote central and north coast of the province is significant habitat for salmon, grizzly bear and an extremely rare subspecies of black bear that has white fur: the kermode, also known as the Spirit Bear. The kermode bears are found primarily on the island of Princess Royal and the valleys of the adjacent mainland coast. Logging threatens their habitat, as well as the habitat for important runs of wild salmon—coho, chinook, sockeye and chum. Old-growth forests in coastal British Columbia play a vital role in the life of wild salmon, and their relationship to bears is a complex one, creating a symbiosis in the fertilization of stream and soils. As the old trees or branches fall, forests feed the streams. As the bears eat the spawning salmon, leaving nutrient-rich bones behind, the streams feed the forest.

Support was growing for the proposed 265,000-hectare Spirit Bear Park to encompass much of Princess Royal Island, as well as neighbouring islands, part of the mainland and interconnecting seas. Such habitat protection is crucial for the survival of the kermode bear and other endangered creatures.

The area known to forest companies as the "Mid-Coast Timber Supply Area" was more aptly named the "Great Bear Rainforest" by Greenpeace and other B.C. environmental groups. In 1996, in response to escalating public concern, the government initiated an ambitious land-use planning process over more than 4.5 million hectares of the central coast. The Central Coast Land and Resource Management Planning (LRMP) brought together local communities, organized labour, industry, small business, tourism, conservation and environmental groups in a marathon seven-year process. Environmental groups came together to commission an independent scientific assessment of the conservation needs of the central coast. The approach taken by the scientific team was to focus on the needs of the large carnivore, the bear, knowing that its preservation would protect many other species as well. It was for this reason that the kermode bear was identified as an umbrella species.[42]

In 2001, the LRMP recommended the protection of twenty pristine valleys from logging, and a further sixty-eight valleys were placed under a logging moratorium while the discussions and negotiations continued. Ultimately, in December 2003, the multi-stakeholder process emerged with a full set of recommendations for the B.C. and First Nations governments. The key recommendation was that, to ensure adequate habitat for the large carnivores and salmon, more than 1 million hectares of the region should be permanently off-limits to logging. Combined with earlier recommended protection, this would result in 1.5 million hectares off-limits to logging, or nearly one-third of the central coast area.

Unfortunately, one-third of the area recommended for protection could remain open for mining exploration, making the solution less than ideal. An independent scientific team sponsored by industry, environmental groups and First Nations called for an ecosystem-based approach to logging and an increase in core habitat protection, 40 to 60 per cent of the land base.[42] Still, conservation representatives who had worked for seven years through the LRMP process were pleased. Nearly one-third of the area being protected from logging in a recommendation with the support of communities, labour and industry was a resounding success. A similar process has nearly been completed for the north coast and Haida Gwaii regions as well. The recommendations are currently part of the "government-to-government" negotiations between provincial and First Nations governments, the outcome of which will be a final land-use plan for the region.[43]

A 1990 report for Conservation International by forest consultant Keith Moore, later the chair of the B.C. Forest Practices Board, confirmed that "Virtually every watershed on the entire south coast, including Vancouver Island, that was identified as unlogged has had logging plans proposed in the recent past."[44]

A B.C. Ministry of Forests report on old growth set out the liquidation policy of the provincial government:

> Within the over-all policy of achieving sustained yield, it appears the *province's implicit old-growth forest policy is to liquidate it in favour of young forest plantations.* The lack of an explicit recognition of the non-timber values within old-growth forests is resulting in continuing conflicts over specific old-growth stands. These conflicts will become increasingly bitter as old-growth forests disappear [emphasis added].[45]

In the face of these short-sighted policies, it is no wonder that the fight to save areas such as Clayoquot Sound took on such urgency and ignited such passion. Of those few remaining unlogged watersheds on Vancouver Island, three are in Clayoquot Sound. The other three were the Klaskish and the East Creek to the north and adjacent to the Brooks Peninsula Provincial Park on the west coast of Vancouver Island and the Shushartie on the northern tip of the island. In September 1997, logging was approved in the Klaskish; a road through the heart of the Klaskish has recently crossed over into East Creek, though the struggle of Vancouver Island activists to save East Creek continues. The Shushartie has also been logged and is no longer considered "undeveloped." The two watersheds of the Klaskish and the East River harbour the last remaining wild chinook salmon runs on the north island and an abundant population of the endangered marbled murrelet.[46] The coastal old-growth Douglas-fir ecosystem is almost completely wiped out, with less than 1 per cent protected.

The battle for Clayoquot Sound

Clayoquot Sound was one of the most contentious areas in the B.C. forest for over a decade. That it was possible to achieve "peace in the woods" in Clayoquot means that it is possible, with enormous levels of effort and good faith, anywhere.

In 1984, the Nuu chah nulth and local residents launched the first forest blockade in British Columbia's history against MacMillan

Bloedel's logging on Meares Island, within Clayoquot Sound. After successfully obtaining an injunction to protect Meares Island's forests, pending resolution of their land claim, the Nuu chah nulth declared Meares Island a Tribal Park in 1985.

The controversy on Meares Island was quickly overshadowed by Haida blockades on Lyell Island in the Queen Charlottes (Haida Gwaii) and by protests by the Lillooet people of the Stein Valley. Clayoquot Sound flared again in the late 1980s as clear-cut logging continued to push into pristine areas. A new logging road into Sulphur Passage, the entrance to the Shelter Inlet and the Megin Valley, was blockaded, and arrests were made in the summer of 1988. But Clayoquot Sound did not become a household name in Canada until the summer of 1993. When the B.C. government announced on April 13, 1993, that 70 per cent of Clayoquot Sound would be logged, the Friends of Clayoquot Sound launched an enormous campaign of non-violent civil disobedience to create global awareness of the threat. In all, nearly one thousand people were arrested at the Kennedy Lake blockades. The protest reverberated around the world.

Following a ruling by the B.C. ombudsman that the government had failed to adequately consult with the Nuu chah nulth, an interim measures agreement (IMA) was negotiated through forty days of intensive discussion and signed in the spring of 1994, giving greater control and the right of veto to First Nations over land-use decisions in Clayoquot. Among other things, the agreement with the First Nations called for protection of critical areas of salmon habitat, as Clayoquot Sound is an important area for salmon runs. It also called for protection of "culturally modified trees," those old trees that, through test holes or bark or plant removal, presented evidence of Nuu chah nulth traditional use and occupation of the area.[47]

As a result of the interim measures agreement, a central regional board (CRB), a local community-based board, was created to review all resource-development plans in Clayoquot. Membership of the CRB was divided equally between provincial and First Nations appointees. As all decisions of the CRB were to be by consensus, the First Nations had, in essence, secured a veto.

The most high-profile effort in British Columbia to assess the impacts of clear-cutting and present logging practices and to make recommendations for ecologically appropriate logging was the Clayoquot Sound Scientific Panel, with co-chairs Dr. Fred Bunnell, wildlife biologist of the University of British Columbia, and Dr. Richard Atleo, a hereditary chief from Ahousat in Clayoquot Sound. The panel was convened by the embattled NDP government of Mike Harcourt in June 1993 as a response to the public outcry over the government's announcement of clear-cut logging of 70 per cent of the Sound's old-growth forests. The panel brought together renowned scientists and Native elders. They were given a mandate to identify how logging could be made ecologically sound, not *whether* logging should take place.

The final recommendations of the panel, published in several volumes, were released in 1995. In July 1995, the Harcourt government accepted all 128 recommendations, including a moratorium on logging in pristine watersheds until extensive inventories could be conducted. In accepting the recommendations, the minister stated that it signified the end of clear-cutting in Clayoquot Sound. The panel recommended a system they called "variable retention silviculture," in which logging approximates the small openings occurring in a natural forest when old giants fall to the forest floor. The panel recommended that no opening, or clearing, should be more than two tree lengths from the next area of standing forest. It also called for a full inventory of the biological characteristics of the forest before logging plans could be approved.

The most significant aspect of the panel's report, however, was not in the nuts and bolts of the specific recommendations, but in the approach to exploiting a renewable natural resource. It could apply to forest ecosystems far beyond the temperate rainforest, as well as to ecosystems beyond forests—fisheries and agriculture. In its approach, the Scientific Panel called for the application of the precautionary principle—that every decision affecting complex ecosystems about which we fundamentally know so little be approached with caution. In terms of logging, in the words of panel chair Dr. Fred Bunnell, traditional forest practice was "turned on its head."[48]

The panel recommended that, when cut plans were prepared, rather than deciding what the industry wanted taken out of the forest, decisions should be based first on what should remain. They were to identify, first, what needed to be retained to protect other values, and, then, what could be logged. This is fundamentally different from the way logging is presently conducted in British Columbia. As in every other province, decisions are driven by the rate of cut, with "non-timber" values viewed as a constraint on logging. In essence, the panel's recommendations recognized that, under the industrial model, foresters may be able to regrow trees but they cannot regrow a forest with the structure of what was logged. The panel's recommendations would ensure that forest management is based on sustaining the ecosystem, not on meeting the needs of the mills.

These recommendations, fully supported by the Nuu chah nulth Central Region Tribal Council, slowed the rate of logging in the Sound. But, despite these parallel accomplishments, and the commitment of the provincial government to implement all of the Scientific Panel's recommendations, clear-cut logging did not end in Clayoquot Sound. The forest industries that held rights within Clayoquot Sound, MacMillan Bloedel and Interfor, interpreted the "no more than two tree heights" opening guideline as permission for long ribbon-like clear-cuts, each devastating areas four very tall tree lengths in width. It resembles nothing in the pattern of normal forest disturbance.

But then something unexpected occurred. A new CEO at MacMillan Bloedel, Tom Stephens, decided that the ongoing "war in the woods" was not good for his company. In initial efforts at quiet diplomacy, he invited leaders of the environmental movement and First Nations to talk about what might be possible. So often in history it is not the big movement, but the one person who is willing to take a chance who drives fundamental change. Gorbachev picked up the phone and asked Reagan directly, Why not get rid of all the nuclear weapons? Tom Stephens, in an issue where the stakes were smaller, but with comparable career and personal risk, started a process that would lead to the unimaginable.

On June 16, 1999, the province's major environmental groups issued a press release supporting a new logging company in Clayoquot Sound, Iisaak Forest Resources.[49] In April 1997, MacMillan Bloedel and the Central Region First Nations of the Nuu chah nulth Tribal Council established the new joint venture company, 51 per cent owned by the Nuu chah nulth and 49 per cent by MacBlo (later bought by Weyerhaeuser). By 1999, Iisaak Forest Resources had signed a memorandum of understanding with environmental groups in which the company committed to log only within the strict guidelines set out by the Scientific Panel, achieve

eco-certification of its operations and voluntarily stay out of undis-
turbed watersheds. In exchange, environmental groups, including
Greenpeace, the B.C. chapter of Sierra Club of Canada, Western
Canada Wilderness Committee and the U.S.-based Natural Resources
Defence Council, agreed to promote the sale of ecologically certified
products from Iisaak.

On February 10, 2000, the federal government announced
that UNESCO had designated Clayoquot Sound a United Nations
Biosphere Reserve. This international recognition of the area's
extraordinary beauty, biodiversity and Aboriginal heritage is a tribute
to every person who was arrested on the logging roads, every activist
who took a chance by talking with an industry CEO, every producer
of paper products from catalogues to phone books who refused to buy
Clayoquot-sourced paper. It is especially a tribute to the indomitable
Friends of Clayoquot Sound.

Despite all the unexpected good news after decades of conflict,
there is still a threat to the area. Interfor still holds a TFL in the heart
of Clayoquot Sound. In 2003, a local Native group sent Interfor an
"eviction notice" for its failure to consult about its logging plans.
Meanwhile, the anti-environmental Campbell government gave
expanded cutting rights to Interfor, allowing it to retroactively cut
from an AAC that was left uncut in previous years and thus significantly increasing the rate of logging overall. As well, the degree of
local control afforded the Central Region Board was significantly
undermined, as the Ministry of Forests approved the Interfor plans
despite their rejection by the CRB. The battle is far from over.[50]

Many observers credit the controversy over Clayoquot Sound, and
the international black eye it gave the B.C. government, with a host
of protected areas. It directed a public spotlight on logging practices.
It ignited public outrage. The denuded hills of Clayoquot Sound drew
attention to what was happening throughout British Columbia's
forests.

Biodiversity at risk

As the forest disappeared, woodland creatures lost their homes. For
much of British Columbia, logging continues to move into pristine
forests—some of the last remaining ancient temperate rainforests on
earth. These areas are home to grizzly bears, salmon, marbled murrelets, spotted owls, northern goshawks and cougars. So, too, is

logging bringing down the older montane and boreal forest ecoregions.

A large number of species are dependent on the structural characteristics of the ancient forest. More than 65 per cent of Vancouver Island's bird species, as well as more than 80 per cent of mammals, and many amphibians and reptiles, require old-growth habitat. A total of 70 per cent of these forests are already logged, and the remaining forests are severely fragmented. The connections between flora and fauna are intricate and intriguing. The endangered marbled murrelet, for example, nests in the mossy forest, tumbling to the ground as a hatchling and heading straight to the sea.[51] The pine marten and the long-eared Keene's myotis bat are also dependent on old-growth habitat and so are in decline. In British Columbia, the grizzly bear and kermode bear are in serious trouble, losing ground as access and logging roads as well as clear-cuts fragment and destroy habitat.

In 1996, three new forest-dependent species were added to the list of endangered species by the Committee on the Status of Endangered Wildlife in Canada (COSEWIC). Of these, two are in British Columbia: the Queen Charlotte Islands goshawk and the cryptic paw lichen.[52] Numerous plant species have already joined the extirpated column in the endangered-species list. In 2000, COSEWIC confirmed the 1986 designation of the northern spotted owl to the list of species at risk, with the status of most imperilled, "endangered." Despite the designation, little to nothing was being done to keep the owl from slipping into extinction. Between 1992, six years after the initial listing as "endangered," and 2002, the spotted owl population declined by 76 per cent. By 2003, only fourteen adult owls were recorded, making it the most endangered bird in Canada. In response, the B.C. government eliminated funding to monitor the owl's dwindling population and allocated only 3 per cent of the funds requested by the spotted owl recovery team. The government continues to allow logging in areas where the handful of remaining birds had been seen, ignoring recommendations from its own biologists calling for a halt to old-growth logging in these areas.[53] Due to pressure from environmental groups, Canfor and Interfor have voluntarily agreed to stay out of these areas but the B.C. government has continued to log.

In 2002, the Species at Risk Act became the law of the land. Although much criticized for its limited approach to federal jurisdiction, with immediate application only to species on federal land, there was a section that appeared to apply perfectly. In the event that a species was at risk and the province in question was not taking adequate steps to ensure its recovery, the federal Minister of Environment was mandated to bring a request for federal regulation forward to the Cabinet, and, upon approval, to ensure that the federal act be enforced.

After the May 2001 election victory of the Gordon Campbell Liberals, the new forestry laws explicitly placed timber supply as a goal above other environmental values. It seemed the ideal circumstance in which to use the new legal tools provided federally. In February 2004, Western Canada Wilderness Committee, ForestEthics, the David Suzuki Foundation and Sierra Club of Canada brought forward a legal petition calling upon the federal minister to protect the spotted owl with an emergency order.[54] If the federal endangered species law could not be made to apply to the most endangered bird in Canada in circumstances in which the provincial government was prevailing over an extinction plan, then when would the act ever come to the aid of any species? The answer may be "never." The request for an emergency order was denied.

The loss of old-growth deciduous forests has caused declines in numerous species, including the yellow-breasted chat, Lewis' woodpecker and Vaux's swift. The rare Garry oak forests, reduced to less than 5 per cent of their original range, harbour a unique insect, the robber fly, which disappears with its habitat. Most of this forest loss is due to urbanization.

Meanwhile, the rate of cut in southeastern British Columbia has endangered the woodland caribou. More than half of their habitat has been removed. And as old-growth forests disappear, the new growth managed on planned rotations of clear-cuts will never again provide the habitat that was lost when the ancient forest was felled. The woodland caribou are dependent on lichen that grow only in old-growth forest. Forests on a permanent cycle of logging at "maturity" will never develop the characteristics of the natural forest. It could take 350 years for coastal clear-cut forests to reach the first stages of old growth. The caribou in the Chilcotin are especially at risk; they roam an area of two extinct volcanoes, the Itcha and Ilgachuz. The Itcha-Ilgachuz herd belong to a distinct type, known as the northern caribou. This internationally significant herd of fifteen hundred caribou is at risk as clear-cut logging threatens the lichen-bearing forests upon which the animals depend for sustenance.[55]

Of particular concern in British Columbia has been the devastation of critical fish habitat. In patterns similar to the collapse of the East Coast cod fishery, in British Columbia there have been drastic declines in specific runs and races of salmon, the economic mainstay of the West Coast commercial, sport and Aboriginal fishery. While many factors have played a role—overfishing and higher water temperatures consistent with climate change—clear-cut logging operations have been a major contributing factor. An independent audit of logging operations, commissioned by the province in 1992, found that of the twenty-one Vancouver Island clear-cuts surveyed, every one had had a major or moderate impact on stream quality. Damage was so substantial from clear-cut logging that 35 per cent of the streams in the studied clear-cuts had "complete habitat loss." More than 90 per cent of the streams had been polluted to some extent by logging debris.[56]

A provincial government review in 1994 found that hundreds of streams on the coast had been degraded by clear-cutting. Clear-cutting can increase the severity of flooding, alter stream flows, cause channel instability, and increase erosion. Logging roads, in particular, have been identified as a cause of landslides, erosion and the clogging and destruction of what had been ideal fish-spawning habitat. Even siltation can clog the stream, coating fish eggs and young fish (alevin) and thereby reducing reproductive success.[57] There have been 142 documented salmon and trout stock extinctions in the Yukon and British Columbia associated with habitat degradation from logging, urbanization and hydropower developments. Currently, more than 624 stocks are considered at "high risk."[58]

While the federal government does have legislation to protect wild salmon stocks, requests for emergency protection of some salmon runs have been delayed for years to allow consultation. The Department of Fisheries and Oceans is loath to offend commercial fishing interests, and so wild salmon populations continue to dwindle. The current government of British Columbia has no intention of bringing in legislation to protect species.

While the plight of the endangered spotted owl is well known, fewer people are aware that the canopy of a temperate old-growth forest offers unique conditions for an array of insect life. In fact, when the Western Canada Wilderness Committee built the world's first ancient-forest-canopy research station in the treetops of the Carmanah Valley, scientists identified sixty-seven species previously unknown in the world. According to Neville Winchester, an entomologist, a further three hundred insect species are still under review and may be unique. Ultimately, based on the research thus far, Dr. Winchester estimates that more than six hundred species previously unknown to science will be identified. These are predator and parasitoid species that prey on forest pests and are an integral part of the forest ecology. Canopy-dwelling insects of the ancient forest help maintain forest health.[59]

Lichen expert Trevor Goward announced that he had established a new class of old-growth forests, which he dubbed "antique oroboreal rainforests." Based in part on the presence of lichens, and their abundance and diversity, Goward determined that the oldest inland rainforests have been standing in place for a thousand years or more, and are probably much older than the oldest trees within them. The presence of certain lichen structures is an indicator for ancient forests because such stratified lichen appear only in forests that have not seen a disturbance for hundreds of years. While the forest service declares a forest "mature" and ready for logging, the forest continues to change and develop old-growth characteristics long after that point. In fact, it has been found that a five-hundred-year-old forest will contain significantly more and different lichens, including rare species, than a relatively "young" two-hundred-year-old forest. Noted Goward, "By their very patterns of distribution, these old-growth dependent lichens are powerful allies in our efforts to locate and set aside the oldest of our old-growth forests."[60]

As logging moves ever farther north, logging pressures are being felt even in the Yukon and northern British Columbia. It is in these unallocated northern boreal forests that one of the most progressive of B.C. land-use processes took place. Beginning in 1990, an LRMP process was launched to review the 6.31 million hectares known as the Muskwa-Kechika.[61] This largely untouched wilderness contains mountains, valleys and fifty undisturbed watersheds, each larger than 5,000 hectares. Wildlife in the area is varied and plentiful—moose, caribou, Stone's sheep, deer, bison, mountain goats, wolverines and foxes, as well as a host of large carnivores, such as lynxes, grizzly bears, black bears and wolves. Five years of hard work led to consensus recommendations, accepted by the NDP government of the day in 1997. New protected areas of 1.75 million hectares were established, and 4.5 million hectares were zoned for resource development to be guided by ecological principles. The government brought in stand-alone legislation in 1998 to ensure adequate funding and implementation of the multi-use plans for the entire territory. Sadly, the Campbell government cut the available funding to one-third of the original allocation in 2002. Despite the erosion of political support, the Muskwa-Kechika represents a large opportunity for protection of tundra and boreal plains.

Where industrialized logging took place through the 1980s in the absence of land-use planning, the impacts on wildlife and old growth were predictable. A government study in British Columbia concluded: "The clear-cutting silvicultural system that is typically used in the range of the two ecotypes of caribou...in British Columbia is not compatible with maintaining their habitat."[62]

Clogged streams and endangered species grew in public consciousness as clear evidence of wilderness and habitat decimation. And so the public pressure grew on the government to overhaul its forestry policies. For one brief political moment, it looked as though British Columbia might lead Canada in progressive reforms.

Reforming B.C. logging practices

Faced with the legacy of "sympathetic administration" and overcutting, the government of former Premier Mike Harcourt made valiant efforts both to protect more forest and to reform the practice of logging across the landscape. Unfortunately, those efforts were continually undermined by a recalcitrant bureaucracy and an arrogant forest industry used to having its own way.

The Harcourt government created a host of new regulations, laws and acronyms. Announcing the proposed Forest Practices Code in November 1993, Harcourt declared, "Our objective is to dramatically change the way B.C.'s forests are managed and to better protect both the environment and wildlife. Until now, the attitude has been that the forests were there to be exploited. Those days are over."[63]

The Forest Practices Code, launched in June 1995 with promises to fully implement it by June 1997, was designed to ensure that biodiversity protection is an integral aspect of forest management, with far stricter rules for protecting riparian zones and the structural characteristics of old growth. A Forest Practices Board was established to respond to public complaints about Code violations. With revenues gained from increasing stumpage rates by 80 per cent, Forest Renewal B.C. (FRBC) funded intensive silviculture, watershed

rehabilitation, research and inventory efforts. Overall, FRBC rein-
vested about $400 million a year in forest renewal, including
watershed restoration to rehabilitate degraded fish habitat. In 1997,
the head of the Watershed Restoration Program estimated the cost of
attempting to rehabilitate the province's most abused watersheds at
somewhere between $1 billion and $4 billion. For many watersheds,
of course, it was too late.

Harcourt's Forest Minister, Andrew Petter, explained that decades
of mismanagement and overcutting had created a situation requiring
dramatic reforms. Overall, new Code measures to reduce the environmental damage of logging were predicted to reduce the cut rate by
6 per cent—on top of the expected reductions due to a newly established Timber Supply Review to set AACs.[64] Petter made a commitment to the loggers' union, the IWA-Canada, that the 6-per-cent
estimate would be the cap on impacts.

In February 1996, the government released a Timber Supply
Analysis that provided an estimate of the Code's impact. To no one's
surprise, it matched the political commitment of a 6-per-cent impact
on the short-term timber supply. While the overall provincial impact
was predicted to be approximately 8 per cent, this was reduced by
2 per cent through increased logging in scenic areas using more sensitive techniques.

Implementation of the Forest Practices Code was sabotaged by the
government's determination to hold the impact on the AAC at no
more than 6 per cent. Thus, Code requirements for protection of biodiversity and other non-timber values were immediately undercut by
an artificial directive to hold the Code's impact on timber supply at a
certain level. Biodiversity goals set in 1995 stipulated only that in
10 per cent of the forest, biodiversity will be high priority in forest
management. Even within this 10 per cent of the forest, the requirements of many key species were never considered in the Code. Chief
Forester Larry Pederson admitted that nobody knew what impact protecting the grizzly bear or spotted owl would have on timber supply.[65]
Outside the 10-per-cent high-priority areas, 90 per cent of the landscape would see considerable risk to biodiversity.

The Forest Code's Biodiversity Guidebook itself was already a
compromise document between science and demands for logging.
Since it was brought in, interpretation after interpretation continues
to weaken measures that protect biodiversity.

In low-priority areas, covering 45 per cent of the forest, the impact on biodiversity, according to the Code's Guidebook, will be significant: "The pattern of natural biodiversity will be significantly altered and the risk of some native species being unable to survive in the area will be relatively high."[66]

Industry played a difficult public-relations game. Out of one side of its mouth, industry tried to benefit from the Code's "strict protection of biodiversity" goals. It is extremely useful in speaking tours through Europe and the United States to quote from the Code's sustainability rhetoric and commitment that logging not interfere with the spiritual values of forests. Out of the other side of its mouth, industry opposed the Code, arguing that it was too costly and that the wood supply would be jeopardized.

Harcourt's immediate successor, Glen Clark, at the helm of the NDP government, issued warnings to the forest industry that it must process more wood in B.C., increasing employment through "value-added" activities. Clark signed a Jobs and Timber Accord with industry, in which industry was expected to create 21,000 new forest industry jobs. The accord was a failure, as job losses due to economic pressures and the ongoing softwood lumber war with the United States took a further toll on employment in the woods.

Throughout 1996–1997, global prices for pulp plummeted. For the first time in years, MacMillan Bloedel posted losses in each quarter.[67] Repap was forced to declare bankruptcy over its B.C. operations as part of its failed restructuring during the abortive bid by Avenor to buy Repap's assets from coast to coast. Overall, B.C. pulp company operations lost $625 million in 1996.[68] The plywood sector was in trouble as well. When Evans Forest Products of Golden, British Columbia, was flirting with bankruptcy in spring 1997, Glen Clark delivered $14 million in subsidies and twisted arms in the trade unions to gain wage concessions. Mill owner Georges St. Laurent, an Oregon banker, reciprocated with commitments to keep the mill open and install $25 million in new equipment.[69] Clark has also bailed out the failing Skeena Cellulose Inc. mill with $240 million of public money.

As profits fell, the Code became the industry's scapegoat. A study, jointly commissioned by the provincial government and the industry, claimed the cost per log had increased 75 per cent in four years. The industry used that figure to lobby hard for concessions.[70] The study, conducted by KPMG, used extremely subjective techniques. Lacking accounting systems that allowed any objective assessment of what operations actually cost, KPMG conducted the study via questionnaires sent to timber companies. This questionable method led to claims that costs had increased from an average $49.57 per log in 1992 to a 1997 average of $86.74. The bulk of the increase was attributed to higher stumpage and royalty fees.

Even the increased stumpage rates were estimated to be approximately one-half what forest companies were paying for similar wood in the United States.[71] The increased stumpage rates were, at long last, sufficient to ensure that government forest revenues actually exceed forest costs. The biggest increase attributable to Code requirements was for road building. Companies operating on the coast claimed the price per log had increased $7.80 solely due to more careful road building required on steep slopes in coastal forests.

Environmental groups in British Columbia pointed to a different study, undertaken by Price Waterhouse, which supported the argument that it was companies operating in areas they had largely logged out that faced higher costs in logging remote and inaccessible forests.[72] "The truth is that many companies have already mowed down the best old-growth forests, and what remains is poor-quality wood that is in remote and expensive to access terrain," said Sierra Club of Canada's B.C. Conservation Chair, Vicky Husband.[73]

For all the industry uproar about the Forest Practices Code, not a single charge was laid in the first two years it was in effect. But a study by Sierra Legal Defence Fund found abundant evidence of Code violations. For example, in 1996, there was clear-cutting right up to the banks of streams in 83 per cent of such cases.[74] The David Suzuki Foundation did a status report in 2003 and 2004 on logging practices on the coast that specifically looked at stream management and found that 56 per cent of small fish-bearing tributaries were logged right to the bank.[75]

Old habits die hard. The B.C. industry, accustomed to cheap wood, cozy deals and lax regulation, campaigned against the forest reforms. For generations, British Columbians had been conditioned to believe that their bread and butter, whether they were personally in the forest industry or not, relied on the forest industry. The slogan was that "fifty cents out of every dollar" came from forestry. The truism wasn't true. A recent economic analysis found that since 1970 the contribution of the forest industry to the provincial economy has dropped from approximately 11 per cent to 8 per cent. The 50 per cent figure was a convenient myth. Over the same period, logging increased by 40 per cent, but as mechanization reduced the number of people required per unit of production, employment remained stable.[76] Nevertheless, the forest industry in British Columbia remains a powerful political force.

B.C. forests in the Liberal "New Era"

In May 2001, in a stunning electoral win, the Gordon Campbell Liberals took 77 of the 79 seats in the provincial legislature. In the topsy-turvy world of West Coast politics, the electorate switched from left wing to far right. When thinking of the Campbell government, do not let the Liberal name fool you. With the election of Premier Campbell, the B.C. forest industry had a willing partner in a return to the bad old days of unregulated logging. Campbell promised to increase the rate of logging, raise the AAC, reduce the "regulatory burden" of the Forest Practices Code, slash bureaucracy and reform the stumpage system to accommodate U.S. complaints in the long-running trade war.

One of the Campbell government's first actions was to get rid of the Ministry of Environment and replace it with the new Ministry of Water, Land and Air Protection. Land-use planning and related functions were transferred from the Ministry of Environment to the newly created Ministry of Sustainable Resource Management. Most ministries experienced 30-per-cent staffing cuts.[77] The impact of the firing of civil servants across the province was even more devastating than in Mike Harris's reign in Ontario.[78]

The Liberals' forestry commitments have resulted in some sweeping changes to B.C. forest policy and regulation over the last three years.

The Forest Practices and Range Act

The Forest Practices Code was replaced with the watered-down Results Based Code (RBC), officially called the Forest Practices and Range Act.[79] The new streamlined Code qualified every ecological objective with the following statement: "without unduly reducing the supply of timber from British Columbia forests."[80] Similarly, the discretion of a district manager to disallow logging plans that compromised environmental values was removed. The RBC evolved in part from massive forest industry opposition to the Forest Practices Code Act of 1995. It argued that the FPC was overly prescriptive and administratively burdensome while dramatically increasing the cost of forest operations in British Columbia.[81] The RBC initiative was intended to allay these industry concerns—balanced with demands for increased industry accountability, clear and enforceable environmental outcomes and a scientific approach to forest management. In the end, the new Code did not achieve these goals, but rather reduced the regulatory regime to a point where environmental values are subordinate to the timber industry's needs, corporate control over British Columbia's public resources has been substantially increased, and costs to the public have likely increased.

One of the most significant implications of this change is the potential to reverse previous protection should available timber be reduced. For example, if an endangered species is threatened by logging in its habitat and land has been set aside for its protection, a company could demand access to timber that was previously unavailable or could demand exemptions from other environmental restrictions to ensure no net loss of timber overall. In the first plan submitted under this new regime, Western Forest Products' draft Forest Stewardship Plan, "timber access targets" have been established with built-in mechanisms to ensure timber targets trump other values, such as salmon habitat.[82]

Other objectives in the new results-based act are vague and will be nearly impossible to enforce. A 2001 policy paper by the Compliance and Enforcement Branch stated that objectives need to be "clear, precise and succinct and crafted with an eye to enforcement."[83] That, unfortunately, is precisely what they are not. For example, riparian management goals are described with phrases such as "maintenance of" and "conservation of," which are virtually meaningless without basic information. There are no requirements to establish baseline measures prior to harvesting.[84]

Vague and unenforceable objectives will further compromise the minister's already limited ability to carry out effective enforcement, especially given that compliance and enforcement staff have been dramatically reduced over the past three years. A recent report for Sierra Club of Canada's B.C. chapter showed that 38 per cent of the eight hundred jobs cut from the Ministry of Forests were in compliance and enforcement. On average, each B.C. Forest Service employee is now responsible for 18,000 hectares of forestland—eight times more than their counterparts in the U.S. National Forest Service. Furthermore, the discretion of the government decision-maker to reject plans compromising environmental values has been removed and limited by other legislative provisions.[85]

The Forest Revitalization Act

As part of their new platform, the Liberals introduced the B.C. Heartland Economic Strategy early in their mandate. The forestry component of this plan, the Forestry Revitalization Act (Bills 28, 29, 45), outlines a number of strategies the government claims will reinvigorate the rural economy.

The most significant component requires large licensees to return 20 per cent of their replaceable tenure to the Crown. About half of this allowable annual cut will then be redistributed to woodlots, community forests and First Nations. The other half will bolster the province's timber auction—an attempt to establish a credible and transparent timber market. This market, which will itself account for about 20 per cent of the province's timber supply, is meant to be the basis for a new "market pricing system." The market pricing system will determine the stumpage rates licensees will pay to the Crown. This new system is a response to American complaints over British Columbia's stumpage rates.

This is one of the largest redistributions of tenure since the tenure system was established more than fifty years ago. But the companies who lost tenure are getting a very sweet deal, as the Forest Revitalization Act included a number of goodies for the industry. The minimum cut control was removed, and the minister was also given power to waive penalties. In theory, removing the requirement that a minimum amount of forest must be cut in any given year, even when market conditions are extremely unfavourable, is a progressive move. The problem is that removing minimum cut controls can lead to a boom and bust economy for communities as companies shut down at the low part of the business cycle and go full tilt in the high part.

The government removed the decades-old rule that licensees had to process logs in local mills, thereby providing jobs and community stability. This has led to a wave of mill closures in communities throughout British Columbia and given companies the flexibility to concentrate processing in a few "monster mills." Cutting the link between logging and processing opens up the opportunity to match logs to the highest bidder, breaking the monopolistic link between logger and mill. But this is only possible if real markets for logs are created, which would help channel high-value logs to high-value uses. This was not part of the Liberals' plan; instead, companies were allowed to retain access to public timber without the obligation to provide processing jobs.

Finally, the Forest Revitalization Act also removed the requirement that government take back 5 per cent of a tenure whenever it was transferred from one company to another. As well, it removed the requirement that the Minister of Forests approve all tenure transfers; this relieves companies of the usual hearing process and, so the government claims, the obligation to consult First Nations on tenure transfers. Both of these changes make buying and selling of tenure much easier, while eliminating the public's opportunity to see its interests met in the allocation of these tenures over public land.

All of these changes are enormously valuable to companies, significantly increasing the value of the tenures by giving them more attributes of private ownership. Not surprisingly, these changes have unleashed a flurry of deal-making, with tenure traded like hockey cards as companies scramble to assemble ever-larger holdings of public forest. In addition, the government has set aside more than $200 million of taxpayer money to compensate companies for the tenure take-back. The logging giants have gained enormously, yet lost virtually nothing—except perhaps their subsidized timber prices.

It is still quite possible that they won't lose even those subsidized prices. Many observers assert that at least 50 to 60 per cent of British Columbia's wood supply needs to flow through log markets before a truly credible, fully transparent market can be said to exist.[86] With only 20 per cent of the timber supply going through the market, it is possible for major licensees to depress market prices simply by avoiding the auction, opting instead to barter timber among themselves. Keeping the prices low in the 20 per cent reference market will quite effectively reduce the stumpage charged on the other 80 per cent of timber. If the U.S. timber industry can find any signs of market manipulation, further penalties can be expected.

British Columbia's wood supply

As clear-cutting has increased, so too has the area logged increased in absolute terms. The debate about whether this is an overcut comes back to the question of whether the Long Term Harvest Level (LTHL) is itself sustainable. Bearing in mind the fact that second-growth forests will drastically reduce what is available to the industry, is it reasonable to cut at levels that, even according to the government, exceed the Harvest Level by at least 10 million cubic metres a year?

British Columbia had been ahead of every other province in acknowledging the need to rethink its wood supply and recalculate its AAC. As recently as 2001, resource economist Peter Pearse was commissioned by the province to study, among other things, the timber supply reductions that are necessary to put the coastal forest sector back on a sustainable path.[87] Despite warnings, the government has explicitly stated its intention to increase the provincial cut. Timber supply and corporate profits are once more paramount.

But can this approach that claims to put timber supply first really ensure adequate long-term supply? In 1984, the provincial government issued a timber supply analysis that candidly admitted, "British Columbia's forests are commonly thought to be managed under a policy of constant production over time. This is not true."[88]

It went on to explain the reality that, once the old-growth forest was liquidated, harvest levels would fall: "Many future second-growth stands will yield smaller harvests at maturity than the existing old-growth forests. Application of the sustained yield concept must, therefore, allow for making a transition from using an accumulated inventory of mature timber to relying on annual production from second growth."[89] The policy of cutting old growth, creating logging rates that could not possibly be maintained into the future, was a policy of planned overcut. British Columbians began to realize that logging rates would have to be reduced once all the high-volume old growth was gone.

In 1991, the government conducted a review of the timber supply and the management process for establishing AACs. The study found that: "Allowable annual cuts were based on out-dated information and management practices; there was a lack of recognition of non-timber resources and values such as fish and wildlife habitats, biodiversity, visual quality, recreation, and sensitive resources such as community watersheds; Forest Service Staff had a poor understanding of inventory and timber supply analysis applications."[90] The report's most stunning conclusion may have been that "there is a perception among many staff that AACs are too high."[91]

As a result of this study, in 1992 the former NDP government brought in legislation requiring the Chief Forester to review and set new AACs every five years. Since then, the provincial Chief Forester has been conducting a Timber Supply Review in each Forest District every five years. Reduced levels of cut are now viewed as inevitable, as the AAC is significantly higher than the LTHL in many areas. In fact, the 2000 provincial AAC was 74 million cubic metres, while the forest service calculated the LTHL in 1996 at 60 million cubic metres.[92]

In 1993, Sierra Club issued a court challenge to MacMillan Bloedel's AAC for Tree Farm Licence 44. The Forest Act at that time required the Chief Forester to set "an allowable cut that he determines may be sustained from the tree farm licence area."[93] Sierra Club argued that setting an AAC that was *higher* than a cutting level that could be sustained indefinitely violated the act. The provincial Chief Forester, MacMillan Bloedel and the pro-industry International Woodworkers of America, Canadian branch, disagreed. Government and industry argued that "sustained" meant sustaining the cut through higher rates to remove old growth, eventually lowering the cut to the sustained yield. Harking back to the Fernow model of the "normal" forest, old-growth forest was described as "non-interest-earning capital in an interest-bearing account." Therefore, cutting out all the old growth and reducing the cut levels to accommodate the smaller volumes of the second-growth forest meets the goal of "sustained yield." The court accepted the Chief Forester's view.[94]

Decisions about the appropriate level of cut are first based on the inventory. In British Columbia, as in every other province in Canada, the inventory is not reliable. A 1991 government-appointed Forest Resources Commission concluded that the inventory was out of date and could not be relied upon for accurate information at the stand level. The commission commented that inventory information on non-timber values was "a disgrace."[95] Since then, work has accelerated to improve the quality and coverage of inventory,[96] including spot-check audits to assess the accuracy of inventory information.

Rather than continue to improve government inventory information, the Liberals have decided to hand this over to the licensees who want AACs increased. As part of the Defined Forest Area Management process, licensees will be responsible for timber supply analyses, though the final setting of the AAC still rests with the Chief Forester. This inevitably increases the credibility gap for British Columbia's forest inventory and the AAC. Even professional foresters recognize that "handing over growth and yield determination on public lands to the companies is tantamount to the Bank of Canada handing interest rate determinations to the commercial banks. It's not something that an informed public would consent to."[97]

There is a serious backlog of areas classified as NSR. In fact, over 20 per cent of the area logged between 1976 and 1985 was in the NSR category. In 1995, 27 per cent of harvested Crown land was considered "understocked." Over 90 per cent of all logging in British Columbia was by clear-cutting and still is. Worse still, the industry preferred "progressive clear-cuts," in which an entire valley or mountain is denuded in a series of large clear-cuts, one after the other. Soil degradation, landslides and poor regeneration are the results. A 1988 government-funded Forest Resource Development Agreement (FRDA) study concluded that the potential annual loss in future timber productivity to the B.C. economy due to soil degradation was approximately $80 million per year and growing. Although the area categorized as NSR land has dropped substantially since 1988, it still remains high. By 2003, the percentage was down to 18 per cent, representing 626,700 hectares.[98]

Wood shortages

The debate about the extent to which British Columbia is overcutting depends on the availability of the second-growth forest once the old growth is gone. The AAC will fall, but by how much? The answer to that question is hardly reassuring. There are clear indications from the government's own Timber Supply Review that old-growth forest will run out *before* adequate regrowth has occurred in the logged-over areas. In 1981, then Deputy Minister of Forests, later the president of the Council of Forest Industries, Mike Apsey, warned that there would be "local shortages in every region of the province within the next twenty years."[99]

The reality of wood shortages has arrived in British Columbia. On Vancouver Island, some mills have closed, and others are importing wood from neighbouring provinces, as far away as Saskatchewan and the Yukon. The mills have overbuilt, with capacity considerably above what the B.C. forests can continue to produce. In 1990, it was estimated that the capacity of B.C. mills exceeded the AAC by about 20 per cent. In the Interior, capacity exceeded supply by 30 per cent. These supply shortages are occurring while the province is still overcutting. Once the AAC begins to drop, mill closures will be inevitable.

In some cases, Chief Forester Larry Pederson has angered industry with significant reductions in the AAC. In the Fraser Timber Supply Area (TSA), for example, the Chief Forester's July 1996 inventory audit found that timber volumes in the area had been overestimated by 23 per cent. Logging rates had been reduced in April 1995 by 12 per cent based on the suspicion that the volumes had been overestimated. Further reductions in cut for the Fraser TSA are likely. But the Chief Forester hastened to reassure industry that "the lower estimate does not necessarily mean a corresponding 23-per-cent reduction in the AAC."[100] Industry spokesperson Les Kiss of the Coast Forest and Lumber Association commented, "I hope people don't think this means forest companies have overharvested."[101]

Setting the AAC is not simply a technical process. It is also political. Part of the Chief Forester's mandate is to consider social and economic issues. The review of the Williams Lake Timber Supply Area, in the Cariboo-Chilcotin region of the province, resulted in a minor reduction of only 4 per cent in 1992. The rate of cut remains 35 per cent higher than the LTHL estimated by the Ministry of Forests. The Chief Forester's rationale for keeping the AACs high in the Williams Lake area is clearly the economic dependency of the local mills—four sawmills, a plywood and veneer mill and six "value-added" manufacturing plants—on the rates of overcut established during the beetle-wood salvage (from 1985 to 1989, the AAC was increased by 5 million cubic metres). Commenting on the Williams Lake decision, B.C. environmentalist Jim Cooperman wrote, "Timber companies are stealing from British Columbia's future."[102]

A similar timber review for the Kingcome TSA on northern Vancouver Island and portions of the adjacent mainland also created controversy. The Timber Supply Review in July 1995 determined that the AAC in the Kingcome TSA was 65 per cent too high. This conclusion did not include the impact of the new Forest Practices Code or proposed protected areas. Interfor, with cutting rights in the TSA, vigorously opposed the recommended reduction to its AAC.

Interestingly, Interfor did not debate the reality of wood shortages. Instead, the company argued for a smaller reduction of 15 per cent in the AAC, coupled with the usual magic panaceas of increased silviculture to allow continued overcutting. Sierra Club of Canada's B.C. chapter argued for a 75 per cent reduction. But the Chief Forester reduced the cut by only 25 per cent.[103]

While AACs in southern British Columbia are going down, the AAC is being radically increased in the north. British Columbia's last unlogged frontiers are being opened to logging. A 13.5-million-hectare area, the Cassiar TSA, is also known as the Serengeti of the North. Far from most industrialized development, in the northwestern corner of the province, this huge area boasts an amazing richness of wildlife, from enormous herds of caribou to black and grizzly bears, to Dall sheep and mountain goats. The forests of the Cassiar had been too remote to be considered commercially viable. But with timber shortages to the south, the boreal forests of the Cassiar are becoming more attractive to logging companies. Just as in the forests of Labrador, there are real concerns in northern British Columbia that logging cannot be sustainable. The region's harsh climate and short growing season mean that regrowth will be slow. The region is already feeling the impacts from increased logging roads, affecting critical wildlife habitat. Yet the Chief Forester's Timber Supply Analysis ordered the AAC increased from 140,000 cubic metres to 400,000 cubic metres—an almost threefold increase.[104]

More recently, salvage logging following the mountain pine beetle crisis in British Columbia's interior has pushed AACs to astronomical levels. The implications of the dramatic increase in logging are sobering for local communities.[105]

Logging increased in the northeastern interior forest of the Mackenzie TSA of over 6 million hectares. In 1996, the Chief Forester approved a 50,000-cubic-metre increase in logging, bringing the AAC to nearly 3 million cubic metres for the TSA.[106]

Despite imminent timber shortfalls and dwindling old growth, British Columbia's AAC has remained more or less stable overall, increasing between 1993 and 1994 from 71.9 million cubic metres to 72.4 million cubic metres, going down to 71.3 million cubic metres in 1996, and rebounding to an all-time high of 74 million in 2000.[107]

And the B.C. government seems determined to make the situation worse. The Campbell government's commitment to increase the rate of logging and the amount logged, while reducing the levels of environmental protection in the Forest Practices Code, does not bode well for the environment or for timber supply. Timber supply issues will be particularly urgent in the central interior, where overcutting is compounded by losses to beetles.

Exhausting the inexhaustible

British Columbia's policy of deliberate overcutting and liquidation of old growth has not changed. The unsustainable rates of logging are locked into the system by mill overcapacity. With erosion of the efforts under the Forest Practices Code and the Timber Supply Review, B.C. forest policy is a recipe for economic and ecological disaster.

British Columbia already has wood shortages due to substantial overcutting. In most of the TSAs on the B.C. coast, the government's own analysis confirms that the rate of cut is 12 to 65 per cent too high. The provincial AAC of approximately 74 million cubic metres is higher than the government's designated LTHL. And the LTHL itself is arguably too high at 56 million cubic metres. Overcapacity of mills and a historic industry stranglehold on the provincial governments, of all political stripes, reduces the likelihood of courageous decisions now.

The reality is that industrial logging practices are wholly incompatible with healthy self-renewing forests. Ecologists have known this for years. It is only recently that wood shortages are making the same point evident to economists.

British Columbia

Forest and other wooded land in million hectares	64.1
Stocked harvested Crown land in million hectares (2002)	3.6
Area logged in hectares (2001)	189,277
Volume logged in million cubic metres (2001)	73.6
Annual allowable cut in million cubic metres (2001)	81.5

Source: Natural Resources Canada, Canadian Forest Service, *The State of Canada's Forests 2003–2004* (Ottawa, 2004). These are federal government summaries, based on provincial government data. The figures are not necessarily accurate.

British Columbia Corporate Players

Canfor
International Forest Products
Louisiana-Pacific
NorskeCanada
Riverside (Lignum)
Tembec
Timberwest
Tolko
Western Forest Products
Weyerhaeuser

---

15 | THE TERRITORIES

One of the last unindustrialized areas of Canada—our vast north—is poised for massive change. Most of the onslaught of industrialization comes in the form of mining, especially for diamonds, as well as oil and gas. Still, some significant industrialization is occurring in territorial forests—of the three territories, only Nunavut, with less than 1 million hectares of forest and forestry trade of less than $40,000 in 2003, does not merit a full forest review.

Yukon

The Yukon is a vast, mostly undeveloped territory—nearly 50 million hectares of forests, mountainous wilderness, glaciers and, in the summer, bright purple fields of wildflowers. Grizzly bears, caribou and moose outnumber people in the Yukon. Roughly 60 per cent of the territory is forested, sharing the same ecosystem with forests in Alaska and northern British Columbia. Accounting for 5 per cent of Canada's total forest land, these forests are overwhelmingly coniferous, with a marked predominance of white spruce.[1] Of the Yukon's entire forested area, only 20 to 30 per cent, 7.6 million hectares, is considered productive, or potentially commercially valuable.[2] These productive forests are primarily found in the south, particularly in the southeast upland forest areas and near rivers and streams. There are scattered productive forests as far north as Dawson City. In fact, in the summer of 2004, the northern Yukon came to national attention when forest fires there burned out of control.

Logging is not new to the Yukon. The Gold Rush of 1898 created the first short-lived boom, when the northern boreal was cut to fuel the stern-wheelers and for use as building supplies for early settlements and prospectors' tents. Primitive sawmills provided whip-sawed lumber along the water route between Lake Bennett and Dawson City.[3] At the peak of the Yukon Gold Rush, logging chewed through

210,000 cubic metres of forest in one year.[4] But by 1902, logging rates had plummeted, staying below 60,000 cubic metres for the next forty years. In 1944, another brief spike appears, as timber was required for the construction of the Alaska Highway. But once the highway was finished, so was the logging boom.[5]

A commercially viable forest industry in the Yukon would not seem a likely prospect. For one thing, the harsh climate means that the northern boreal ecoregion is extremely slow-growing and fragile. Soils are low in nutrients, and permafrost conditions militate against any forestry. The cold soil temperatures and short growing season have a major impact on the physiology of the boreal. Water uptake is slower, and the forest animal population is far smaller than in warmer climates, which means that the litter of organic material on the forest floor is broken down very slowly and the availability of nutrients to the trees is low.[6] A government report in 1981 noted that the timber in the Yukon and Northwest Territories was largely inaccessible, physically and economically, and concluded: "There is little likelihood of major forest industry development in the Territories during the next two decades."[7]

But as the forces of history and dwindling resources collide, even the Yukon has been eyed by the expanding forest industry. The economic viability of such efforts is much in doubt, as mills have opened and closed when falling lumber prices drove them to bankruptcy.

Who's in charge here?

For most of its history, despite the existence of an elected legislature, the real power in the North was the federal government. The Minister of Indian Affairs and Northern Development was more powerful than the territorial Premier, the land base being 100 per cent owned by the federal government. All of that changed when, on April 1, 2003, responsibility for public lands, water, forestry, mineral resources and environmental assessment devolved to the Yukon government.

For indigenous peoples of the Yukon, the first contact with white settlers, prospectors and entrepreneurs occurred later than almost anywhere else in Canada—in the late nineteenth and early twentieth century. The fourteen First Nations and Inuvialuit on the North Slope maintain a strong attachment to the land. In recent years, progress has been made in resolving land claims. Agreements are in place for nine self-governing First Nations, with two more moving toward ratification. While the areas turned over to Native self-government sound substantial, the reality is that Yukon First Nations will control only 8.5 per cent of Yukon's total land area. Three claims remain outstanding. Of greatest significance from a forestry viewpoint is the Kaska land claim. The majority of Yukon merchantable forests are within the Kaska traditional territory.

In the last years under federal management, pressure for logging increased. In the mid-1990s, the Yukon had only limited forest inventory, no annual allowable cut (AAC) and no forest policy, but the government proceeded to set an annual harvest ceiling of 450,000 cubic metres. Efforts to develop an inventory began, but as of 1995, one federal forestry official estimated: "At the rate we're going, we may have a first pass of the Yukon's forest inventory within the next decade."[8] Yet by 2000, the Yukon had substantially improved its inventory.

For decades, resource regulations in the Yukon had been based on what was originally designed for the mining industry at the turn of the century. Archaic regulations conspired with benign neglect of the forests. Stumpage rates until August 1995 were set at the rock-bottom price of 20 cents a cubic metre. There were no requirements for reforestation, no long-term tenure arrangements and little regulation of forest operations.

Suddenly, in the early 1990s, the Yukon's forest sparked a second resource rush. In April 1995, a federal government discussion paper on a proposed forest policy put it this way: "Today's challenges are upon us. Improved markets for forest products, fibre shortages within parts of western Canada, coupled with low stumpage prices for Yukon timber, are creating unprecedented demands and pressures on the Yukon forest resource."[9]

The value of forest products in the Yukon in 1992 was $4 million; just two years later, it had more than doubled to $10 million.[10] A 1995 letter from federal Minister of Indian Affairs and Northern Development Ron Irwin to former Yukon Government Leader John Ostashek put the situation in perspective: "Only two years ago, there were 30 to 40 applications for commercial timber permits for 30,000 to 50,000 cubic metres of wood. *This year, there are 1,300 applications for the 450,000 cubic metres of available timber*" [emphasis added].[11]

Playing catch-up

The federal regulators started to realize that they were woefully unprepared for the rush of timber-hungry companies. Logs were being cut and shipped unprocessed to Alaska and to British Columbia, and demand was sharply increasing year to year. Gary Miltenberger, regional manager of forest resources for the Department of Indian Affairs and Northern Development (DIAND), told local media in 1993 that Yukon's forest regulations were "very simplistic and sadly outdated."[12]

Almost immediately, Miltenberger was faced with demands for increased logging and schemes for the export of wood chips to Alaska. First Nations objected to clear-cutting on territory that was likely to fall within their self-government regimes, while the previous territorial government wondered if federal bureaucrats weren't taking too long in clearing the way for development.

In fact, the territorial government was part-owner of the Yukon Development Corporation, which entered into a joint venture with a private company called Envirochip to clear-cut nine harvest blocks of the White Mountain for wood chips. The chips were destined for export to Alaska. In 1993, having spent $700,000 on the wood-chip scheme, the application was withdrawn due to a public outcry over clear-cutting green timber instead of using waste wood to produce chips for export.

To exert some level of control over the new timber rush, in December 1991 the federal government placed a moratorium on the export of raw logs from the Yukon out of Canada. But no one could stop the ongoing export to British Columbia. Even with the costs of transporting wood from the Yukon to southern mills, high prices in those years made Yukon wood a bargain. Stopping the flow to Alaska was proving difficult, as wood cut for other purposes was being trucked out: for example, a contractor clearing 160 hectares for a sewage lagoon near Whitehorse was caught selling wood to Alaska. One local contractor told the press, "I'll stand buck naked in the middle of the road if that's what it takes to stop those trucks. It's not right. That wood should go to locals."[13]

One timber licence, to a First Nations–controlled corporation, Kaska Forest Resources, specifically allowed the export of raw logs— the only exemption from the export moratorium. Tempers flared in 1993, when the Kaska, in partnership with Rayonier Canada of British Columbia, proposed five years' worth of logging for export to Alaska, with the eventual goal of building a mill in the Yukon that would process small-diameter pine logs.[14] Other logging was allowed under agricultural permits and through road-building contracts. Even mining claims included the timber rights, and so the government was unable to completely stop the clearing of Yukon forests for mills in British Columbia and Alaska.

A second moratorium was declared in the spring of 1995 on the issuing of any new Commercial Timber Permits (CTPs) and Timber Harvest Areas (THAs). Logging pressure in the Yukon closely paralleled the increased demand for fibre in northern British Columbia.

In August 1995, the federal Minister of Indian Affairs and Northern Development came forward with the first attempts at modern forest regulation for the Yukon. The interim forest policy established that the two types of tenure agreements would continue: Timber Harvest Agreements, negotiable for up to five years, and the more common Commercial Timber Permits, which allow up to two years' access to no more than 15,000 cubic metres per year. The CTPs, in true Yukon Gold Rush fashion, were to be allocated based on a lottery system in which names are literally drawn from a drum of hopeful contestants. Meanwhile, the THAs cover a larger area. In 1995, Kaska Forest Resources was the only holder of a THA.

Under the new policy, stumpage rates jumped from 20 cents a cubic metre to $5 per cubic metre for wood utilized in the Yukon, and $10 per cubic metre for unprocessed wood for export. The funds raised are placed in a reforestation fund, to begin to address the backlog of not satisfactorily restocked (NSR) lands from previous logging.[15] No tree planting had been done in the Yukon until 1992. Instead, almost the entire government budget for forest management had been spent on fire protection. As fires have been increasing in recent years, with more and larger areas consumed, the territorial governments have become concerned about accepting this responsibility without adequate financial assistance. Far more forest has been burned than felled. In 1994, Yukon lost over 400,000 hectares to fire, and less than 3,000 hectares to logging.[16] In 2003, Yukon lost 49,037 hectares to fire, and 42 hectares to logging.

The Yukon timber rush

Between 1988 and 1994, the total area harvested jumped from 465 hectares to 2,056 hectares, with logging volumes increasing from 160,000 cubic metres in 1993 to more than double that in just one year—390,000 cubic metres logged in 1994. Meanwhile, the mill capacity in the Yukon remained at approximately 155,000 cubic metres, demonstrating that more than half of Yukon logging was feeding mills in British Columbia, Alberta and Alaska.[17]

There was also pressure for industrial expansion within the Yukon. In the spring of 1996, a new company based in Watson Lake, Liard Pulp and Lumber (LPL), announced its intention to build a sawmill, pulp mill and plywood plant, with annual wood-supply requirements of 350,000 cubic metres of wood a year—an amount nearly equal to the entire volume logged in the unprecedented clear-cutting of 1994. Watson Lake in southeastern Yukon is the district with the most merchantable timber. The 5 million hectares of forest in the Watson Lake district accounted for 86 per cent of the 1994–1995 logging.[18]

Fortunately, federal officials took a cautious approach to the new mill complex. They recognized that they still lacked the most basic information on which to base expanded industrial capacity, such as an adequate forest inventory. Moreover, as logging in the Yukon takes place on federal land, new mills and forest projects must undergo an environmental assessment under the federal Canadian Environmental Assessment Act. This particular proposal was called into question by the Liard First Nation and federal officials. Liard Pulp and Lumber, lacking the necessary $165 million for the mill, assumed the capital could be raised as soon as the government granted them cutting rights. In fact, LPL was bankrupt a year later, leaving a trail of creditors and earning the LPL acronym a new meaning: "Let's pay later."

The Watson Lake district attracted another company with grandiose plans and an appetite for government subsidies. In 1998, the South Yukon Forest Corporation (SFYC) completed its sawmill, which was large by Yukon standards. The company then demanded a 200,000-cubic-metre tenure, promising that with that amount of secure supply, it would add a kiln and planing facilities to the mill. SFYC had built the mill without any environmental approvals and was demanding wood from an area subject to land-claim negotiation and for which no forest management planning had yet been done. SFYC convinced the Kaska First Nation to take a 10-per-cent interest in the company, hoping First Nations involvement would grease the wheels for approvals from the federal department. When that didn't work, SFYC sued the federal Department of Indian Affairs and Northern Development, claiming it had received assurances of the wood supply from the government and thus holding the feds responsible for the company's financial losses. It demanded $20 million in loans from the territorial government. By 2000, the company was bankrupt.

The Fort Nelson–based company TransNorth Timber also came in for its share of trouble. In 2000, it received permits within the proposed Kaska settlement area in the ecologically sensitive La Biche watershed. The Kaska First Nation and the Yukon Conservation Society raised the alarm and threatened legal action. Some of the sanctioned logging was within areas that had been declared too sensitive to ever be logged, according to a 1996 environmental screening. There was something fishy about the allocations, with the local press covering news of what appeared to be fraudulent names listed as permit holders, the dismissal of the bureaucrat who initially granted the permits, and $682,000 paid out to the company in compensation for the cancelled permits.[19]

Despite the fact that logging had been at low levels until the early 1990s, the Yukon already had a backlog of over 2,000 hectares of NSR lands by 1993. If trends toward increasingly large expanses being logged every year had continued, this damaged area would have increased sharply. Fortunately, the reduced price of wood lightened the pressure on Yukon forests, which allowed the government, federally and territorially, some time to catch up.

As ecologically disastrous as clear-cutting is in ecosystems across Canada, it is completely untenable in the Yukon, with its poor, fragile soils and permafrost conditions. Logging plans were set on a rotation cycle with the expectation that Yukon forests will re-establish themselves within that time. Foresters probably know less about the dynamics of the northern boreal forest than about any ecoregion on earth. Ecological studies of the Yukon forest are fairly recent and point to some particular problems in clear-cutting Yukon's forests.

Meanwhile, clear-cut logging is wholly incompatible for many species in the Yukon. The caribou are integral to the lives of northern indigenous peoples. Those who now fight for the trees can learn much from the efforts of the northern Gwich'in, who have been at the forefront of efforts to prevent oil and gas development on the Alaska side of the border, in the Arctic National Wildlife Refuge. The sensitive calving grounds of the Porcupine Caribou herds are within those lands, and, as the Gwich'in say, "The caribou are our life."

Farther south, First Nations are dependent on the woodland

caribou herds of the Yukon and northern British Columbia. A government study in British Columbia concluded that logging was incompatible with maintaining caribou habitat.[20] This conclusion also applies to the southern Yukon.

The removal of old growth also threatens the pine marten. While in the rest of Canada threats to pine marten habitat are seen as a biodiversity concern, in the Yukon they are also an economic concern to First Nations. The pine marten is the most important fur-bearing mammal harvested by Watson Lake trappers. The forests along rivers and streams are also home to songbirds found nowhere else in the Yukon. But it is precisely these riparian zones that have the most productive forests.

Northern lights

Of all the jurisdictions in Canada, the Yukon government may be the most likely to learn the lessons of previous devastation to the south. On September 30, 1996, a new territorial government with strong environmental principles came to power. One of the government's first actions was to create a Yukon Forest Commission. The Commission was tasked with developing a forest management policy before the federal government handed over control of natural resources to the territorial government in the spring of 1998. In February 1997, a tripartite agreement was signed by the federal Department of Indian Affairs and Northern Development, the territorial government and the Council of Yukon First Nations.[21] As well, the government established a citizen-led Yukon Forest Advisory Council, including representatives of industry, conservation groups, other forest users and all levels of government—First Nations, territorial and federal.

In response to the demands for a larger wood supply from SFYC, then federal Minister of Indian Affairs and Northern Development Robert Nault appointed a forestry envoy to come to the Yukon and propose solutions. He chose well. George Tough reviewed all facets of the issue, consulted extensively with the local stakeholders and made a series of recommendations. Tough's report supported the Kaska First Nation memorandum of understanding on forest stewardship, recommended a ceiling on logging at current levels and urged that an interim wood supply be located. In July 2002, the Kaska memorandum was officially signed, creating a forest management and planning process underpinned by ecological principles. Forest management planning was delegated to a new forest stewardship council made up of Kaska representatives, appointees of the Yukon government and an independent chair. The Kaska forest stewardship council picked up the suggestion of the Yukon Conservation Society and decided to work toward certification under the boreal standard of the international Forest Stewardship Council. Before devolution occurred, a process was underway to lead the way for the Yukon.

The Yukon government has followed up with a forest policy framework and made significant progress in developing a binding framework with the Kaska First Nation. In January 2004, the Yukon-Kaska Forestry Agreement in Principle was signed, bringing the boreal forests of the Kaska Territory, nearly 80 per cent of all the Yukon forests, one step closer to Kaska management. Thus far, conservationists in the Yukon have been impressed with the Kaska Councils' decisions to protect habitat for pine marten, to protect sensitive watersheds and to ensure that logging is consistent with biodiversity objectives.

Yukon forestry legislation, policy and regulations are being developed. So far the process, while not perfect, has been inclusive. There is the potential for state-of-the-art forestry legislation and policies if the voices of First Nations, non-timber forest users and representatives of industry with a long-term vision are heard. The Yukon's forestry industry is in its infancy, with no long-term tenures or established large-scale companies. An appropriately scaled, economically viable long-term industry could be developed relying on a rate of cut that the forest can sustain, maintaining First Nations traditional lifestyles, wildlife and wilderness.

The first head of the Yukon Forest Commission, Dennis Fentie, a member of the legislature from Watson Lake, had a vision for the Yukon forests. "We are in a unique situation in the Yukon," Fentie said in a speech in March 1997. "Our ecosystems are relatively undisturbed compared with the rest of North America. We have an opportunity to manage them in a way that will not simply save them from the devastation faced in other regions, but will actually preserve them in their natural state."[22]

In November 2002, Dennis Fentie became the Premier of the Yukon. Thus far, his commitment to ecological values appears to have diminished in direct proportion to his political clout. The devolution of the forests to the territory creates the real possibility that the Yukon will be able to avoid the mistakes of other jurisdictions, but the jury is still out.

Yukon

Forest and other wooded land in million hectares	22.8
Stocked harvested Crown land in hectares (2001)	5,700
Area logged in hectares (2002)	42
Volume logged in cubic metres (2002)	70,000
Annual allowable cut in cubic metres (2001)	267,000

Source: Natural Resources Canada, Canadian Forest Service, *The State of Canada's Forests 2003–2004* (Ottawa, 2004). These are federal government summaries, based on provincial government data. The figures are not necessarily accurate.

Yukon Corporate Players

Arctic Inland Resources
Dimok Timber
Yukon Alaska Log Homes
Yukon Forevergreen Wood Products

Northwest Territories

The Northwest Territories is a land of snow, ice and thundering herds of muskoxen. Out of a vast region of 134.6 million hectares of land and water, only 33.3 million hectares are forested. Since 1987, the territorial government has had control over its forests. The devolution of responsibility from the federal government empowered the territorial government to pass laws regulating forest management in 1988.[1] While most of the land base is still owned by the federal government, significant progress in land-claim settlement has created a number of First Nations jurisdictions dealing with forest policy.

In the 1990s the Northwest Territories saw extensive mineral claims and exploration by the diamond mining industry almost wholly within the unforested tundra regions. The South African, British, Canadian and Australian multinationals were digging up the terrain with an intensity that reminds northerners of the Gold Rush. First Nations, environmental groups and Canada's most distinguished scientists expressed outrage at the lack of adequate environmental assessments.

Controversy swirls around plans for a Mackenzie Valley pipeline, drawing on Mackenzie Delta gas reserves, which are located under the Kendall Island Bird Sanctuary. The pipeline would run through 1,200 kilometres of permafrost to fuel the tar sands operations of northern Alberta. Oil and gas looms on the horizon as a threat to biodiversity and the traditional way of life, or as a long-waited economic salvation. It all depends on your point of view. In the short term, these interests have replaced the brief timber rush as attention turns to the proposed Mackenzie Gas Project.

While most diamond mining activity occurs on the tundra, a majority of the projected Mackenzie pipeline and the oil and gas development that is expected along its route would take place in forested zones. The Mackenzie Valley is a rich ecosystem, used by several distinct caribou herds, migratory waterfowl and large carnivores. As in Alberta, the oil and gas industry impacts the forest primarily through the clearing of seismic lines, drilling and road building. A recent assessment of the Fort Liard region, conducted for two national conservation organizations, found that existing levels of activity had left a physical impact on 148 square kilometres of the study area of 14,173 square kilometres (or 1 per cent). When researchers examined the broader impact on wildlife habitat, that impact extended over 7,655 square kilometres, or 55 per cent of the study area.[2] Given the low level of forest industry activity in the Northwest Territories, the oil and gas industry impact is the major threat to the intact boreal forests.

The forest of the Northwest Territories

Out of the 61 million hectares of the Northwest Territories that have any forest cover at all, just over 14 million hectares could be considered commercially viable. The forests are owned by the federal government but are under the jurisdiction of the territorial government. First Nations governments and regional conservation boards have developed their own approaches to forest management. Both the Deh Cho First Nation and the Gwich'in Renewable Resource Board have integrated forest management plans. Land claims have been settled with the Inuvialuit, the Gwich'in, the Sahtu Dene, the Tlicho and the Métis. All of these lands include some forests. The largest area of intact boreal wilderness along the Mackenzie River is found in the Deh Cho territory, where a land claim has not yet been resolved.

While the rates of logging are low, the productive forest land supports the richest biodiversity in the northern boreal. The riparian zones are fertile habitat for a range of wildlife. The NWT government is currently working on the recovery of a number of forest-dependent species: wood bison, woodland caribou and peregrine falcon are threatened; grizzly bear, wolverine, northern leopard frog and western toad are listed as species of special concern. The largest threat to species in the Northwest Territories is the coming onslaught of climatic disruption from fossil fuel use far to the south. The polar bear and Peary caribou are already at risk due to changes in their environment brought on by increases in greenhouse gases.[3] The territorial government is developing its own species at risk legislation, complementing the federal act.

As in the Yukon, stumpage rates in the Northwest Territories could be considered a subsidy to industrial forestry. In 1993–1994, for example, the government collected $189,000 in stumpage and reforestation levies, while spending $518,000 in forest management costs. This figure was exclusive of fire protection costs, which are primarily directed to protecting people and property, rather than forests.[4] The government set stumpage rates based on a number of variables. The goal is to discourage raw log export and reward local users, providing jobs locally, with reduced stumpage.[5]

In the late 1980s and into the 1990s, growth was exponential in the NWT forest industry. In 1988, a total area of 399 hectares was logged; by 1994, logging had increased to 604 hectares. The Northwest Territories had set an annual allowable cut (AAC) at 300,000 cubic metres, and as of 1994 was logging about half that. In 1996–1997, 164,000 cubic metres was logged. But then the price of lumber fell, the sawmills opened in the 1990s closed, and by the early years of the current century, the volume logged was inconsequential—as little as 1,000 cubic metres. Currently, the Northwest Territories has no AAC.

Basic research has not yet been done on forest regeneration in conditions such as those found in the Yukon and the Northwest Territories. Logging in the Northwest Territories is 100 per cent by clear-cutting or by smaller 20-hectare cuts called "patch-cuts."[6] Clear-cutting is likely responsible for the highest percentage of any jurisdiction in Canada of not satisfactorily restocked (NSR) lands within logged-over areas. Fully 85 per cent of the NWT harvested areas are reported to be "understocked"—even though the actual amount of land in question is smaller than that impacted by other industries.[7] Replanting in these areas has begun.

The Northwest Territories, First Nations and Inuvialuit governments have made large strides in recent years in sustainable forest management planning. Inventories of the forest base are underway for the first time. The concept of the AAC has largely been jettisoned in preference to a more ecological approach to setting limits on logging. Increasingly, an index of sustainability is applied that considers a variety of ecosystem-based indicators to measure the amount of change a forest can experience while maintaining itself in perpetuity. Timber harvesting is just one of the possible uses for the forest, and all users must be considered. The index of sustainability is still under development.

The threat of industrial forest expansion in the Northwest Territories receded with recent economic conditions and reduced demand. But, as has been demonstrated over and over again in Canadian forest history, pricing and demand are cyclical. What has been a receding tide could easily rebound. The progressive trends for forest management in the Northwest Territories give reason for hope that if and when logging pressures begin to build over the remote NWT forests, the governments and Aboriginal resources boards will be ready to protect their forests.

Northwest Territories

Forest and other wooded land in million hectares	33.3
Stocked harvested Crown land in hectares (2001)	547
Area logged in hectares (2002)	50
Volume logged in cubic metres (2002)	3,000
Annual allowable cut in cubic metres	N/A

Source: Natural Resources Canada, Canadian Forest Service, *The State of Canada's Forests 2003–2004* (Ottawa, 2004). These are federal government summaries, based on provincial government data. The figures are not necessarily accurate.

Part III
The Future of the Forests

16 | Signs of Hope

Since the publication in 1998 of this book's first edition, significant changes have occurred across Canada. Admittedly, there is still widespread overcutting, with old-growth forest being systematically eliminated in the move to even-aged forest management. Stumpage rates have risen, but not enough to capture all the economic costs of logging a forest, much less the full environmental ones. Some provinces, such as Ontario, are promising better forest practices following a change in government, while in other provinces, such as British Columbia, the rollback of regulations and slashing of staff are threatening earlier progress. In Alberta, at least one major multinational has expressed concerns in partnership with environmental groups.

In many specific areas, a number of forest companies are making improvements in industrial practices in the normal course of events. For example, roads are, for the most part, more carefully constructed than they were twenty years ago. Roads represent a significant risk to biodiversity by their very existence, fragmenting wildlife habitat, but at least they are now less likely to erode and choke streams with silt. Some of the big forest companies have started employing forest biologists to assist in maintaining habitat for certain species, such as moose and marten. Some are opening up their management methods through public advisory committees. Such changes might make a difference site by site, but they fail to address larger issues, such as species conversion and the need to maintain intact and old-growth forests.

Nonetheless, a number of trends give cause for hope. The last decade has seen a greater use of integrated land-use planning prior to timber allocations. As well, Aboriginal people are taking a greater role in forest management decisions and playing a key role in more land-use decisions than ever. Lastly, the new five-year National Forest Strategy for 2003–2008 includes a number of important commitments. These trends, combined with increased public pressure, could still protect Canada's forests.

Integrated land-use planning

The first objective of the 2003–2008 National Forest Strategy is to "manage Canada's natural forest using an ecosystem-based approach that maintains forest health, structure, functions, composition and biodiversity, and includes . . . using integrated land-use planning, especially before tenure allocations."[1]

This practical approach to ensuring that planning proceeds in accordance with ecosystem-based management has been a long time coming. Ecosystem-based management is founded on the principle that forest-based cultures, communities, industries and wildlife depend on healthy ecosystems.

In general, integrated land-use planning is still more the exception than the rule across Canada.[2] Nevertheless, the Canadian traditions of consensus building and stakeholder participation support the process of making decisions for large areas with many voices and interests at the table. In the 1990s, British Columbia pioneered integrated land-use decisions in Canada through the CORE process under the Harcourt government. The Commission on Resources and the Environment (CORE), chaired by Stephen Owen (who later became a federal cabinet minister), sought to resolve divergent views and intense conflicts between forest companies, First Nations, local communities and environmental groups across much of British Columbia. As described in the chapter on British Columbia, many of the province's most significant decisions on protected areas emerged from the land-use planning exercise. Ongoing efforts to manage areas such as the Muskwa-Kechika, within a plan developed through a well-run process, hold real promise for sustainability but are threatened by the current Campbell government.

Recent history demonstrates that integrated land-use planning alone is not a solution. However, when it occurs before tenure allocations and in concert with meaningful consultation, it can lead to decisions that protect healthy forest ecosystems.

Canada still has large areas of unallocated forests in the northern boreal. The first and best land-use choice would be to follow the Quebec lead and simply prohibit industrial-scale logging in those remote forests. That decision is clearly in the best interests of the earth's atmosphere, as the intact boreal is a significant carbon reservoir. It is in the best interests of the woodland caribou and the waterfowl and songbirds nesting and breeding in the boreal.

But where development is moving forward, land-use planning is a better approach than logging rates based on mill requirements. Ideally, land-use planning engages all those concerned with the health of the forest. Ideally, it ensures sustainability. Canada is on the cusp of land-use planning within an ecosystem-based management framework. Although some planning processes have failed to meet ecosystem-based objectives (such as retaining wildlife habitat), some are moving in the right direction. To the limited extent that Canada has relied on such processes, there are a number of examples from which we can learn.

The most ambitious land-use planning process outside British Columbia was the Ontario government's Lands for Life exercise in the late 1990s, described in more detail in the Ontario chapter. Under the former Harris government, the Lands for Life process lacked the transparency and full inclusion of stakeholders that had characterized the processes in British Columbia. At stake was about 45 per cent of the provincial land base—39 million hectares of Crown land. Unfortunately, all of the forested area in question had *already* been allocated to large forest companies. Any new protected areas thus represented clawbacks from existing leases. The process also suffered from a wholly unrealistic timeline. Consultations about nearly half of the province, covering thirty-two different natural regions and home to forty-eight Aboriginal communities, were to be concluded, from start to finish, within eighteen months. Interests from the provinces' major urban areas were excluded, biasing the process toward those communities that are economically dependent on logging and mining.

In the end, the decision-making moved behind closed doors, with a handful of large environmental groups, large industries and the provincial government reaching agreement. The Ontario Forest Accord was announced on March 12, 1999. A stunning conservation achievement, the Accord resulted in 2.4 million hectares in new protected areas. It also resulted in a commitment to the forest industry that there would be no overall reduction in wood supply to industry as a result of the creation of the new protected areas, and that permanent increases in wood supply would be shared between additional protected areas and increased supply to industry.

As outlined in the Prairies chapter, Manitoba has also embraced integrated land-use planning. The significant forested areas along the

East Side of Lake Winnipeg, over 8 million hectares, are being treated to a consensus-based, multi-stakeholder process. Although a long time getting from political promise to active engagement, the East Side Planning Initiative has the potential for resolving conflicts over more than 12 per cent of the province. From March 2002 to June 2004, a Round Table comprised of First Nations, community, conservation and environmental stakeholders met with forest and mining industry representatives. In March 2004, the Round Table members requested more time to develop their recommendations. Much will depend on whether the provincial government allows the Round Table to meet until the issues are resolved.

Saskatchewan is just starting down the road of integrated land-use planning, with the Athabasca Planning Area process. Over 15 per cent of the province is on the table for consensus decision-making, engaging community groups, First Nations, conservation organizations, trappers, forest industry and mining companies. As well, integrated land-use planning is underway for the Fort a la Corne forest, the Great Sand Hills, North Central La Ronge and the Pinehouse-Dipper forest—a total of more than 5 million hectares of forested lands undergoing multi-stakeholder planning.

Most of Canada's commercially accessible forest has already been leased to forest companies. The unallocated areas are virtually all in the boreal zone north of the 51st parallel. Ontario's Northern Boreal Initiative (NBI) was established in response to interest in logging by Aboriginal communities. The NBI covers eleven communities in different stages of land-use planning. As in the Lands for Life process, interests based outside the local areas are excluded. Ideally, the Initiative could lead the way in setting aside huge tracts of boreal forest for wildlife species while offering sustainable economic opportunities for community-based forestry.

While ecosystem-based, integrated land-use planning has the potential to change the way that forests are allocated in some provinces, other provinces are not in the game at all. In the Maritimes, virtually everything is already allocated. In Alberta, the provincial government of Ralph Klein does not use public consultation as a tool in planning. It is not clear that there are any factors in planning beyond what the oil and gas sector wants. Even the large Japanese corporations, seduced into opening pulp mills in Alberta, have complained that there was no prior resolution of land claims over the forested areas they were leased and that the oil and gas sector is taking nearly as many trees over the same territory as logging. There is only 1 per cent of unallocated forest land in Alberta. The Klein government has indicated that it might open those decisions to public consultation. The National Forest Strategy is supported by the federal government, nine provinces and the territories; Alberta is the only hold-out, refusing to endorse the strategy or even to offer the tepid support offered by FPAC.[3]

The protection of the northern boreal forest has become an increasingly important focus for environmental groups in Canada. On December 1, 2003, some of the largest paper companies in Canada— Domtar, Tembec and Al-Pac—joined with one of the largest oil and gas companies, Suncor, as well as with several First Nations—the Innu, Poplar River First Nation and the Deh Cho—and four environmental groups—World Wildlife Fund, Ducks Unlimited, Canadian Parks and Wilderness Society (CPAWS) and ForestEthics—to formulate principles to protect the boreal. Styling themselves the Boreal Leadership Council, the companies, environmental groups and First Nations signed a Boreal Forest Conservation Framework, calling for protection of at least half of Canada's boreal forests. For the other half of the boreal, the group urged that current development meet high environmental and social standards, and new development be tightly controlled.

The scale of the initiative was breathtaking. Without any government involvement, major industries, First Nations and civil society were attempting to make land-use decisions over half of the landmass of Canada. Then CEO of Al-Pac, Bill Hunter, spoke of his nervousness in signing the Framework. "I'm scared," he said. "But if this works, man oh man, what a model it will be for the world!"[4]

The Framework was assembled by the Canadian Boreal Initiative (CBI), a relatively new conservation group launched by the Philadelphia-based Pew Charitable Trusts. With several million dollars in support from Pew, the Canadian Boreal Initiative has funded extensive research and conservation projects in the boreal forest. Information about the boreal's role as habitat for billions of songbirds, migratory waterfowl and caribou was unearthed through CBI funding. But the announcement of the Boreal Forest Conservation Framework was not embraced by all conservationists, some of whom feared that the decision to protect half of the boreal was inadequate and would result in unrestricted development of the other half.

Nevertheless, the boreal framework may prove to be a useful starting point. For the first time, major industry and some First Nations with increasing control over large areas of forest were thinking ahead about conservation of frontier forests. CBI pointed out that the Framework called for *at least* half of the boreal being protected—the more, the better. In fact, approximately half of the boreal is already allocated to industry. Meanwhile, the Framework suggests the need for a more participatory process.

Protecting all of the unallocated boreal from industrial exploitation is the only reasonable position when the boreal's role as a carbon reservoir is considered.

The rise of First Nations forestry

Another noticeable trend of the last decade has been the increase in forestry operations owned and managed by Aboriginal peoples. The National Forest Strategy 2003–2008 endorses greater engagement of First Nations and Aboriginal peoples in forest management. Forest Stewardship Council certification also requires that Aboriginal rights be respected, offering some hope of marketplace reward for those companies that involve First Nations in decisions affecting resource use on their lands. Numerous court decisions have secured the rights of First Nations to access resources on their lands and territories, whether in fishing or logging. The obligations of the Crown to ensure First Nations rights are protected in relation to their natural resources have been set out in court rulings.

Over the past fifteen years, a number of court rulings have strengthened the obligations of the government to consult with Aboriginal peoples about forest management decisions. In 1990, the Supreme Court of Canada confirmed in the Sparrow case that Aboriginal rights to traditional uses of natural resources must be respected. The Supreme Court decision in Delgamuukw in 1997 requires governments to consult with Aboriginal peoples in cases where government actions may infringe on Aboriginal and treaty rights.[5]

In 1997, a precedent-setting New Brunswick case, *R v. Paul*, confirmed an Aboriginal treaty right to harvest trees from Crown land to earn a moderate livelihood. Although the case was successfully appealed, it was reconfirmed in the 2003 Bernard case. Most recently, in 2004, in *Haida Nation v. BC and Weyerhaeuser*, the Supreme Court of Canada confirmed the government's obligation to consult with Aboriginal peoples affected by industrial activity. The Supreme Court of Canada ruled that the province of British Columbia had failed to engage in meaningful consultation with the Haida.

A non-judicial step forward in defining appropriate mechanisms for consultation has been developed—the Forest Stewardship Council's standard for the boreal forest. The standard requires forest managers to obtain written consent from affected Aboriginal communities verifying that their interests and concerns are clearly incorporated into the management plan.[6]

First Nations have played a major role in the restrictions on logging in Quebec's boreal through the Peace of the Braves agreement. Partnerships between First Nations and industry have become far more common in British Columbia, Saskatchewan, Manitoba and Ontario. In New Brunswick, pending court cases over Aboriginal rights to the forest were a major factor in the big power grab in which the forest industry tried to entrench guaranteed rights to fibre.

No automatic association between First Nations ownership interests and more sustainable forestry should be assumed. After all, the longest running blockade in Canada was against logging conducted by a company owned by the Meadow Lake Tribal Council in Saskatchewan. Still, many of the most promising examples of locally run forest operations are those with First Nations involvement. Unlike stateless capital, First Nations communities have a long-term stake in the land and a relationship that within traditional thinking requires planning for seven generations.

One of the best-known North American examples of community forestry is the Menominee forest in northeast Wisconsin. It is the first commercial forest operation in the United States to receive certification as sustainably managed. It is owned and managed by the people of the Menominee Nation. In 1854, when the lands were established as a reservation for the Menominee, it was estimated that the land contained 1.5 billion board feet of usable timber. More than a hundred years later, in 1988, 2 billion board feet of timber had been logged, yet the estimate of timber volume available for logging remained at least as high as it had been in 1854. The Menominee maintain their own mill and run their own woodlands operation, employing nearly five hundred people on a full-time basis.[7]

First Nations leadership has been a significant factor in conflicts between logging and conservation from Temagami to Haida Gwaii, and from Cree territory in Quebec to Clayoquot Sound. The existence of a Nuu chah nulth–owned forestry company in Clayoquot Sound made possible the shift to more ecologically sensitive logging. The Algonquin of Barrière Lake and the Innu of Labrador have forged new understandings of the forests in their territories through the application of traditional knowledge.

Arguably the most progressive forest planning in Canada has taken place over the Innu lands in Labrador. Thanks to the tenacity of Innu negotiators and an unprecedented flexibility on the part of the provincial Department of Forests, the 2001 Forest Practices Agreement has become a model for the country and First Nations. Covering an area of approximately 10,000 square kilometres, the five-year plan allows for the establishment of a network of protected areas as well as modest logging. For over two years, community members worked with scientists and loggers, listened to their elders and forged a new understanding of what was possible across their land. Innu community members are playing a significant role in forest operations, both in harvesting and monitoring. Peter Penashue, president of the Innu Nation, described the effort as "trying to get out of the pit that was dug for us, by reclaiming our land, reaffirming our rights, and restoring the health and vitality in our communities."[8]

As a partner in the Boreal Forest Conservation Framework, Penashue made a spirited defence of the leadership of First Nations in not waiting for provincial governments to address conservation concerns. "Forgive me if I sound cynical," he wrote in an opinion column, "but I'm not convinced that governments alone can protect the boreal forest or people who live off the land."[9]

The National Forest Strategy

Beginning with a forest strategy that was largely focused on industry objectives in 1981, through progressively greater use of environmental rhetoric in the 1990s, the Canadian government has developed a number of forest strategies over the past few decades. By 1992, the federal Canadian Forest Service had turned over responsibility for developing a strategy to the Canadian Council of Forest Ministers (CCFM), comprised of all provincial, territorial and federal ministers. The CCFM assisted in the creation of a non-government effort called the National

Forest Strategy Coalition (NFSC) to oversee implementation. The coalition was chaired by a major player in the forest industry, a former B.C. Deputy Minister of Forests, Mike Apsey. Some environmental groups participated, as well as provincial governments and the forest industry. The National Aboriginal Forestry Association represented Aboriginal interests. Accompanied by National Forest Accords, complete with ceremonial signing photo ops with industry leaders and provincial ministers of forests, the documents made impressive commitments.

The last National Forest Strategy, with goals to be achieved between 1998 and 2003, contained over one hundred separate commitments. Apsey wanted to get an unbiased assessment of whether the Strategy was effective. He pulled together a high-level audit committee, including scientists, academics and environmental, First Nations and industry representatives.[10] The audit committee found that few of them had been acted upon and advised the industry-government-environment coalition to focus on key goals and limit the number of individual targets to a manageable level. The next strategy to be developed (the current one) is more focused and is the most ambitious of all the National Forest Strategies.

The National Forest Strategy for the five-year period 2003 to 2008 contains eight themes.[11] Throughout the document is the notion of public engagement and consensus decision-making about the future of Canada's forests. The first theme is dedicated to ecosystem-based management. Should it be effective, the forests of Canada and the ecological services they provide could be far better protected. The strategy calls for completion of the network of protected areas, use of integrated land-use planning before allocations are made, maintaining the forests as carbon reservoirs while "managing the forests to be a net carbon sink," conserving old-growth forests and threatened forest ecosystems. Greater specificity in meeting each objective is included in specific action items, from developing guidelines for integrating watershed-based management and wildlife habitat conservation into forest management plans to better understanding Kyoto and integrating the impacts of climate change into planning. The second addresses community engagement in decisions. The third establishes targets for Aboriginal engagement and empowerment to participate in decisions about their lands and territories.

Sadly, the language regarding the rights and participation of Aboriginal people was watered down in the Forest Accord—somewhere between the Coalition's final document and the one provincial ministers were willing to sign. Nevertheless, the Aboriginal groups remain active in implementing the new strategy. Other themes address issues of enhancing the urban forest, supporting the role of private woodlot owners, the diversification of markets through greater value-added processing, strengthening science and technology to assist the forest industry and improvement of the national reporting of data and research.

To ensure that the commitments are not forgotten, the NFSC established a system of "champions" for each theme. Many of them are already engaged in monitoring progress, establishing templates for reporting and engaging more participants in the process of achieving the strategy's goals.

The strategy is undermined by Alberta's refusal to sign. Still, it has the imprimatur of all other federal, provincial and territorial governments, as well as a number of leading forest companies. Environmental groups—notably Wildlife Habitat Canada, whose executive director, Jean Cinq-Mars, is the new chair of the Coalition, and Sierra Club of Canada—are playing active roles in the strategy's implementation. In fact, Sierra Club of Canada has been chosen as one of the champions for the implementation of the ecosystem-based management objectives.

It is the hope of all coalition members that an audit at the end of this five-year strategy will find it has made a difference. During thirty years of working as an activist on forest issues, I have mostly found myself at loggerheads with forest companies. Shared land-use planning, the Boreal Forest Conservation Framework, responsible First Nations forestry and the National Forest Strategy are signs that change is possible. It is encouraging to feel the potential of collaborative effort.

17 | Where Do We Go
from Here?

Throughout this book, an analogy has been drawn between current conditions in Canada's forests and those that led to the collapse of the East Coast cod fishery. Canada will not run out of wood the way we've run out of many fish species. Nevertheless, the analogy is valid. With the advantage of hindsight, many people can now see what could have been done to prevent the loss of the fishery. There were too many fish plants. Some should have been closed. Far too much damage was being done by draggers. If draggers had been banned outright, the fish catch would have been cut in half, but only 10 per cent of the workforce would have been affected. The industry was over-subsidized and overcapitalized. Economic ambitions should have been aligned with conservation goals. These are the factors that find their uncanny parallel in the forestry sector.

Much was learned from the collapse of the East Coast fishery—through autopsies. Canada's forests need a proper diagnosis *before* it is too late. Every indicator points to significant wood shortages to meet mill demand across the country within fifteen to twenty years. While the shortfalls may be described as local, the "local" shortages extend from coast to coast. British Columbia is already importing wood from the Yukon and the prairie provinces. New Brunswick is importing from Nova Scotia and Prince Edward Island. Although the volume of wood imports to Quebec has recently decreased, Quebec is still importing 13 per cent of its fibre requirements from Maine and New Brunswick. Newfoundland is still in a wood shortage. Alberta is 99 per cent allocated, with cumulative impacts well beyond those of its forest industry alone. Across the board, there are far more hungry mills then Canadian forests can feed. So, while there will always be forests and trees, there will be far fewer mature, commercially accessible trees than the industry needs to keep operating at anything close to its current levels.

The overcapacity of mills is becoming a competitive disadvantage for the Canadian forest industry. As provincial governments bail out old mills, newer facilities are kept out. In British Columbia, for example, where the wood supply is completely committed, the government's determination to subsidize old mills may cost jobs. "Provincial government policy that favours preserving jobs in obsolete sawmills is discouraging a $60-million investment," said the president of Primex Forest Products, George Malpass, in April 1997.[1]

The second-growth forests will not have the same volume as the primary forest. Nor will they have the same biodiversity. Production levels will fall, and technology will shift to what are currently considered "weed" species. After aspen, maybe someone will figure out how to make building materials from raspberry bushes. Given Canada's forest history, the industry will keep moving through the ecosystem to species of less economic and ecological value. The move toward pulp and less value-added products threatens Canada in the global market, as many countries have climates that enable them to grow fibre for pulp more cheaply and quickly.

This historical pattern can be changed. Canadians have a right to demand that forest management not be dictated by the interests of a small group of multinationals. The goal of governmental forest policy should be to create the maximum economic value to Canadian society, while maintaining First Nations homelands and critical ecological functions, including carbon sequestration and protection of biodiversity.

The debate must move to fundamentals. The reliability of inventories needs urgent reassessment. The questionable assumptions that go into the annual allowable cut calculations need to be laid bare. Perverse subsidies, in all forms, must stop.

The federal government should take responsibility, not for the forest resource, which is provincial, but for the potential national economic disaster that sudden mill closures and wood shortages will have on Canadian society. A national review of wood supply needs to be undertaken with full involvement of all stakeholders—government, environmental groups, labour unions and the public, with First Nations having a prominent role.

The rate of cut must be re-examined. The wisdom of premising today's rate of cut on unproven benefits from future silviculture—the "allowable cut effect"—must be questioned. Justifying current overcutting on the basis of speculative future efforts is more than a gamble. It is voodoo forestry. Overcutting is a critical issue everywhere; nationwide, the cut is too high. Let's just say so and fix it. Responsibly.

The "precautionary principle," developed at the Earth Summit in 1992, should be adopted by foresters as part of their professional code of ethics: "Where there are threats of serious or irreversible damage, lack of full scientific certainty shall not be used as a reason for postponing cost-effective measures to prevent environmental degradation."

Foresters like to believe that they can make management decisions based on their vast knowledge and expertise. Just as fisheries scientists were confident in their theories, so foresters, with confidence in their expertise, set logging rates at the upper end of what they believe to be available. Given what humanity does not know about forests, any land-use decisions should be premised on our collective ignorance rather than on presumptions of knowledge. Pumping up the estimates of what we hope may be available in order to deliver wood to the mills now is a dangerous course. We need to reassess our wood supply, including healthy margins for error. The allowable cut effect is wholly incompatible with the precautionary principle. In fact, it has entrenched risky behaviour as the norm, for decades.

We must anticipate an inevitable level of climate change in practical ways and begin serious efforts to reduce fossil fuel emissions now. To ensure the survival of key ecosystems, large tracts of wilderness must be set aside with ecologically viable north-south corridors as buffers against sudden climate change. We must recognize the enormous value of the northern boreal to global climatic balance. We cannot afford to drain our carbon sink for cheap paper.

As the wood-supply crunch hits, some process will be needed to equitably decide which mills remain open and which must be shut down. British Columbia's former Forest Minister David Zirnhelt acknowledged in 1997 that there was too much capacity in sawmilling and that older mills might have to close.[2] It will, of course, be politically difficult to make such decisions, but once a sound information base is agreed upon by all participants, it should be apparent that the approaching shortages will have serious economic impacts. If these can be managed in such a way as to protect workers and forest-dependent communities, the hardship experienced by the small coastal communities of Newfoundland need not be repeated. Those mills demonstrating high levels of labour-intensity, value-added products and modern pollution controls should be assured wood supply, as less environmentally responsible mills are closed. Worker relocation, retraining and unemployment insurance should be devised in advance, so that large and ineffectual subsidy programs can be avoided. Assuming that mills will be forced to close due to wood shortages, funds should be collected now from the forest industry and redirected from subsidies in order to assure that its misuse of the resource will not lead to economic hardship for employees.

Canadian provinces should continue the reform of stumpage policies, allowing the most valuable wood to move to the most valuable end use while ensuring that stumpage rates reflect the full costs of logging. Internalized costs will increase the cost of forest products and ensure that sufficient revenues are collected to protect other resources associated with forests.

The value of forests is more than their worth as board feet or cubic metres. One fascinating case before the Supreme Court of Canada attempted to estimate the full value of a forest.[3] The B.C. government brought the case for damages against Canfor as a result of a 1992 fire in northern British Columbia. The Stony Creek fire consumed 1,500 hectares of forest within the Canfor lease area, as well as adjacent areas that had been protected. The B.C. courts had already found Canfor to be 70 per cent responsible for the losses, but the courts refused to find damages above the costs the B.C. government incurred in fighting the fire and replanting in the area. Worse, the Court of Appeal decided that the trees on the protected area were worth less than the trees in the commercial area. The Court of Appeal ordered Canfor to pay one-third the value of the commercial trees for those in the protected area. Sierra Club of Canada intervened in the case to make the argument that the value of the forest exceeds its commercial worth. It is the first case in Canadian history to raise the issue of the value to the Canadian public of a healthy forest ecosystem.

Including the full value of a forest in forest products may mean paying more and using less. Individual citizens can support the transition to sustainably logged forest products. As a first step, consumption levels must be reduced. Currently, it is estimated that global demands for wood products will increase by 56 per cent by the year 2010.[4] That trend spells disaster for forests around the world. Think about your consumption. Whether you live in Canada or the United States, you are participating in deforestation.

Most of the paper made from Canadian forests—pulp, newsprint, catalogue paper, magazines—ends up in landfills in the United States. According to the U.S. Environmental Protection Agency, the largest item in the waste stream is wood and paper products. American citizens use more paper, collectively and per capita, than any other nation or people on earth. Most of that paper comes from Canada. In 2002, 80 per cent of all Canadian forest products was shipped to the United States.[5] It ends up in single-use and throwaway marketing. Catalogues now use more paper than magazines, while junk mail makes up 10 per cent of the total use of U.S. paper—from Canadian forests to unwanted mail without a thought of the consequences. The United States also consumes a huge volume of tissue products—toilet paper, paper towels, disposable diapers, sanitary napkin products, and tissues. All told, over 7.4 million tons are thrown out, flushed down the toilet or tossed in the trash, every year. Of that total, 300,000 tons come from Canadian forests.[6]

Canadians also use huge amounts of paper per capita, actually creating more solid waste per person than our neighbours south of the border. While we may think we are recycling aggressively, the truth is Canadian industry requires more post-consumer paper than is currently being recycled in Canada. Canadians consume about 7.6 million tons of paper a year. Unfortunately, less than half of that gets recycled. The Canadian forest industry needs 4.9 million tons a year to meet current market demand for recycled paper content. With only 3.3 million tons making it to blue boxes across Canada, the industry has to import 1.6 million tons from outside Canada.[7] By recycling more, Canadians can directly assist the forest industry in meeting demand, without additional environmental costs in shipping and trucking waste paper to Canada.

The movement to demand recycled paper is sweeping university campuses in Canada. Through Sierra Youth Coalition's *Greening the Ivory Towers*, all campuses in Canada, with only four exceptions, have a student-run organization to reduce paper waste. The changes face opposition from administration and purchasing staff. At the University of Victoria, student activism continues to bring motions to the board of governors for the phase-in of photocopiers that have a two-sided copying function and that can handle recycled paper. It should be easy, but it's not. The head purchaser for the university commented, "How much do you want to see tuition fees go up? 100 per cent post-consumer recycled paper is dramatically more expensive."[8] The student response is that with two-sided copying the university could use half as much paper. The costs to the environment do not even need to be factored in for the switch to make economic sense.

The federal government, the biggest paper purchaser in the country, must shift to 100 per cent post-consumer recycled paper. If the federal government committed to recycled paper, it would improve access and price for everyone. The greater the consumer demand, the more the price will fall.

The role of certified forest products is increasing. The success of market-based campaigns in the 1990s demonstrated to forest activists new approaches beyond changing government policy. Reaching out to other countries, either to influence public opinion in a company's home territory or to influence its customers, has proven to be a powerful tool. When a multinational is threatening a Canadian forest, it may be prepared to put up with bad publicity in Canada. But when Olof Palme, the Prime Minister of Sweden, endorsed the concerns of Nova Scotia environmentalists in their opposition to herbicide spraying by Stora, which is based in Sweden, the impact was significant. Large shareholders in Stora, such as Volvo, pressured Stora management for changes.

When Fletcher Challenge, the New Zealand company that was clear-cut logging in one of the last unlogged valleys of the lower mainland of British Columbia, the Stein Valley, began to receive bad press at home, it made a difference. It took only one Canadian conservationist, armed with a slide show of Fletcher Challenge logging, to make the company sit up and take notice. Friends of Nature executive secretary Martin Rudy Haase travelled in New Zealand in 1989, spoke in several cities and rallied New Zealand groups to the cause of the Stein. The bad press undoubtedly played a part in Fletcher's decision to leave British Columbia.[9]

The first highly successful "market" campaigns were undertaken by Friends of Clayoquot Sound. Valerie Langer, Tzeporah Berman and other leaders in the Clayoquot struggle did their homework to identify the companies buying the pulp that came from the ancient temperate rainforests of Clayoquot Sound. Then they travelled to the boardrooms of major paper purchasers—the publishers of the California Yellow Pages and printers of large magazines in Germany. As customers refused to buy pulp from Clayoquot Sound, the bottom line of the forest industry in British Columbia was at risk. The changes to forest policy in British Columbia in the 1990s had more to do with market campaigns than with protests. Convincing European catalogue makers and California phone book publishers to avoid old-growth rainforest products from British Columbia led to a focus on the ultimate market for Canadian forest products.

The potential for using voluntary certifications to distinguish more sustainably harvested forest products from those that are from industrialized clear-cuts has made it even more feasible to focus on markets. Organizations such as ForestEthics that did not even exist five years ago have found a niche in campaigns for changes in the retail chain. Environmental groups have established a "push-pull" or "incentive-disincentive" dynamic, promoting change in forestry practices. Environmentalists say not only where and how *not* to log, but where and how to log more sustainably. As a result, a revolution in forestry is underway.

Currently, only 1.4 per cent of Canadian forests are certified by the Forest Stewardship Council, but that amount is growing. Forest Stewardship Council certification remains the most trusted of the various labelling schemes, providing performance-based standards over particular areas, combined with assurances that the product you buy has been monitored from harvesting in its woodlot of origin through to production into a chair or piece of paper, ensuring it actually came from the certified forest area.

Other certification schemes have come under direct attack from environmental groups. In 2003, ForestEthics, Greenpeace and Sierra Club of Canada's B.C. chapter co-authored a report on the rival and environmentally far less friendly CSA and SFI certification systems. Warning "buyer beware," the groups charged that under CSA or SFI, tree farms could be expanded, water courses damaged, fisheries and streamside forests logged and forest ecosystems eroded.[10]

The campaigns to protect Canada's boreal are relying on consumer demand, particularly from big catalogues, to reduce logging pressure on forests through greater use of recycled content, coupled with a commitment to FSC-certified product. Mountain Equipment Co-op, Canada's leading co-operatively owned supplier of outdoor clothing and camping gear, has worked with suppliers to develop its own paper, combining one-third post-consumer paper with about 20 per cent FSC-certified virgin pulp. The rest of the paper is pre-consumer recycled plus uncertified virgin paper. Not perfect, but it's a great improvement. Norm Thompson Outfitters in Oregon is making similar efforts to get all ancient forest pulp, unless FSC certified, out of its catalogues.[11]

Major publishers are also finding a demand for Ancient Forest Friendly paper. Thanks to the efforts of Markets Initiative, which promotes the use of 100 per cent post-consumer recycled paper in the publishing industry in Canada, Raincoast Books in British Columbia published J.K. Rowling's *Harry Potter and the Order of the Phoenix* on Ancient Forest Friendly paper. The author added the following note: "Because the Canadian editions are printed on Ancient Forest Friendly paper, the Harry Potter books are helping to save magnificent forests in the muggle world."[12] Raincoast Books has subsequently made a commitment to publish all its books on Ancient Forest Friendly paper.

We can also help to reduce the pressure on forests by supporting "tree-free" paper products manufactured from agricultural waste, hemp, kenaf or straw. Within Canada, the potential for non-THC hemp to replace tobacco as a crop in southern Canada could alleviate the strain on tobacco farmers *and* the forests.

The goal of the new era of forest management should be to reduce the cut substantially, while ensuring that employment is maintained and, ideally, expanded, in a new sustainable forest industry. As Pulp and Paper Workers of Canada has said, "We need to create more jobs while cutting fewer trees."[13] Doing this effectively will require innovative mechanisms and better timber pricing systems to ensure that value-added producers can get access to the timber they need to generate those additional jobs.

Individual forest owners provide a model for sustainable forest management through selection logging. Leonard Otis, a seventy-two-year-old Quebec farmer, has husbanded his 283 hectares of forest land for forty years, providing a steady flow of wood products to sawmills and pulp mills, while producing $200,000 worth of maple syrup every year.[14] Merv Wilkinson in British Columbia is another venerable example of long-term forest stewardship, producing high-value forest products through selection logging of his B.C. forest.

Meanwhile, communities are coming to grips with the necessity of planning new approaches to economically viable and ecologically sustainable forestry. The Slocan Valley in British Columbia, for example, is at a turning point. All evidence points to critical timber shortages as clear-cutting significantly above sustainable levels continues and pristine areas are opened to industrial forestry. Community conflict escalated in the late 1990s. Thirty-five local residents, including one of Canada's leading forest ecologists, the late Dr. Stanley Rowe, were part of a blockade by 350 people. They were arrested in the summer of 1997, protesting to protect their water supply from planned logging. As one of those arrested, Eloise Charest, said, "When they are down to your watersheds, they have logged everything else around."[15]

An alternative vision has been promoted by the Slocan Valley Watershed Alliance and the Silva Forest Foundation. In August 1996, Herb Hammond, one of Canada's leading ecological foresters, unveiled a comprehensive ecosystem-based plan for the valley. The goal of the plan was to provide enhanced economic opportunities for the area through environmentally integrated activities. It set standards for "ecologically responsible forest use that leaves a fully functioning forest after logging." Water quality, tourism values and "wildcrafting"—the collection of non-timber forest products such as mushrooms—are all protected.

"The plan maintains logging and milling jobs, even though the allowable annual cut is greatly reduced." Hammond said. In fact, the plan would reduce the AAC for the area to 10 per cent of what the government currently projects as the allowable harvest over the next one hundred years. But jobs would be maintained, even at one-tenth the rate of cut. Hammond explained, "This is possible because logging is done with small machines that require more people to cut fewer trees, and because value is added to wood products before they leave the local area. This means that far more people can be employed cutting and milling much less wood than is currently cut."[16]

Instead of racing for the bottom, this approach means racing for the top. If the ecosystem-based approach advocated by Hammond and others was applied across the country, Canada would no longer export low-value, unprocessed forest products. Everything about Canadian forest products would aim for quality, in both economic and ecological terms. Canadian forest products would no longer come from unrestricted clear-cuts. Canadian forest products would qualify for the best possible eco-labelling scheme, guaranteeing markets in Europe, perhaps even with a "green premium."

While it is unrealistic to expect such widespread transformation to take place overnight, the phase-out of destructive forestry practices should begin immediately. In its place, we need to adhere to the principles underlying the recommendations of the Clayoquot Sound Scientific Panel. At the heart of the Science Panel report was the proposal that logging plans should focus on what must be left undisturbed to maintain the ecological integrity of the forest. FSC standards show how this can be done in the various forest regions of Canada.

The method of logging to replace conventional clear-cutting will vary by region and forest type across Canada, but some elements are common to all forests. Begin with landscape planning to establish protected areas and wilderness reserves, and to preserve and/or restore large unfragmented forest areas, old-growth forests and other forests that have special value. Where logging does take place, there must be a higher level of retention of intact forests stands and individual trees, more closely emulating the kinds of forests left behind after natural disturbances typical in that ecoregion, landscape and topography. Special attention needs to be paid to the quality of what gets left behind—the living trees, the dead snags and the coarse woody debris, all of which provide vitally important wildlife habitat.

How the forests are cut and tended is also an important consideration. Feller-bunchers are the equivalent of the mechanized industrial fishing apparatus that devastated the East Coast fishery. We need to search for ways to increase meaningful employment in the forest industry; both in value-added processing and in logging itself. Selection logging is one way of doing this, as it requires workers to walk through the forest and make decisions. Selection logging, as well as partial harvesting and variable retention logging that meets FSC standards, have both ecological and social benefits.

The purely economic calculation that displaces forest workers by introducing highly mechanized operations rarely gives adequate consideration to the social impacts faced by displaced workers and their families. Nor does the economic analysis begin to value the benefits of intact ecosystems for wildlife and the irreparable cost of species at risk becoming extinct.

In the end, Canadians must weigh the economic, ecological and social costs of the current energy-intensive approach to forestry. Industry will have a large role in redesigning the system, but government must also play a key role. To maintain Canadian markets, the tax system will have to be reformed to ensure that Canadian forest companies can compete, even as they shift to a quality-driven product.

Strong evidence from government and industry sources throughout this book makes the case that Canada's forests are being overcut. The rate of overcutting threatens the economic base of the forest industry, as well as irreplaceable forest biodiversity, wildlife and fish habitat, and the myriad of ecological functions offered by a healthy forest. The humbling experience of walking through a grove of venerable trees—hearing birds in the canopy overhead, listening to a brook gurgling over pebbles and smelling the pungent richness of layers of moss—is beyond economic valuation.

A national overview is required. Otherwise, each province will continue to lay plans based on the vain hope that when the wood-supply crunch hits, fibre supplies can be boosted through silviculture or imported from a neighbouring province. The National Forest Strategy calls for better national data and an enhanced information base for decisions about forest management. But in times of serious budget cutbacks in forest services, how can this goal be met? No one can focus on the big picture—assessing what is a truly sustainable level of logging to supply what number of mills—without this kind of information. No one can assess the loss of habitat, of species, of sacred creation. And so new mills are added, more logging roads are driven through wilderness, more forest is strip-mined for the Athabasca Tar Sands, more forest is clear-cut by fewer and fewer workers. At some point, there will be nowhere to go to borrow wood, and the green mantle will be so reduced worldwide as to affect all life on this planet.

In *A Short History of Progress*, Ronald Wright offered a devastating critique of humanity's infatuation with technology and historical inability to read the danger signs of impending societal and ecological collapse. "'A culture,' said W.H. Auden, is no better than its woods.' Civilizations have developed many techniques for making the earth produce more...some sustainable, others not. The lesson I read in the past is this: that the health of land and water—and of woods, which are the keepers of the water—can be the only lasting basis for any civilization's survival and success."[17]

We are at the cutting edge.

Acknowledgments

Of the four books I have written, *At the Cutting Edge* is without a doubt the book for which I am less the author than the midwife. Pulling together data and stories from all across Canada required a team of researchers. Short biographies follow these Acknowledgments, but I want to thank each of them here as well: many thanks to Karen Baltgailis, Lance Bishop, Alexandre Boursier, Catherine Boyd, Allyson Brady, Justin Calof, Karin Clark, David Coon, David Nickarz, Dave Pearce, Olivia Schliep, Gary Schneider, Rick Schneider, Inuk Simard and Don Sullivan.

Our own editorial team was headed by the wonderfully unflappable Cendrine Huemer. This book could never have happened without her. Rachel Plotkin, Sierra Club of Canada's National Forests and Biodiversity Director, donated a huge amount of her energy to steering the book and keeping me on the forest policy course our organization has set. SCC's brilliant Executive Coordinator, Debra Eindiguer, has made it possible for me to handle a zillion competing demands. Martin von Mirbach, SCC's National Conservation Director, has been a constant factor in this project. In 1995 when the first edition was just a germ of an idea, Martin provided indispensable advice from his academic role in Newfoundland. We have been so fortunate to have him move to Ottawa and take on leadership of our conservation program. Many thanks to all.

A number of colleagues have provided sound counsel, helping me by reading over drafts and freely offering their views. Thanks in particular to Alan Appleby, Susan Casey-Lefkowitz, Jim Cooperman, Peter Demarsh, Gaile Whelan Enns, Tim Gray, Vicky Husband, Peter Lee, Dan McDermott, Gillian McEachern, Lisa Matthaus, Len Moores, Jennifer Morin, Stephen Price, Jocelyne Rankin, Joanne Roberge, Dan Soprovich and Ray Travers.

As is always the case, any mistakes are my own. In addition, owing to rapid shifts in ownership and logging rates, some details of particular situations may well have changed by the time this book reaches the public. The opinions expressed are also my own, although they are in line with Sierra Club of Canada policies.

The man without whom the book would never have happened, in first or second edition, is Glen W. Davis. Glen is friend, mentor, critic, funder and eagle-eyed editor. The funny thing about his support for this project is that he really wanted me to be working on a completely different book—a book on Canada's Dirty Dozen, the twelve most spectacular environmental disasters in Canada. Without his financial support, we would never have been able to assemble the team of researchers across Canada. Having made it possible, I hope he forgives me for delaying the book he really wants!

Thanks to my publisher in the amazing person of Anna Porter, who is also friend and supporter. Meg Taylor has been a wonderful editor. She became excited about the book and committed to saving Canada's forests at the same time.

I can never thank Farley Mowat enough for all his love and support. He offered the Foreword to both editions and continues to be a mentor for my writing, while he and Claire help keep me sane.

Last but not least, I cannot acknowledge anything in my work without thanking the most important person in my life. My daughter, Victoria Cate, continues to be a constant source of joy, offering her tired Mom support and love. She puts up with a lot when a "book project" comes along, and she never complains. I don't know how I got so lucky.

BIOGRAPHIES OF RESEARCHERS

National Research Coordinators
CENDRINE HUEMER
Cendrine Huemer has a B.Sc. in Behavioural Ecology. She has worked for fifteen years for environmental and naturalist organizations, including as biodiversity campaigner for Sierra Club of Canada, and as communications manager for the Canadian Nature Federation. She is now working as a consultant and is also editor of Sierra Club of Canada's national newsletter. She lives with her husband and daughter in an R2000 house in the shadow of three enormous white pines at the edge of a conservation area in Ottawa.

RACHEL PLOTKIN
Rachel Plotkin decided to become a forest campaigner while living in Bamfield, British Columbia, where she was surrounded by spectacular old-growth forests and witnessed one too many a logging truck whisking them off to the mill. She has worked with Sierra Club of Canada to protect forests and biodiversity for over three years, and has a master's degree in Environmental Studies and an Outdoor and Experiential teaching degree.

The following researchers worked to update data from the first edition of the book in their respective provinces.

Newfoundland and Labrador
CATHERINE BOYD
A native of Lewisporte, Newfoundland, Catherine Boyd is a graduate of the B.A. Environmental Studies program at Sir Wilfred Grenfell College and started working for Sierra Club of Canada in May 2003. As the Forest Campaigner for Newfoundland and Labrador, Catherine has been busy participating in multi-stakeholder groups within the CSA certification process, organizing a workshop that brought together forest activists from around the province and across the country, and mobilizing groups in response to government policy. Through this work, Catherine has established solid working relationships with people within government departments, as well as members of the activist community and Aboriginal groups.

Nova Scotia
LANCE BISHOP
Lance Bishop grew up and still lives in Baxter's Harbour, Nova Scotia. In 1996, he graduated from Acadia University with a B.Sc.H. in Biology, and in 1998 from Carleton University with an M.Sc. in Biology. His thesis research compared the effects of forestry disturbance with the effects of natural disturbance on forest beetle communities in red spruce forests in Nova Scotia. In response to witnessing large-scale clear-cutting across Nova Scotia, Lance started a logging contracting business that specializes in managing woodlots in the context of Acadian forest restoration. In 2001, Lance founded the North Mountain Old Forest Society, a non-profit organization devoted to helping landowners who want to restore the ecological integrity of private woodlots. Lance believes deeply that forests can and should be managed to protect and enhance their capacity to provide diverse benefits in perpetuity.

New Brunswick
DAVID COON
David Coon is Policy Director of the Conservation Council of New Brunswick. His first encounter with a tree was tapping an ancient maple as soon as he could walk—a rite of passage in his family for generations. He lives in Waweig with his wife and two daughters, where they own a small woodlot. He is a founding Director of the New Brunswick Community Land Trust, which seeks to keep woodlots and farm land in ecologically sound production through

conservation easements and trust agreements. Back in the analog age he obtained a B.Sc. in Biology from McGill University. He currently directs the Conservation Council's Endangered Acadian Forest Campaign.

INUK SIMARD

Inuk Simard holds a B.Sc. in Forestry Sciences and has done Environmental Studies at Université de Moncton. He has been involved in forest management and conservation through various governmental, non-governmental and private organizations. He has been involved in the scientific and GIS aspects of conservation projects in New Brunswick, including the establishment of large protected areas. He lives in Penniac with his wife and daughter.

Prince Edward Island
GARY SCHNEIDER

Gary Schneider is a founding member of the Environmental Coalition of Prince Edward Island and began the Macphail Woods Ecological Forestry Project in 1991. Sited on the 140-acre Macphail Homestead in Orwell, the restoration and education project offers school tours and workshops throughout the year. Macphail Woods includes demonstrations of a variety of restoration techniques, a nature centre and a 4-acre native plant nursery. In 2004, Gary won *Canadian Geographic's* Environmental Award in the Restoration and Rehabilitation category. He lives on a certified organic farm that includes 50 acres of forest.

Quebec
ALEXANDRE BOURSIER

Alexandre Boursier is a multilingual professional forester from Quebec with a master's degree in Social Forestry. He has extensive experience in Quebec and in the Majority World (Latin America and Africa) in the areas of conservation, certification according to FSC principles, knowledge transfer and international development projects pertaining to governance and public sector reform. Recently, Alexandre has worked as an independent consultant for forestry companies, for environmental organizations such as Greenpeace, World Wildlife Fund and Sierra Club of Canada, and for governmental organizations such as the National Round Table on the Environment and the Economy, and the Commission for Independent Study of Quebec's Public Forest Management (Coulombe Commission).

Ontario
DAVID PEARCE

Dave Pearce is Forest Conservation Analyst for the Wildlands League, a chapter of the Canadian Parks and Wilderness Society. After completing his master's in Forest Conservation in 2001, he worked for the Ontario Ministry of Natural Resources on a team writing a silvicultural assessment manual and for the University of Toronto in wildlife biology fieldwork. He initiated a sustainable forestry endeavour in a friend's woodlot. Dave also holds a degree in Biology from Trent University and a B.Ed. from Lakehead. He is a certified Ontario Tree Marker and Managed Forest Plan Approver. From White Lake in the Ottawa Valley, Dave now calls another lakeside community (Toronto) home.

Manitoba
DON SULLIVAN

Don Sullivan is an award-winning environmental writer, researcher, photographer and activist. He is the Executive Director for the Boreal Forest Network. Don was the recipient of the 1995 Manitoba Eco-Network Award for his outstanding contribution to the awareness and protection of Manitoba's environment. Don was the lead project coordinator for the North American Forest Forum held in September of 1996. The forum was endorsed by over thirty organizations and attracted some 150 environmentalists, First Nations representatives and youth from across Canada, the United States and Mexico to discuss forest-related issues in North America. In 2002, Don received the Queen's Golden Jubilee Medal in recognition of his significant contribution to his fellow citizens, his community and to Canada.

DAVID NICKARZ

David Nickarz has been active in forest issues since 1990. In 1993, he participated in the Clayoquot Sound logging blockades in British Columbia. He was arrested and fined $1500 for blockading a logging road and violating a B.C. Supreme Court order. Dave has volunteered and worked for many forest conservation groups in Manitoba, including the Boreal Forest Network and the Western Canada Wilderness Committee (Manitoba Chapter). Dave's specialty is the east side of Lake Winnipeg and Nopiming Provincial Park. He led logging protests in the park in 1995 and a citizen's watch campaign in 1996–1999. He helped expose more than two dozen illegal logging bridges built by the logging company in Pine Falls. Currently, Dave is helping with efforts to get United Nations World Heritage status for a First Nations–protected area on the east side of Lake Winnipeg.

Saskatchewan
ALLYSON BRADY
Allyson Brady is the Coordinator of the Saskatchewan Environmental Society and has spent the past thirteen years working in the environmental NGO sector. In additional to her appointments on government and industry advisory bodies on forest issues, Allyson has served, for the past ten years, on the Canadian Environmental Network Forest Caucus steering committee. Allyson coordinated and wrote a national critique of the Canadian Model Forest project, and published a report titled "Deforestation: the Lack of Regeneration in Saskatchewan Forests" as part of the Global Forest Watch initiative, a project of the World Resources Institute. More recently, she has authored two backgrounders on economic alternatives for forest-dependent communities: one on ecotourism and the other on non-timber forest products.

OLIVIA SCHLIEP
Olivia Schliep is a relative newcomer to the environmental movement. Since moving to Saskatoon in 2002, she has been a member of the Saskatchewan Environmental Society (SES) and currently serves as the President of their Board of Directors. As part of her commitment to SES, she sits on the steering committee of the Saskatchewan Eco-Network as vice-chair. Growing up in the interior of British Columbia, Olivia was exposed to many aspects of the local forest industry, which led her to begin studies in Forestry at the University of Alberta. After meeting her husband, also a student in the Forestry program, Olivia switched paths and completed a degree in Biological Science with a minor in Anthropology. Her interest in environmental issues is shared by her husband and two-year-old son, a true nature lover and explorer.

Alberta
RICHARD SCHNEIDER
Dr. Richard Schneider obtained a degree in Veterinary Medicine from the University of Saskatchewan in 1985 and a Ph.D. in Wildlife Epidemiology from the University of Guelph in 1992. He then completed an NSERC postdoctoral fellowship at the University of Alberta, studying the interrelationships between wolves, bison and disease in northern Canada. More recently, as a consultant for the governments of Alberta, Newfoundland and Ontario, and for various forestry companies, Dr. Schneider has conducted research on wildlife–habitat relationships in a variety of wildlife species including pine martens, fishers, moose and caribou. He also has been actively involved in several landscape-level forest management initiatives in Alberta and has written a book on the management of Alberta's forests. Dr. Schneider is currently Executive Director of the Canadian Parks and Wilderness Society, Edmonton Chapter.

British Columbia
JUSTIN CALOF
Justin Calof has a technical diploma in Forestry from the British Columbia Institute of Technology and a B.Sc. in Forest Resource Management from the University of British Columbia. He has worked throughout the province of British Columbia as a forest technician and forest manager for a number of large forest companies for eight years. He has worked overseas on a sustainability research project for the Canadian Government. He began working for the ENGO sector two years ago, and is now the Forest Management Specialist for Sierra Club of Canada, B.C. Chapter. He is registered as a forester in training (FIT) in British Columbia.

Yukon
KAREN BALTGAILIS
Karen Baltgailis has worked on forestry issues for more than twelve years, and has been Forestry Coordinator for the Yukon Conservation Society since 1998. Being self-taught in forestry, she has faith in communities' ability to take over management of their forests from people who have credentials, but lack long-term vision. Karen worked for Western Canada Wilderness

Committee, Alberta, for several years. She led the Alberta research for the first edition of *At the Cutting Edge*, and has written and produced two forestry documentaries. From 2000 to 2004, Karen was a member of the International Reference Group (board) of the Taiga Rescue Network—an international network with 220 participating organizations.

Northwest Territories
KARIN CLARK
Karin Clark has a B.Sc. in Ecology from the University of Calgary and an M.Sc. specializing in Tundra Plant Ecology from the University of British Columbia. She has been working for ten years in the environmental field in Yellowknife, where she shares her passion for the outdoors with her husband and three children. She is a member of the Board of Directors of a local environmental organization, Ecology North, which focuses on sustainable living, climate change and environmental education.

The following researchers provided invaluable assistance in the writing of the first edition:

Erica Konrad (National Research Coordinator)
Greg Mitchell (Newfoundland)
Charlie Restino (Nova Scotia)
Matthew Betts (New Brunswick)
Gary Schneider and Ruth Richman (Prince Edward Island)
Pierre Dubois and Henri Jacob (Quebec)
Tim Gray and Lorne Johnson (Ontario)
Don Sullivan (Manitoba)
Joys Dancer (Saskatchewan)
Karen Baltgailis and Erin McGregor (Alberta)
Jim Cooperman (British Columbia)
Laurel Jenkins and Juri Peepre (Yukon and Northwest Territories)

CONTACT ORGANIZATIONS

SIERRA CLUB OF CANADA

Sierra Club of Canada
1 Nicholas St., Suite 412
Ottawa, ON K1N 7B7
Phone: (613) 241-4611
Toll-free: (888) 810-4204
Fax: (613) 241-2292
Email: info@sierraclub.ca
www.sierraclub.ca

Sierra Youth Coalition
1 Nicholas St., Suite 406
Ottawa, ON K1N 7B7
Phone: (613) 241-1615
Toll-free: (888) 790-7393
Fax: (613) 241-2292
Email: info@syc-cjs.org
www.syc-cjs.org

Sierra Club of Canada—
Atlantic Canada Chapter
1657 Barrington St.
Roy Building, Suite 502
Halifax, NS B3J 2A1
Phone: (902) 444-3113
Fax: (902) 444-3116
Email: emilym@sierraclub.ca
www.sierraclub.ca/atlantic

Sierra Club of Canada—
British Columbia Chapter
733 Johnson St., Suite 302
Victoria, BC V8W 3C7
Phone: (250) 386-5255
Fax: (250) 386-4453
Email: info@sierraclub.bc.ca
www.sierraclub.ca/bc

Sierra Club of Canada—
Ontario Chapter
24 Mercer St., Suite 101
Toronto ON M5V 1H3
Phone: (416) 960-9606
Fax: (416) 960-0020
Email: ontariochapter@
sierraclub.ca
www.sierraclub.ca/ontario

Sierra Club of Canada—
Prairie Chapter
2nd Floor, 6328-104 St.
Edmonton, AB T6H 2K9
Phone: (780) 439-1160
Fax: (780) 437-3932
Email: prairiechapter@
sierraclub.ca
www.sierraclub.ca/prairie

Sierra Club of Canada—
Quebec Chapter
Phone: (514) 571-5139
Email: quebec@sierraclub.ca
www.sierraclub.ca/quebec

SIERRA CLUB—U.S.

Sierra Club
National Headquarters
85 Second St., 2nd Floor
San Francisco, CA
94105 U.S.A.
Phone: (415) 977-5500
Fax: (415) 977-5799
Email: information@
sierraclub.org
www.sierraclub.org

Sierra Club
Legislative Office
408 C St., N.E.
Washington, DC
20002 U.S.A.
Phone: (202) 547-1141
Fax: (202) 547-6009
www.dc.sierraclub.org

NATIONAL GROUPS

Assembly of First Nations
1 Nicholas St., Suite 1002
Ottawa, ON K1N 7B7
Phone: (613) 241-6789
Fax: (613) 241-5808
Email: imcleod@afn.ca
www.afn.ca

Canadian Environmental
Network Forest Caucus
945 Wellington St.,
Suite 300
Ottawa, ON K1Y 2X5
Phone: (613) 728-9810
Fax: (613) 728-2963
Email: info@cen-rce.org;
chantal@cen-rce.org
www.cen-rce.org/eng/
caucuses/fores

Canadian Parks and
Wilderness Society
(CPAWS)
880 Wellington St.,
Suite 506
Ottawa, ON K1R 6K7
Phone: (613) 569-7226
Toll-free: (800) 333-WILD
Fax: (613) 569-7098
Email: info@cpaws.org
www.cpaws.org

Grand Council of the Crees
81 Metcalfe St.
Ottawa, ON K1P 6K7
Phone: (613) 761-1655
Fax: (613) 761-1388
Email: cree@gcc.cs
www.gcc.ca

Greenpeace Canada
250 Dundas St. West,
Suite 605
Toronto, ON M5T 2Z5
Phone: (416) 597-8408
Toll-free: (800) 320-7183
Fax: (416) 597-8422
Email: members@yto.
greenpeace.org
www.greenpeace.ca

Nature Canada
1 Nicholas St., Suite 606
Ottawa, ON K1N 7B7
Phone: (613) 562-3447
Toll-free: (800) 267-4088
Fax: (613) 562-8208
www.cnf.ca

Sierra Legal Defence Fund
131 Water St., Suite 214
Vancouver, BC V6B 4M3
Phone: (604) 685-5618
Toll-free: (800) 926-7744
Fax: (604) 685-7813
Email: sldf@sierralegal.org
www.sierralegal.org

Taiga Rescue Network
c/o Don Sullivan
70 Albert St., Suite 2
Winnipeg, MB R3B 1E7
Phone: (204) 947-3081
Fax: (204) 947-3076
Email: don.sullivan@
shawbiz.ca
www.taigarescue.org or
www.borealnet.org

World Wildlife Fund Canada
245 Eglinton Ave. East,
Suite 410
Toronto, ON M4P 3J1
Phone: (416) 489-8800
Toll-free: (800) 26-PANDA
Fax: 416-489-8055
Email: panda@wwfcanada.
org
www.wwf.ca

NEWFOUNDLAND &
LABRADOR

Humber Environment Action
Group
P.O. Box 1143
Corner Brook, NF A2H 6T2
Phone/Fax: (709) 634-2520

Innu Nation
P.O. Box 119
Sheshatshiu, NL A0P 1M0
Phone: (709) 497 8398
Fax: (709) 497-8396
www.innu.ca

Newfoundland Lichen
Education and Research
Group
Email: lockyerswaters@
erioderma.com
www.erioderma.com

NOVA SCOTIA

Ecoforestry School in the
Maritimes
RR#2, New Germany, NS
B0R 1E0
Phone: (902) 543-0122
Fax: (902) 543-9950
Email: jim@windhorsefarm.
org
www.windhorsefarm.org

Ecology Action Centre
1568 Argyle St., Suite 31
Halifax, NS B3J 2B3
Phone: (902) 429-2202
Fax: (902) 422-6410
Email: eac@ecologyaction.ca
www.ecologyaction.ca

Margaree Environmental
Association
P.O. Box 55
Mabou, NS B0E 1X0
Tel: (902) 258-3354/
248-2211

NEW BRUNSWICK

Conservation Council of
New Brunswick
180 St. John St.
Fredericton, NB E3B 4A9
Phone: (506) 458-8747
Fax: (506) 375-4221
ccnb@nb.aibn.com
www.conservationcouncil.ca

Fallsbrook Centre
125 South Knowlesville Rd.
Knowlesville, NB E7L 1B1
Phone: (506) 375-8143
Fax: (506) 375-4221
Email: ja@fallsbrookcentre.ca
www.fallsbrookcentre.ca

PRINCE EDWARD ISLAND

Environmental Coalition of
Prince Edward Island
126 Richmond Rd.
Charlottetown, PEI C1A 1H9
Phone: (902) 569-2215
Fax: (902) 566-4037
Email: mail@ecopei.ca
www.ecopei.ca

QUEBEC

Algonquin of Barrière Lake
Kitiganik—Rapid Lake
La Vérendrye, PQ J0W 2C0
Tél/Fax: (819) 824-1734

L'Union québecoise pour la
conservation de la nature
1085 avenue de Salaberry,
bureau 300
Québec, PQ G1R 2V7
Tél: (418) 648-2104
Fax: (418) 648-0991
Email: courrier@uqcn.qc.ca
uqcn.qc.ca

ONTARIO

CPAWS-Wildlands League
401 Richmond St. West,
Suite 380
Toronto, ON M5V 3A8
Tel: (416) 971-9453
Fax: (416) 979-3155
www.wildlandsleague.
org

Earthroots
401 Richmond St. West,
Suite 410
Toronto, ON M5V 3A8
Phone: (416) 599-0152
Fax: (416) 340-2429
Email: info@earthroots.org
www.earthroots.org

Federation of Ontario
Naturalists (Ontario Nature)
355 Lesmill Rd.
Toronto, ON M3B 2W8
Phone: (416) 444-8419
Toll-free (within Ontario):
(800) 440-2366
Fax: (416) 444-9866
Email: info@ontarionature.
org
www.ontarionature.org

Northwatch
P.O. Box 282
North Bay, ON P1B 8H2
Phone: (705) 497-0373
Fax: (705) 476-7060
Email: northwatch@
onlink.net
www.northwatch.org

Ontario Public Interest
Research Group
Carleton—Forest Working
Group
326 Unicentre,
Carleton University
1125 Colonel By Drive
Ottawa, ON K1S 5B6
Phone: (613) 520-2757
Fax: (613) 520-3989
Email: opirg@opirg-
carleton.org
www.opirg-carleton.org

MANITOBA

Manitoba Future Forest
Alliance
275 Broadway Ave.,
Suite 503
Winnipeg, MB R3C 6M6
Phone: (204) 947-3081
Fax: (204) 947-3076

Manitoba Naturalists Society
63 Albert St., Suite 401
Winnipeg, MB R3B 1G4
Phone/Fax: (204) 943-9029
Email: mns1@mts.net
www.manitobanature.ca

SASKATCHEWAN

Saskatchewan Eco-Network
203-115 2nd Avenue North
Saskatoon, SK
Phone: (306) 652-1275
Fax: (306) 665-2128
Email: sen@the.link.ca

Saskatchewan Environmental
Society
Box 1372
Saskatoon, SK S7K 3N9
Phone: (306) 665-1915
Fax: (306) 665-2128
Email: info@
environmentalsociety.ca
www.environmentalsociety.ca

ALBERTA

Alberta Wilderness
Association
P.O. Box 6398, Station D
Calgary, AB T2P 2E1
Phone: (403) 283-2025
Toll-free: (866) 313-0713
Fax: (403) 270-2743
Email: awa.info@shawcable.
com
www.albertawilderness.ca

Bow Valley Naturalists
P.O. Box 1693
Banff, AB T1L 1B6
Phone/Fax: (403) 762-4160
Email: mcivor@telusplanet.
net

Friends of the Athabasca
P.O. Box 1351
Athabasca, AB T0G 0B0

Western Canada Wilderness
Committee
10168 100A St., Suite 310
Edmonton, AB T5J 0R6
Phone: (780) 420-1001
Fax: (780) 420-1475
www.wcwc.ab.ca

BRITISH COLUMBIA

East Kootenay
Environmental Society
495 Wallinger Av., #2
Kimberley, BC VIA 1Z6
Phone: (250) 427-9325
Fax: (250) 427-3535
Email: ekes@ekes.org
www.ekes.org

Friends of Clayoquot Sound
P.O. Box 489
Tofino, BC V0R 2Z0
Phone: (250) 725-4218
Fax: (250) 725-2527
Email: info@focs.ca
www.focs.ca

Silva Forest Foundation
P.O. Box 9
Slocan Park, BC V0G 2E0
Phone: (250) 226-7222
Fax: (250) 226-7446
Email: silvafor@netidea.com
www.silvafor.org

Valhalla Wilderness Society
Box 329
New Denver, BC
V0G 1S0
Phone: (250) 358-2333
Email: info@vws.org
www.savespiritbear.org

Western Canada Wilderness
Committee
227 Abbott St.
Vancouver, BC V6B 2K7
Phone: (604) 683-8220
Toll-free: (800) 661-9453
Fax: (604) 683-8229
www.wildernesscommittee.
org

YUKON

Canadian Parks and
Wilderness Society
Yukon Chapter
P.O. Box 31095
211 Main St.
Whitehorse, YK Y1A 5P7
Tel: (867) 393-8080
Fax: (867) 393-8081
Email: cpaws@cpawsyukon.
org
www.cpawsyukon.org

Yukon Conservation Society
302 Hawkins St.
Whitehorse, YK Y1A 1X6
Phone: (867) 668-5678
Fax: (867) 668-6637
Email: ycs@ycs.yk.ca
www.yukonconservation.org

NOTES

Introduction
[1] Roderick Nash, *Wilderness and the American Mind* (New Haven: Yale University Press, 1967), pp. 134–35.
[2] Samuel P. Hayes, *Conservation and the Gospel of Efficiency* (Cambridge, MA: Harvard University Press, 1972), p. 42.
[3] Nash, *Wilderness and the American Mind*, p. 188.

PART 1: AT THE CUTTING EDGE

Chapter 1: A Forest Nation
[1] Natural Resources Canada, Canadian Forest Service, *The State of Canada's Forests 2002–2003: Looking Ahead* (Ottawa, 2003), p. 7.
[2] Ibid. Data based on employment in 2002. Indirect employment data from 2001: Price Waterhouse Coopers, *The Forest Industry in Canada 2001* (Ottawa: Forest Products Association of Canada, July 2002).
[3] Jim Cooperman, "British Columbia's Forest Crisis: A BC Environmental Network Forest Caucus Discussion Paper," *British Columbia Environmental Report* (undated); Global Forest Watch Canada, *Canada's Forests at a Crossroads: An Assessment in the Year 2000* (Washington, D.C.: World Resources Institute, 2000), p. 13.
[4] D. Bryant et al., *The Last Frontier Forests: Ecosystems and Economies on the Edge*, (Washington, D.C.: World Resources Institute, 1997), p. 21.
[5] Natural Resources Canada, Canadian Forest Service, *The State of Canada's Forests, 2003–2004* (Ottawa, 2004).
[6] Ibid.
[7] Natural Resources Canada, Canadian Forest Service, *The State of Canada's Forests 1993* (Ottawa, 1993), p. 91.
[8] Andrew Nikiforuk and Ed Struzik, "The Great Forest Sell-Off," *Globe and Mail, Report on Business*, November 1989. Figures updated to 1999.
[9] L.A. Sandberg, ed., *Trouble in the Woods: Forest Policy and Social Conflict in Nova Scotia and New Brunswick* (Fredericton: Acadiensis Press, 1992), p. 5.
[10] Elizabeth May, *Paradise Won: The Struggle for South Moresby* (Toronto: McClelland and Stewart, 1990), p. 244.
[11] Don Sullivan, *Suspension of Liquidation of Canadian Lumber is Critical to*

Provide Short-term Relief to the U.S. Lumber Industry, pp. 11-12.

[12] Ibid., pp. 13–14.

[13] Environment Probe is a project of Energy Probe, a Toronto-based environmental non-government organization, which has championed the use of market forces and private property rights for environmental protection.

[14] Quoted in Terry Glavin, "Much ado about APEC," *Globe and Mail*, November 7, 1997, p. A23.

[15] Canadian Press, "Nova Scotia tree-cutting assailed: Government not protecting resource, independent foresters say," *Globe and Mail*, March 28, 1997.

[16] Environment Canada, "Building Momentum: Sustainable Development in Canada," Canada's Submission to the Fifth Session of the United Nations Commission on Sustainable Development, April 7–25, 1997, p. 18.

[17] Allan Swift, "Americans, Canadians at odds over 'sustainable forestry' plan," *Ottawa Citizen*, February 1, 1997, p. H3. The minister clarified her remarks in a letter to Sierra Club asserting that nations using trade barriers based on sustainable forest practices were the target of her remarks, not environmental groups. Nevertheless, it is clear that the federal role in forestry is one of defending industry interests in a global propaganda war.

[18] Global Forest Watch Canada, *Canada's Forests*.

[19] Global Forest Watch Canada, *Canada's Forests*; Environment Canada, "Forests," *State of the Environment Bulletin* 95, no. 4 (Summer 1995); Environment Canada for 1950 and 1970; 1994 data from Natural Resources Canada, Canadian Forest Service, *The State of Canada's Forests 1995–1996* (Ottawa, 1996); Natural Resources Canada, Canadian Forest Service, *The State of Canada's Forests 2002–2003* (Ottawa, 2003).

[20] Natural Resources Canada, Canadian Forest Service, *The State of Canada's Forests 1994* (Ottawa, 1994); *The State of Canada's Forests 2002–2003* (Ottawa, 2003).

[21] Quoted in Okanagan TSA Rationale, 1996, p. 19.

Chapter 2: Myths and Propaganda

[1] Natural Resources Canada, Canadian Forest Service, *The State of Canada's Forests 1991* (Ottawa, 1992), p. 41.

[2] Greenpeace, *Broken Promises: The Truth About What's Happening to British Columbia's Forests* (April 1997). A full 97 per cent of the Forest Alliance's funds are from the forest industry.

[3] Ibid., p. 20.

[4] Credit for unmasking industry myths goes particularly to Herb Hammond, *Seeing the Forest Among the Trees: The Case for Holistic Forest Use* (Vancouver: Polestar Press, 1991); Mitch Lansky, *Beyond the Beauty Strip* (Gardiner, ME: Tilbury House, 1992); and Dr. Chris Pielou, "A Clear-cut Decision," *Nature Canada* (Spring 1996).

[5] R. Locke, "Regeneration status of black spruce and balsam fir sites after cutting in district 12." *Silviculture Notebook* 3 (St. John's: Newfoundland Forest Service, May 1994).

[6] T.J. Carleton and P. MacLellan, "Woody Vegetation Responses to Fire Versus Clear-cut Logging: A Comparative Survey in the Central Canadian Boreal Forest," *Ecoscience* 1, no. 2 (1994).

[7] Official number: Natural Resources Canada, Canadian Forest Service, *The State of Canada's Forests 2003–2004* (Ottawa, 2004).

[8] Nova Scotia Department of Lands and Forests, *The Forest Resources of Nova Scotia* (Halifax, 1958), p. 59.

[9] Ibid., p. 60.

[10] Natural Resources Canada, Canadian Forest Service, *The State of Canada's Forests 2002–2003* (Ottawa, 2003).

[11] Royal Commission on Forest Protection and Management, Report (St. John's: Queen's Printer, 1981).

[12] Hammond, *Seeing the Forest*.

[13] I am grateful to Dr. Chris Pielou for pointing this out.

[14] Clayoquot Sound Scientific Panel, cited in Greenpeace, *Broken Promises*, p. 9.

[15] B. Freedman et al., "Forestry practices and biodiversity, with particular reference to the maritime provinces of Eastern Canada," *Environmental Review* 2 (1994), p. 54.

[16] Chris Maser, "Ancient Forests: Priceless Treasures," *The Mushroom Journal* (Fall 1988).

[17] G.R. Parker, D.G. Kimball and B. Dalzell, "Bird Communities Breeding in Selected Spruce and Pine Plantations in New Brunswick," *Canadian Field Naturalist* 108, no. 1 (1994).

[18] Pielou, "Clear-cut Decision," p. 23.

[19] Freedman et al, "Forestry practices and biodiversity."

[20] R. Silen, "Nitrogen, Corn and Forest Genetics," U.S. Department of Agriculture Forest Service, Pacific North West Range Experiment Station, General Technical Report, PNW137 (June 1982).

[21] Patrick Moore, *Pacific Spirit: The Forest Reborn* (West Vancouver: Terra Bella Publishers, 1995).

[22] Pielou, "Clear-cut Decision," p. 25.

[23] Canadian Council of Forest Ministers, *Compendium of Forestry Statistics 1994* (Ottawa, 1995), p. 88.

[24] "Protected areas" for this purpose is defined in conformity with the International Union for the Conservation of Nature (IUCN) protected levels 1,2 and 3, i.e., no logging.

[25] Global Forest Watch Canada, *Canada's Forests at a Crossroads: An Assessment in the Year 2000* (Washington, D.C.: World Resources Institute, 2000), p. 76.

[26] Ontario Ministry of Natural Resources, "Red and White Pine in Ontario," Fact Sheet (October 1996). Available at www.mnr.gov.on.ca.

[27] Debate on *Face-Off*, CBC Newsworld, January 3, 1996.

[28] Hammond, *Seeing the Forest*, p. 62.

[29] Ontario Ministry of Natural Resources, *Forest Management Guide for Natural Disturbance Pattern Emulation* (Toronto, November 2001).

[30] Ibid.

[31] M. Reeder, "Individual tree selection: More than forestry without chemicals," *Journal of Pesticide Reform* 8, no. 3 (Fall 1988).

[32] Ibid., p. 2.

[33] Hammond, *Seeing the Forest*, p. 63.

[34] Paul Hawken, *The Ecology of Commerce* (New York: Harper Business, 1993).

[35] Wayne Roberts, *Get a Life!* (Toronto: Get a Life Publishing House, 1995).

[36] M. Rauter, *Expert Panel on Information Technology Development and Use*, presentation by the president of the Ontario Forest Industries Association, "Proceedings Decision Support: 2001," vol. 2, 17th Annual Geographic Information Seminar Resource Technology 1994, Symposium. (Toronto, September 12–16, 1995), eds., J.M. Power, M. Strome and T.C. Daniel (Bethesda, MD: American Society for Photogrammetry and Remote Sensing), pp. 1111–16. Sponsored by the Canadian Forest Service, the Ontario Ministry of Natural Resources and the Resource Technology Institute.

[37] Jamie Swift, *Cut and Run: The Assault on Canada's Forests* (Toronto: Between the Lines, 1983), p. 139.

[38] M. McCormack, "Overview," *Proceedings of the Conference on the Impacts of Intensive Harvesting*, January 22, 1990 (Fredericton: Forestry Canada, Maritime Region, 1991). The discussion of the evolution of logging technology is based on Dr. McCormack's paper, especially Figure 5.

[39] Environment Canada, "Forests," *State of the Environment Bulletin* 95, no. 4 (Summer 1995).

[40] Statistics Canada, *Principle Statistics in the Logging Industry, 1967–1995*, Cat. no. 25-201 (Ottawa: Minister of Supply and Services, January 1996). Note that the figures from 1967–1987 and 1987–1993 are not completely comparable as, after 1987, the data collected included more small operators. In other words, if the data were readjusted to take this factor into account, the job-loss figures would be greater.

[41] Forest Allies, *Wood Consumption Increases…Jobs Decrease*, Fact Sheet (1995). (Originally in cords: 200,000 cords = 724,920 cubic meters; 900,000 cords = 3,262,140 cubic meters.)

[42] Cited in Wildlands League, *Cutting the Future out of Prosperity?*, Forest Diversity/Community Survival Series, Fact Sheet 2 (1995).

[43] Ibid. Wildlands League sources for these statistics were drawn from Statistics Canada, *Canadian Forestry Statistics*, Cat. no. 25-202 (Ottawa: Minister of Supply and Services, 1996); Forestry Canada, *Selected Forestry Statistics, 1988*, Info Report E-X-41 (Ottawa, 1989); Forestry Canada, *Selected Forest Statistics, 1991*,

Info Report E-X-46 (Ottawa, 1992); and Price Waterhouse, *The Canadian Pulp and Paper Industry: A Focus on Human Resources* (Ottawa: Minister of Supply and Services, 1994).

[44] Quoted in Sierra Club of Canada, "Forests," Fact Sheet (Ottawa, 1996).

[45] J. Berthiaume, *Research Note: Evolution of Employment in the Forestry Industry between 1970 and 1992* (Ottawa: Economic Studies Division, Canadian Forest Service, August 1993).

[46] GPI Atlantic, "Jobs plus...or minus?" *Reality Check: The Canadian Review of Well-Being* 2, no. 2 (Tantallon, NS: Genuine Progress Indicators—NS, August 2002).

[47] R. Wood, "Analysis of the Forest Industry Employment Situation in Port Alberni," *Forest Planning Canada* 8, no. 2 (March/April 1992).

[48] Statistics Canada, *Canadian Forestry Statistics,* Cat. no. 25-202; Price Waterhouse, *The Forest Industry of British Columbia* (1993-1994 annual).

[49] Cited by Wildlands League, *A New Appetite in the Forest,* Forest Diversity/Community Survival Series, Fact Sheet 3 (1995).

Chapter 3: Voodoo Forestry

[1] Ken Drushka, *Stumped: The Forest Industry in Transition* (Vancouver: Douglas & McIntyre, 1985), p. 23.

[2] N.S. Nicholas et al., "The reliability of tree crown position classification," *Canadian Journal of Forest Research* 21 (1991), p. 699.

[3] R.E. McRoberts et al., "Variation in forest inventory field measurements," *Canadian Journal of Forest Research* 24 (1994), p. 1766.

[4] Ibid., p. 1769. For similar studies and conclusions, see also G. Gertner et al., "Effects of measurement errors on an individual tree-based growth projection system," *Canadian Journal of Forest Research* 14 (1984), p. 311; S.A. Omule, "Personal Bias in Forest Measurements," *The Forestry Chronicle* (October 1980), p. 222; W. Dahms, "Correction for a possible bias in developing site index curves from sectioned tree data," *Journal of Forestry* (January 1963), p. 25.

[5] S. Magnussen, "Recovering time trends in dominant height from stem analysis," *Canadian Journal of Forest Research* 26 (1996), pp. 9–22. Abstract: "Site-index curves derived from stem analysis of trees with dominant height at the time of selection will underestimate dominant height of young trees and thus overestimate the performance and yield expectations of young stands."

[6] Drushka, *Stumped*, p. 34.

[7] The Manitoba Provincial Parks Act (Assented to July 27, 1993).

[8] Natural Resources Canada, Canadian Forest Service, *The State of Canada's Forests 1992* (Ottawa, 1993), p. 109.

[9] Chris Pielou, Speech to the University of British Columbia Law School Conference on Biodiversity and the Law.

[10] Donald MacKay, *The MacMillan Bloedel Story: Empire of Wood* (Vancouver: Douglas and McIntyre, 1982), p. 335.

[11] Ibid., p. 336.

[12] D.H. Kuhnke, "Silvicultural statistics for Canada: An 11-year summary," *Forestry Canada* (1989), p. 12.

[13] Global Forest Watch Canada, *Canada's Forests at a Crossroads: An Assessment in the Year 2000* (Washington, D.C.: World Resources Institute, 2001), p. 11.

[14] Report of the British Columbia Royal Commission on Forestry, *Timber Rights and Forest Policy*, vol. 1 (1976), p. 228.

[15] Tom Clark, *Timber Supply and Endangered Spaces: A World Wildlife Fund Canada Discussion Paper* (Toronto: World Wildlife Fund Canada, 1996), p. 54.

[16] Natural Resources Canada, Canadian Forest Service, *The State of Canada's Forests 1990* (Ottawa, 1991), pp. 32–33.

[17] Darcie L. Booth, *The Sustainability of Canada's Timber Supply* (Policy and Economics Directorate, Forestry Canada, June 1993), p. 3.

[18] Government of Newfoundland, *20-Year Forestry Development Plan, 1990–2009* (February 1992), p. 67.

[19] Clark, "Timber Supply," p. 47, quoting Ray Addison on the philosophy of the 1945 Sloan Commission.

[20] Monique Ross, *Forest Management in Canada* (Calgary: Canadian Institute of Resources Law, University of Calgary, 1995), p. 90.

Chapter 4: The Lungs of the Planet

[1] M. Apps and W. Kurz, "Assessment of Carbon Flows in Canadian Boreal Forests," in M.J. Apps and D.T. Price, eds., *Forest Ecosystems, Forest Management and the Global Carbon Cycle*, series 1, vol. 18 (Heidelberg, Germany: Springer-Verlag, 1995).

[2] Sierra Club of Canada, "Forest Fires and Climate Change," Fact Sheet (Ottawa, 1996).

[3] Quoted in Mitch Lansky, *Beyond the Beauty Strip: Saving What's Left of Our Forests* (Gardiner, ME: Tilbury House, 1992), p. 277.

[4] Ibid., citing D. Cayle, "From Commons to Catastrophe: The Destruction of the Forests," Transcript, Part V (Toronto: Canadian Broadcasting Corporation, 1989).

[5] J.P. Hall et al., *Health of North American Forests* (Ottawa: Natural Resources Canada, Canadian Forest Service, 1996).

[6] J. Hoddinott, "Global Warming and the Forest Flora," *Boreal Conference Proceedings* (Athabasca: Athabasca University, 1992), pp. 172–78.

[7] Shawna L. Naidu et al., "The Effects of Ultraviolet-B Radiation on Photosynthesis of Different Aged Needles in Field-Grown Loblolly Pine," *Tree Physiology* 12 (1993), pp. 151–62.

[8] Natty Urquizo, Jamie Bastedo, Tom Brydges and Harvey Shear, eds., *Ecological Assessment of the Boreal Shield Ecozone* (Ottawa: Environment Canada, 2000), p. 38.

[9] David Schindler, "A dim future for the boreal waters and landscapes: Cumulative effects of climate warming, stratospheric ozone depletion, acid precipitation and

other human activities," *Bioscience* 48, no. 3, pp. 157–64. Cited in Urquizo et al., *Ecological Assessment*.

[10] Intergovernmental Panel on Climate Change, "Palaeo CO_2 and Natural Changes in the Carbon Cycle," *Third Assessment Report: Climate Change 2001—The Scientific Basis: Contribution of Working Group I to the Third Assessment Report*, Section 3.3 (Cambridge, England: Cambridge University Press, 2001).

[11] Peter Bunyard, "Is it too late to put a brake on climate change?" *The Ecologist* (October 2001).

[12] Peter Graff, "Tarzan-style jungle vines choke trees, impede gas absorption: Scientists record first plant composition change in the virgin Amazon," *Ottawa Citizen*, August 15, 2002.

[13] R. Prins and D.G. Roberts, *The Role of Forests in Global Warming: A Problem Analysis* (Ottawa: Economic Studies Division, Forestry Canada, March 1991), p. 7.

[14] Global Change Strategies International Inc., *Disaster Mitigation and Preparedness in a Changing Climate: A Synthesis Paper Prepared for Emergency Preparedness Canada, Environment Canada, and the Insurance Bureau of Canada* (Ottawa, 1998), p. 13.

[15] Natural Resources Canada, Canadian Forest Service, *The State of Canada's Forests 1997–1998* (Ottawa, 1998).

[16] Murray Brewster, "Hurricane Juan mystifies scientists," *Globe and Mail*, August 12, 2004.

[17] Kurz, W.A. and M.J. Apps. 1996. Retrospective assessment of carbon flows in Canadian boreal forests. Pp. 173–182 in M.J. Apps and D.T. Price (eds). Forest Ecosystems, Forest Management and the Global Carbon Cycle, NATO ASI Series 1: D.H. Peterson (ed.) Global Environmental Change, Springer-Verlag, Heidelberg, Germany, Vol. 40.

[18] Sheila Copps, "Global warming and Canada's forest fires," *Globe and Mail*, July 10, 1995; Seth Borenstein "2002 The Second-Hottest Year," *Detroit Free Press*, January 18, 2003.

[19] World Meteorological Organization, "2003 Is Third-Hottest Year On Record, WMO Says," press release, December 17, 2003.

[20] Natural Resources Canada, Canadian Forest Service, *The State of Canada's Forest 1995–1996* (Ottawa, 1996).

[21] Natural Resources Canada, Canadian Forest Service, *The State of Canada's Forests 1999–2000* (Ottawa, 2000), p. 15.

[22] Mark Hume, "Filmon will probe BC forest fires," *Globe and Mail*, September 27, 2003, p. A8; Jim Beatty, "Rebuild firefighting corps, BC urged," *Ottawa Citizen*, February 29, 2004, p. A4.

[23] J. Saunders, "Forest fires raise expensive questions," *Globe and Mail*, July 20, 1995, quoting Dr. Jag Maini, former Assistant Deputy Minister, Forestry Canada.

[24] Canadian Food Inspection Agency, Plant Health Division, "Emerald Ash Borer: Questions and Answers." Available at www.inspection.gc.ca.

25 Natural Resources Canada, Canadian Forest Service, *The State of Canada's Forests 2002–2003* (Ottawa, 2003), p. 62.

26 BC Ministry of Water, Lands, and Air Protection, *Indicators of Climate Change for British Columbia 2002* (Victoria, 2002). Available at www.wlap.gov.bc.ca.

27 Mark Wilson, "BC pine beetle infestation reaches 'emergency' levels," *Ottawa Citizen*, November 10, 2000.

28 Frances Bula, "Logging in parks may be necessary: Campbell," *Vancouver Sun*, September 27, 2003.

29 Dennis Bueckert, "Fire fumes burn hole in ozone, experts say," *Ottawa Citizen*, June 27, 1995.

30 M. Harmon et al., "Effects on Carbon Storage of Conversion of Old-Growth Forests to Young Forests," *Science* 247 (February 9, 1990), p. 699.

31 A.M. Gordon et al., "Seasonal patterns of soil respiration and CO_2 following harvesting in white spruce forests of interior Alaska," *Canadian Journal of Forest Research* 17 (1987), pp. 304-19. Cited in Greenpeace International, *The Carbon Bomb: Climate Change and the Fate of the Northern Boreal Forests* (Toronto, 1994).

32 National Forest Strategy Coalition, *National Forest Strategy 2003–2008: A Sustainable Forest, a Canadian Commitment* (Ottawa, 2003), p. 10.

33 Nicola Ross, "Carbon Sinks, Forest Rises," *Alternatives Journal* 30, no. 3 (Summer 2004).

34 Ibid., p. 12.

35 *State of Canada's Forests 2002–2003*, p. 61.

36 National Climate Change Process, Forest Sector Table, *Options Report: Options for the Forest Sector to Contribute to Canada's National Implementation Strategy for the Kyoto Protocol* (Ottawa: Natural Resources Canada, November 1999), p. 137.

37 Martin von Mirbach, *Forests, Climate Change and Carbon Reservoirs: Opportunities for Forest Conservation*, A Sierra Club of Canada Discussion Paper (Ottawa: Sierra Club of Canada, September 2003).

38 Ross, "Carbon Sinks," p. 12.

Chapter 5: Pollution, Pesticides, and Politics

1 Warner Troyer, *No Safe Place* (Toronto: Clarke, Irwin, 1977).

2 National Climate Change Process, Forest Sector Table, *Options Report: Options for the Forest Sector to Contribute to Canada's National Implementation Strategy for the Kyoto Protocol* (Ottawa: Natural Resources Canada, November 1999).

3 W. Sinclair, *Controlling Pollution from Canadian Pulp Manufacturers: A Federal Perspective* (Ottawa: Environment Canada, March 1990).

4 Ibid., p. 34.

5 Theo Colborn, D. Dumanoski and J. Peterson Myers, *Our Stolen Future* (New York: Dutton, 1996).

6 During this period, I was Senior Policy Advisor to the federal minister. This is a personal recollection of events. Dr. Ranata Kroesa of Greenpeace did an invaluable

service in running the tests and in sharing her results before going public with them.

[7] D. Meagher, "Restrict pulp mills' organochlorines," *Fredericton Daily Gleaner*, September 1, 1989.

[8] J. Myrden, "Stora tops pulp mill pollution list," *Chronicle-Herald* (Halifax), March 17, 1989.

[9] J. Myrden, *Chronicle-Herald* (Halifax), October 1, 1988. Cited in Green Web Bulletin 26 (Saltsprings, NS, April 1991).

[10] Myrden, "Stora tops pulp mill pollution list."

[11] Natural Resources Canada, Canadian Forest Service, *The State of Canada's Forests 1993: Fourth Report to Parliament* (Ottawa, 1993), p. 107.

[12] Colborn, Dumanoski and Peterson Myers, *Our Stolen Future*.

[13] Northern River Basins Study, "Some fish under stress and nutrients affect river system," *River Views* (Winter 1996).

[14] Colborn, Dumanoski and Peterson Myers, *Our Stolen Future*.

[15] Natural Resources Canada, Canadian Forest Service, *The State of Canada's Forests 1993* (Ottawa, 1993).

[16] See the Manitoba section of Chapter 13, "The Prairies," for details.

[17] National Climate Change Process, Forest Sector Table, *Options Report*, p. 14.

[18] Robert Hornung, *Corporate Action on Climate Change, 1996: An Independent Review* (Edmonton: The Pembina Institute, April 1997), p. 39.

[19] National Climate Change Process, Forest Sector Table, *Options Report*, p. viii.

Chapter 6: The Softwood Lumber Dispute

[1] Natural Resources Canada, Canadian Forest Service, *The State of Canada's Forests 2002–2003* (Ottawa, 2003).

[2] Natural Resources Canada, Canadian Forest Service, *The State of Canada's Forests 1995–1996* (Ottawa, 1996), p. 62.

[3] J. Cartwright, "Wither Canada's Forests?" unpublished paper prepared for *Policy Options* (Institute on Research on Public Policy).

[4] Natural Resources Canada, Canadian Forest Service, *The State of Canada's Forests 1997–1998* (Ottawa, 1998).

[5] Natural Resources Canada, Canadian Forest Service, *The State of Canada's Forests 1999–2000* (Ottawa, 2000).

[6] Natural Resources Canada, Canadian Forest Service, *The State of Canada's Forests 2000–2001* (Ottawa, 2001).

[7] Natural Resources Canada, Canadian Forest Service, *The State of Canada's Forests 2002–2003* (Ottawa, 2003).

[8] Mary Lynn Young, "Forest firms on right track with focus on productivity," *Globe and Mail, Report on Business*, April 1, 2004, p. B2.

[9] Peter Kennedy, "Tembec, Domtar report steep losses: companies blame punitive U.S. lumber duties and higher fibre costs," *Globe and Mail, Report on Business*,

April 30, 2004, p. B12; Robert Gibbens, "Abitibi, Domtar face further cost cutting: rising product prices not enough," *Financial Post*, January 29, 2004, p. FP6; Bertrand Marotte, "Abitibi shutting down two paper-making plants: cutting 1,220 jobs; cites higher dollar and excess supply," *Globe and Mail, Report on Business*, December 11, 2002, p. B5.

10 Peter Kennedy, "BC lumber firms agree to merger: Riverside Forest to acquire Lignum," *Globe and Mail, Report on Business*, February 3, 2004, p. B7. Laurie Cater is publisher of Madison's Canadian Lumber Directory.

11 Young, "Forest firms on right track."

12 G. Kuehne, "On the Softwood Lumber Tariff—An Update," *Forest Planning Canada* 7, no. 3 (September/October 1991).

13 Adam Zimmerman, *Who's in Charge Here, Anyway?* (Toronto: Stoddart, 1997), p. 78.

14 Ibid.

15 Ibid.

16 Elizabeth May, *Paradise Won: The Struggle for South Moresby* (Toronto: McClelland & Stewart, 1990), p. 164.

17 Ken Drushka, *Stumped: The Forest Industry in Transition* (Vancouver: Douglas & McIntyre, 1985), p. 279.

18 Coalition for Fair Lumber Imports, *Suspension of Liquidation on Canadian Lumber is Critical to Provide Short-Term Relief to the U.S. Lumber Industry* (1995).

19 G. Shannon, "It's time to solve the softwood issue," *Globe and Mail, Report on Business*, August 1, 1996.

20 Zimmerman, *Who's in Charge*, p. 103.

21 P. Lush, "Lumber shipments flooding into U.S.," *Globe and Mail, Report on Business*, July 4, 1996.

22 Steven Chase and Peter Kennedy, "Eco-probe of softwood trade urged," *Globe and Mail, Report on Business*, April 18, 2002, p. B2.

23 Tim Gray, Elizabeth May, Linda Nowlan and Cliff Wallis, "Let's stop blaming the U.S.," *Globe and Mail*, February 19, 2002, p. A15.

24 Barrie McKenna, "Lumber deal pledged: Chrétien, Bush vow to reach an agreement on softwood before U.S. duties are finalized," *Globe and Mail*, March 15, 2002, p. A1.

25 Natural Resources Canada, Canadian Forest Service, *The State of Canada's Forests 2001–2002* (Ottawa, 2002).

26 Barrie McKenna, "Lights, camera, but no lumber action for Campbell," *Globe and Mail, Report on Business*, October 24, 2003.

27 Amy Carmichael, "Domtar slams proposed softwood deal: Proposal pits Ontario, Quebec firms against Western Canada," *Ottawa Citizen*, December 9, 2003.

28 Susan Casey Lefkowitz, briefing note to Elizabeth May (December 6, 2003).

29 Naomi Koppel, "WTO upholds U.S. softwood duties: Trade body rules rates miscalculated," *Ottawa Citizen*, April 14, 2004, p. D3.

[30] Steven Chase, "Softwood counteroffer not seen any time soon," *Globe and Mail*, *Report on Business*, May 14, 2004, p. B3.

[31] Steven Chase, "Hold softwood challenge, Canada asks U.S.," *Globe and Mail*, *Report on Business*, August 25, 2004, p. B3.

[32] "NAFTA rejects U.S. softwood claims," CBC News online, www.cbc.ca/ stories/2004/08/31/softwood_ruling040831 (Updated August 31, 2004).

[33] Nigel Sizer, "Perverse habits: The G8 and subsidies that harm forests and economies," *Forest Notes* (Washington, D.C.: World Resources Institute, June 2000).

[34] McKenna, "Lumber deal pledged."

Chapter 7: The Certification Debate

[1] I was approached to sit on the Canadian Standards Association forest-certification advisory committee, but declined in view of time constraints. I became extremely dissatisfied with the CSA only after I learned I was being listed as a committee member who consistently sent regrets for not attending meetings. I subsequently asked the CSA to remove my name from the members' list, only to discover I was then listed as an associate member. Monte Hummel of World Wildlife Fund Canada had a similar experience.

[2] C. Elliott and A. Hackman, *Current Issues in Forest Certification in Canada* (Toronto: World Wildlife Fund Canada, April 1996).

[3] The six criteria under CCFM for sustainable forest management are: conserving biodiversity; maintaining and enhancing forest ecosystems; conserving soil and water, contributing to global ecological cycles; providing multiple benefits to society; and accepting society's responsibility for sustainable development. A seventh criterion, relating to the rights of Aboriginal peoples was rejected by the CCFM. Thus, there are no specific obligations to First Nations in the CSA process.

[4] Martin von Mirbach, *The Canadian Standards Association SFM standard Review and Analysis* (Ottawa: Sierra Club of Canada, 2004, prepared for FERN).

[5] Ibid.

[6] Ibid.

[7] *Alternatives Journal* staff, "Setting the standard: *Alternatives* interviews Martin von Mirbach on the Forest Stewardship Council's new guidelines for good logging practices in the boreal forest," *Alternatives Journal* 30, no. 3 (Summer 2004).

[8] "World Wildlife Fund and Tembec Inc. Reach Historic Accord to Promote Long-Term Sustainability of Canadian Forestry," joint press release, January 25, 2001. Available on World Wildlife Fund Canada's website: www.wwf.ca.

[9] *Alternatives Journal* staff, "Setting the standard."

[10] Canadian Newswire, "Report on boreal forest decimation hot lists Canadian logging companies," *ForestEthics* release, July 21, 2004.

[11] Martin von Mirbach, "Much ado about nothing: FSC and Ontario announce-

ment," *Forest Caucus Report* 3, no. 1 (Ottawa: Canadian Environmental Network, Summer 2001).

[12] Elliott and Hackman, *Current Issues*, Appendix 6.

[13] See the Nova Scotia section of Chapter 10, "Atlantic Provinces."

[14] Sean Silcoff, "Ontario accused of dragging heels on smog reduction," *Globe and Mail*, June 13, 1996.

Chapter 8: Other Pressures on Canada's Forests

[1] Peter Lee, "Boreal Canada: State of the Ecosystem, State of Industry, Emerging Issues and Projections," Report to the National Round Table on the Environment and the Economy (Edmonton: Global Forest Watch Canada, 2004).

[2] Ducks Unlimited, *Canada's Boreal Forest: A Vision for and Commitment to World-Leading Conservation by Ducks Unlimited* (undated, post-2002).

[3] Mining Watch Canada, *The Boreal Below: Mining Issues and Activities in Canada's Boreal Forest Region* (Ottawa, December 2001).

[4] Ibid.

[5] Lee, "Boreal Canada."

[6] Ducks Unlimited, *Canada's Boreal Forest*.

[7] Lee, "Boreal Canada."

[8] Shell Canada, "Submission to the Alberta Energy and Utility Board Joint Federal-Provincial Environmental Assessment Hearing" (Jackpine Mine, October 2003).

PART 2: ONCE A LAND OF TREES

Chapter 9: The Lost Forests

[1] Paul Senez, "Letter from the President," *SCAN Newsletter* 5, no. 4 (Ottawa: Sierra Club of Canada, December 2003).

[2] Ken Farr, *The Forests of Canada* (Ottawa: Natural Resources Canada, 2003).

[3] Global Forest Watch Canada, *Canada's Forests at a Crossroads: An Assessment in the Year 2000* (Washington, D.C.: World Resources Institute, 2000).

[4] Sierra Club of Canada, BC Chapter, *Canada's Ancient Rainforest: Home of the Great Bears and Wild Salmon* (Victoria, 1999).

[5] Report of the Sub-committee on Boreal Forest of the Standing Senate Committee on Agriculture and Forestry, *Competing Realities: The Boreal Forest at Risk*, Chair, Nicholas Taylor, Deputy Chair, Mira Spivak (June 1999), p. i.

[6] Peter Lee, "Boreal Canada: State of the Ecosystem, State of Industry, Emerging Issues and Projections," Report to the National Round Table on the Environment and the Economy (Edmonton: Global Forest Watch Canada, 2004).

[7] Ducks Unlimited, *Canada's Boreal Forest: A Vision for and Commitment to World-Leading Conservation by Ducks Unlimited* (undated, post-2002).

[8] Senate Sub-committee, *Competing Realities*.

[9] Lee, "Boreal Canada."

[10] David Neave, Erin Neave, Tony Rotherham and Brenda McAfee, *Canada's Forest Biodiversity: a Decade of Progress in Sustainable Management* (Ottawa: Natural Resources Canada, Canadian Forest Service, 2002).

[11] Senate Sub-committee, *Competing Realities.*

[12] Lee, "Boreal Canada." See Peter Lee's footnote number 190.

[13] Lee, "Boreal Canada."

[14] Tzeporah Berman, "Boreal Time Has Come," *Taiga News* 41 (Winter 2002).

[15] Senate sub-committee, *Competing Realities*, p. i.

[16] Global Forest Watch, "Forest companies increase their mill capacity to handle increased cutting in Canada's boreal forest," press release, May 7, 2004. Available at www.globeforestwatch.ca.

Chapter 10: Atlantic Provinces

NEWFOUNDLAND

[1] Department of Forest Resources and Agrifoods, Newfoundland Forest Service, *20-Year Forestry Development Plan 1996–2015* (St. John's: Government of Newfoundland and Labrador, 1998), reported shortfalls of 27 per cent. *20-Year Forestry Development Plan 1990–2009* (1992), reported shortfalls of 10 to 15 per cent. Department of Forest Resources and Agrifoods, Forest Service of Newfoundland and Labrador, *Provincial Sustainable Forest Management Strategy 2003* (St. John's: Government of Newfoundland and Labrador, 2003), p. 36, projects an ongoing shortfall of 776,600 cubic metres to run the mills at current levels.

[2] Farley Mowat, *Sea of Slaughter* (Toronto: McClelland and Stewart, 1984).

[3] W. Meades, "Stability in the Boreal Forest/Ericaceous Dwarf-Shrub Heath Ecotone of Eastern Newfoundland," Proc. of 1989 IUFRO Working Party 51, 05-2, Information Report N-X-271 (St. John's: Forestry Canada, 1989); W. Meades, "Successional Status of Ericaceous Dwarf Heath in Eastern Newfoundland," doctoral dissertation (University of Connecticut, 1986).

[4] Royal Commission on Forestry, *Report* (St. John's: David R. Thistle, 1955), p. 10.

[5] John Gray, *The Trees Behind the Shore: The Forests and Forest Industries of Newfoundland and Labrador* (St. John's: Economic Council of Canada, 1981), p. 17.

[6] Gray, *Trees Behind the Shore*, p. 16.

[7] A "board foot" is a timber term for a piece of wood 1-inch (2.5 cm) thick and 1-foot (30 cm) square. It takes 15 cubic feet (4.6 cubic metres) of round logs to make 1,000 board feet of lumber.

[8] In an ironic footnote, Ontario Hydro actually traded in carbon futures with Abitibi-Consolidated, "buying" 840,000 tons from Star Lake at an estimated $3 per ton.

[9] D. Haley and M.K. Luckert, *Forest Tenures in Canada: A Framework for Policy Analysis*, Information Report E-X-43 (Ottawa: Forestry Canada, 1990), p. 99.

[10] Gray, *Trees Behind the Shore*, p. 18.

[11] Greg Mitchell, "Newfoundland's Giant Trees of the Past," *Newfoundland and*

Labrador Environment Network News 7, no. 1 (January 1996), citing Anglican Bishop Edward Field's travels of 1849.

¹² Ibid. The Poole Royal Commission is cited as the source for the 6-million-board-feet-per-year figure, and John Munroe, "Public Timber Allocation Policy in Newfoundland," Ph.D. thesis (Vancouver: University of British Columbia, 1978), is credited for the 1884 and 1910 production levels.

¹³ Laura Jackson, *Parks Privatization: Concerns and Solutions* (St. John's, Newfoundland: Protected Areas Association of Newfoundland and Labrador, April 1997), p. 1.

¹⁴ Government of Newfoundland and Labrador, Provincial Parks Act (2003).

¹⁵ See Chapter 2, "Myths and Propaganda."

¹⁶ R. Locke, "Regeneration status of black spruce and balsam fir sites after cutting in district 12." *Silviculture Notebook* 3 (St. John's: Newfoundland Forest Service, May 1994).

¹⁷ Natural Resources Canada, Canadian Forest Service, *The State of Canada's Forests 2002–2003: Looking Ahead* (Ottawa, 2003). Actual area: 2.6 million hectares, or 15 per cent of harvested Crown land, based on data from 2000.

¹⁸ Ibid. Actual area: 80,000 hectares, or 19 per cent of harvested Crown land, based on data from 2000.

¹⁹ Briefing note, Greater Gros Morne Ecosystem Connectivity Working Group, open house June 9, 2004, p. 2. This group is comprised of the forestry and wildlife divisions of the provincial government, the Park, Corner Brook Pulp and Paper and Sir Wilfred Grenfell College (Memorial University). Collectively they facilitate research on the impact of activities outside the park on habitats and species within the park. This is particularly important for the Main River area, which is rich in biological diversity and adjacent to the park to the East.

²⁰ Greg Mitchell, logging contractor, personal correspondence to Elizabeth May, 1997, referring to Upper Glide, Pine Brook and Copper Lakes, to be logged by Kruger (Corner Brook Pulp and Paper, Newfoundland).

²¹ Greg Mitchell, "Newfoundland's Newest Endangered Species," *Newfoundland and Labrador Environment Network News* 7, no. 3 (April 1996).

²² The Species at Risk Act (SARA) became law in June 2003. It limits its scope to federal lands and waters unless the federal Cabinet acts on a determination by the federal Minister of the Environment that the relevant province is failing to protect a particular species.

²³ Gray, *Trees Behind the Shore*, p. 5.

²⁴ Natural Resources Canada, Canadian Forest Service, *The State of Canada's Forests 2002–2003* (Ottawa, 2003), p. 23. Note that the area of total land and area of total forest land are different in *Provincial Sustainable Forest Management Strategy 2003*, p. 35, note 1. The provincial document estimates total forest land at 23.2 million hectares.

²⁵ *20-Year Forestry Development Plan, 1990–2009.*

[26] Ibid., pp. 2–4.

[27] Gray, *Trees Behind the Shore*, p. 20.

[28] *20-Year Forestry Development Plan, 1996–2015*, p. 84.

[29] Canadian Council of Forest Ministers, *Compendium of Canadian Forestry Statistics, 1994* (Ottawa, 1995), p. 60. The 964,000 cubic metres figure is from 1993.

[30] *20-Year Forestry Development Plan, 1990–2009*, p. 85.

[31] Natural Resources Canada, Canadian Forest Service, *The State of Canada's Forests, 2001–2002: Reflections of a Decade* (Ottawa, 2002), p. 8.

[32] "Government shall issue to the Company licences...to cut timber on all or any part, as requested by the Company": Labrador Linerboard Limited Agreement Act, Statutes of Newfoundland, 1979, Chapter 11, section 1(2), p. xxv.

[33] Timber Licence, Province of Newfoundland: Agreement between Newfoundland and Abitibi Paper Company Ltd., November 2, 1987.

[34] Gray, *Trees Behind the Shore*, p. 23.

[35] Greg Mitchell, logging contractor, personal communication to Elizabeth May, 1996.

[36] *20-Year Forestry Development Plan 1990–2009*, p. 69.

[37] *State of Canada's Forests 2002–2003*, p. 23. Data from 2000 used.

[38] Martin von Mirbach, *Newfoundland's Wood Supply: A Critique of the Assumptions Used in the "20-Year Forestry Development Plan, 1990–2009,"* (Humber Environment Action Group, November 1993).

[39] Government of Newfoundland and Labrador, Poole Royal Commission, "Report of the Royal Commission on Forest Protection and Management" (St. John's: Queen's Printer, 1981), pp. 14–15. The figure was stated as 805,000 cords. Since 2.2 cubic meters makes up to 1 cord, the metric figure is 1.6 million cubic meters.

[40] *20-Year Forestry Development Plan, 1996–2015*, p. 84.

[41] Quoted in Larry Innes, "Adaptive Mismanagement Proposed for Nitassinan Forests," American Indian Heritage website: www.indians.org.

[42] Ibid.

[43] Statistics are from Department of Forest Resources and Agrifoods, Newfoundland Forest Service, *Forest Management* (St. John's: Government of Newfoundland and Labrador, 1995).

[44] Progressive Conservative Party of Newfoundland and Labrador, *Blue Book 2003: Danny Williams' Plan for Newfoundland and Labrador*. Retrieved May 27, 2004 from www.pcparty.nf.net/plan2003d.htm.

NOVA SCOTIA
[1] Nova Scotia Department of Lands and Forests, *The Forest Resources of Nova Scotia* (Halifax, 1958).

[2] Ibid.

[3] Quoted in Ken Drushka, *Stumped: The Forest Industry in Transition* (Vancouver: Douglas & McIntyre, 1985), p. 27.

4 L.A. Sandberg, "Forest Policy in Nova Scotia: The Big Lease, Cape Breton Island, 1899–1960"; in L.A. Sandberg, ed., *Trouble in the Woods: Forest Policy and Social Conflict in Nova Scotia and New Brunswick* (Fredericton: Acadiensis, 1992), p. 65. (Note: 25 cm = 10 inches).

5 Andrew D. Rodgers, *Bernhard Edward Fernow: A Story of North American Forestry* (Durham, England: Forest History Society, 1991).

6 Quoted in *Forest Resources of Nova Scotia*, p. 1.

7 *Forest Resources of Nova Scotia*, p. 55.

8 Sandberg, "Forest Policy," pp. 65–89.

9 Quoted in L.A. Sandberg, "Introduction: Dependent Development and Client States: Forest Policy and Social Conflict in Nova Scotia and New Brunswick," in L.A. Sandberg, ed., *Trouble in the Woods: Forest Policy and Social Conflict in Nova Scotia and New Brunswick* (Fredericton: Acadiensis, 1992), p. 1–21.

10 *Forest Resources of Nova Scotia*, p. 62.

11 Ibid.

12 *Forest Resources of Nova Scotia*, pp. 63–64.

13 John S. Donaldson, General Manager of Halifax Power and Pulp Co. Ltd, of Sheet Harbour, Nova Scotia, cited in *Pulp and Paper Primer: Nova Scotia*, Green Web Bulletin 26,(Saltsprings, NS, April 1991).

14 Quoted in H. Thurston, "Nova Scotia: Squandering Tomorrow," in A. Schneider, ed., *Deforestation and "Development" in Canada and the Tropics* (Sydney, NS: Centre for International Studies, University College of Cape Breton, 1989), p. 163. Originally published as "Prest's Last Stand," in *Harrowsmith* 50 (August/September 1983).

15 Ibid.

16 Sierra Club of Canada, *Rio Report Card 1998* (Ottawa, 1998). Available at www.sierraclub.ca; Nova Nada Monastery, "Nova Nada sold as solitary haven," press release, March 15, 2002. Available at www.spirituallifeinstitute.org.

17 Elizabeth May, *Budworm Battles* (Tantallon, NS: Four East, 1982).

18 L.A. Sandberg, ed., *Trouble in the Woods: Forest Policy and Social Conflict in Nova Scotia and New Brunswick* (Fredericton: Acadiensis, 1992), especially P. Clancy, "The Politics of Pulpwood Marketing in Nova Scotia, 1960–1985."

19 May, *Budworm Battles*.

20 Quoted in ibid., p. 31.

21 Quoted in Farley Mowat, "Introduction," in Elizabeth May, *Paradise Won: The Struggle for South Moresby* (Toronto: McClelland and Stewart, 1990).

22 Stora Kopparberg, *Annual Report* (1992).

23 C. Shaw, "Stora announces $650 m plant," *Chronicle-Herald* (Halifax), December 12, 1995.

24 Robert Hirtle, "Bowater to halt cutting at Kaizer Meadow for one year," *The Lighthouse* (April 2002), quoting Bowater vice-president of operations Roger Loney.

25 Information from Sierra Club of Canada website: atlantic.sierraclub.ca/camp_kaizer.htm.

26 Ron Stang, "Environmentalist's claims 'ridiculous,' says Stora president," *Cape Breton Post*, July 6, 1988.

27 Quoted in K. Cox, "Cape Breton forestry program stirs debate," *Globe and Mail*, November 6, 1991.

28 Quoted in D. MacNeil, "Fight for the Keppoch," *Cape Breton Post*, October 26, 1991.

29 Nova Scotia Legislature, *Hansard*, September 25, 2001, testimony of Tourism Industry Association of Nova Scotia, per Jennifer Archibald.

30 "Wildlife Species Protected under the Endangered Species Act in Nova Scotia," Government of Nova Scotia website: www.gov.ns.ca/natr/wildlife/endngrd/species-list.htm.

31 P. Neily, "Nova Scotia Status Report on Timber Supply," in *Timber Supply in Canada: Challenges and Choices*, Canadian Council of Forest Ministers Conference, held November 16–18, 1994. Kananaskis, Alberta (Ottawa: Natural Resources Canada, November 1994), p. 64.

32 Forestry Canada and Nova Scotia Department of Natural Resources, *Nova Scotia's Forest Management Strategy*, printed under the Canada-Nova Scotia Cooperation Agreement for Forestry Development (July 1994), p. 2.

33 Neily, "Nova Scotia Status Report."

34 Total area harvested: Forestry Canada, *The State of Forestry in Canada, 1990, First Report to Parliament* (Ottawa, 1990), p. 12; demand for wood to mills: Gardner Pinfold Consulting Economists, *An Evaluation of the Forest Resource Development Agreement and the Forest Renewal Agreement*, prepared for the Nova Scotia Department of Lands and Forests and the Canadian Forestry Service (March 1987).

35 Natural Resources Canada, Canadian Forest Service, *The State of Canada's Forests 1995–1996* (Ottawa, 1996), p. 94.

36 Natural Resources Canada, Canadian Forest Service, *The State of Canada's Forests 2002–2003: Looking Ahead* (Ottawa, 2003), p. 22.

37 Gardner Pinfold Consulting Economists, *Evaluation of the Forest Resource Development Agreement*, pp. 106-8.

38 Observations based on a series of workshops held with stakeholders in the Maritime forest industry, organized by the National Round Table on Environment and Economy, on the subject of small private woodlots. (Workshops held throughout winter/spring 1996–97; I was a member of the NRTEE Taskforce on Small Private Woodlots and Vice-Chair of the NRTEE through this period.)

39 Keith Elwood, Representative of Nova Scotia Joint Venture, "Presentation to the National Round Table on Environment and Economy: Panel Discussion on Private Woodlots" (Miramichi, NB, May 24, 1996).

40 Based on estimates of rotation ages from NS Department of Natural Resources staff (personal communication between Lance Bishop (researcher for Nova Scotia chapter) and Tim McGrath (Forest Planning & Research Section, Nova Scotia, Department of Natural Resources, Truro, Nova Scotia, 2004).

[41] ATi Consulting, "CAFD 2: Evaluation of the Canada-Nova Scotia Cooperation Agreement for Forestry Development, 1991-1995" (March 1995)," Ex-3 and p. 96.

[42] Ibid., p. 103.

[43] Natural Resources Canada, Canadian Forest Service, *The State of Canada's Forests 2000–2001: Sustainable Forestry: a Reality in Canada* (Ottawa, 2001), p. 19.

[44] Canadian Press, "Nova Scotia tree-cutting assailed: Government not protecting resource, independent foresters say," *Globe and Mail*, March 28, 1997.

[45] National Forest Strategy Coalition, *Canadian Accomplishments: Our evolving journey toward sustainable forests 1997–2000* (Ottawa, 2000), p. 1.

[46] "Forests are devastated by two centuries of clear cutting: GPI report," *The Masthead News*, January 2002, p. 8.

[47] "Forests are devastated," *Masthead News*; Sara Wilson and Ron Coleman, with Minga O'Brien and Linda Pannozzo, *The Nova Scotia Genuine Progress Index Forest Accounts* (November 2001). Available at www.gpiatlantic.org.

[48] *State of Canada's Forests 2000–2001: Sustainable Forestry*, p. 12.

[49] Nova Scotia Department of Natural Resources, "2002 Wood Acquisition Plan Program Summary" (2003). Available at www.gov.ns.ca.

[50] Bob Bancroft, "Providing more Acadian forest wildlife habitats in today's managed forests," Nova Forest Alliance Forest Forum (November 19-20, 2003).

[51] Richard Hurlbut, Minister of Natural Resources, letter to Lance Bishop, December 23, 2003.

[52] Wilfred Creighton, "The Old Man and the Trees," transcript of comments made by Dr. Wilfred Creighton at the forum Sustainability or Liquidation: The State of Nova Scotia's Forests (September 24, 1998), in *Clearcutting in Perspective* (Halifax: Nova Scotia Public Interest Research Group, Spring 2000), p. 3.

[53] Nova Scotia's Future Forest Alliance, "Fantasy Gardens East: Nova Scotia's Annual Allowable Cut," Information report, no. 1 (1990).

NEW BRUNSWICK

[1] Richard Foot, "Timber Land," *The New Brunswick Reader*, February 17, 1996, p. 8.

[2] M. Betts and D. Coon, *Working with the Woods: Restoring the Forest and Communities in New Brunswick* (Fredericton: Conservation Council of New Brunswick, 1996), citing Webster (1991).

[3] Department of Natural Resources and Energy, Timber Management Branch, *New Brunswick Forest Inventory Report 1986* (St. John, 1989), p. 23. A more recent inventory has been completed and is expected to be on the DNR website as of June 2005. At this writing, it is unavailable. Personal communication from Michael H. McDonald, Forest Inventory Unit coordinator for New Brunswick Natural Resources to Inuk Simard, New Brunswick researcher, confirms that the amount of hemlock remains as 1 per cent or less.

[4] R. Foot, "Fibre Crunch: Now," *The New Brunswick Reader*, March 2, 1992, p. 8.

[5] Betts and Coon, *Working with the Woods*. In 2001, the New Brunswick govern-

ment added nearly 150,000 hectares of protected areas, bringing the percentage from 1.2 per cent to 3.4 percent (Sierra Club of Canada, *Rio Report Card 2001*. Available at www.sierraclub.ca.

[6] Quoted in Foot, "Fibre Crunch," p. 8.

[7] Quoted in L.A. Sandberg, "Introduction: Dependent Development and Client States," in L.A. Sandberg, ed., *Trouble in the Woods: Forest Policy and Social Conflict in Nova Scotia and New Brunswick* (Fredericton: Acadiensis, 1992), p. 6.

[8] Bill Parenteau, "Pulpwood Marketing in New Brunswick," in L.A. Sandberg, ed., *Trouble in the Woods: Forest Policy and Social Conflict in Nova Scotia and New Brunswick* (Fredericton: Acadiensis, 1992), p. 117.

[9] Ibid., pp. 95-96.

[10] Ibid., pp. 116-17.

[11] Quoted in ibid., p. 122.

[12] Steve Llewellyn, "We're talking about resource being destroyed," *Fredericton Daily Gleaner*, September 22, 1995.

[13] Foot, "Fibre Crunch," p. 6.

[14] Foot, "Timber Land," p. 11.

[15] Quoted in Elizabeth May, *Budworm Battles* (Tantallon, NS: Four East, 1982), p. 46.

[16] Ibid.

[17] Ibid.

[18] Quoted in ibid., p. 26.

[19] It should be noted that the federal decision on fenitrothion left the door open to its use against insects other than budworm if an economically acceptable alternative insecticide could not be found.

[20] David Coon, Conservation Council of New Brunswick, personal communication with Elizabeth May, 1997.

[21] Compiled from data from the Department of Natural Resources and Department of Natural Resources and Energy, Timber Management Branch, annual reports, 1952 to 1994 (St Johns, 1952-1994).

[22] Matthew Betts, Department of Natural Resources and Energy, official interview, 1997.

[23] R. Clearwater and D. Coon, *Biodiversity Primer 1995* (Fredericton: Conservation Council of New Brunswick, 1995); R.C. Waldick, B. Freedman and R.J. Wassersug, "The consequences for amphibians of conversion of natural, mixed-species wood forests to conifer plantations in southern New Brunswick," *Canadian Field Naturalist* 113, no. 3 (July–September 1999), pp. 408–18.

[24] Canadian Nature Federation, "New Brunswick forests and economy threatened by forest industry proposal," press release, January 21, 2004. Available at www.naturecanada.ca.

[25] B. Freedman et al., "Forestry practices and biodiversity, with particular reference to the maritime provinces of Eastern Canada," *Environmental Review* 2 (1994), p. 54.

[26] Ibid.

[27] Clearwater and Coon, *Biodiversity Primer 1995*.

[28] Foot, "Timber Land," p. 7.

[29] New Brunswick Department of Natural Resources, *Forest Management Plan Highlights 1992*, Crown Licence 1-10 (St. Johns, New Brunswick, 1992).

[30] Natural Resources Canada, Fish and Wildlife Branch, *Management of Forest Habitat in New Brunswick* (Fredericton, 1995).

[31] New Brunswick Department of Natural Resources, *A Vision for New Brunswick Forests: Goals and Objectives for Crown Land Management* (St. Johns, New Brunswick, December 1999; revised March 2000).

[32] New Brunswick Department of Natural Resources, *Forest Management Plan Highlights 1992*.

[33] Ibid., p. 10.

[34] The residual 2 per cent is federal land, mostly in the Fundy National Park.

[35] Tom Clark, *Timber Supply and Endangered Spaces: A World Wildlife Fund Canada Discussion Paper* (Toronto: World Wildlife Fund Canada, 1996), p. 55.

[36] Natural Resources Canada, Canadian Forest Service, *The State of Canada's Forests 1994* (Ottawa, 1994) and *The State of Canada's Forests 1995–1996* (Ottawa, 1996).

[37] Natural Resources Canada, Canadian Forest Service, *The State of Canada's Forests 2002–2003: Looking Ahead* (Ottawa, 2003), p. 22

[38] Department of Natural Resources and Energy, Timber Management Branch, annual reports 1952-2003 (St Johns, New Brunswick, 1952-2003).

[39] J.D. Irving Ltd., *Queens-Charlotte Forest Management Plan 1992*, Crown Licence 6 (St. Johns, New Brunswick, 1992).

[40] T. Erdle, "Timber Management in New Brunswick," in D. Brand, ed., *Canada's Timber Resources: Proceedings of a National Conference* held June 1990 at the Victoria Conference Centre, Victoria (Chalk River: Petawawa National Forestry Institute, 1991). Petawawa National Forestry Institute, Information Report PI-X-101 (Fredericton, 1994), p. 94.

[41] *Queens-Charlotte Forest Management Plan 1992*, p. 26.

[42] See Chapter 8, "Other Pressures on Canada's Forests," on job loss and mechanization pressures.

[43] Peter DeMarsh, *Presentation to the National Round Table on the Environment and the Economy* (Miramichi, NB, May 24, 1996).

[44] Matthew Betts, Department of Natural Resources, personal communication with Elizabeth May, 1997.

[45] The National Round Table on the Environment and the Economy, *State of the Debate on the Environment and the Economy: Private Woodlot Management in the Maritimes* (Ottawa, 1998).

[46] Natural Resources Canada, Canadian Forest Service, *The State of Canada's Forests 2001–2002: Reflections of a Decade* (Ottawa, 2002), p. 11.

[47] Peter DeMarsh, New Brunswick Woodlot Owners Association, personal communication to Elizabeth May, September 2004.

[48] R. Foot, "The Miller's Tale," *Telegraph-Journal* (New Brunswick), April 20, 1996.

[49] *R. v. Sappier and Polchies*, 2004 NBCA 56. (In this decision, the court found Aboriginal people in New Brunswick have both an Aboriginal and a treaty right to harvest wood from Crown lands for personal use for such things as building homes and furniture, etc. The decision has been stayed for a year to permit time to work out a reasonable management regime, however the province is considering an appeal to the Supreme Court.); *R v. Bernard*, 2003 NBCA 55. (In this decision, the court found Aboriginal people in New Brunswick have a treaty right to earn a "moderate livelihood" from harvesting wood on Crown lands. The decision was stayed for a year to permit negotiation over its application, but the province has appealed the decision to the Supreme Court, with arguments to be heard beginning January 13, 2005.)

[50] *State of Canada's Forests, 2001–2002: Reflections of a Decade*, p. 8.

[51] Jaakko Pöyry, *New Brunswick Crown Forests: Assessment of Stewardship and Management*,(New York: New Brunswick Department of Natural Resources and Energy and the New Brunswick Forest Products Association, November 2002). Available at www.gnb.ca.

[52] Pöyry, *New Brunswick Crown Forests*, p. 5.

[53] David Coon, Conservation Council of New Brunswick, personal communication to Elizabeth May, November 2004.

[54] Chris Morris, "Irving issues dire warning about future of forestry industry," Canadian Press, *Telegraph-Journal* (New Brunswick), November 20, 2003, pp. A1, A6.

[55] Ibid.

[56] "Legislative Assembly Select Committee on Wood Supply releases report," NB 1000 (September 15, 2004).

[57] Sierra Club of Canada, Atlantic Canada Chapter, "Environmental group happy with NB Select Committee Report on Wood Supply," press release, November 4, 2004. Available at www.nben.ca.

PRINCE EDWARD ISLAND

[1] Natural Resources Canada, Canadian Forest Service, *The State of Canada's Forests 1994* (Ottawa, 1994), p. 89.

[2] Gary Schneider, Environmental Coalition of Prince Edward Island, personal communication to Elizabeth May, 1996.

[3] Department of Agriculture, Fisheries and Forestry, Forestry Division, *Report on Forest Resource Issues, An Update of the 1990 Forest Inventory* (Charlottetown, August 1995).

[4] National Round Table on Environment and Economy, *State of the Debate Report on Maritime Small Woodlots* (Spring 1997).

5 PEI Forestry Branch, "Forestry cuts its own future," press release, quoted in *The Guardian* (Prince Edward Island), February 1, 1996.

6 Gary Schneider, "Acadian Calamity," *Rural Delivery* (March 1990), p. 32.

7 Ibid., p. 33

8 Government of PEI, Ministry of Agriculture, Fisheries, Aquaculture and Forestry, "New forestry director named," press release, May 29, 2003.

Chapter 11: Quebec

1 Ministry of Natural Resources, *Quebec's Forest Ecology—Biodiversity—Forest Resource Protection* (Quebec: Government of Quebec, June 1996).

2 Hugh Gray, letters from Canada written in 1806, 1807 and 1909, cited in A.R.M. Lower, *North American Assault on Canadian Forests* (New York: Greenwood Press, 1938).

3 M. Ross, *Forest Management in Canada* (Calgary: Canadian Institute of Resources Law, 1995), p. 65.

4 Jim Cooperman, "Cutting Down Canada," in B. Devall, ed., *Clearcut: The Tragedy of Industrial Forestry* (San Francisco: Sierra Club Books, 1993).

5 Pierre Dubois, "Une 'old-growth' québécoise au Temiscamingue," *Forest Conservation* 59, no. 5 (September 1992).

6 Ministère des ressources naturelles, de la faune et des parcs, *Rapport sur l'état des forêts québécoises: 1995–1999* (Quebec: Bibliothèque nationale du Québec, 2002).

7 Ministère des ressources naturelles, de la faune et des parcs, *Document d'information sur la gestion de la forêt publique pour l'usage de la commission d'étude sur la gestion de la forêt publique* (Quebec, 2003), p. 166. Available at www.commission-foret.qc.ca.

8 J. Gauvin, "Forest development in Quebec: New Models on the Horizon?" in *Timber Supply in Canada: Challenges and Choices*, Canadian Council of Forest Ministers Conference, held November 16–18, 1994. Kananaskis, Alberta (Ottawa: Natural Resources Canada, November 1994), p. 158. Latest statistics: Conférence des coopératives forestières du Québec. Available at www.ccfq.qc.ca.

9 Ministère des ressources naturelles, de la faune et des parcs website: www.mrn.gouv.qc.ca/publications/forets/connaissances/stat_edition_complete/ch10/f031000.xls.

10 Mitch Lansky, *Beyond the Beauty Strip: Saving What's Left of Our Forests* (Gardiner: Tilbury House, 1992), p. 47.

11 Cooperman, "Cutting Down Canada."

12 Lansky, *Beyond the Beauty Strip*, p. 206.

13 Cooperman, "Cutting Down Canada."

14 Ross, *Forest Management in Canada*, p. 80.

15 Felice Page, "Cultural Clearcuts: The Sociology of Timber Communities in the Pacific Northwest," in Bill Devall, ed., *Clearcut: The Tragedy of Industrial Forestry* (San Francisco: Sierra Club Books/Earth Island Press, 1993), p. 162.

[16] D. Haley and M.K. Luckert, *Forest Tenures in Canada: A Framework for Policy Analysis*, Information Report E-X-43 (Ottawa: Forestry Canada, 1990), p. 76.

[17] Gauvin, "Forest development in Quebec," pp. 203-9.

[18] Ross, *Forest Management in Canada*, p. 80-81.

[19] Miller Freeman Inc., *Company Profiles: Abitibi-Price* (St. John's, 1994).

[20] J. MacFarland, "An unusual team, on paper," *Globe and Mail, Report on Business*, February 19, 1997, p. B1.

[21] Grand Council of the Cree, *Crees and Trees* (Ottawa, 1996), p. 4.

[22] While the companies are responsible for planting, the province provides the seedlings and restocks for NSR areas: Haley and Luckert, *Forest Tenures in Canada*, p. 75.

[23] "La Forêt publique: Nouvelles règles du jeu," *Forêt Conservation* supplement (September 1987); my translation.

[24] *Document d'information sur la gestion de la forêt publique*, p. 133.

[25] Jules Dufour, "Towards Sustainable Development of Canada's Forests," in B. Mitchell, ed., *Resource and Environmental Management in Canada: Addressing Conflict and Uncertainty*, Second Edition. (Toronto: Oxford University Press, 1995) p. 100, 183–206.

[26] Ibid., p. 199, quoting Vanier.

[27] Boyce Richardson, *The Algonquins Defend the Forest*, National Film Board video (Barrière Lake, PQ, 1990).

[28] World Commission on Environment and Development, *Our Common Future* (New York: Oxford University Press, 1987), p. 79.

[29] Elizabeth May, "Cultural Survival Canada Report—Algonquins of Barrière Lake," *Cultural Survival Quarterly* 15, no. 2 (1991), p. 79.

[30] In this period, 1991–1992, I worked for the Algonquin of Barrière Lake in the implementation phase of the agreement. I was constantly amazed by their patience and forbearance in the face of the complete unreliability of government assurance. I honestly do not know how they kept such a principled focus on the outcome of the Trilateral Agreement during the face of daily provocative actions. The conflict that centred on the existing permits finally resulted in arbitration. The agreement is still in place and is now entering its third phase.

[31] Tony Wawatie, "Algonquins of Barrière Lake—Update," unpublished (April 1997).

[32] Vincent Malenfant Inc., *Economic Output from the James Bay Forest*, forest economics report commissioned by the Grand Council of the Cree (July 1996).

[33] Grand Council of the Cree, *Crees and Trees*, p. 1.

[34] Robert Monderie and Richard Desjardins, *L'Erreur Boréale* (National Film Board 1999).

[35] Brigitte Voss, "L'Erreur Boréale: Serious Situation in Quebec's Forests Exposed," *Forest Caucus Report* 2, no. 2 (Ottawa: Canadian Environmental Network, Spring 2000), p. 4.

[36] Ottertooth.com website, www.ottertooth.com.

[37] Ministère des ressources naturelles, de la faune et des parcs, *La gestion forestière québécoise et les communautés autochtones: Présentation à la commission d'étude sur la gestion de la forêt publique québécoise* (Quebec, 2004). Available at www.com-mission-foret.qc.ca; National Aboriginal Forestry Association, *Aboriginal-Held Forest Tenures in Canada* (2003), pp. 29-31.

[38] G. Drouin, "Les parcs, trois ans plus tard," *Forêt Conservation* 61, no. 1 (March/April 1995), p. 23.

[39] Sierra Club of Canada, *Rio Report Card 2003* (Ottawa, 2003), p. 31. Available at www.sierraclub.ca.

[40] *Document d'information sur la gestion de la forêt publique*, p. 133.

[41] Ministère des ressources naturelles, de la faune et des parcs website, www.mrn.gouv.qc.ca.

[42] Ministère des ressources naturelles, de la faune et des parcs, *Liste des espèces fauniques, menacées our vulnérables au Québec* (Quebec, 2004).

[43] The other Canadian provinces to ban 2,4,5-T use were Ontario and Saskatchewan.

[44] Grand Council of the Cree, *Crees and Trees*, p. 10.

[45] Environmental News Service, "World Forest Congress Harmony Broken By Canadian Logging" (September 30, 2003).

[46] Yves Bergeron and Brian Harvey, "Basing silviculture on natural ecosystem dynamics: An approach applied to the southern boreal mixedwood forest of Quebec," *Forest Ecology and Management* 92 (1997), p. 242.

[47] Natural Resources Canada, Canadian Forestry Service, *The State of Canada's Forests 2002–2003: Looking Ahead* (Ottawa, 2003), p. 21.

[48] Vérificateur Général du Québec, *Rapport à l'Assemblé Nationale pour l'année 2001–2002*, Volume 2 (Quebec, 2002), p. 309.

[49] *Rapport à l'Assemblé Nationale*.

[50] Commission d'étude sur la gestion de la forêt publique québécoise, "The main priorities for improving the management of Québec's public forests," press release, December 14, 2004. Available at www.commission-foret.qc.ca.

[51] Ibid.

[52] Miller Freeman Inc., *Company Profiles: Kruger* (St. John's, 1993), p. 380.

[53] Ross, *Forest Management in Canada*.

[54] *Timber Supply in Canada: Challenges and Choices*, Canadian Council of Forest Ministers Conference, held November 16-18, 1994. Kananaskis, Alberta (Ottawa: Natural Resources Canada, November 1994), in which Quebec is not mentioned.

Chapter 12: Ontario

[1] Jimmy Kennedy, "Teddy Bears' Picnic" (1933).

[2] Natural Resources Canada, Canadian Forestry Service, *The State of Canada's Forests 1995–1996* (Ottawa, 1996), p. 95.

[3] Ontario Ministry of Natural Resources, "Northern Boreal Initiative: A Land Use

Planning Approach, Concept Document" (July 2001); Wildlands League, "The Boreal Forest, Ontario's Big Wild," *Seasons* and *Wildland News*, supplement (Spring 2002).

[4] Natural Resources Canada, Canadian Forestry Service, *The State of Canada's Forests 1994* (Ottawa, 1994), p. 22.

[5] B. Bynes, *Saving the Countryside: Conserving Rural Character and the Countryside of Southern Ontario* (Conservation Council of Ontario, 1994).

[6] G.M. Allen, P.F.J. Eagles and S.D. Price, *Conserving Carolinian Canada* (Waterloo, ON: University of Waterloo Press, 1990).

[7] Anna Brownell Jameson, *Winter Studies and Summer Rambles (1836–37)*, (Toronto: McClelland & Stewart Ltd., 1990), p.6.

[8] John Theberge, *Legacy: The Natural History of Ontario* (Toronto: McClelland and Stewart, 1989).

[9] Peter A. Quinby, "Old-growth eastern white pine—an endangered ecosystem," *Forest Landscape Baselines*, no. 2 (1993).

[10] R.H. Bonnycastle, *Canada and the Canadians in 1846* (London, England: Henry Colburn, 1846), cited in P. Quinby et al., *An Ancient Forest Atlas of the Lake Temagami Site Region (4E)* (Ottawa: Canadian Nature Federation, April 1996).

[11] Ontario Ministry of Natural Resources, Old Growth Public Advisory Committee, *Interim Report on Conserving Old Growth Red and White Pine* (1993); Ontario Ministry of Natural Resources, *The State of the Forests Report 2001* (Toronto, 2001).

[12] Wildlands League, "Eastern White Pine Forests in Ontario: Ecology, Threats and Survival," Forest Ecology Series, Fact Sheet 1 (1995).

[13] From a letter written in 1871 by Sir John A. Macdonald, cited in *Forest History* 11, no. 3 (New Haven: Forest History Society, 1968: National Archives of Canada C3207).

[14] "Ontario," in Department of Energy and Resources Management, *Mississippi Valley Conservation Report 1970* (1970).

[15] Letter by Sir John A. Macdonald, cited in *Forest History* 11, no. 3.

[16] Bernard Fernow, "Forest Resources and Forestry in Ontario," in Adam Shortt and Arthur G. Doughty, eds., *Canada and its Provinces*, Vol. 18 (Toronto: Glasgow, Brook and Company, 1914), p. 599.

[17] Ontario Ministry of Natural Resources "Red and White Pine in Ontario," Fact Sheet (October 1996). Available at www.mnr.gov.on.ca.

[18] L.L. Rogers and Edward L. Lindquist, "Supercanopy White Pine and Wildlife," *White Pine Symposium Proceedings* (1992).

[19] Mark Stabb, *Ontario's Old Growth: A Learner's Handbook* (Ottawa: Canadian Nature Federation, 1996).

[20] Charles Wilkins, "Beset by disease, Ontario's provincial tree is not regenerating," *Canadian Geographic* 114 (1991), pp. 59–66.

[21] G.P. Buchert, "Genetics of white pine and the implications for management and conservation," *The Forestry Chronicle* 70, no.4 (1994), pp. 427–432.

22 Ontario Ministry of Natural Resources, *A Silvicultural Guide for the Great Lakes–St. Lawrence Conifer Forest in Ontario* (Toronto, 1998).

23 *State of the Forests Report 2001*, pp. i–9.

24 T.J. Carleton and P. MacLellan, "Woody vegetation responses to fire versus clear-cut logging: A comparative survey in the central Canadian boreal forest," *Ecoscience* 1, no. 2 (1994).

25 A. Perera, Ontario Forest Research Institute, Paper presented at Global to Local: Ecological Land Classification Conference (1994).

26 Ibid.

27 Natural Resources Canada, Canadian Forestry Service, *The State of Canada's Forests 2002–2003: Looking Ahead* (Ottawa, 2003), p. 21.

28 B. Hodgins and J. Benidickson, *The Temagami Experience* (Toronto: University of Toronto Press, 1989).

29 Ibid., p. 293.

30 Ibid.

31 Ibid.

32 Tim Gray, "Temagami update: What's it going to be, Mr. Harris?" *Wildland News* (Summer 1996); most recent information from personal communication between Tim Gray and Elizabeth May, November 2004.

33 Ontario Ministry of Natural Resources, *Temagami Land Use Plan for the Temagami Comprehensive Planning Area* (1997), based on the work of the Temagami Advisory Council (1989–1991), and the Comprehensive Planning Council (1991–1996). Available at crownlanduseatlas.mnr.gov.on.ca.

34 C. Henschel, *The Road Less Travelled? A Report on the Effectiveness of Controlling Motorized Access in Remote Areas of Ontario: A Case Study in Temagami* (Toronto: Wildlands League, 2003). Available at www.wildlandsleague.org.

35 Ontario Native Affairs Secretariat, "Update on Elements of the Proposed Temagami Land Claim Settlement," *The Temagami Land Claim* (July 2003). Available at www.nativeaffairs.jus.gov.on.ca.

36 Wildlands League, "Red Squirrel Road re-opened," *Wildland News* (Spring 2002).

37 Warner Troyer, *No Safe Place* (Toronto: Clarke, Irwin, 1977).

38 Grassy Narrows, "Abitibi makes offer, Grassy Narrows to consider," press release, November 13, 2003.

39 Elizabeth May, *Paradise Won: The Struggle for South Moresby* (Toronto: McClelland and Stewart, 1990).

40 Wildlife Habitat Canada, *The Status of Wildlife Habitat in Canada: Realities and Visions* (Ottawa, July 1991).

41 F.T. Flemming and K. Kloski, *Moose Habitat Studies and Moose Management Unit 40 with Particular Reference to the Effects on Roads and Cutovers* (Temagami: Ontario Ministry of Natural Resources, 1976).

42 Ontario Ministry of Natural Resources, "Strategy to Halt Decline in Moose

Populations," Fact Sheet (March 1997). The study encompassed Wildlife Management Units 38, 39, 40 and 41.

43 G. Racey et. al., *Forest Management Guidelines for the Conservation of Woodland Caribou: A Landscape Approach* (Thunder Bay, Ontario Ministry of Natural Resources, 1999). Available at www.mnr.gov.on.ca.

44 Wildlands League, *Restoring Nature's Place: How We Can End Logging in Algonquin Park, Protect Jobs and Restore the Park's Ecosystems* (Toronto, 2000). Available at www.wildlandsleague.org.

45 Sierra Club of Canada, *Rio Report Card 1998* (Ottawa, 1998). Available at www.sierraclub.ca.

46 Ontario Ministry of Natural Resources, "Ontario restructures forest management," press release, April 1996.

47 Gray, "Temagami update."

48 Partnership for Public Lands members were World Wildlife Fund Canada, CPAWS-Wildlands League and the Federation of Ontario Naturalists (now Ontario Nature).

49 OraclePoll Research Ltd., "September 2001 Omnibus Survey Results," prepared for Earthroots, Wildlands League, and the Federation of Ontario Naturalists.

50 Evan Ferrari, Canadian Parks and Wilderness Society, personal communication to David Pearce, Ontario researcher, November 2004. These regulated sites include 45 Provincial Parks, 216 Conservation Reserves, 26 Provincial Park additions, 1 Conservation Reserve Addition and 2 amalgamated CRs.

51 Wildlands League, "The Goulais Project Breaks New Ground," *Goulais River Watershed Project* (Toronto, 2001). Available at www.wildlandsleague.org.

52 World Wildlife Fund Canada, *The Nature Audit: Setting Canada's Conservation Agenda for the 21st Century*, Report No. 1-2003 (Toronto, 2003), p. 76.

53 *State of Canada's Forests 1994*, p. 91.

54 Ontario Ministry of Natural Resources, *Forest Information Manual* (Toronto, April 2001) and *OMNR Forest Management Planning Manual* (Toronto, September 1996).

55 B. Callaghan, "Ontario Status Report," in *Timber Supply in Canada: Challenges and Choices*, Canadian Council of Forest Ministers Conference, held November 16–18, 1994. Kananaskis, Alberta (Ottawa: Natural Resources Canada, November 1994).

56 Canadian Council of Forest Ministers, *Compendium of Canadian Forestry Statistics 1994* (1995).

57 K.A. Armson, *Forest Management in Ontario* (Toronto: Ontario Ministry of Natural Resources, 1976).

58 G. Baskerville, *An Audit of the Crown Forests of Ontario* (Toronto: Ontario Ministry of Natural Resources, 1986), cited by M. Levy, "Timber Supply in Ontario: Environmentally Sensitive and Transparent," in *Timber Supply in Canada: Challenges and Choices*, Conference Proceedings 16–18 (Ottawa: Natural Resources Canada, November 1994).

[59] Levy, "Timber Supply in Ontario," citing the Lakehead Report to the Royal Commission on the Northern Environment and the Baskerville audit (1986).

[60] Callaghan, "Ontario Status Report," p. A71.

[61] D. Kloss, *Strategic Forest Management Model, Version 2.0 User Guide* (Toronto: Ontario Ministry of Natural Resources, 2002).

[62] R. Sawn, "Legal Implications of the Crown Forest Sustainability Act," in *Operating under Ontario's New Crown Forest Sustainability Act* (Toronto: Insight Press, 1995).

[63] Tim Gray, Wildlands League, personal communication to Elizabeth May, 1998.

[64] Ontario Ministry of Natural Resources, Industry Relations Branch, *Forest Industry at a Glance* (2004).

[65] D. Haley and M. Luckert, *Forest Tenures in Canada: A Framework for Policy Analysis*, Information Report E-X-43 (Ottawa: Forestry Canada, 1990).

[66] Haley and Luckert, *Forest Tenures*.

[67] The renewal charges set in May 1995 were: $11 per cubic metre for red and white pine, $6 per cubic metre for all other conifers, $0.50 per cubic metre for poplar and birch, $8 per cubic metre for grade 1 hardwoods, and $1.50 per cubic metre for grade 2 hardwoods.

[68] If the market price goes above a certain ceiling, the government's share of industry windfall profits falls to 10 per cent.

[69] Ontario Ministry of Natural Resources, *Historical Stumpage Matrix* (1998). Available at www.mnr.gov.on.ca.

[70] Ontario Ministry of Natural Resources, *Forest Values: Sustainable Forestry Programme, Forest Management Accounting Framework* (1993).

[71] Office of the Provincial Auditor, *2002 Report on Natural Resources Forest Management Program* (Toronto, 2002).

[72] M. Ross, *Forest Management in Canada* (Calgary: Canadian Institute of Resources Law, 1995), citing the brief from the Forest for Tomorrow coalition before the Class EA.

[73] Chris Henschel, Wildlands League, personal communication to Elizabeth May, 2004.

[74] Ontario Environmental Assessment Board, 1994, cited in Tom Clark, *Timber Supply and Endangered Spaces: A World Wildlife Fund Canada Discussion Paper* (Toronto: World Wildlife Fund Canada, 1996), p. 19.

[75] *State of Canada's Forests 1994*, p. 8. The report claims that the 115 requirements of the Ontario Class EA "will change the way forests are managed."

[76] M. Kaiser, *Ontario's New Reality: The Timber E.A. and the Crown Forest Act* (Canadian Forest Industries, March 1996), p. 34.

[77] Crown Forest Sustainability Act, 1994, S.O. 1994, chapter 25, Amended by: 1996, c. 14, s. 1; 1998, c. 18, Sched. I, ss. 15–18; 2000, c. 18, s. 64; 2000, c. 26, Sched. L, s. 3; 2001, c. 9, Sched. K, s. 2.

[78] Henschel, "Road Less Travelled?"

[79] Ontario Ministry of Natural Resources, *Forest Management Guide for Natural Disturbance Pattern Emulation*" (November 2001).

[80] Environmental Commissioner of Ontario, *2001–2002 Annual Report Supplement: Developing Sustainability* (Toronto, 2002), p. 155.

[81] Ibid., p. 153.

[82] Ibid., p. 157.

[83] Ibid., p. 156.

[84] Levy, "Timber Supply in Ontario," p. 78, citing Bob Carman, "New Forest Industry/Ontario Government Relationship," Treasury Board presentation (1994).

[85] Mike Innes, Abitibi-Price, in *Timber Supply in Canada: Challenges and Choices*, Canadian Council of Forest Ministers Conference, held November 16–18, 1994. Kananaskis, Alberta (Ottawa: Natural Resources Canada, November 1994)., p. 74.

[86] Ontario Ministry of Natural Resources, *Ontario Forest Products and Timber Resource Analysis*, vols. I and II (1992), cited in Levy, "Timber Supply in Ontario," p. 79.

[87] Wildlands League, "Cutting the Future out of Prosperity?" Ontario's Forest Product Industry Fact Sheet #2 (Toronto, 1994).

[88] *State of the Forests Report 2001*.

[89] Environmental Commissioner of Ontario, *2001–2002 Annual Report Supplement*, p. 149.

[90] Callaghan, "Ontario Status Report," p. A74.

[91] Ibid., p. A83.

[92] Ontario Ministry of Natural Resources, "Forest industry developments," press release, February 15, 1995.

[93] Ontario Ministry of Natural Resources, "$9-million investment will help create 40 new jobs in Hearst," press release, December 16, 1994.

[94] SBA and Resources Information Systems Inc., *Wood Products Review* (July 1997).

[95] R. Forrest, "Jury out on Ontario Forest Act," *Logging and Sawmilling Journal* 26, no. 1 (February/March 1995).

[96] Ibid.

[97] Callaghan, "Ontario Status Report," p. A81.

[98] Ontario Ministry of Natural Resources, *Provincial Wood Supply Strategies* (Ontario, 2004), p. 11.

Chapter 13: The Prairies

MANITOBA

[1] D. Haley and M.K. Luckert, *Forest Tenures in Canada: A Framework for Policy Analysis*, Information Report E-X-43 (Ottawa: Forestry Canada, 1990), p. 9.

[2] V. Werier, "Keeping data from public shows up in Repap fiasco," *Winnipeg Free Press*, May 13, 1989.

[3] Ibid.

4 J. Saunders, "Petty ponders sale of Repap," *Globe and Mail, Report on Business,* July 16, 1996, p. B1.

5 R. Foot, "Fibre Crunch: Now," *The New Brunswick Reader,* March 2, 1996, p. 5.

6 Quoted in V. Werier, "Manfor decision raises environmental concerns," *Winnipeg Free Press,* March 25, 1989.

7 Werier, "Keeping data from public."

8 Quoted in Werier, "Manfor decision."

9 Roy Adams, ed., *Proceedings of the Aspen Symposium,* July 25–27, 1989 (Duluth, MN: Natural Resource Research Institute, 1989).

10 Don Sullivan, "Louisiana-Pacific's Forest Management Licence: Not a clear-cut issue," *Canadian Dimension* (April/May 1995).

11 Ibid.

12 Manitoba Department of Conservation, "Towards a Management Plan for Duck Mountain Provincial Park," Newsletter #1 (July 2001). Thirty-three per cent is protected, 66 per cent is under resource management and recreational development, which is not protected from logging. There have been logging and gravelling operations in areas designated for recreational development.

13 Manitoba Government, "Repap and Manitoba finalize development agreement," press release, November 6, 1995.

14 Patricia Lush, "Repap close to the financial brink: Sources say company must find buyer or obtain more credit next week—otherwise it could go under," *Globe and Mail, Report on Business,* April 11, 1997, p. B1.

15 D. Kuxhaus, "Repap wins injunction," *Winnipeg Free Press,* April 2, 1996; A. Bray, "Band halts Repap road," *Winnipeg Free Press,* April 9, 1996.

16 Don Sullivan, "Manitoba whitewashes environmental process," *Canadian Dimension* (October/November 1994).

17 Quoted in Council on Economic Priorities, *Louisiana-Pacific: A Report on the Company's Environmental Policies and Practices* (New York: Corporate Environmental Clearing House, May 1992).

18 The Manitoba Environment Act, Licence #1900S4 (January 1998), amends the list of pollutants from the Louisiana-Pacific mill to only acrolein, acetaldehyde and benzo(s)pyrene. The original licence listed toluene, propionaldehyde, m-xylene, acetone, 2-kethones and benzo(a)pyrene.

19 See the discussion of doubling the AAC for hardwood in Chapter 3, "Voodoo Forestry."

20 Manitoba, press release, November 6, 1995.

21 Manitoba Conservation Department, *Next Steps: Priorities for Sustaining Manitoba's Forests* (Winnipeg, March 2002).

22 Robert Lamont, "Manitoba Status Report," in *Timber Supply in Canada: Challenges and Choices,* Canadian Council of Forest Ministers Conference, held November 16–18, 1994. Kananaskis, Alberta (Ottawa: Natural Resources Canada, November 1994), pp. A84–A92.

[23] Manitoba Conservation Department, Forestry Branch, (Winnipeg, October 2004).

[24] Lamont, "Manitoba Status Report," p. A85.

[25] World Wildlife Fund Canada, *Report on Conservation and Protected Areas for the National Round Table on the Environment and the Economy.*

[26] Sierra Club of Canada, *Rio Report Card 2000* (Ottawa, 2000). Available at www.sierraclub.ca.

[27] Natural Resources Canada, Canadian Forestry Service, *The State of Canada's Forests 1999–2000: Forests in the New Millennium* (Ottawa, 2000), p. 13.

[28] World Wildlife Fund Canada, *The Nature Audit: Setting Canada's Conservation Agenda for the 21st Century*, Report No. 1-2003 (Toronto, 2003), p. 76.

[29] Dan Soprovich, *Progress on Protected Areas in Manitoba's Northern Boreal Forest: Case Study of the Tolko Industries Ltd. (formerly Repap Manitoba Inc.) FMLA* (Swan River, Manitoba: Bluestem Wildlife Services, September 2000). Research undertaken for Senator Mira Spivak.

[30] H. Williams, "Paper trail of broken promises."

[31] Sierra Club of Canada, *Rio Report Card 2000*, p. 35, quoting from a letter from Premier Gary Doer to the Manitoba Chapter of the Canadian Parks and Wilderness Society, May 30, 2000.

[32] Canadian Environmental Network, "Manitoba: Opening up the East Side of Lake Winnipeg," *Forest Caucus Report* 3, no. 1 (Summer 2001), p. 6.

[33] Rachel Plotkin, *Integrated Land-Use Planning and Canada's New National Forest Strategy* (Ottawa: Sierra Club of Canada, 2004), p. 27–28.

[34] Sierra Club of Canada, "Sierra Club evaluates East Side planning," press release, July 29, 2004.

[35] Global Forest Watch, *Canada's Forests at a Crossroads: An Assessment in the Year 2000*, (Washington, D.C.: World Watch Institute, 2000).

[36] Western Canada Wilderness Committee, Manitoba Chapter, "Eastern Region Woodland Caribou Advisory Committee Map of Woodland Caribou Home Ranges" (Winnipeg, 2004), compared with Tembec 2004 *Annual Operating and Renewal Plan, Owl Lake Cut Block.*

[37] Tolko, 2004 *Annual Operating Plan.* Available at www.tolkomanitoba.com.

[38] KPMG Management Consulting, *Manitoba's Forest Plan: Towards Ecosystem-Based Management*, Report to Manitoba Natural Resources, funded by Canada-Manitoba Partnership Agreement in Forestry (Winnipeg, 1995), pp. 4-10; Manitoba Natural Resources, *Five-Year Report to the Legislature on Wildlife 1987–1992* (Winnipeg, 1992).

[39] KPMG, *Manitoba's Forest Plan.*

[40] "Pitre honoured with gift of appreciation," *The Community Voice* (Pine Falls, MB), September 8, 1994.

[41] Jeff Delaney, Forest Management and Development, Forestry Branch, Manitoba Conservation, Schedule A, Revision 19B (2004–2005). Dues per cubic metre of

roundwood per forest section. This relates only to aspen/poplar for OSB in the Mountain Forest Section and in the aspen parkland and pineland section. Otherwise, the rates vary from $0.75 to $2.95.

[42] Don Sullivan, *Louisiana-Pacific's Forest Management Licence Agreement: Analysis and Implications* (Winnipeg: Manitoba's Future Forest Alliance, December 11, 1994).

[43] KPMG, *Manitoba's Forest Plan*, p. 4-58.

[44] Manitoba Natural Resources, Forestry Branch, *The First 5-Year Review of Manitoba's Forest Royalty System* (Winnipeg, September 1986).

[45] KPMG, *Manitoba's Forest Plan*, p. 3-25.

[46] Letter from Dr. R.A. Westwood, Acting Director of Forestry, Department of Natural Resources, Government of Manitoba, to Don Sullivan, April 5, 1996.

[47] Dan Soprovich, "A submission to the Manitoba Clean Environment Commission," text of an oral presentation made during hearings, November 30, 1995.

[48] Environment Canada, Prairie and Northern Region, "Environment Canada's Response to Louisiana-Pacific Canada Ltd., Letter of January 3, 1996," January 18, 1996, p. 8.

[49] A. Santin, "Swan River biologist sacked after faulting province over Louisiana-Pacific," *Winnipeg Free Press*, Dec. 9, 1995, p. A4.

[50] Letter from Jim W. Ball, Manitoba District Office, Forestry Canada, Department of Natural Resources, to Dr. Floyd Phillips, Chairman, Forestry TAC, August 17, 1995.

[51] Letter from Jim W. Ball, Manitoba District Office, Forestry Canada, Department of Natural Resources, to Larry Strachan, Director Environment Act, Manitoba Department of Environment, December 15, 1995.

[52] Ibid., p. 2.

[53] Ibid.

[54] Ball, letter to Strachan: "I apologise for not appearing at the CEC [environmental review] hearings as previously agreed; however, I received instructions that Thursday morning [the day he was to have testified] not to appear."

[55] *Manitoba Government Detailed Estimates of Expenditures by Department* 1990–2003, one per year since the amalgamation.

[56] Report on Abitibi-Price Inc. FML #01 Forest Resource Management Plan 1991-1998.

SASKATCHEWAN

[1] J.H. Richards and K.I. Fung, "Natural History of Saskatchewan Forest," in R.T. Coupland and J.S. Rowe, eds., *Atlas of Saskatchewan* (Saskatoon: University of Saskatchewan Press, 1969).

[2] R.T. Coupland and J.S. Rowe, "Early history of logging in Saskatchewan," in J.H. Richards and K.I. Fung, eds., *Atlas of Saskatchewan* (Saskatoon: University of Saskatchewan Press, 1969).

[3] National Research Council, Canadian Forest Service, "Saskatchewan Environment and Resource Management: Focus on Forests in Saskatchewan, 1994," draft.

[4] Saskatchewan Environment and Resource Management, Forestry Branch, "Draft Concept Plan for Forest Management in the Hudson Bay and Cumberland House Supply Areas" (August 1994).

[5] Delcan Western Ltd., *State of the Resource Report* (Prince Albert: Saskatchewan Environment and Resource Management, April 1993), p. 143, figure 5-13.

[6] "Environmental Impact Statement for OSB Plant, Hudson Bay, Saskatchewan" (September 29, 1995), p. 1.9.

[7] "Weyerhaeuser Canada Ltd.—Prince Albert Pulp Company Ltd. and UCFS Paper Mill Development," *Government-Weyerhaeuser Agreement*, vol. 1 (September 8, 1986).

[8] Weyerhaeuser, "Weyerhaeuser to acquire MacMillan Bloedel," press release, June 21, 1999. Available at www.weyerhaeuser.com.

[9] *The Norsask Forest Management Project, Vol. 3: Technical Summary* (November 1995); MISTIK Management Ltd., Meadow Lake, Saskatchewan, and Crown Investment Corporation of Saskatchewan, *Annual Report 1995*.

[10] D. Haley and M.K. Luckert, *Forest Tenures in Canada: A Framework for Policy Analysis*, Information Report E-X-43 (Ottawa: Forestry Canada, 1990),p. 54.

[11] Province of Saskatchewan, "Dues and Fees, 2004–2005" (Saskatoon, 2004).

[12] Delcan Western, *State of the Resource Report*, p. 145.

[13] Isidore Campbell, "Employment and Sustainable Development: Opportunities for Canada," Jobs and Environment Conference 1994, International Institute for Sustainable Development, Winnipeg, MB, 1994.

[14] Protectors of Mother Earth, "Action Alert," undated.

[15] P. Hanley, "Forest adventure faces legal morass," *Star-Phoenix* (Saskatoon), November 2, 1992.

[16] Gerry Ivanochko, Provincial Specialist, Northern Agricultural Crop Development, Saskatchewan Agriculture and Food, cited in *Non-Timber Forest Products: Economic Development While Sustaining Our Northern Forests* (Saskatoon: Saskatchewan Environmental Society, June 2002).

[17] Bonnie Baird, research manager, Saskatchewan Tourism, 2003, personal communication to Cendrine Huemer, Jan 15, 2005.

[18] Environment Canada, *Importance of Nature to Canadians: Economic Significance of Nature-Related Activities* (Ottawa, 1996), p. 30.

[19] Al Balinksy, Planning Manager, Mistik Management Ltd., personal communication to Allyson Brady, Saskatchewan researcher, May 20, 2004.

[20] Andrea Atkinson, Forest Service, Saskatchewan Environment and Resource Management, personal communication to Allyson Brady, Saskatchewan researcher, June 9, 2004.

[21] Sierra Club of Canada, *Integrated Land-Use Planning and Canada's New National Forest Strategy* (Ottawa, July 2004).

[22] Michael Fitzsimmons, "Saskatchewan Biodiversity Conference: Community Review—Forested Farmland," in D. Nernber and M.R.T. eds., *Proceedings of the Saskatchewan Biodiversity Conference* (Regina, April 11-13, 1995), p. 1-2.

[23] David Lindenas, "Saskatchewan Status Report" in *Timber Supply in Canada: Challenges and Choices*, Canadian Council of Forest Ministers Conference, held November 16-18, 1994. Kananaskis, Alberta (Ottawa: Natural Resources Canada, November 1994)., p. A93.

[24] Saskatchewan Economic and Co-operative Development, "Major forest industry expansion announced: Industry plans could create up to 10,000 new jobs," press release, April 26,1999.

[25] World Wildlife Fund Canada, *The Nature Audit: Setting Canada's Conservation Agenda for the 21st Century*, Report No. 1-2003 (Toronto, 2003); Sierra Club of Canada, *Rio Report Card 2002* (Ottawa, 2002), p. 27. Available at www.sierraclub.ca.

[26] C. Varcoe, "New forestry law may force Weyerhaeuser to kill expansion," *Leader-Post* (Regina), March 18, 1996.

[27] B. Bradon, "Timber companies fuming," *Star-Phoenix* (Saskatoon), March 15, 1996.

[28] Varcoe, "New forestry law."

[29] Bradon, "Timber companies fuming."

[30] Personal communication to Elizabeth May from Joys Dancer, Saskatchewan researcher for the first edition, 1996.

[31] Lindenas, "Saskatchewan Status Report," p. A93.

[32] Delcan Western, *State of the Resource Report*, section 4.1.6.

[33] Sierra Club of Canada, *Rio Report Card 2001* (Ottawa, 2001). Available at www.sierraclub.ca.

[34] Delcan Western, *State of the Resource Report*, pp. 143-44. Again, the provincial 1993 review concluded: "Definite softwood supply shortages occur in the south-eastern portion of the commercial Forest Zone...the young age classes are under-represented...and a large component of NSR land is present in this area... This pattern suggests a history of severe softwood overcutting in the last fifty years and minimal softwood reforestation...the bulk of the uncommitted [to FMLAs] area is in the eastern portion, most seriously overcut in the past and under significant commercial pressure."

Other government documents acknowledge the problem as well. See, for example, Environment Canada, *Saskatchewan Forests*, Saskatchewan-Canada Partnership Agreements (Saskatoon, March 1994): "Some of this surplus [above harvest level] timber is located in remote areas and its harvest is not, at present, economically feasible. At the same time, some regions of the province are experiencing shortages of harvestable conifers"; Lindenas, "Saskatchewan Status Report," p. A100: "Over-utilization of the timber resource is currently limited to our eastern timber supply areas. In this area softwood harvest levels exceed softwood (AAC) primarily because the existing mill facilities cannot utilize the small softwood timber."

35 Delcan Western, *State of the Resource Report*, p. 121.

36 *The State of Canada's Forests*, 2002. Latest available data.

37 Natural Resources Canada, Canadian Forestry Service, *The State of Canada's Forests 2002* (Ottawa, 2002). Latest available data.

38 Global Forest Watch Canada, *Canada's Forests at a Crossroads: An Assessment in the Year 2000* (Washington, D.C.: World Resources Institute, 2000), p. 70.

39 Allyson Brady and Alan Appleby, *Deforestation: Lack of Regeneration in Saskatchewan Forests* (Toronto: Global Forest Watch Canada, 2000).

40 Ibid., citing Saskatchewan Environment and Resources Management, 1993.

41 Al Gore, *Earth in the Balance: Ecology and the Human Spirit* (Boston, New York, London: Houghton Mifflin Company, 1992), p. 191. See also H. Daly and John B. Cobb, *For the Common Good* (Boston: Beacon Press, 1989).

ALBERTA

1 Bill Devall, ed., *Clearcut: The Tragedy of Industrial Forestry* (San Francisco: Sierra Club Books/Earth Island Press, 1993), p. 154.

2 C. Henderson, "Status Report on Alberta," in *Timber Supply in Canada: Challenges and Choices*, Canadian Council of Forest Ministers Conference, held November 16-18, 1994. Kananaskis, Alberta (Ottawa: Natural Resources Canada, November 1994).

3 Canadian Council of Forest Ministers, *Compendium of Canadian Forestry Statistics 1994* (Ottawa, 1995).

4 M. Ross, *Forest Management in Canada* (Calgary: Canadian Institute of Resources Law, 1995), p. 85.

5 Andrew Nikiforuk and Ed Struzik, "The great forest sell-off," *Report on Business Magazine* (November 1989).

6 Henderson, "Status Report on Alberta," p. A10.

7 J. McInnis, "The sale of Alberta's forests," *Newest Review* 20, no. 5 (June/July 1995).

8 Government of Alberta, Ministry of Sustainable Resource Development, *Annual Report 2002–2003* (Edmonton, 2003).

9 Barry Sadler, "International Study of the Effectiveness of Environmental Assessment: Final Report," *Canadian Environmental Assessment Agency, International Association for Impact Assessment* (Ottawa, June 1996), p. 213.

10 Based on 1993 prices: Jim Cooperman, "Cutting Down Canada," in B. Devall, ed., *Clearcut: The Tragedy of Industrial Forestry* (San Francisco: Sierra Club Books, 1993), p. 57.

11 Andrew Nikiforuk, *Saboteurs: Wiebo Ludwig's War Against Big Oil* (Toronto: Macfarlane Walter & Ross, 2001).

12 J. Goddard, *Last Stand of the Lubicon Cree* (Vancouver: Douglas & McIntyre, 1992).

13 Ibid.

[14] Cooperman, "Cutting Down Canada," p. 57.

[15] Natural Resources Canada, Canadian Forest Service, *The State of Canada's Forests 1996–1997* (Ottawa, 1997).

[16] Alberta Liberal Caucus, press release, January 24, 1995.

[17] Henderson, "Status Report on Alberta."

[18] Alberta Lands and Wildlife Department, *Impact of Forest Industry Development on the Alberta Forest Service* (Edmonton, 1991).

[19] Ibid.

[20] Henderson, "Status Report on Alberta," pp. A110, A111.

[21] Alberta-Pacific Forest Industries Inc., *1995 Detailed Forest Management Plan* (Boyle, AB, 1995).

[22] D. Haley and M.K. Luckert, *Forest Tenures in Canada: A Framework for Policy Analysis*, Information Report E-X-43 (Ottawa: Forestry Canada, 1990).

[23] D. Dancik et al., *Forest Management in Alberta, Report of the Expert Review Panel* (Edmonton: Alberta Energy/Forestry, Lands and Wildlife, 1990), p. 26.

[24] McInnis, "Sale of Alberta's Forests."

[25] Ibid., p. 9.

[26] Rick Schneider, "The Forestry Sector Today: Overview of the Forest Industry in Alberta," *Alternative* Future (2001).

[27] Natural Resources Canada, Canadian Forest Service, *The State of Canada's Forests 2003–2004* (Ottawa, 2004).

[28] Alberta Resource Development, *Annual Report 2000–2001* (Edmonton, 2001), p. 43.

[29] Natural Resources Canada, Canadian Forest Service, *The State of Canada's Forests 1995–1996* (Ottawa, 1996). Newfoundland, Prince Edward Island, Nova Scotia, New Brunswick, Quebec and Manitoba include private lands in the AACs; Alberta, Ontario and Saskatchewan do not.

[30] McInnis, "Sale of Alberta's forests," p. 8.

[31] Ross, *Forest Management in Canada*, citing Andrew Nikiforuk, "The great Alberta timber rush," *Environment Views* 17, no. 2 (1994), p. 11.

[32] Andrew Nikiforuk, "The Great Alberta Timber Rush," *Environment Views* 17, no. 2 (1994); excerpts from an article that appeared in *The Georgia Straight*, in "Logging and Private Land: Not in my Own Backyard," Western Canada Wilderness Committee, Boreal Forest Campaign, *Educational Report* 14, no. 8 (Summer 1995).

[33] B.C. mills were offering $65 per ton at the stump in 1994. Since 1 cubic metre equals 750 kilograms of conifer, 1 cubic metre yields $48.75. Source: Ken Glover, Alberta Provincial Government Private Woodlot Program, Ministry of Forests (personal communication to Karen Bartgailis, Western Canada Wilderness Committee Edmonton, 1995).

[34] J.B. Stelfox, *Relationships between Stand Age, Stand Structure, and Biodiversity in Aspen Mixedwood Stands in Alberta* (Vegreville and Edmonton: Alberta Environmental Centre and the Canadian Forest Service, 1995).

[35] The Honourable Ty Lund, Minister of Environmental Protection, Government of Alberta, personal communication to Erin McGregor Alberta researcher, first edition, 1997.

[36] Evidence from Environment Canada representatives in answer to a Sierra Club of Canada question in the hearings of the Alberta Energy and Utilities Board and the Canadian Environmental Assessment Agency, *Jackpine Mine Phase 1 EIA Proposed by Shell Canada, Chevron Canada and Western Oil Sands, Application No. 1271285, 1271307, and 1271383* (October 2003).

[37] Alberta Resource Development, *Annual Report 2000–2001.*

[38] Richard R. Schneider, J. Brad Stelfox, Stan Boutin and Shawn Wasel, "Managing the cumulative impacts of land-uses in the western Canadian sedimentary basin: a modeling approach," *Conservation Ecology* 7, no. 1 (April 2003).

[39] Bob Weber, "Canada: Energy, Forestry on collision course in northern Alberta, scientists say," Canadian Press, Edmonton, April 20, 2003.

[40] Tom Knudson, "New alarm sounded for Canada's forest," *Sacramento Bee*, May 4, 2003, quoting an April 27, 2003 editorial in the *Edmonton Journal.*

[41] Schneider et al., "Managing the cumulative impacts," p. 3.

[42] Ibid.

[43] Richard Schneider, "Whatever happened to the Alberta Forest Conservation Strategy?" *Encompass* 5 (December 2001).

[44] Cooperman, "Cutting Down Canada," p. 57.

[45] Sierra Club of Canada, *Rio Report Card 1996* (Ottawa, 1996). Available at www.sierraclub.ca.

[46] J. Stelfox, *Effect of Clear Cut Logging and Scarification on Wildlife Habitats in West Central Alberta* (Ottawa: Canadian Wildlife Service, 1984), p. 271

[47] K. Timoney, "The logging of a World Heritage Site: Wood Buffalo National Park," *The Forestry Chronicle* 72 (1996), pp. 485–90.

[48] Natural Resources Canada, Canadian Forest Service, *The State of Canada's Forests 2001–2002* (Ottawa, 2002), p. 19. The 2002–2003 report lists the amount of unstocked harvested Crown land in Alberta as "unavailable."

[49] V. Lieffers and E. MacDonald, "Ecology and Control Strategies for *Calamagrotis canadensis* in Boreal Forest Sites," *Canadian Journal of Forest Research* 23: 2070-2077 (September 1993).

[50] Henderson, "Status Report on Alberta," p. 86.

[51] Alberta Environmental Protection, "Summary of Joint LSF/F and W Enforcement Activities, March 6, 1995–May 1, 1995"; R. Volman, "City not told about Mill's pollution violations," *Fort McMurray Today*, July 2, 1992; Alberta Environmental Protection, *Enforcement History Report, 1988–1996.*

[52] T. Marr-Laing, "Regulatory Reform: Deregulation by any other name," *Environment Network News* 44 (March/April 1996).

[53] *Pollution Control Division Enforcement Action Report, September 1, 1993, to December 31, 1994.*

54 Schneider, "Whatever happened to the Alberta Forest Conservation Strategy?"

55 Global Forest Watch Canada, *Canada's Forests at a Crossroads: An Assessment in the Year 2000* (Washington, D.C.: World Resources Institute, 2000), p. 86.

Chapter 14: British Columbia

1 B.C. Ministry of the Environment, Lands and Parks/Environment Canada, *State of the Environment Report for British Columbia* (Victoria, 1994).

2 D. MacKay, *Empire of Wood: The MacMillan Bloedel Story* (Vancouver: Douglas & McIntyre, 1982).

3 Ibid.

4 Ibid., p. 19.

5 Ken Drushka, *Stumped: The Forest Industry in Transition* (Vancouver: Douglas & McIntyre, 1985).

6 John Gray, "Royal Commission and Forest Policy in British Columbia: A Review of the Pearse Report," *Canadian Public Policy* 3 (1977), p. 218.

7 Drushka, *Stumped*.

8 M. Ross, *Forest Management in Canada* (Calgary: Canadian Institute of Resources Law, 1995), p. 74.

9 Drushka, *Stumped*, p. 74.

10 Canadian Council of Forest Ministers, *Compendium of Canadian Forestry Statistics 1994* (Ottawa, 1995).

11 B.C. Ministry of Forests, *Annual Reports*: 1991–1992: 166,000 hectares; 1992–1993: 196,000 hectares; 1993–1994: 180,000 hectares; 1994–1995: 160,000 hectares, plus another 30,000 hectares on private land. 1998–1999: 191,309 hectares (170,680 hectares, or 89 per cent, clear-cut); 1999–2000: 198,268 hectares (194,121 hectares, or 98 per cent, clear-cut); 2000–2001: 198,268 hectares (170,660 hectares, or 86 per cent, clear-cut) 2001–2002: 163,922 hectares (144,358 hectares, or 88 per cent, clear-cut). Natural Resources Canada, Canadian Forest Service, *The State of Canada's Forests 2002–2003* (Ottawa, 2003) records the total annual harvest in the year 2000 at 204,472 hectares, a figure that includes private land logging.

12 Natural Resources Canada, Canadian Forest Service, *The State of Canada's Forests 2002–2003* (Ottawa, 2003): Ontario, 28 million cubic metres, plus Quebec, 43.5 million cubic metres, plus Manitoba, 2.2 million cubic metres, equals 73.7 million cubic metres.

13 In British Columbia, the total harvest may exceed the AAC, as the latter does not include logging on private and unregulated Crown land.

14 World Wildlife Fund Canada, *The Nature Audit: Setting Canada's Conservation Agenda for the 21st Century*, Report No. 1-2003 (Toronto, 2003), p. 76.

15 Tim D. Janzen, Issues Manager, Office of the Deputy Minister, B.C. Ministry of Water, Land and Air Protection, personal communication to Justin Calof, Sierra Club of Canada, B.C. Chapter, April 19, 2004.

[16] Reed F. Noss, "Protected Areas: How Much is Enough?" in R.I. Vane-Wright, ed., *National Parks and Protected Areas* (Cambridge, MA: Blackwell Science, 1996), pp. 91–120.

[17] Jim Cooperman, "BC's old growth forest crisis," *British Columbia Environmental Report* (Summer 1996).

[18] B.C. Ministry of Water, Air and Land Protection, "Is the Ecological Diversity of British Columbia's Forests Adequately Protected?" wlapwww.gov.bc.ca.

[19] Elizabeth May, *Paradise Won: The Struggle for South Moresby* (Toronto: McClelland and Stewart, 1990).

[20] Forest Resources Commission, *The Future of Our Forests* (Victoria, 1991).

[21] B.C. Forest Sector Strategy Committee, Resource Working Group, *Interim and Final Reports* (Victoria, 1994).

[22] *Future of Our Forests.*

[23] Drushka, *Stumped.*

[24] B.C. Ministry of Forests, *Annual Reports* (1960–1990). Includes private lands.

[25] Gray, "Royal Commission and Forest Policy."

[26] Quoted in Drushka, *Stumped*, p. 84.

[27] D. Haley and M.K. Luckert, *Forest Tenures in Canada: A Framework for Policy Analysis*, Information Report E-X-43 (Ottawa: Forestry Canada, 1990), p. 99.

[28] May, *Paradise Won*, p. 131.

[29] Ibid., p. 53.

[30] B.C. Ministry of Forests, *Annual Reports* (1998–2002).

[31] Ibid.

[32] Ian Miller, "British Columbia Status Report on Timber Supply," in *Timber Supply in Canada: Challenges and Choices*, Canadian Council of Forest Ministers Conference, held November 16–18, 1994. Kananaskis, Alberta (Ottawa: Natural Resources Canada, November 1994)), p. A129.

[33] B.C. Ministry of Water, Air and Land Protection, "Is the Ecological Diversity of British Columbia's Forests Adequately Protected?" wlapwww.gov.bc.ca.

[34] B.C. Ministry of Forests, *Forest Range and Recreation Resource Analysis and Addendum* (Victoria, 1994).

[35] Sierra Club of Western Canada, *Ancient Rainforests at Risk* (Victoria, 1993).

[37] B.C. Ministry of Forests, *An Inventory of Undeveloped Watersheds in British Columbia*, Recreation Branch Technical Report (Victoria, 1992), p. 2.

[37] The term "coast" encompasses the coastal fringe, not including Vancouver Island or Haida Gwaii (the Queen Charlottes). Sierra Club mapping of the coastal forest is of the larger area, encompassing both Vancouver Island and Haida Gwaii.

[38] Sierra Club of Canada, B.C. Chapter, "Half of BC's ancient temperate rainforest gone," press release, March 19, 1997. Data based on satellite information and six years of mapping and research.

[39] T. Jones and F. Depey, "An Inventory of Undeveloped Watersheds in the Southern Interior of British Columbia," unpublished report (1991).

⁴⁰ K. Moore, "An Inventory of Watersheds in the Coastal Temperate Forests of British Columbia," *Earthlife/Ecotrust* (Victoria: Sierra Club of Canada, B.C. Chapter, 1991).

⁴¹ Richard M. Jeo, M.A. Sanjayan and Dennis Sizemore, *A Conservation Area Design for the Central Coast Region of British Columbia, Canada: A Report Prepared by Round River Conservation Studies for the Sierra Club of British Columbia, Greenpeace, the Forest Action Network, and the Raincoast Conservation Society* (Utah: Round River Conservation Studies, August 2000).

⁴² Coast Information Team web site: www.citbc.org.

⁴³ Rainforest Solutions Project web site: www.savethegreatbear.org.

⁴⁴ K. Moore, "Where is it and how much is left? The state of temperate rainforest in British Columbia," *Forest Planning Canada* 6, no. 4 (1990), p. 17.

⁴⁵ Ibid., citing B.C. Ministry of Forests, *Executive Summary: Towards an Old-Growth Strategy* (Victoria, March 1990).

⁴⁶ Jim Cooperman, "Cutting Down Canada," in B. Devall, ed., *Clearcut: The Tragedy of Industrial Forestry* (San Francisco: Sierra Club Books, 1993); 1993 Sierra Club Mapping Project Report (1993), p. 32.

⁴⁷ G. Hamilton, "Clayoquot Sound's quieter, gentler face of logging," *Vancouver Sun*, June 29, 1996.

⁴⁸ Keith Baldrey, "New code not clear, forest industry says: it doesn't go far enough, wilderness group claims," *Vancouver Sun*, November 10, 1993, p. D1.

⁴⁹ Iisaak Forest Resources, *Historic Agreements*, www.iisaak.com.

⁵⁰ Update from Sierra Club of Canada, B.C. Chapter, July 2004.

⁵¹ May, *Paradise Won*.

⁵² Natural Resources Canada, Canadian Forest Service, *The State of Canada's Forests 1995–1996* (Ottawa, 1996).

⁵³ Devon Page, counsel, *Petition to the Honourable David Anderson, Minister of the Environment, in Support of an Emergency Order Pursuant to Section 80 of the Species at Risk Act, 2002, c.29 for Protecting the Northern Spotted Owl; On Behalf of the Petitioners: Western Canada Wilderness Committee, the David Suzuki Foundation, ForestEthics and the Sierra Club of Canada*, (Vancouver: Sierra Legal Defence Fund, February 27, 2004).

⁵⁴ Ibid.

⁵⁵ BC Wild, *Over-cutting the Chilcotin: Putting at Risk Southern BC's Great Herd* (Vancouver, 1997).

⁵⁶ R. Tripp, "Findings from the Application and Effectiveness of the Coastal Fisheries Forestry Guidelines in Selected Cutblocks on Vancouver Island, 1992," cited in BC Wild, *Forest Practices in British Columbia: Not a World Class Act* (Vancouver, 1995).

⁵⁷ Ministry of Environment, Land and Parks, Ministry of Forests and Department of Fisheries and Oceans, *A Preliminary List of Watershed Assessment, Restoration and Evaluation Projects for the Watershed Restoration Program* (Vancouver, 1994).

⁵⁸ T.L. Slaney, K.D. Hyatt et al., "Status of Anadromous Salmon and Trout in BC

and the Yukon," *American Fisheries Society Journal* 21, no. 10 (1996), pp. 20–35. (Most recent data available.) The study reported that 142 of those stocks have now become extinct, and a further 624 are at high risk. A total of 4,417 stocks were identified as not threatened and 4,172 stocks were of unknown status.

[59] L.E. Harding. and E. McCullum, eds, *Biodiversity in British Columbia: our changing environment,* (Delta, BC: Environment Canada, 1994), p. 263; personal communication from Jim Cooperman, B.C. Environmental Network, to Elizabeth May.

[60] Trevor Goward, communication with Elizabeth May. See also Trevor Goward and A. MacKinnon, "BC's Inland Rainforests," *The Log* (Fall 1996), p. 13; Trevor Goward, Research Branch, B.C. Ministry of Forests and Habitat Protection Branch, B.C. Ministry of Environment, Lands and Parks, "Lichens of British Columbia: rare species and priorities for inventory," working paper (Victoria, August 1996).

[61] Sierra Club of Canada, *Integrated Land-Use Planning and Canada's New National Forest Strategy* (Ottawa, July 2004).

[62] H. Armleder and S. Stevenson, "Silvicultural Systems to Maintain Caribou Habitat in Managed British Columbia Forests," in B.C. Ministry of Forests, *Innovative Silvicultural Systems in Boreal Forests,* Land Management Handbook (Victoria, 1986), p. 83.

[63] G. Hamilton, "Forest code change allows more logging," *Vancouver Sun*, March 2, 1996.

[64] Greg Utzig and Donna Macdonald, "Citizens' Guide to Allowable Annual Cut Determinations" (Vancouver: B.C. Environmental Network Education Foundation, March 2000). Available at www.bcen.bc.ca.

[65] *Forest Practices Code of British Columbia Act, Biodiversity Guidebook,* September 1995. Available at www.for.gov.bc.ca.

[66] Ibid.

[67] C. Osterman, "MacBlo set to report record large losses," *Globe and Mail, Report on Business*, February 7, 1997, p. B2.

[68] Price Waterhouse report, March 4, 1997, cited in B.C. Environment Network Forest Caucus, "Environmentalists tell industry, don't destroy the environment to make a profit," press release, March 1, 1997.

[69] Miro Cernetig, "Under Siege," *Report on Business Magazine* (May 1997), p. 51.

[70] P. Lush, "Cost of BC logs soars 75 per cent in 4 years: Study: Industry blames provincial forest policy, higher stumpage, royalty and compliance fees," *Globe and Mail, Report on Business*, April 7, 1997, p. B5.

[71] Greenpeace, *Broken Promises: The Truth About What's Happening to British Columbia's Forests* (Vancouver, April 1997).

[72] The solid wood portion of the B.C. industry was profitable, with profits of $475 million in a year when pulp companies lost $625 million. Companies operating in the interior made a profit of $510 million. The average cost per log in the interior was just $4 above costs in Ontario and Quebec. It was only companies operating on the coast, along the steeper slopes, who lost money.

73 B.C. Environment Network Forest Caucus, "Environmentalists tell industry, don't destroy the environment to make a profit," press release, March 1, 1997.

74 Greenpeace, *Broken Promises*.

75 David Suzuki Foundation, *Clearcutting Canada's Rainforest Status Report 2004* (Vancouver, April 6, 2004), p. 11. Available at www.canadianrainforests.org.

76 R. Schwindt and T. Heaps, *Chopping Up the Money Tree: Distributing the Wealth from British Columbia's Forests* (Vancouver: David Suzuki Foundation, June 1996).

77 Sierra Club of Canada, *Rio Report Card 2002* (Ottawa, 2002). Available at www.sierraclub.ca.

78 West Coast Environmental Law, *Please Hold, Someone Will Be with You: A Report on Diminished Monitoring and Enforcement at the Ministry of Water, Air and Land Protection* (Vancouver, 2004). Available at www.wcel.org.

79 Forest and Range Practices Act, SBC 2002, c. 69, Consolidated to December 31, 2004 (last amendments: 2004 Bill 47, B.C. Reg. 547/2004).

80 Ibid.

81 Subsequent analyses that attempted to quantify these increases were based on arbitrary assessments by field staff of forest companies and were of questionable validity. In fact, the increases in planning costs were a conjured excuse the forest industry used to justify more subsidies from the province. See Tom Green and Lisa Matthaus, "Cutting Subsidies, or Subsidized Cutting? Subsidies to the BC Forest Industry and the BC Liberals' Commitment to End Them," (Vancouver: BC Coalition for Sustainable Forest Solutions, July 2001), pp. 5–6. Available at www.forestsolutions.ca.

82 Western Forest Products and Nootka Sound Economic Development Corporation, "Draft Zeballos Forest Stewardship Plan 2004" (Gold River, BC, 2004). Available at www.westernforest.com. The plan proposes that, in the event that the Timber Supply Review-established Timber Harvesting Landbase is reduced through the designation of habitat for wildlife, biodiversity, riparian areas or species at risk, other areas previously designated for protection or retention for visual quality, water quality or fisheries needs will be ranked and prioritized for re-inclusion in the THLB so the net loss to the THLB does not exceed 0.5 per cent.

83 Roberta Reader, Director, Compliance and Enforcement Branch, "Developing a Legal Framework for the Results Based Code" (Victoria, 2001).

84 Sierra Club of Canada, B.C. Chapter, "Submission on Results Based Code," discussion paper (June 2002).

85 The government can decide to turn over the job of determining whether plans meet the legal requirements of the FPRA to a private sector professional who is not accountable to the public. For example, the minister might be required to approve logging plans if a registered professional forester, employed by the logging company, assures the minister that the logging plans meet the minimum requirements of the FPRA. See West Coast Environmental Law, "Deregulation Backgrounder Bill 33 Forest Statutes Amendment Act 2004" (Vancouver, May 2004).

[86] See www.forestsolutions.ca. These log markets must include regional log markets, not just options of standing timber.

[87] Peter H. Pearse, *Ready for Change: Crisis and Opportunity in the Coast Forest Industry, A Report to the Minister of Forests on British Columbia's Coastal Forest Industry* (Vancouver: B.C. Ministry of Forests, November 2001). Available at www.for.gov.bc.ca.

[88] B.C. Ministry of Forests, *Range and Timber Analysis* (Victoria, 1984), cited in J. Cooperman, "The elephant under the table: A critique of BC's Timber Supply Review," *British Columbia Environmental Report* 5, no. 3 (September 1994), p. 7.

[89] Ibid.

[90] Miller, "British Columbia Status Report," p. A131.

[91] Jim Cooperman, "The Elephant under the Table: A Critique of B.C.'s Timber Supply Review," *BC Environmental Report.* Vol. 5, No.36 (1994). Available at www.bcen.bc.ca; B.C. Ministry of Forests, *Review of the Timber Supply Analysis Process for BC Timber Supply Areas: Final Report* (Victoria, March 1991), p. 4.

[92] B.C. Ministry of Forests, Timber Supply Review documentation, 1995–1996; K.L. Runyon, *Canada's Timber Supply: Current Status and Outlook*, Information Report E-X-45 (Ottawa: Forestry Canada, 1996).

[93] *Ministry of Forests Act, Revised Statutes of BC* 1979, c. 140, s. 28(g)(i).

[94] *Sierra Club of Western Canada* v. *British Columbia (Chief Forester)* (1993) 13 C.E.L.R. (N.S.) 13 (B.C.S.C.).

[95] Forest Resources Commission, *The Future of Our Forests* (Victoria, 1991).

[96] B.C. Ministry of Forests, *Annual Report 1993/94* (Victoria, 1994).

[97] Ben Parfitt, *Axing the Forest Service: How British Columbians Are Losing Their Eyes and Ears in the Forest*, report for Sierra Club of Canada, B.C. Chapter (Victoria, December 2004), p. 22. Available at www.sierraclub.ca.

[98] B.C. Ministry of Forests, *2003/04 Annual Service Plan Report* (Victoria, 2004), p. 25. Available at www.bcbudget.gov.bc.ca.

[99] Drushka, *Stumped*, p. 116.

[100] Jim Cooperman, "End the Overcut!" editorial, *The British Columbia Environmental Report* (Spring 1997), p. 2.

[101] B.C. Ministry of Forests, "Audit results show Fraser TSA inventory is overestimated," press release, July 16, 1996.

[102] B. Bouw, "Fraser area tree harvest slashed again," *Vancouver Sun*, July 17, 1996.

[103] Cooperman, "End the Overcut!" For example, in the Vanderhoof district in the Prince George Timber Supply Area, the 2004 cut was increased to such an extent that it will need to be reduced by 81 per cent within ten years, according to the emergency timber supply analysis that was done, and will only be able to rise back to a Long Run Sustainable Yield (LRSY) situation fifteen years after that.

[104] Justin Calof and Lisa Matthaus, "Difficult road ahead for new chief forester," *Times Colonist* (Victoria), October 12, 2004.

[105] BC Wild, *The Cassiar* (Vancouver, March 1996); BC Wild, *Begging Questions: The Cassiar Timber Supply Analysis and the Ruin of BC's Northwest Wilderness* (Vancouver, February 1995).

[106] B.C. Ministry of Forests, "New Allowable Annual Cut announced for Mackenzie Timber Supply Area," press release, July 17, 1996.

[107] 1993 AAC: Natural Resources Canada, Canadian Forest Service, *The State of Canada's Forests 1994* (Ottawa, 1994); 1994 AAC: Natural Resources Canada, Canadian Forest Service, *The State of Canada's Forests, 1995–1996* (Ottawa, 1996); 1996 AAC: B.C. Ministry of Forests, Timber Supply Review documentation 1995–96 (Victoria, 1996); 2000 AAC: Natural Resources Canada, Canadian Forest Service, *The State of Canada's Forests 2002–2003* (Ottawa, 2003).

Chapter 15: The Territories

YUKON

[1] Canadian Forest Service, Whitehorse, *Yukon Forestry Fact Sheet* (Whitehorse, 2000). The current estimates of species composition place white spruce at 306 million cubic metres, with the next most prevalent species, lodgepole pine, at only 75 million cubic metres.

[2] Forestry Canada, *The State of Forestry in Canada, 1990: First Report to Parliament* (Ottawa, 1990), p. 16.

[3] Department of Indian and Northern Affairs, "Yukon Development Strategy: Forestry," in *Yukon 2000: Building the Future* (Whitehorse, October 23, 1986).

[4] C. Heartwell, *The Forest Industry in the Economy of the Yukon*, report prepared for the Department of Renewable Resources, the Government of Yukon, Department of Economic Development, Indian and Northern Affairs Canada and Forestry Canada (Whitehorse, February 1988).

[5] Ibid.

[6] Herb Hammond, "The Boreal Forest: Options for Ecologically Responsible Human Use," paper prepared for the Yukon Conservation Society (April 1994).

[7] Ministry of Environment, "A Forest Sector Strategy for Canada," discussion paper (Ottawa, 1981), cited in R. Grenier, "In Search of a Forest Policy for the Yukon and the Northwest Territories," policy document submitted to the Northern Renewable Resources Branch, Department of Indian and Northern Affairs (Ottawa, December 1982).

[8] Don White, "State of Yukon's Forests," *Symposium Proceedings for Yukon Forests: A Sustainable Resource, February 2–4, 1995* (Whitehorse: Government of Yukon, 1995), p. 11.

[9] Indian and Northern Affairs Canada, "Discussion Paper on Policy Changes to Stumpage Pricing, Reforestation and Forest Tenure in the Yukon" (Ottawa, April 26, 1995), p. 1.

[10] Yukon Council on the Economy and the Environment, *The Future of Yukon's Forests: Conference Summary, Watson Lake, Yukon, November 4–5, 1995* (Watson Lake, 1996).

[11] The Honourable Ron Irwin, Minister of Indian Affairs and Northern Development, letter to Government Leader John Ostashek, published in the *Whitehorse Star*, November 20, 1995.

[12] L. Jenkins, "Mountain clear-cutting proposal is called off," *Whitehorse Star*, November 24, 1993.

[13] R. Mostyn, "Logs still being exported despite ban," *Yukon News*, May 26, 1995, quoting Jerry Armstrong, local contractor.

[14] L. Jenkins, "Logging companies grilled about plans," *Whitehorse Star*, March 30, 1994.

[15] Indian and Northern Affairs Canada, "Announcement of Interim Yukon Forest Policy, Including a Yukon Forestry Advisory Committee and the Edward Elijah Smith Reforestation Program," communiqué (Whitehorse, August 4, 1995).

[16] Natural Resources Canada, Canadian Forest Service, *The State of Canada's Forests 1995–1996* (Ottawa, 1996).

[17] Figures on volume and areas logged are from Forestry Canada, *The State of Forestry in Canada: 1990 Report to Parliament* (Ottawa, 1990); Natural Resources Canada, Canadian Forest Service, *The State of Canada's Forests 1994* (Ottawa, 1994); and Natural Resources Canada, Canadian Forest Service, *The State of Canada's Forests 1995–1996* (Ottawa, 1996).

[18] Watson Lake Management Office, *Yukon Forest Management Plan* (Sterling Wood Group Corp., August 1991).

[19] "Local group forecasts forestry blunder," *Whitehorse Star*, December 18, 2000.

[20] H. Armleder and S. Stevenson, "Silvicultural Systems to Maintain Caribou Habitat in Managed British Columbia Forests," in *Proceedings: Innovative Silvicultural Systems in Boreal Forests: A Symposium Held in Edmonton, Alberta, Canada, October 2–8, 1994*, p. 83.

[21] Yukon Government, "Governments agree to further work on devolution," press release, February 3, 1997.

[22] Dennis Fentie, Yukon Forest Commissioner, "Ecosystems know no political boundaries," speech delivered at Ecosystem Management Workshop (Whitehorse, March 24, 1997).

NORTHWEST TERRITORIES

[1] *The Northwest Territories Forest Management Act and Regulations*, 1988, *The NWT Forest Protection Act*, 1988. Both are currently under review.

[2] Cizek Environmental Services, *Fort Liard Area Cumulative Impacts Mapping Project, Technical Report*, prepared for the Canadian Arctic Resources Committee and the Canadian Parks and Wilderness Society (Ottawa, 2002).

[3] Northwest Territories Biodiversity Team, *Northwest Territories Biodiversity Action Plan: Major Initiatives on Biodiversity* (Yellowknife, 2004).

[4] Canadian Council of Forest Ministers, *Compendium of Canadian Forestry Statistics, 1995* (Ottawa, 1996).

[5] Government of the Northwest Territories, Forest Management Act, R.S.N.W.T. 1988, c. F-9, Schedule B, Timber Cutting Charges.

[6] Tom Lakusta, Forest Management Division, Government of the Northwest Territories, personal communication to Karin Clark, Yukon researcher, June 17, 2004.

[7] Natural Resources Canada, Canadian Forest Service, *The State of Canada's Forests 1996–1997* (Ottawa, 1997).

PART 3: THE FUTURE OF THE FORESTS

Chapter 16: Signs of Hope

[1] National Forest Strategy Coalition, *National Forest Strategy 2003–2008* (Ottawa, 2003), p. 10.

[2] For an excellent review of integrated land-use planning and a systematic analysis of the elements that make for sound process, see Rachel Plotkin, *Integrated Land-Use Planning and Canada's New National Forest Strategy* (Ottawa: Sierra Club of Canada, July 2004).

[3] Although Quebec has not officially signed the Accord, it has committed to supporting the Strategy.

[4] Alanna Mitchell, "Coalition aims to save boreal forest: Natives, environmentalists, industry allied in bid to preserve half the country's area," *Globe and Mail*, December 1, 2003, p. A6.

[5] National Aboriginal Forestry Association, "Canada forest policy inconsistent with legal requirements for addressing Aboriginal issues," press release, September 2003. Available at www.nafaforestry.org.

[6] Forest Stewardship Council, Canada Working Group, *National Boreal Standard* (August 6, 2004). Available at fsccanada.org.

[7] Wildlands League, Fact Sheet #6; also read about this success story in Paul Hawken's *Ecology of Commerce*.

[8] Peter Penashue, "We *are* protecting a treasure," *Ottawa Citizen*, May 6, 2004, p. A19.

[9] Ibid.

[10] I was a member of this committee, along with Dr. Jag Maini, formerly of the Canadian Forest Service and the United Nations Forum on Forests; Joe O'Neil, former woodlands director, Repap, New Brunswick; Prof. Gilles Frisque of Laval University; Steve Thorlakson, Mayor of Fort St. John, B.C.; Ron Vrancart, Deputy Minister, Ontario Ministry of Natural Resources; and Grand Chief Edward John.

[11] National Forest Strategy Coalition, *National Forest Strategy 2003–2008: A Sustainable Forest; a Canadian Commitment* (Ottawa, 2003).

Chapter 17: Where Do We Go from Here?

[1] G. Hamilton, "Primex discouraged by NDP," *Vancouver Sun*, April 25, 1997, p. E1.

[2] Ibid.

[3] Kirk Makin, "Supreme Court will hear claim for lost timber: BC government seeks damages for loss of revenue from forest fire, 11 years ago," *Globe and Mail*, October 14, 2003, p. A8.

[4] D. Bryant, Daniel Nielsen and Laura Tangley, *The Last Frontier Forests: Ecosystems and Economies on the Edge* (Washington: World Resources Institute, 1997).

[5] ForestEthics, *Bringing Down the Boreal: How U.S. Consumption of Forest Products Is Destroying Canada's Endangered Northern Forests* (San Francisco, 2004).

[6] Ibid. All U.S. consumption figures come from ForestEthics.

[7] Natural Resources Canada, Canadian Forest Service, *The State of Canada's Forests 2002–2003* (Ottawa, 2003).

[8] Patrick White, "Movement starts to dump Weyerhaeuser: Activists challenge paper purchasing policy at the University of Victoria," *The Martlet* (University of Victoria newspaper), March 15, 2004.

[9] Jane Dunbar, "Fletcher's logging unpopular," *The Press* (Christchurch, New Zealand) March 16, 1989; Martin Rudy Haase, "Visiting New Zealand helps BC forest," *Friends of Nature Newsletter* (Chester, NS), May 30, 1989.

[10] Sierra Club of Canada, B.C. Chapter, "Environmentalists release report warning 'Buyers Beware' of bogus forest certification schemes," press release, May 26, 2003.

[11] ForestEthics, *Bringing Down the Boreal*.

[12] J.K. Rowling, *Harry Potter and the Order of the Phoenix* (Vancouver: Raincoast Books, 2003).

[13] Sierra Club of Canada, "Forests," Fact Sheet (Ottawa, 1995).

[14] Wildlands League, "Ecological Forestry...A Cut Above," Fact Sheet #6, *Forest Diversity and Community Survival* (Toronto, 1995).

[15] "Slocan Residents Behind Bars for Water," *BC Environmental Report* 8, no 3 (Fall 1997), p. 7.

[16] Slocan Valley Watershed Alliance and Silva Forest Foundation, "Ecosystem-based planning provides win/win solution to logging conflicts," press release, August 15, 1996.

[17] Ronald Wright, *A Short History of Progress* (Toronto: Anansi, 2004), p. 105.

Selected Bibliography

Brown, Lester R., Christopher Flavin and Hilary French. *State of the World 1997: A Worldwatch Institute Report on Progress Toward a Sustainable Society.* New York: Worldwatch Institute/W.W. Norton, 1997.

Brown, Lester R., and Hal Kane. *Full House: Reassessing the Earth's Population Carrying Capacity.* Worldwatch Environmental Alert Series. New York: W.W. Norton, 1994.

Brown, Lester R., Michael Renner and Christopher Flavin. *Vital Signs 1997: The Environmental Trends That Are Shaping Our Future.* New York: Worldwatch Institute/W.W. Norton, 1997.

Carson, Rachel L. *Silent Spring.* Boston: Houghton Mifflin, 1962.

Clark, Tom. *Timber Supply and Endangered Spaces.* A World Wildlife Fund Canada Discussion Paper.

Cohen, Joel E. *How Many People Can the Earth Support?* New York: W.W. Norton, 1995.

Devall, Bill, ed. *Clearcut: The Tragedy of Industrial Forestry.* San Francisco: Sierra Club Books/Earth Island Press, 1993.

Drushka, Ken. *Stumped: The Forest Industry in Transition.* Vancouver: Douglas & McIntyre, 1985.

Erlich, Paul R., and Anne H. Erlich. *The Population Explosion.* New York: Touchstone, Simon and Schuster, 1990.

ForestEthics. "Bringing Down the Boreal: How U.S. Consumption of Forest Products Is Destroying Canada's Endangered Northern Forests." 2004.

Gordon, Anita, and David Suzuki. *It's a Matter of Survival.* Toronto: Stoddart, 1990.

Hammond, Herb. *Seeing the Forest Among the Trees: The Case for Wholistic Forest Use.* Vancouver: Polestar Press, 1991.

Hodgins, Bruce, and Jamie Benidickson. *The Temagami Experience.* Toronto: University of Toronto Press, 1989.

Howard, Ross. *Poisons in Public: Case Studies of Environmental Pollution in Canada.* Toronto: James Lorimer, 1980.

Hummel, Monte, ed. *Endangered Spaces: The Future for Canada's Wilderness.* Toronto: Key Porter Books, 1989.

———. *Protecting Canada's Endangered Spaces: An Owner's Manual*. Toronto: Key Porter Books, 1995.

Lansky, Mitch. *Beyond the Beauty Strip: Saving What's Left of Our Forests*. Gardiner, ME: Tilbury House, 1992.

Lee, Peter. "Boreal Canada: State of the Ecosystem, State of Industry, Emerging Issues and Projections." Report to the National Round Table on the Environment and the Economy. Global Forest Watch Canada. Edmonton: 2004.

Marchak, M. Patricia. *Logging the Globe*. Montreal and Kingston: McGill-Queen's University Press, 1995.

Maser, Chris. *The Redesigned Forest*. San Pedro, CA: R. & E. Miles, 1988.

May, Elizabeth. *Budworm Battles*. Tantallon, NS: Four East Publishers, 1982.

———. *Paradise Won: The Struggle for South Moresby*. Toronto: McClelland & Stewart, 1990.

Meyer, William B. *Human Impact on the Earth*. Cambridge, England: Cambridge University Press, 1996.

M'Gonigle, Michael, and Ben Parfitt. *Forestopia: A Practical Guide to the New Forest Economy*. Madeira Park, BC: Harbour Publishing, 1994.

National Forest Strategy Coalition. "National Forest Strategy 2003–2008: A Sustainable Forest, the Canadian Commitment." Ottawa.

Natural Resources Canada. Canadian Forest Service. *The State of Canada's Forests: 2003–2004*. Ottawa: 2004.

Peattie, Donald, and Paul H. Landacre. *A Natural History of Trees: Eastern & Central North America* and *A Natural History of Western Trees*. Boston: Houghton Mifflin, 1991.

Pielou, E.C. *The World of Northern Evergreens*. Ithaca, NY: Cornell University Press, 1988.

Ross, Monique. *Forest Management in Canada*. Calgary: Canadian Institute of Resources Law, 1995.

Suzuki, David. *Time to Change*. Toronto: Stoddart, 1994.

Swift, Jamie. *Cut and Run: The Assault on Canada's Forests*. Toronto: Between the Lines, 1983.

Troyer, Warner. *No Safe Place*. Toronto: Clarke, Irwin, 1997

World Wildlife Fund Canada. *The Nature Audit: Setting Canada's Conservation Agenda for the 21st Century*. Report No. 1-2003. Toronto.

Wright, Ronald. *A Short History of Progress*. Toronto: Anansi, 2004.

Zimmerman, Adam. *Who's in Charge Here, Anyway? Reflections from a Life in Business*. Toronto: Stoddart, 1997.

Websites

www.canadian-forests.com
An independent gateway to many forest and forestry-related sites.

www-eosdis.ornl.gov/BOREAS/bhs/BOREAS_Home.html
The Boreal Ecosystem-Atmosphere Study

www.borealnet.org
Boreal Forest Network

www.ccfm.org
Canadian Council of Forest Ministers

www.nrcan.gc.ca/cfs-scf/
Canadian Forest Service

www.canadianforestry.com
Canadian Forestry Association

pubs.nrc-cnrc.gc.ca
Canadian Journal of Forest Research

www.ecoforestry.ca
Ecoforestry Institute Society of Canada

www.globalforestwatch.org
Global Forest Watch

www.borealforest.org/index.php
An initiative of Lakehead University, Ontario.

www.nrcan-rncan.gc.ca
Natural Resources Canada

www.geocities.com/RainForest/7317/mainfl.html
World Forestry Libraries (partial listing)

www.nswooa.ca
Nova Scotia Woodlot Owners' and Operators' Association

INDEX